Mastering Third-Party Risk

Mastering Third-Party Risk

A Practical Handbook for Managing Vendor, Third-Party, and Supply Chain Threats in Every Organization

Bill Bonney
Chris Forbes
Gary Hayslip
Dr. Andrea Little Limbago
Matt Stamper

Mastering Third-Party Risk
A Practical Handbook for Managing Vendor, Third-Party, and Supply Chain Threats in Every Organization

CISO DRG Publishing
P.O. Box 581
Paso Robles, CA 93447
<www.CISODRG.com>
info@cisodrg.com
ISBN 978-1-955976-28-2

To contact the authors, write the publisher at the address provided above, "Attention: Author Services."

Edited by Bill Bonney
Artwork by Gwendolyn Peres
Copyediting by Nadine Bonney

Acknowledgments

Bill Bonney: I would like to thank my partner, Nadine, for her loving support. She has always been my biggest fan and a source of constant strength. Thank you to my partner, Christine, for the special bond that I have come to cherish and depend on for joy and inspiration.

Chris Forbes: My heartfelt gratitude and appreciation to the CISO DRG team for allowing me the opportunity to contribute my insights and opinions. Thank you to my wife and kids for their patience and understanding over the past 40+ years, as careers in Technology, Risk, and Security often pull us away from the ones we love most.

Gary Hayslip: I would like to thank my co-authors, Andrea, Bill, Chris, and Matt, for their dedication to this project and for providing this valuable resource for our community. I want to tell my wife of 36 years, Sandi, thank you for your patience and calming influence. Your love and support have allowed me to stay focused on this project. You are my best friend, and I thank you for putting up with my late-night rewrites and rambling debates with Matt and Bill.

Dr. Andrea Little Limbago: Thank you to my co-authors and the CISO DRG team for the opportunity to share my perspective on such an important topic. I am grateful for the colleagues throughout academia, industry, and government who have supported and educated me and am indebted to my family and extended family for their flexibility, love, and humor.

Matt Stamper: I want to thank my co-authors, Andrea, Bill, Chris, and Gary, for their perspectives and dedication to this topic. I'd also like to thank the extended crew at CISO DRG Publishing, including Nadine, Chris, and Wendy. None of this would happen absent the support at home. I'm indebted to my wife Lisa, the love of my life, and our two daughters, Danielle and Lauren. I also thank my parents for their love and support.

Table of Contents

Preface

Every company desires greatness and success; what sets them apart is the quality of their strategies. Michael Porter said, "The essence of strategy is choosing what not to do." Henry Mintzberg said, "Strategy is not the consequence of planning, but the opposite: its starting point." Sun Tzu said, "Strategy without tactics is the slowest route to victory. Tactics without strategy is the noise before defeat."

Supply Chain Management Challenges

As we'll show, especially in Section 1, "Foundations of Third-Party Risk Management," and Section 2, "Operations Considerations for Third-Party Risk Management," third-party risks that are the result of relationships external to our organizations grow greater and more complex as the number of third parties we deal with grows and the complexity of our supply chains increases. In the ever-expanding and rapidly evolving global marketplace, supply chain management (SCM) has become increasingly critical for businesses of all sizes. SCM is a necessary lifeline for organizations that depend on external providers for their products, services, intellectual property, and integration of extended partner networks. As supply chains become increasingly complex, often spanning multiple countries, they become more vulnerable to geopolitical risks and logistical challenges. Unplanned events, such as natural disasters, supplier bankruptcies, trade disputes, and cyberattacks, can lead to significant operational disruptions and economic losses, and have profound implications for a company's financial stability. The World Economic Forum reported that supply chain disruptions cost organizations an average of $184 million annually. Let's take a look at the most significant sources of change driving companies to rethink their entire approach to SCM.

Supply chains are growing in size and complexity

Adam Smith's Wealth of Nations promoted the concepts of specialization and division of labor as the most effective means to increase productivity and efficiency. Smith believed the underlying problem was a person's limitation in mastering many complex concepts and tasks. When followed to its logical conclusion, the Division of Labor principle had driven significant increases in the number of participants involved in supply chains. As suppliers and participant numbers increase, a more comprehensive and robust SCM program is required. A prime example of a growing supply chain is the average smartphone, which requires components from over 200 suppliers.

Supply chains are constantly changing and less mature

Globalization has introduced new sources of talent, service partners, raw materials, and manufacturing locations, thereby increasing opportunities for innovation, novel uses of intellectual property, and the ability to leverage growing distribution channels to reach new customers. Unfortunately, newer supply chains may not have been proven or may be unstable, bringing different market dynamics and risks. These newer supply chains must evolve and optimize before settling into more predictable patterns and may be replaced or obsolete before they fully mature. In 2020, global e-commerce sales grew by 27.6% to reach $4.28 trillion. The 2021 MHI Annual Industry Report stated that 60% of supply chain leaders reported an accelerated adoption of digital technologies due to the COVID-19 pandemic, with the adoption of artificial intelligence and predictive analytics increasing by 44%. A 2020 survey by Deloitte found that 48% of supply chain leaders identified rapid technological changes as a significant risk, affecting their ability to keep pace with innovations and integration.

Supply chain globalization has increased exposure to geopolitical volatility

Relying on a global supply chain and its underlying global workforce increases the likelihood that geopolitical issues in one part of the world could cause supply shortages on the other side of the planet. For example, Indonesia's nickel ore export ban led to a 30% increase in global prices, impacting supply chains in the stainless steel and electric vehicle industries.

Supply chain threats and risks are becoming more diverse and unpredictable

When a company relies on a single supplier, usually in the same geographic region, it can more easily anticipate the issues and challenges its suppliers might face. Suppliers are also increasing their use of material fourth-party suppliers, making monitoring and predicting supply chain threats and risks more difficult. This layering of suppliers also increases the likelihood of concentration risks and cascading failures from supply chain disruptions that can trigger a domino effect, disrupting large sections of the supply chain. According to a report by Accenture, the number of cyberattacks on supply chains increased by 42% in the first half of 2020 compared to the same period in the previous year. The report also noted that supply chain attacks accounted for 11% of all cybersecurity incidents.

Supply chains are increasingly affected by climate change and environmental disasters

Climate change is proving to be a substantial and unpredictable threat to global supply chains. A recent example of this was experienced in the Panama Canal, where drought reduced the flow of rivers into the canal, causing long shipping delays for materials and finished products. This slowed passage through the waterway or required circumnavigation around South America's Cape Horn and Drake's Passage, adding weeks to the journey. Another example is the 2021 ice storms in Texas, which disrupted power utilities and caused regional supply chain disruptions that lasted for several weeks. The 2020 BCI Supply Chain Resilience Report reported that 37% of organizations identified environmental risks, such as climate change and resource scarcity, as significant threats to their supply chains.

Supply chain risk information is stifled by litigation and intellectual property theft

The fear of litigation and the risk of intellectual property theft drive companies to share less and less risk-related information. While some government intervention is underway to counter supplier reluctance to disclose risks, much more needs to be done before we achieve complete transparency of supply chain risks. According to a report by the Risk and Insurance Management Society (RIMS), 62% of risk managers cited litigation concerns as a reason for withholding information about supply chain risks. A 2019 survey by Deloitte found that 45% of supply chain executives cited competitive concerns as a reason for limiting the sharing of supply chain information. According to a study by the Association for Supply Chain Management (ASCM), 54% of supply chain professionals reported that confidentiality agreements with suppliers limited their ability to share risk information with other stakeholders.

Supply chain inventory reserves are reduced by just-in-time manufacturing

Over the past century, we have seen a dramatic shift away from companies trying to maximize their utilization of manufacturing capacity as a means to drive down individual unit construction costs. The Economies of Scale approach focused on spreading fixed costs of equipment and facilities across the maximum number of units possible. This approach resulted in inventory fluctuations that ranged from surplus to shortages based on consumer demand cycles. It also raised the risk of inventory spoilage when supply exceeded demand for an extended period. To counteract these weaknesses, management at Toyota developed the Toyota Production System, which reduced inventory holding costs and space requirements by

60% compared to traditional manufacturing systems, demonstrating the impact of the Just-in-Time approach on inventory reserves.

While history has credited this evolution with further reducing the construction costs per unit, it introduced the unintended consequence of removing the buffer that previously cushioned minor supply chain shocks. The 2011 Japan earthquake and tsunami, for example, led to a 20% reduction in global automotive production in the months following the disaster, illustrating the far-reaching effects of such events on supply chains.

Supply chain underinvestment and reduced staffing hinder risk management and compliance

Many companies have focused on short-term cost reductions as their best option to increase their stock price and company value. This tendency often considers SCRM to be overhead and an expense that should be limited and minimized. One could argue that investments in mastering supply chains have contributed to the emergence of some of the world's largest and most financially successful companies. For example, Walmart and Amazon have demonstrated that investments in supply chain management (SCM) can provide substantial economic benefits and competitive advantages. A survey by McKinsey & Company found that 85% of supply chain leaders acknowledged a need for more investment in risk management tools and processes as a critical challenge in building resilient supply chains.

The World Bank reported that compliance with international regulations and standards has become a significant factor in global supply chains, impacting over 50% of global trade flows. The Institute for Supply Management (ISM) reported that 47% of companies experienced supply chain disruptions due to compliance issues, underscoring the importance of investing adequately in compliance capabilities.

When your raw material is data, supply chains can change instantaneously

Every organization depends on data and information to succeed in business. An increasing number of companies are entirely digital, meaning they provide only products and services that collect, process, and distribute electronic information. As such, these companies may have multiple options for sourcing their data and instantly switch to other suppliers offering the same data at a lower price or with a higher quality guarantee. While picking and choosing among multiple suppliers may appear financially advantageous, it increases the need for substantial risk information before making a change.

Supply chains are increasingly subject to cybersecurity attacks and disruptions

Ransomware is just one example of how a supplier may suddenly be rendered inoperative or disabled by a cyberattack. Other extreme examples include the financial impacts of a data breach, which can lead to a class action lawsuit or loss of customer trust, resulting in significant economic losses and ultimately causing the company to go bankrupt or cease operations. The NotPetya attack resulted in an estimated $10 billion in damages globally, underscoring the vulnerability of supply chains to cyber threats. According to a report by Accenture, 43% of cyberattacks targeted supply chains, and underinvestment in cybersecurity was a significant factor contributing to the increased vulnerability of these supply chains.

Introduction

The essays within each chapter of this book often present the topic from the perspectives of two or three authors. This allows us to examine the topics in a manner similar to how a panel discussion might provide different viewpoints and flesh out concepts that are more relevant to various segments of the audience. This technique affords us the luxury of offering multiple fully-formed positions, rather than either rotating between different authors chapter by chapter or trying to blend the thoughts of multiple authors into a single narrative. There are also a few chapters in the latter sections where the topic is unique enough to the author's experience that those essays stand alone for the subject of that chapter.

This is an action-oriented book. Each chapter has a summary titled "Insights and Actions." In the summary, we aim to identify the key takeaways and provide advice that you can apply immediately in your program. While there is no requirement to follow every recommendation at the end of every chapter, if you are wondering, "Now what?" we've got you covered. Third-party risk management is anything but passive—it demands active engagement at every turn.

In Section 1, we'll make clear how we use the terms "Vendor Risk Management," "Third-Party Risk Management," and "Supply Chain Risk Management." For this Introduction, the term "Third-Party Risk Management" will serve as a proxy for all three models.

How to Use This Book

We have organized the book into five sections. We start in Section 1 by presenting the foundations of third-party risk management governance. There are three chapters, covering high-level governance, required resources, and a discussion of roles and responsibilities. Bill Bonney, Matt Stamper, and Chris Forbes cover these topics. In Section 2, we examine the lifecycle of third-party risk management, covering onboarding, operating and stewardship, incident response, and offboarding. Bill, Matt, Chris, and Gary Hayslip contribute essays in Section 2.

In Section 3, we address managing and optimizing by providing a reset on global supply chain risks, followed by an exploration of managing these risks and optimizing the global supply chain. Chris and Dr. Andrea Little Limbago are the authors of Section 3. In Section 4, we present five essays, spread across two chapters, on the legal and regulatory impacts on the supply chain, as well as guidance on navigating the legal and regulatory landscape. Matt, Chris, and Andrea contribute the content for Section 4.

After the legal and regulatory discussion, we transition in Section 5 to a technical discussion of risk within the context of global supply chains, first by examining the unique risks to the AI supply chain and then delving into a quantitative assessment of supply chain risk. Chris and Andrea provide their expertise on these topics.

Sections 1, 2, and 4 consist of a preamble for the section, and an introduction and a summary with insights and actions for each chapter. For Sections 3 and 5, there is a section introduction, and each chapter concludes with a summary that includes insights and actionable steps.

Finally, the legal and regulatory landscape continues to evolve. We've made every effort to provide the most current guidance. To help you stay current, we've provided links and references in several hundred footnotes and scores of other sources. We encourage you to bookmark the links relevant to you and consult these references as you keep your program up to date.

Section 1

Foundations of Third-Party Risk Management Programs

A house must be built on solid foundations if it is to last. The same principle applies to man, otherwise he too will sink back into the soft ground and becomes swallowed up by the world of illusion.

~ Spiritual Master, Sai Baba of Shirdi

Preamble

In Section 1, authors Bill Bonney, Matt Stamper, and Chris Forbes present their perspectives on the foundational requirements for vendor, third-party, and supply chain risk management. Throughout the first two sections of this book, you will see the terms vendor risk management (VRM), third-party risk management (TPRM), and supply chain risk management (SCRM) used seemingly interchangeably. They are not interchangeable, but they are closely related, and you'll notice that each term is used accurately within the context of the problem and solution being discussed. You'll also see an instructive hierarchy where techniques used to help solve vendor management issues can mature into techniques used to address broader third-party management issues. These same techniques, in their newly matured form, can serve as a foundational basis for supply chain management.

It is helpful to present the foundations in this way because it allows us to establish several principles in the less complex vendor management scenario and then show how these same principles apply to more complex programs. It also allows us to present a process maturity journey conceptually. Using a Capability Maturity Model Integration (CMMI) scale of 1 to 5, with 1 being "Initial" and 5 being "Optimizing," we can follow this journey starting with a maturity level of 1 in some of Bill's early anecdotal experiences and see how he established the level of management and definition that his smaller companies needed. We can pick up the journey as Matt describes how to define goals, objectives, accountability, and standards, and introduces data-driven metrics to ensure the organization achieves the desired outcome in terms of risk reduction. Finally, we can end the journey with Chris as he applies supply chain management principles to show how optimizing critical components of the supply chain can lead to outcomes beyond risk reduction and deliver significant competitive advantages.

Chapter 1

Third-Party Risk Management Governance

Introduction

In Chapter 1, we begin the foundations section of this book with a discussion about the fundamental elements of governance. Bill leads off by emphasizing the central importance of governance in vendor (third-party) risk management (VRM), arguing that third-party governance should address a broad range of risks that can impact an organization. He discusses the key elements of a charter and shares real-world anecdotes illustrating the consequences of poor governance. Bill then highlights some of the risks that smaller organizations must manage and demonstrates how tools such as the RACI matrix and Three Lines of Defense model can be used together to identify ownership of the various risks.

Matt looks deeper at the cross-functional nature of third-party risk management (TPRM) in modern organizations, arguing for an entity-wide program that addresses the complexity of vendor and supply chain risks and the necessity to rely on expertise from across the organization. He shows that TPRM should be closely aligned with an organization's strategy and risk tolerance to ensure executive and board sponsorship. Matt then illustrates a lifecycle approach to TPRM and dives into governance, administrative functions, and technical solutions that are critical for TPRM program success.

Chris argues that a company's most important competitive advantage lies in its ability to sense customer demand changes, efficiently gather materials or talent, integrate manufacturing or service capacity, and optimize logistics and customer support. He believes that when companies excel at these supply chain activities—faster and cheaper than competitors—they grow market share and thrive. Conversely, he contends that weaknesses in these areas lead to lagging performance and cause firms to struggle to survive. Chris defines the collective oversight of these activities as Supply Chain Management (SCM), which includes all vendors and third parties essential to business operations.

Collectively, Bill, Matt and Chris demonstrate that in addition to helping the organization identify risks originating in its third-party relationships, a robust TPRM program also allows it to remain agile and resilient, and when optimized, provides a true competitive advantage.

In Chapter 1, we provide the foundations for TPRM program structure and begin to identify the foundational tools to successfully manage third-party risks.

Immediately following Chris' essay is a list of publications he references throughout.

Central to Risk Management

Bill Bonney

VRM should be an integral part of enterprise risk management, not just a compliance exercise, ensuring the organization's resilience and long-term success.

In this first chapter, I provide a high-level discussion reviewing a vendor risk management charter, drawing attention to what I believe are the essential areas of focus. After that, I'll share my insights on the governance objectives for vendor management and the criticality of watching and solving for more than just the budget issues involved in using third parties. Then, I will build on my governance anecdote to show how these same governance objectives relate to vendor management risk categories. Next, I address the three lines of defense (TLOD) model and the RACI matrix as essential tools for managing vendor risk. Finally, I provide my take on how to identify critical vendors.

Creating the Charter

When tasked with creating a charter for any program, most of us start by grabbing a file from somewhere to use as a template. Where we get the template depends on the maturity of the organization or the program. Do we have an existing charter? If we're just now spinning up a program or spinning off a program from a more comprehensive parent program, we'll need a new charter. If we do program governance well, we can take almost any recent internal example and modify it to our needs. If not, we might consult a colleague or look for one online. Then we modify that one to our needs.

What we probably don't do, or hopefully, do fully aware of the risk of overlooking key inputs, is start with a vendor management solution provider. We know that their (simplistic) view is usually constructed to fit their solution and tends to group risks otherwise worthy of individual scrutiny. For example, while it is true that supply chain interruption does have a potential financial impact and could be a source of financial risk, it can come with several other risks that their approach overlooks. Likewise, because their solution typically skews toward organizational outcomes versus managing risks, they might conflate legal risks with regulatory risks, whilst larger, more complex entities would be wise to deal with legal and regulatory risks individually with the appropriate internal and external expertise.

Whatever the source and however you produce it, the vendor risk management program, informed by its parent, the enterprise risk management program, is so essential to an organization that the program charter must enable the organization to staff and address vendor risk. It cannot be window dressing or exist only to check a box for the latest in-vogue metrics for internal governance. The charter must clearly lay out roles and duties, provide an enforceable mandate, and establish accountability with visibility at the board or enterprise risk management levels, assuming that accountability within that function is ultimately to the board.

The Components of the Charter

Given the ease with which you can acquire a template for a charter, I'm not going to provide one here. Instead, I'll address the purpose of several of the components of your charter. Call it a charter for your charter. As you read through these sections, focus most on where you need to be prescriptive in your language and exert or have the appropriate senior leader assert appropriate authority.

- **Authority** – Assuming there will be times when risk or expediency will require senior leadership to make and communicate decisions, you must establish executive sponsorship as early as possible as you build up your vendor risk management program.

- **Purpose** – Beyond the need to identify, assess, and mitigate risks, there also needs to be an appropriate high-level focus on maintaining the visibility of vendor risks for the entire company and defining the program's role (separate from the role of the contributing individuals). This focus will help determine the objectives and scope and identify the contributors and their roles and responsibilities.
- **Objectives and Scope** – The way I look at the differences between these two components of the charter and the responsibilities is that the objectives and scope speak more to executive leadership so you can get the needed buy-in, and the responsibilities speak more to the business leaders to ensure you are addressing the areas of risk specific to your company. They should reflect your executive leadership's requirements and the unique risks to your company.
- **Responsibilities** – The only generic role I'd define here is for the leader of the vendor risk management program. Beyond that, I'd be definitive about integrating with the business units. In my experience, the greater risk is with a corporate function too detached from the business, where most vendor engagements live. By too detached from the business, I mean vendor risk management, when run in a corporate silo, is prone to create procedures that are ignorant of the needs or abilities of the business unit(s) they are designed to protect. It's also important to keep in mind that the same dynamic can play out across back-office functions. Think of the many disconnects between procuring, accounting, and governance functions.
- **Principles** – It's easy to list the elements that make up your key principles, but it's much harder to live them. You might not find it difficult to maintain a risk-based approach. However, maintaining due diligence before and during vendor engagement and continuing to uphold your stated goals for transparency can be a challenge. These principles must drive your day-to-day actions. Failure here creates the

impression and then the reality that vendor risk management has detached from the business and become a check-the-box function.

Senior leadership must hold the leader of the vendor management program accountable for providing appropriate visibility of vendor risks and mitigation strategies and provide the mandate that vendor risk management integrates with the business units to achieve the visibility and mitigation of vendor risks.

Proper Governance Is Essential to VRM

My first exposure to vendor management, and by extension vendor risk management, came almost immediately after I created a new central IT function at a small, 300-person software company in the mid-1980s. One of the reasons I got this assignment was that our spending on telephony was the largest line item after payroll. A little digging uncovered more than spending risk. We were woefully under-capacity in our in-house telecom equipment. The equipment itself was not well maintained and was out of warranty. The group that managed our telephony received constant complaints about a lack of outgoing capacity and dropped inbound customer calls. At a minimum, we had cost issues, intermittent service disruption, and the risk of imminent collapse. However, the real problem was a lack of competent governance.

The group responsible for telephony was the HR department. Well, of course, telecom was about phones. HR managed the receptionists and ensured everyone had a phone when they started work as part of the personnel onboarding process, so they should manage telephony, right? They had no background or expertise and drove decisions purely on upfront cost. Every new fax machine came with a long-distance contract by whoever was having a sale. We, therefore, had multiple long-distance contracts with AT&T, MCI, and Sprint. Each contract was for a single phone line.

My point is not to trash the company's HR department. They were not experienced in telephony management. The lack of attention to vendor management and the risks of any third-party relationship was a failure by the board and executive management. This example is illustrative and sadly true, and by no means was the last time I inherited a collection of third-party relationships that, by their mismanagement, created third-party risks that were disproportionate to the strategic value of the third-party relationship. In a fascinating twist, all three times that I had to clean up one of these messes, the problem initially came to management's attention because of a spending problem that caught someone's eye. No risk committee conducted a vendor risk assessment, and no auditor (internal or external) raised any red flags. Someone was trying to free up cash to invest elsewhere. You could certainly make the point that they uncovered spending risk, which led to better governance, but in all three cases, the hit to the operating budget was the least of the risks we faced.

Without going into the details, we experienced service failures, financial fraud, and the requirement to devote resources to fix the short-term and long-term problems at all three companies. A properly implemented and resourced vendor risk management program would likely have surfaced each of these problems in the department that owned the relationships. Uncovering the risk of customer attrition due to an inability to reach us would have raised a red flag. These events were before the Internet and email, so calling us was our customers' only option.

The problem at the second company was that a hiring manager received a finder's fee for contractors supplied by a sourcing firm for contractors on his team, which ran the risk of exposure to bribery charges, though not likely at the senior leadership level. That exposure, though, could easily have jeopardized contracts with our most important client, the U.S. federal government, which was undoubtedly concerned about integrity within its supplier network for airport security.

The third company had both the risk of legal sanctions for financial fraud and a gap in capabilities that left us vulnerable to a security breach that could have been catastrophic. In this case, a manager agreed to purchase equipment in exchange for having the vendor cover the cost of employee morale-building exercises. This maneuver allowed him to make capital expenditures, which were less scrutinized, and save on his expense budget, allowing him to deploy those resources elsewhere. While company number two could have caught its problem with a sound financial fraud risk mitigation strategy (60% of personnel were contractors, which would likely have required a risk assessment and mitigation program for supplier risk), company number three would have uncovered the risk sooner had they been looking at the over-coverage of specific security controls.

I spent almost two pages going through these examples from my past to call attention to the importance of cooperative governance by the relevant parties, illustrate how embedded these vendors were with operations, and show that relying on only financial governance is clearly inadequate. While financial triggers caused investigations that eventually uncovered operational and strategic risks, they were invisible and, therefore, not managed for too long. Because vendor relationships did not receive appropriate ongoing governance, we missed the risks, and problems occurred. Management was not as engaged in each case because these third-party vendors provided us with at least some of the services.

Categories of Risk

In my anecdote above, I identified and began articulating six vendor risk categories. Rather than provide a series of textbook definitions for the various types of risks, I'll provide below the six I identified and how they could apply.

- **Financial** – The wrong or mismanaged vendor could cost rather than save the company money. However, a greater financial risk comes from management's distance from operations managed by vendors and the potential cost overruns and fraud that can occur when they are not monitored.

- **Reputational** – Companies are routinely held accountable for and suffer reputational harm from the misdeeds and failings of their vendors.

- **Operational** – We primarily use third-party vendors for their expertise, to save management the operational burden of managing the delivery of an outcome, or to reduce costs. Ideally, you can achieve all three. Poorly chosen or poorly managed vendors could cost more but also deliver an inferior outcome or even bog management down in operational overhead.
- **Security** – How your vendor implements security controls over proprietary, customer, or sensitive corporate data exposes you, as does how you each secure the pathways by which this data flows. Additionally, these access points potentially open unrelated data protection and financial control gaps.
- **Regulatory** – The company and its vendors share regulatory responsibility for data protection in multiple regulatory regimes. Still, offloading operations to a vendor does not transfer regulatory responsibility. Therefore, failures with your vendor can expose you to regulatory sanctions.
- **Legal** – All the risk categories listed above also create potential legal risks for the company. Additionally, your failure to perform due diligence and govern your vendors properly exposes you to regulator, shareholder, and customer litigation.

In addition, as my co-authors have articulated, you'll want to consider strategic risk, technology risk in general, country risk, and environmental, social, and governance risk.

Defending Against the Risks and the Three Lines of Defense Model

Here are a couple of illustrations that are likely familiar to most of you. The sample RACI in Figure 1.1 is just a small number of tasks related to the contracting phase for acquiring a vendor. The Three Lines of Defense in Figure 1.2 is a general TLOD model that can apply to any mega process.

Task	Vendor Managament	Executive Sponsor	Business Owner	Legal	IT & Info Sec
Identify standard items & conditions for contract	C	-	R/A	C	C
Negotiate contract	C	C	R/A	C	-
Review final draft against standards	C	C	C	R/A	C
Execute contract	I	R/A	I	I	I
Store contract managemnet system	R/A	-	I	-	-
Assign contract owner	R/A	I	I	I	I
Intergrate new vendor through onboarding process	C	I	R/A	-	C

Figure 1.1 – Sample RACI

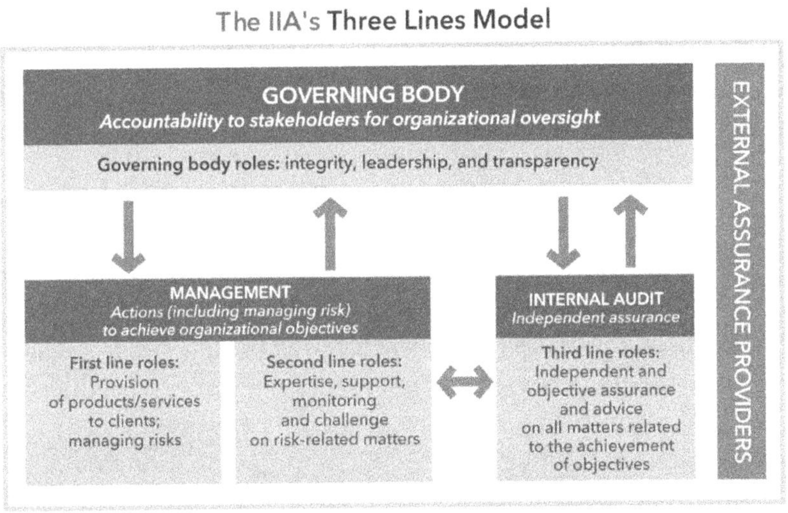

Figure 1.2 – Sample Three Lines of Defense Model

I'll refer to these illustrations for context as I walk through an analysis of high-level governance for the vendor risk management program.

Even if the process is poorly documented and executed with an outdated or unenforced policy, there is some informal process performed by people using one or more tools. We can fill in the knowledge gaps by interviewing the personnel involved. Vendors must get paid, and the accounting department is likely paying them. Let's start there and begin gathering tasks and names. From this list, we can build a process document and a RACI matrix.

Then, we can apply the Three Lines of Defense (TLOD) model by taking our RACI matrix, looking for the responsible and accountable individuals, and using that to build the first (responsible) and second (accountable) lines of the defense model. This will likely be an iterative process and must be checked and rechecked with the responsible and accountable individuals, the leaders of those functions, and the people who comprise the consulted ranks. Including a few check-ins with the informed individuals and the internal audit team is probably necessary. While your auditors can't tell you how to construct the program, they can consult on properly implementing an oversight function. Changes to the policy will ultimately reflect what you learned from the discovery phase.

At the end of this chapter, I have provided a very typical policy template for vendor risk management. Here, I'd like to make a few points:

- Draft your initial team using the current mega process for vendor management/vendor risk management. Ensuring you have representation and, eventually, buy-in from each stakeholder group is essential. While you are in process discovery, this will help you catch all the one-off process forks and help to reduce potential friction when you begin driving changes to how you manage vendors or vendor risk.
- Remember to keep any resulting policy, process definitions, and program element definitions separate. I often advise keeping the policy document as constitutional as possible to avoid burdening the board with oversight of operational details. In this case, we hope the board is engaged in ERM and VRM. However, vendor risk management is often a subject of external audit review, and it is essential to keep the policy free of process and program elements because deviation from the board-approved policy is a hazard during an external audit.

- Ensure that the policy echoes, amplifies, and enables, where appropriate, the purpose, objectives, scope, and responsibilities contained in the program charter.
- In anticipation of external audit review, consider how you define enforceability, conflict resolution, and exemptions or exceptions.
- Have the policy approved or reapproved and the commitment of senior leadership communicated.

It's also helpful to have a RACI matrix early in your assessment. In addition to defining the primary responsibilities, this will allow you to construct a TLOD model in the definition phase. As you draft the process and create the RACI, ensure you have identified the essential personnel underpinning your three lines of defense (TLOD). When reviewing how you implement the TLOD model, safeguard against typical mistakes companies make when relying on the TLOD. In Chapters 2 and 3, we'll do a deep dive into necessary resources and roles and responsibilities.

- Validate that the personnel that make up the first (responsible) and second (accountable) lines of defense understand the process and the red flags to look for.
- Don't assume you'll catch any problems during audits. It's the third line of defense, not the primary line of defense. Even if you do see all or most issues during audits, it may be too late to avoid serious failure.
- Guard against an over-reliance on the third line by ensuring assurance activities are integrated throughout the process as lines one and two interact so they are not an add-on burden. Those burdens can lead to duplication of effort and complacency. Design your process controls to preemptively manage the risks and allow the audit function to understand management's risk assessment and test the effectiveness of control design in addition to process and control execution.

Identifying Critical Vendors

While common, conflating two or more related but distinct concepts can confuse how we think about each, leading to problems managing high-risk business processes. Like my advice to keep policy free of process, I also think limiting the factors that determine vendor criticality is essential. We often see myriad factors listed when considering a vendor's criticality. However, in my experience, these are often added by tool and service vendors motivated to make the process seem as difficult as possible.

Eliminate from your criteria anything that restates or helps define another factor. For example, "Specific Services Provided" and "Business Disruption Factors" would be related, not different factors. The business disruption caused by the inability to deliver the specific service that a vendor provides is one criterion, not two. The potential business disruption is the factor driving criticality. "Regulatory Requirements" is another misused factor. Regulators don't require certain services to be provided by a third party and, in many cases, don't require you to provide a service at all. Regulators are concerned with business disruption for industries like banking and other critical infrastructure sectors and unauthorized disclosure of certain data types. And finally, don't conflate the difficulty of recovering with the vendor's criticality. The difficulty of recovering a service matters only if the service is critical; difficulty alone doesn't cause the vendor to become critical.

I consider the materiality of business disruption and data disclosure as my criteria for vendor criticality. Obviously, your situation may vary, but apply these principles to keep the analysis focused and relatable to your business objectives.

Conclusion

In conclusion, effective vendor risk management (VRM) requires a comprehensive and well-structured governance framework that extends beyond financial oversight. A strong VRM program must be rooted in clear accountability, strategic risk assessment, and continuous monitoring to mitigate financial, operational, reputational, security, legal, and regulatory risks. The examples I provided underscore the consequences of weak governance and the critical need for leadership's proactive engagement to ensure the company manages vendors with the same rigor as internal operations. By leveraging tools like the Three Lines of Defense model, the RACI matrix, and a well-defined charter, organizations can establish a sustainable VRM program that aligns with broader enterprise risk management objectives. Ultimately, VRM should not be a compliance exercise but an integral part of an organization's strategy, safeguarding its reputation, operational resilience, and long-term success.

Vendor Risk Management Policy Template

[Company Name]
Effective Date: [MM/DD/YYYY]
Version: [Version Number]
Owner: [Department Responsible]

1. Purpose

The purpose of this Vendor Risk Management (VRM) Policy is to establish a framework for assessing, managing, and mitigating risks associated with third-party vendors that provide products, services, or technology to [Company Name]. This policy ensures that vendor relationships align with regulatory, operational, security, and financial requirements while protecting the company's reputation and interests.

2. Scope

This policy applies to all departments and business units within [Company Name] that engage with vendors. It covers all third-party vendors, suppliers, contractors, and service providers that interact with or impact business operations, finances, security, or compliance.

3. Roles and Responsibilities

- Executive Sponsor: Provides oversight and ensures vendor risk management aligns with company strategy.
- Vendor Risk Management Team: Responsible for assessing, managing, and monitoring vendor risks.
- Procurement Team: Ensures vendor selection follows due diligence and approval processes.
- Business Unit Owners: Own vendor relationships and ensure adherence to risk mitigation strategies.
- Legal and Compliance: Reviews vendor contracts to align with regulatory and legal requirements.
- IT Security Team: Assesses cybersecurity and data protection risks associated with vendors.

- Internal Audit: Reviews and monitors vendor compliance with company policies and regulatory requirements.

4. Vendor Risk Management Process

4.1 Vendor Identification and Classification

All vendors must be categorized based on their risk exposure and criticality to business operations. The classification levels include:

- Critical Vendor: Directly impacts core business operations, regulatory compliance, financial stability, or security.
- High-Risk Vendor: Handles sensitive data, critical business processes, or regulatory-sensitive functions.
- Medium-Risk Vendor: Provides essential but non-critical services with limited operational impact.
- Low-Risk Vendor: Has minimal impact on operations, finances, or security.

4.2 Vendor Due Diligence and Onboarding

Before engaging with a vendor, the following due diligence steps must be performed:

- Conduct a background check and financial health review.
- Assess security and data protection policies.
- Review regulatory compliance status (e.g., GDPR, HIPAA, SOC 2).
- Evaluate prior performance and industry reputation.
- Identify potential conflicts of interest.

And the following onboarding tasks must be completed:

- Set up accounts, access, and systems for the vendor.
- Communicate expectations and integrate vendor processes with internal processes.
- Train staff on new systems or processes related to the vendor's products or services.

4.3 Risk Assessment and Approval

A risk assessment must be conducted based on:

- Operational Risk: Disruptions to business processes.
- Financial Risk: Cost overruns, fraud, and contractual risks.
- Reputational Risk: Negative impact on brand and customer trust.
- Security Risk: Cyber threats, data breaches, and system vulnerabilities.
- Regulatory and Legal Risk: Compliance with industry-specific regulations.

Approval authority:

- Critical and High-Risk Vendors: Require executive-level approval and periodic reviews.
- Medium and Low-Risk Vendors: Require department-level approval.

4.4 Contract Management

Vendor contracts must include:

- Service level agreements (SLAs) defining performance expectations.
- Security and data protection clauses.
- Compliance with applicable regulations.
- Right to audit and compliance reporting.
- Termination and exit strategy clauses.

4.5 Ongoing Monitoring and Auditing

Vendors must be continuously monitored based on their risk classification:

- Critical and High-Risk Vendors: Quarterly reviews, annual risk assessments, and security audits.
- Medium-Risk Vendors: Semi-annual performance reviews.
- Low-Risk Vendors: Annual check-ins.

Monitoring includes:

- Regular performance evaluations.
- Compliance audits.
- Cybersecurity risk assessments.
- Financial health tracking.

4.6 Incident Response and Vendor Breach Management

In the event of a security or operational incident involving a vendor:

- Immediate Notification: Vendors must report security incidents within [X] hours.
- Investigation: Internal teams must assess the impact and root cause.
- Remediation Plan: The vendor must provide a corrective action plan.
- Reporting and Documentation: All incidents must be documented and reviewed for potential policy updates.

4.7 Vendor Offboarding and Termination

- Define exit strategies for discontinuing vendor relationships.
- Ensure secure transition of services and data.
- Revoke system access and recover company assets.
- Conduct a post-offboarding risk review.

5. Compliance and Enforcement

- Non-compliance with this policy may result in contract termination or legal action.
- Employees and departments must adhere to VRM processes, and violations will be subject to disciplinary actions.
- This policy will be reviewed annually or as needed to reflect regulatory changes.

6. Approval and Acknowledgment

Approved by: [Name], [Title]
Approval Date: [MM/DD/YYYY]
Next Review Date: [MM/DD/YYYY]

Essential Components of a Third-Party Risk Management Program

Matt Stamper

Third-party risk management (TPRM) is critically important in modern organizations and requires an entity-wide program to manage the complexity and cross-functional nature of vendor and supply chain risks.

Few topics warrant more executive attention than vendor and supply chain risk management—collectively, third-party risk management (TPRM). Whether shocks to global supply chains, security risks associated with enterprise software, labor strikes, or the geopolitical risks that threaten computer chip manufacturing in Taiwan, our organizations confront numerous risks and dependencies on external providers that necessitate well-managed and high-assurance TPRM programs.

As discussed in Chapter 3, TPRM programs have unique characteristics that make them inherently challenging to implement, given that core functions of the TPRM process reside within different corporate functions, including notably accounting, legal, IT, operations, and security. Where accountability and resourcing are muddied, risk factors are accentuated. This is the core reason why TPRM should be considered an entity-wide program versus a specific function or set of tasks tied to a single department.

Equally important, the TPRM program should be contextualized to the organization's strategy and its operating environment. Few organizations operate in isolation, and most organizations have material dependencies on third parties to help drive enterprise value. Clearly aligning vendor and supply chain risk management functions to organizational initiatives will help justify the commitments required by the TPRM program. Like security, if the TPRM program is not adequately aligned with the organization's risk tolerances and strategy, the program will be inherently challenged and lack executive and board sponsorship.

Building a successful TPRM program is underpinned by proactive organizational leadership and requires diligence, clear demarcation of roles and responsibilities, adequate resourcing, project and program management, and a governance model that is risk-informed and aligned with organizational strategy and priorities. Accordingly, let's outline the constituent elements of a successful TPRM program. These elements are grouped into the following three categories: governance, administration, and technical functions.

Governance Is Foundational

Governance is foundational to any organizational function that needs to be managed programmatically with predictable and defined outcomes. Good governance underpins risk management and the assurance that organizations require when addressing the operational complexity of TPRM programs. There are some foundational tools that help ensure good governance over the program. Of note are the following:

- **TPRM Program Charter** – Charters are great tools to help establish organizational expectations related to identified programs. Charters should clearly define priorities, key risks that are being managed by the TPRM program, roles and responsibilities, accountabilities for key functions and stakeholders within the program, and how disputes among stakeholders should be arbitrated and by whom. Charters identify governance tasks and their cadences (e.g., meetings with stakeholders, audits, assessments). The charter should also highlight key resource requirements for the TPRM program and how the budgeting for these resources is managed and approved. In short, the charter sets the tone for the TPRM program.

- **TPRM Target Operating Model** – The target operating model (TOM) for the TPRM program is a foundational governance tool. The TOM should clarify organizational expectations as to which TPRM functions will be in-sourced, co-sourced, or outsourced and whether these functions will be centralized or federated across the organization. The TOM should include criteria to evaluate material changes to the TPRM program and organizationally agreed-upon definitions for materiality. TOMs should identify requisite organizational skills and competencies, stakeholders in the program, arbitration mechanisms as noted in the charter to address conflicting priorities within the organization, how vendors and suppliers should be classified or categorized, and some of the basic control mechanisms desired to keep TPRM risk factors within organizationally defined risk tolerances. Ideally, the identified TPRM controls outline inherent risk (e.g., before the control is implemented) and residual risk (e.g., the level of risk that remains once a control has been successfully implemented). The TOM will also define how frequently the TPRM program should be evaluated, whether from a third-party audit (or similar assessment) or an internal review. The TOM should establish a shared calendar and repository for TPRM program documentation as part of the operating model. The calendar should schedule key functions as part of the program, including reports to organizational stakeholders, assessments of material vendors, and other activities. Effectively, the TOM outlines the basic operating model for the TPRM program.

- **RACI Matrix for Stakeholder Roles** – RACI matrices take time to develop, notably as they relate to clarifying who is responsible for a given task or function and who is ultimately accountable for that function's outcome. However, when done correctly, RACI matrices eliminate ambiguity regarding program functions. Build a RACI matrix that contemplates all phases of the TPRM lifecycle, including key tasks, and documents the core deliverables associated with the TPRM function. Spend the time necessary to ensure that all members of the TPRM ecosystem within the organization are aware of their specific or departmental functions and validate if they have the resourcing, time, and requisite competencies to address these items appropriately. I strongly recommend revisiting the RACI matrix annually to see if adjustments or other changes are necessary. RACI matrices, when done correctly, are great governance tools that reduce, if not eliminate, program ambiguity. The time invested in drafting the RACI matrix for the TPRM program is time well spent.

- **TPRM Budget** – Budgets reflect priorities. A TPRM program that does not have a defined budget to address the core risk factors that are material to the organization will likely not meet organizational objectives. Budgets can be drafted to address financial requirements (e.g., licensing for tools, audit and assessment fees, training) and the time needed to perform given functions. Determine how frequently the program's budget should be reviewed and validated. Larger organizations will frequently perform monthly or quarterly budget-to-variance analyses to ensure that stakeholders are not surprised by unanticipated expenses. Ensure that the budget contemplates some contingency—aka rainy day—expenses. Where resources are not sufficient to address identified risks, this should be conveyed to key organizational stakeholders, likely some form of a risk committee.

- **Policies and Standards** – Your TPRM program should be codified with an organizationally defined policy and accompanying standard that outlines how third-party and vendor risks should be managed by the organization. Like all policies, the TPRM policy should be reviewed annually, have a defined scope, and clearly indicate who the accountable party is for the policy and the TPRM program. More detailed expectations may accompany the policy via a TPRM standard and more detailed TPRM procedures. The standard and contemplated procedures provide operational guidance on how vendor and supply chain risks should be evaluated.

- **Key Risk and Performance Indicators (KRIs/KPIs)** – Metrics are integral to good governance. Absent metrics, notably KRIs and KPIs, decisions regarding vendor and supplier risk may be made off the cuff versus informed by data. Developing KRIs/KPIs takes time, but like the RACI matrix, it's time well spent. One of the most important KRIs that should be part of this effort would be the percentage of "material" vendors assessed within the last twelve months. How that percentage is ultimately defined serves as a reflection of the organization's risk tolerance. As a case in point, if there's an expectation that all material third parties are reviewed annually, this data point should be tracked and reviewed. If only, as a hypothetical, eighty percent of material vendors are evaluated given resource constraints, how should this be addressed? Should the risk tolerance change such that 80% of material vendors be assessed annually, or should additional resources be allocated to the TPRM program? Metrics allow for dispassionate, data-driven reviews of the TPRM and other programs. As your organization builds out its KRIs/KPIs, keep the initial batch of metrics to the critical few. Target a workable number—say less than 10—that can inform the status of the program. Keep in mind that if the data associated with a metric is too onerous to obtain, that metric will likely atrophy.

Collectively, the charter, target operating model, RACI matrix of identified functions, coupled with the roles and responsibilities related to the same, the budget, TPRM policy (and standards where applicable), and KRIs/KPIs provide a governance foundation for the TPRM program.

Document Administrative Functions

Administrative functions related to the TPRM process should be documented and aligned to the TPRM program. Ideally, these functions can be mapped to specific job roles and associated job descriptions. Absent this mapping, there is the risk that stakeholders who should be engaged in the TPRM program fail to recognize why that particular objective is placed on their proverbial desk. Preempt this ambiguity and ensure that all participants in the TPRM process know their roles, required resources, and the cadence of the work. Charge these participants with identifying bottlenecks and constraints to the TPRM program. These risks should be captured in a risk register that senior stakeholders can review and address. There's value in explicitly calling out a duty to inform regarding risks. Participants should know how and to whom they can report challenges with the TPRM program.

The diagram that follows provides a simplified view of the TPRM lifecycle. Each phase has administrative functions and tasks that should be captured in the RACI matrix noted above. These administrative functions should be assigned, resourced, documented, and managed with key risk indicators or other metrics as the circumstances warrant. Mature organizations will call out TPRM functions in job descriptions that are consistent with what's been captured in the RACI matrix.

Figure 1.3 – TPRM Lifecycle (Abbreviated)

Here are some foundational activities for each phase. Each organization's specific target operating model and the identified risks will inform the overall nature and extent of tasks and functions by phase.

- **Identification** – The identification phase centers on determining the universe of potential vendors or suppliers that may address a given organizational requirement. Part of the identification phase may include basic pre-filtering exercises that determine if there are geographic or environmental, social, and governance (ESG) factors that constrain the universe of options. Procuring entities within the organization should clearly define the functional requirements, budget, and operational constraints that may impact identified options and relevant factors for the successful use of the service, product, component, or raw material. As part of the identification phase, the organization should evaluate the materiality and potential dependencies that would result from the desired service, product, component, or raw material. The level of diligence that comes in the assessment and selection phases is ultimately risk-based. Not all vendors or suppliers are equal. Material vendors (more on this later) are those that have an inherent capability to impact the organization's reputation, financial well-being, operations, compliance with laws and regulations, or other such factors deemed material by executive stakeholders. Given the concentration of risks found in many areas of our economy, organizations would be well served to expand the universe of options available. For certain industries, geopolitical factors may require looking at options across multiple geographies.

- **Assessment** – The assessment phase is where the rubber meets the road when it comes to challenges with TPRM programs. Line-of-business stakeholders may have well-defined criteria for the identified product, component, or service they are looking to procure. From their operating context, they know what they want and believe that they have identified an option that will help them address specific business objectives. While this functional assessment may be accurate, it frequently lacks a broader operational context. Depending upon the type of product or service, there may be security and privacy topics that need to be addressed but were not evaluated by business stakeholders. There will undoubtedly be finance and accounting issues (e.g., payment terms, W-9s) that need attention and contracting provisions that legal counsel may want to incorporate into the agreement with the identified provider. As an example, from a security perspective, there's value in having breach notification, right to audit, confidentiality, and minimum-security practices clauses added to service agreements. Where personal data may be in scope, it's also recommended to include a data protection addendum (or similar) to the agreement. Operational considerations, including lead times and performance metrics, notably service level agreements

(SLAs) and service level objectives (SLOs), may need to be incorporated into the relationship. When assessment criteria are vague or managed in isolation, there's a proclivity to onboard suppliers and vendors who may not fully meet broader organizational criteria but only those of a given department or function. This is why it's advisable to have standardized requirements established and shared across the organization. For this reason, many larger organizations have drafted their own customized versions of master service agreements (MSAs) and statements of work (SOWs) that are used ubiquitously across the organization.

- **Selection** – The criteria noted in the identification phase should be weighted to provide a holistic perspective on the prospective vendor or supplier. Your organization may have specific criteria that are effectively binary (yes/no) in nature. The vendor or supplier cannot be onboarded without an appropriate response to these criteria. While difficult, it's important to have a consensus on the weightings of the various inclusion/exclusion factors with the key stakeholders for the contemplated good or service. Anticipate some tension when the calculus produces results that frustrate key stakeholders, notably a line of business executive who preferred a given option only to have that option excluded from the selection process given the pre-established criteria. Ensure that there's a process to facilitate arbitrating these "professional" disagreements (as outlined in the charter) with a documented exception process where warranted. The selection process is well-served to look internally at the beginning of the phase to see if any existing suppliers or vendors can meet the specific requirement. For many larger organizations, there may be viable, well-vetted solutions used by other divisions or subsidiaries that are effectively already onboarded and delivering value. The selection process should validate if these options exist. Stakeholders should also seek input from colleagues and peers in other organizations and see if they have recommendations or insights on the prospective candidates. Within our CISO community, these insights are invaluable. Lastly, and to overstate the obvious, it's preferable from a negotiating perspective to have two or more viable providers identified. This competition can be used to support strategic sourcing options where the prospective vendors or suppliers are assessed in such areas as pricing, legal terms, and delivery dates. While not the topic of this book, strategic sourcing should inform the selection criteria and be brought into the selection and negotiation efforts. Before the selection phase is concluded, stakeholders should take a pause and ask if there are any additional factors or risks that have not been identified as part of the process and why they were omitted. This offers everyone in the effort an opportunity to surface any additional concerns that warrant attention. Ideally, structure this risk review to ensure that key risk categories are specifically assessed (e.g., risks operations, data, regulatory compliance).

- **Onboarding** – The onboarding process, frequently referred to as the honeymoon phase, is one in which early warning signs may surface but are dismissed or ignored prematurely. Cases in point may include "minor" service issues such as a slipped delivery date, the wrong products or components being shipped, changes to service delivery, capacity issues, changes to support teams to less senior or skilled staff, or a plethora of other issues that indicate that what was negotiated during the selection process may not be reflective of the current reality. While there's a tendency to accept these minor issues as one-off challenges, don't make this mistake. The onboarding phase requires diligence and vigilance to frame the relationship correctly. By permitting minor issues to occur during this honeymoon phase, the organization implicitly conveys that requirements established during the selection phase were hypothetical and not germane to the relationship. This is a critical mistake. If your organization requires a given feature, service, product, or item and the service or product quality is not to the agreed-to standard, escalate directly with the vendor's or supplier's senior management. Be heard. Ask the provider to provide a written explanation as to the variance between what was contracted versus what was delivered. Establishing the right tone and expectations during the onboarding phase is critical to avoiding surprises and performance issues throughout the contract period. Establish the cadence for service and product reviews during the onboarding phase. These stewardship meetings should evaluate issues to date, changes to either organization that may impact contracted services or products, or any other issue that may be material to the relationship. Use these meetings to validate understandings among the parties.

- **Performance Management** – The tone of the relationship established during the onboarding phase will have a lasting impact on the performance management phase of the lifecycle. During this phase, stewardship meetings and reviews occur with more critical vendors and suppliers. For service providers, it's important to review the fulfillment of SLAs (e.g., uptime and delivery times) and SLOs (e.g., response time to tickets). How effective are remediation and other responses to these concerns if issues surface? For suppliers, are delivery dates and quality consistent to date? Compile your own set of factors that should be reviewed with the third party and ensure that agreed-to schedules for these reviews don't slip. It's too easy to fall into complacency only to be caught off guard by a service-impacting issue or supply chain interruption that impacts your organization. When I was a CISO at an international managed services and data center provider, I welcomed these discussions with our clients. I wanted to review what our team had done to protect their business and learn more about the client's upcoming initiatives and requirements. Well-executed stewardship programs offer an opportunity to share best practices, discover new potential solutions, and improve services and supplies. I strongly recommend that the tone not be adversarial with the supplier or vendor but rather one of professional oversight. As the contracting organization, it's important to recognize that the supplier or vendor's products and services are likely integral to the organizational strategy for your firm. The goal is to ensure that their product or service has predictable quality and commensurate assurance that forms of enterprise risk are mitigated to acceptable levels throughout the engagement or contract.

- **Reassessment** – Over time, requirements and expectations will change, necessitating a reassessment of current providers. While this process is similar to the selection process, this phase benefits from the lessons learned during the performance management phase of the lifecycle. Specifically, stakeholders can evaluate if there were material quality issues with the incumbent or if the current business process requires a new set of services, components, or supplies to deliver enterprise value. In the spirit of a virtuous cycle and continuous improvement, evaluate the lessons learned during the previous selection, onboarding, and performance management phases and bring the TPRM current accordingly. Key topics to review may include dependencies on the provider and the provider's supply chain and vendors. Like your organization, your vendors and suppliers rely upon their vendors and suppliers for key services that ultimately impact their ability to service your organization correctly. Validate if there are material risks in their supply chain or with their service providers that could affect your use of their services or products. Third- and fourth-level risks should be evaluated with your most critical third parties. Additionally, determine if there are material changes to the underlying technology used for the product or service and whether these changes present new options and approaches to meet the desired end state. As part of the reassessment phase, there may also be a need to evaluate if changes are required to service agreements and contracts. Before the European Union's General Data Protection Regulation (GDPR) was adopted, using data protection addendums was uncommon. Now, they are commonplace. The advent of new technologies such as artificial intelligence (AI) and large language models such as ChatGPT, Copilot, and Gemini may require additional contractual considerations. The reassessment phase offers an opportunity to bring current not only that particular relationship (or an alternative) but also key areas within the TPRM program, such as performance and risk management considerations related to the provider.

- **Offboarding** – Business is never static, and for various reasons vendors and suppliers are sometimes changed. The offboarding process introduces important risk considerations that span data and intellectual property protections at one end to technological and supply chain issues at the other. If your organization has shared data with a third party, it's essential that this information is either returned or verifiably deleted. This verification must extend to that vendor's vendors and suppliers if they have had to use third parties to service your organization and these third parties have received your firm's data. As an example, software as a service (SaaS) providers frequently use cloud service providers (CSPs) such as Amazon Web Services (AWS), Google Cloud Platform (GCP), or Microsoft Azure to host their applications. You must ensure that these and other sub-service providers are in scope from a data return or deletion perspective. Ideally, this context would have been captured during the selection and vetting processes above. Knowing where and how your organization's data may have been shared with third parties is foundational and impacts each phase of the TPRM lifecycle, but the offboarding phase is critical. Given the many regulatory requirements that impact data governance, don't accept assurances from the third party unless they are documented. At a minimum, require pre- and post-verification that data has been deleted (e.g., a screenshot showing the database or files before deletion and a screenshot or similar assurance that the data has been deleted). Be sure to validate that any recycle bins or similar have been emptied. All these activities should have appropriate timestamps.

Technical Solutions Are Required

Technical solutions are also required to support our TPRM programs. For organizations that have vendors numbering in the hundreds, if not thousands, performing TPRM functions manually is simply not an option. The number of TPRM tools available to help automate and support key functions has grown dramatically over the last few years. Of note are the many service providers who evaluate and score vendors and allow for routine security and diligence questionnaires to be made available in a vetted marketplace. Certain applications, beyond scoring a vendor or supplier based on common factors such as IP address reputation, disclosed breaches, and dark web analysis, also bring predictive modeling to quantify third-party risk. These services effectively create dossiers on vendors and suppliers that can be queried to evaluate a number of considerations such as ESG, debarment status, availability of audits and certifications, and security and privacy factors. These assessment services can be queried prior to onboarding or at various times throughout the lifecycle with the contracting entity. High-quality TPRM applications provide an interactive dashboard that assesses the contracting organization's exposure to third-party risk in near real time. This telemetry is invaluable when managing a large portfolio of third parties and their associated risk factors.

These same applications frequently allow for the creation of custom diligence questionnaires or the incorporation of common questionnaires and shared assessments. Once ingested or enabled by the application, the questionnaire can be sent to all applicable third parties and responses can be automatically tracked and calendared. Effectively, these tools take many of the administrative burdens of overseeing diligence manually and automate key functions. The applications will also evaluate if responses to specific questions warrant a proverbial double-click by a member of the TPRM team. These services continuously monitor news feeds, disclosures to regulators, and social media posts for providers with negative issues or other challenges. Think of this as a glorified RSS feed at scale.

Contracts also require technical support and automation. With the advent of generative AI (GenAI) tools, many firms are now using applications to scan contracts for specific required terms. These tools have proven especially beneficial in looking back at contracts that may have been executed before required security and privacy language was incorporated into service agreements. The insights gathered from these contract reviews can help stakeholders determine if a new agreement may be in order, or if ongoing diligence should be increased, or if they should seek alternative providers. As a quick example, GenAI services can scan an organization's existing contracts and compile a list of those that don't have desired data protection addendums or breach notification clauses. The ability to query and analyze the status of required contract terms benefits from this innovative use of GenAI technology. These services, clearly, must be well-governed to ensure that MNPI and other forms of IP are not inadvertently exposed publicly. Given the advent of GenAI tools, data access controls have never been more key.

Throughout this book, we'll be highlighting areas where TPRM technology, administrative practices, and governance are front-and-center for the program. Our hope is that the insights and perspectives we share in the chapters that follow will ultimately lead to your organization being more resilient and adaptive as it confronts the challenges of managing third-party risk.

Mastering Supply Chain Management

Chris Forbes

Robust and agile SCM is essential for business success in a complex, rapidly changing world. A resilient supply chain is not just a strategic advantage but a fundamental pillar of long-term sustainability and prosperity.

1.0 Essay Overview

I would argue that a company's most important competitive strength is its ability to sense changes in customer demands, gather appropriate materials or talent, integrate sufficient manufacturing capacity or service delivery models, and optimize logistics and customer support. If they can do these basic activities faster and cheaper than their competition, they will grow their market share and thrive. If weak in these areas, they will likely lag behind the competition and struggle to survive. While most organizations have distributed these functions across many departments and multiple geographies, I refer to the collective oversight of these activities as Supply Chain Management (SCM). To put this into context, I view vendors and third parties that the company relies on to run its operations as part of its supply chain. In a sense, they are supplying intellectual property or supplemental labor.

A growing problem with most legacy SCM programs is their primary focus on minimizing costs. The lowest-expense approach was adequate in previous generations when significant supply chain changes occurred infrequently or took decades to unfold. Today, the lowest-expense model hinders an organization's ability to rapidly recognize new information, adapt to changes in the ecosystem, and evolve faster than the competition.

This essay emphasizes that a company must acknowledge the weaknesses in its legacy SCM practices and invest in developing a more comprehensive understanding of its entire supply chain. Companies must recognize the strategic value of leveraging detailed supply chain data, a more profound knowledge of supply chain risks, building a dynamic SCM decision framework, and continuously monitoring supply chains to produce positive outcomes.

According to McKinsey, Harvard Business, and Deloitte, companies should build their businesses on solid foundations of Vision, Mission, Strategy, Critical Success Factors, Goals, Objectives, Key Results (OKRs), Operations, Governance Risk and Compliance (GRC), Financial Management, and Culture and Values.

This essay highlights why the SCM program is critical to a company's success. It discusses the emerging challenges putting pressure on current and future supply chains and explores the key design elements for SCM's Strategy and Critical Success Factors (CSFs).

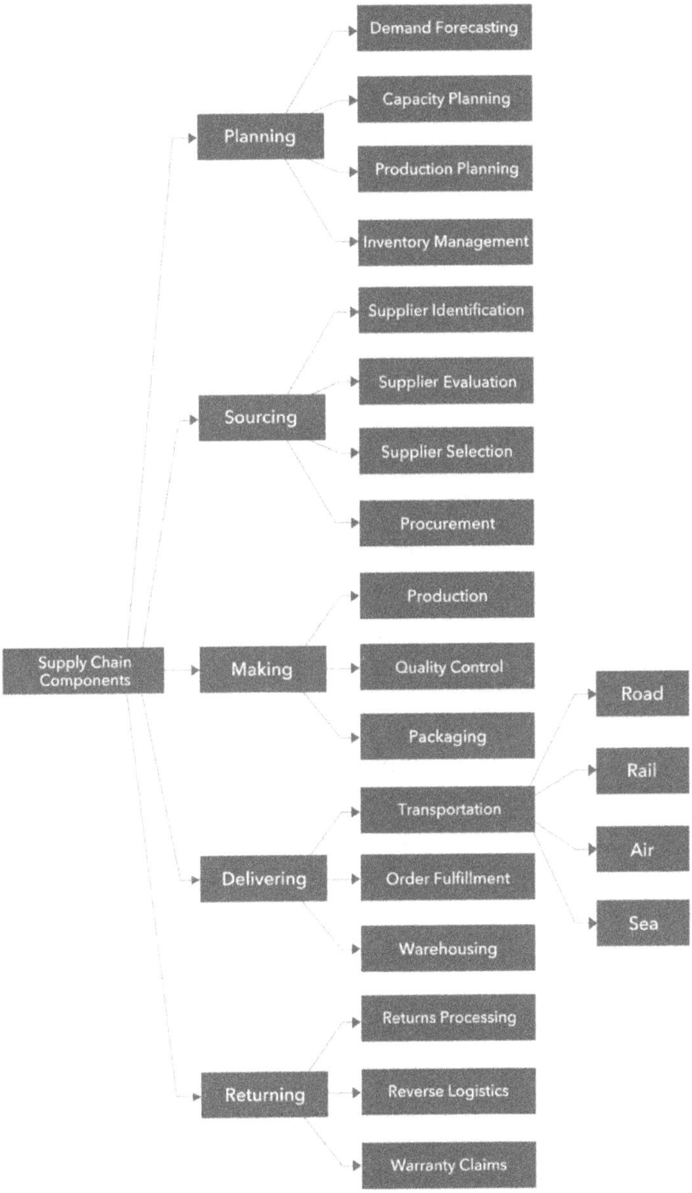

Figure 1.4 – Mindmap for Supply Chain Functions

2.0 SCM Program Benefits and Importance

Industry experts have written extensively about the importance of an effective SCM program and its role in improving efficiency, cost savings, and competitive advantage. For example:

2.1 Reduced Cost

Deloitte's Global Chief Procurement Officer Survey found that companies that invest in supply chain optimization can see a 15% reduction in procurement costs, a 20% decrease in supply chain costs, and up to a 50% reduction in inventory costs. McKinsey & Company found that businesses implementing advanced supply chain technologies, such as AI and automation, can reduce operational costs by 25% to 40%. Gartner's Supply Chain Cost Optimization study found that enhancing supply chain visibility can lead to a 10% reduction in overall inventory costs and a 7% increase in order fill rates, noticeably improving efficiency.

2.2 Enhanced Revenue

Businesses with advanced supply chain capabilities achieve two to three times faster revenue growth than those with less mature capabilities (Deloitte). A PwC survey found that companies with advanced supply chain practices have 50% higher revenue growth and 20% higher profitability than those with less advanced practices. These companies are more agile and can better respond to market changes.

2.3 Raised Customer Satisfaction

79% of companies with high-performing supply chains achieve revenue growth above the industry average (PWC). HBR reports that companies emphasizing supply chain excellence achieve 20% higher customer satisfaction and 30% better perfect order performance. These factors contribute to stronger customer loyalty and higher sales, boosting profitability.

2.4 Optimized Inventories

Effective supply chain management can reduce inventory carrying costs by 20% to 50% (PWC). A BCG report found that companies with advanced supply chain capabilities see a 40% increase in EBIT (Earnings Before Interest and Taxes) margins. These companies also experience a 25% reduction in working capital requirements, further enhancing their financial performance.

2.5 Extended Market Leadership

Supply chain management leaders have 15% lower supply chain costs, less than 50% of the inventory holdings, and more than three times the inventory turns of their competitors (Gartner). Gartner's analysis shows that companies in the Supply Chain Top 25 consistently outperform the market, with stock prices growing 2.5 times faster than the industry average.

2.6 Increased Operational Efficiency

Companies that digitize their supply chains can increase efficiency by 20% to 25% (McKinsey & Company). Research by the MIT Center for Transportation and Logistics indicates that companies with best-in-class supply chain capabilities achieve 75% higher operating margins and 50% less inventory than their peers, leading to significantly improved financial performance.

2.7 Strengthened Profitability

Companies with optimized supply chains have 50% higher net margins and 20% lower cost of goods sold (COGS) than those with less efficient supply chains (Deloitte). According to Deloitte's Global Supply Chain Survey, companies with superior supply chain capabilities achieve 15% higher profitability than their peers. These companies also enjoy better customer service levels and lower operational costs.

2.8 Lowered Risk

70% of companies believe supply chain resilience is essential to protecting long-term business performance (BCI). McKinsey & Company found that companies with advanced supply chain practices can reduce supply chain risk by 50%. Business Continuity Institute (BCI) reports that 70% of businesses with well-established SCRM practices recover from disruptions within a month, compared to 30% for those without. A study by the World Economic Forum highlights that organizations with resilient supply chains can recover 30% faster from economic disruptions.

2.9 Improved Supply Chain Visibility

87% of respondents in a GEODIS survey stated that they believe supply chain visibility is crucial for their operations, yet only 6% have complete visibility. Accenture's Strategy Report on Supply Chain Performance found that companies investing in digital supply chain capabilities can reduce operational costs by up to 30% and increase revenue by up to 10%. These improvements directly contribute to higher profitability.

2.10 Elevated Competitive Advantage

According to a Deloitte report, companies prioritizing supply chain management are 73% more likely to achieve a competitive market advantage. According to an APQC study, top-performing organizations in supply chain management report 50% lower supply chain costs, ten times faster order-to-delivery times, and three times lower inventory levels than their peers. These efficiencies translate into substantial cost savings and higher profits.

These statistics underscore the critical role that effective supply chain management plays in enhancing business performance, reducing costs, improving customer satisfaction, and achieving sustainable growth. We could also argue that improvements in the supply of goods and services lead to greater economic prosperity for a more significant portion of the population and potentially reduce geopolitical unrest. Supply chain stability and the ability to provide life's essentials could lead to fewer wars, less poverty, and more resources spent on innovation and extending the quality of life.

3.0 SCM Strategic Goals and Priorities

The ultimate goal of an SCM program is to create a resilient, continuous, and stable supply chain that can withstand unexpected events, minimize disruptions, and maintain a profitable flow of goods and services to customers. The SCM Strategy describes the steps a company plans to take to achieve its next growth stage, transformation, or repair.

SCM strategies vary from year to year, depending on maturity levels and the desired future state. SCM strategies also differ from one company to another, depending on many internal and external factors.

Regardless of the differences in the strategic plans, all organizations must communicate their plans effectively throughout the company and supplier network. To improve plan understanding and buy-in, I recommend including the following information:

1. Background and Context: Where are we coming from?
2. Vision and Mission: What do we hope to become?
3. Situational Assessment: Where are we now?
4. Value Proposition and Drivers: How does SCM create value?
5. Biggest Challenges and Risks: What is holding us back?
6. Proposed Initiatives: What options did management consider?
7. Decision and Selection Framework: How do we prioritize and rationalize options?
8. Selected Strategic Initiatives: What changes did we commit to?
9. Multi-year Roadmap: How do we sequence optimally?
10. Organization and Oversight: How will we lead and manage change?

3.1 Background and Context

This section provides a historical overview of the company's supply chain operations and past performance. It includes the origins of the current supply chain strategies, key milestones, previous challenges faced, and the evolution of the supply chain over time. This context helps stakeholders understand the current strategic direction's starting point and rationale.

3.2 Vision and Mission

The vision outlines the long-term aspirations for supply chain management, and the mission defines the fundamental purpose and role that SCM plays in the company's success. This vision describes what the company hopes to achieve, such as becoming its industry's most efficient supply chain.

The mission statement identifies the core activities and goals, such as delivering high-quality products and services to customers. Together, they provide direction and motivation for the entire organization.

According to the Value Disciplines model developed by Michael Treacy and Fred Wiersema, companies can adopt one of three strategic approaches to create value and achieve competitive advantage: Operational Excellence, Product Leadership, and Customer Intimacy.

3.3 Situational Assessment

This section analyzes the current state of the supply chain, including its strengths, weaknesses, opportunities, and threats (SWOT analysis).

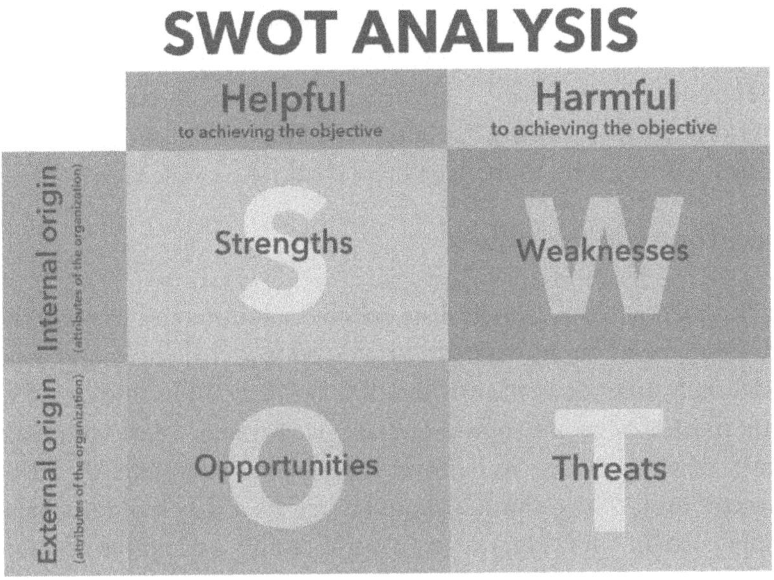

Figure 1.5 – High-level SWOT Diagram

This section also evaluates current performance metrics, supply chain capabilities, market conditions, competitive landscape, and internal resources. It provides a clear picture of the supply chain's current state and identifies areas for improvement.

3.4 Value Proposition and Drivers

This section emphasizes SCM's specific contributions to the organization and customers and goes beyond just describing the tasks performed. The value proposition distills raw data into the bottom-line benefits to financial health and customer satisfaction. Typically, companies define benefits in terms of cost efficiency, speed to market, quality and reliability, or innovation. This section also identifies the primary drivers of supply chain performance, such as technology, talent, and partnerships.

3.5 Biggest Challenges and Risks

This section describes, summarizes, and ranks the various challenges that could hinder the supply chain's success—describing challenges in terms of cause and effect. Ishikawa diagrams (a.k.a. fishbone) are helpful in highlighting how management thinks about possible solutions. This section outlines the key challenges, such as supply disruptions, regulatory changes, geopolitical issues, and environmental concerns. It also includes risk assessments and mitigation strategies to manage these challenges proactively.

3.6 Proposed Initiatives

In this section, management lists possible solutions and changes that are best poised to address the prior section's challenges and risks. Essentially, management provides their rationale and justification for why these actions are appropriate and well-timed. Most companies limit these solutions to "shovel-ready" and commercially viable projects only. The proposals should detail how they would enhance supply chain performance and profitability. Example projects include implementing new technologies, optimizing logistics, or improving supplier relationships.

3.7 Decision and Selection Framework

This section focuses on building stakeholder buy-in by explaining management's thought process when considering and analyzing potential projects. Management should strive to apply a consistent decision-making framework to help train and reinforce organizational muscle memory. This section typically includes specific targets and thresholds that all projects must deliver or achieve, for example, minimum Return on Investment (ROI), Capital requirements, changes to steady-state operating costs and resources, risk-weighted return on assets (ROA), Return on Capital Employed (ROCE), and Internal Rate of Return (IRR).

This framework explains how the company evaluates and chooses among the proposed initiatives.

3.8 Selected Strategic Initiatives

This section outlines the specific initiatives the company has decided to pursue. It includes detailed descriptions, objectives, expected outcomes, and timelines for each initiative. These are the prioritized steps that will drive the supply chain strategy forward.

3.9 Multi-Year Roadmap

This section provides a unified timeline and project calendar showing when each project should begin, which projects can run concurrently, and which projects must wait for prior project completion or resource availability. The multiyear roadmap typically includes requirements to commence, key milestones, deadlines, and dependencies. This information helps the organization and supply chain partners better plan, allocate resources, and track progress.

3.10 Organization and Oversight

This section emphasizes the adage that "everything begins and ends with people." All strategic plans rely on organizational alignment, resource coordination, adequate oversight, and timely feedback. This section describes the structures and processes for managing and monitoring the implementation of the supply chain strategy. It specifies each strategic initiative's leadership roles, governance forums, accountability mechanisms, and success measures.

Conclusion

This essay underscores the multifaceted nature of supply chain management in today's rapidly evolving global landscape. It highlights the escalating complexities, risks, and challenges businesses face, from geopolitical volatility and climate change to cybersecurity threats and the relentless pace of technological advancement. While acknowledging these challenges, the essay emphasizes the substantial benefits of a robust and agile supply chain management program. These benefits encompass cost reduction, revenue enhancement, improved customer satisfaction, and a competitive advantage. A steadfast commitment from the board and executive levels is paramount to navigating this intricate terrain. Their leadership is essential in fostering a proactive approach to SCRM, ensuring that organizations can anticipate, mitigate, and adapt to possible disruptions. Ultimately, a resilient supply chain is a strategic advantage and a fundamental pillar of long-term business success and sustainability.

REFERENCES

- Accenture. “Supply Chain Cybersecurity Attacks.” Accenture, 2020.
- Association for Supply Chain Management (ASCM). 2019. "Supply Chain Risk Management and Information Sharing Survey."
- Business Continuity Institute (BCI). Supply Chain Resilience Report 2020. Business Continuity Institute, 2020.
- Council of Supply Chain Management Professionals (CSCMP). State of Logistics Report 2020. CSCMP, 2020.
- Deloitte. Global Chief Procurement Officer Survey. Deloitte, 2020.
- Deloitte. Global Supply Chain Survey. Deloitte, 2020.
- Gartner. Supply Chain Cost Optimization Study. Gartner, 2020.
- Gartner. Supply Chain Top 25 Report. Gartner, 2020.
- GEODIS. Supply Chain Worldwide Survey. GEODIS, 2020.
- Harvard Business Review. “Supply Chain Excellence and Customer Satisfaction.” Harvard Business Review, 2020.
- Institute for Supply Management (ISM). “ISM Report on Procurement and Supply Chain Trends 2019.” Institute for Supply Management, 2019.
- Institute for Supply Management (ISM). “ISM COVID-19 Supply Chain Survey 2020.” Institute for Supply Management, 2020.
- McKinsey & Company. “Supply Chain Adaptability Survey 2020.” McKinsey & Company, 2020.
- McKinsey & Company. “Supply Chain Flexibility and Resilience Survey.” McKinsey & Company, 2020.

- McKinsey & Company. "Supply Chain Cost and Efficiency Analysis." McKinsey & Company, 2020.
- MHI. MHI Annual Industry Report 2021. MHI, 2021.
- PwC. "Advanced Supply Chain Practices and Profitability Study." PricewaterhouseCoopers, 2020.
- Risk and Insurance Management Society (RIMS). Supply Chain Risk and Litigation Report 2020. Risk and Insurance Management Society, 2020.
- The Commission on the Theft of American Intellectual Property. Report on the Theft of American Intellectual Property. Commission on the Theft of American Intellectual Property, 2019.
- World Bank. "Compliance Costs and International Trade." World Bank Group, 2020.
- World Economic Forum. "The Impact of Supply Chain Disruptions." World Economic Forum, 2020.
- Treacy, Michael, and Fred Wiersema. The Discipline of Market Leaders. Addison-Wesley, 1995.
- Gartner. Supply Chain Top 25 Report. Gartner, 2020.
- MIT Center for Transportation and Logistics. "Best-in-Class Supply Chain Capabilities Report." Massachusetts Institute of Technology, 2020.
- Accenture. "Strategy Report on Supply Chain Performance." Accenture, 2020.
- Association for Supply Chain Management (ASCM). "Supplier Confidentiality and Risk Management Study." ASCM, 2020.
- Risk and Insurance Management Society (RIMS). "Litigation Concerns in Supply Chain Risk Management Report." RIMS, 2020.
- Gartner. "Supply Chain Cost Optimization Study." Gartner Inc., 2020.
- Business Continuity Institute (BCI). "Business Continuity and Supply Chain Resilience Survey." BCI, 2020.
- GEODIS. "Supply Chain Visibility Survey." GEODIS, 2020.

- APQC. "Supply Chain Management Performance Benchmarking Study." American Productivity & Quality Center (APQC), 2020.
- Commission on the Theft of American Intellectual Property. "Economic Impact of Intellectual Property Theft." Commission on the Theft of American Intellectual Property, 2019.
- Texas State Controller. "Economic Impact of 2021 Texas Ice Storm Report." Texas State Controller, 2021.

Insights and Actions

Chapter 1 begins by emphasizing the central importance of governance in vendor (third-party) risk management (VRM), arguing that VRM is not just about budget control but about addressing a broad range of risks that can impact an organization. VRM should be an integral part of enterprise risk management, not just a compliance exercise, ensuring the organization's resilience and long-term success.

Organizations must meticulously document core supplier relationship requirements, including business integration architecture, raw material flows, intellectual property exchanges, identity and access management, data exchanges, product flows, service delivery, performance communications, incident response, and business continuity plans.

Organizations must establish baseline Supplier Risk Assessments (SRA) that enumerate and prioritize risk scenarios, identify existing vulnerabilities, estimate threat likelihood and impact magnitude, calculate inherent risk, map threats to enterprise controls, identify compensating factors, document control gaps, and calculate aggregate residual risk for executive decision-making.

Effective supplier risk management requires a thorough analysis of threats across critical asset categories: supplier facilities, raw materials, fourth-party dependencies, transportation and logistics, technology infrastructure, digital data, labor and workforce, other customers, economic and financial sources, and government and geopolitical factors.

Determine the criticality of each third-party relationship by the potential for significant business disruption or data disclosure, not by the difficulty of recovery or regulatory requirements alone. The focus should remain on materiality and business impact.

Supply Chain Management (SCM) Program Benefits and Importance

- Reduced Costs: Significant cost savings across procurement, inventory, and operations through optimization and technology.
- Enhanced Revenue: Companies with advanced SCM capabilities experience faster revenue growth and higher profitability.
- Raised Customer Satisfaction: High-performing supply chains lead to greater customer satisfaction and loyalty.
- Optimized Inventories: Lower inventory carrying costs and improved financial performance.
- Operational Efficiency: Digitization and best practices lead to higher margins and lower inventory.
- Lowered Risk: Resilient supply chains recover faster from disruptions and reduce overall risk exposure.
- Improved Visibility: Digital investments enhance supply chain visibility and performance.

SCM Strategic Goals and Priorities

The ultimate goal of SCM is to create a resilient, continuous, and stable supply chain that withstands disruptions and maintains profitable operations. SCM strategies should be clearly communicated and include:

- Background and Context: Historical overview and rationale for current strategies.
- Vision and Mission: Long-term aspirations and core purpose of SCM.
- Value Proposition and Drivers: SCM's specific contributions and performance drivers.

- Biggest Challenges and Risks: Key obstacles and proactive risk management.
- Organization and Oversight: Leadership, governance, and accountability structures.

Actions to Take

Develop a Charter:

- The VRM charter should not be a mere formality or copied from external sources without critical review. It must be tailored to the organization's unique needs and risks.
- The charter must clearly define roles, responsibilities, and accountability, with visibility and authority extending to the board or enterprise risk management level.
- Essential components include executive sponsorship, purpose, objectives and scope, responsibilities, and principles that guide day-to-day actions.

Review these six core vendor risk categories:

- Financial: Cost overruns, fraud, and mismanagement.
- Reputational: Harm from vendor misconduct or failure.
- Operational: Poor service delivery and increased management burden.
- Security: Exposures from vendor security practices.
- Regulatory: Non-compliance and regulatory sanctions.
- Legal: Litigation and legal exposure from vendor relationships.

Additional risks to consider include strategic, technology, country, and ESG (environmental, social, and governance) risks.

Consider implementing these governance tools to identify and manage third-party risks:

- A RACI Matrix to clarify who is Responsible, Accountable, Consulted, and Informed for each task.
- The Three Lines of Defense (TLOD) Model when combined with the RACI matrix can ensure risks are appropriately managed
- A Target Operating Model (TOM) to define which TPRM functions are in-sourced, co-sourced, or outsourced, and whether they are centralized or federated.
- Policies and Standards to codify how third-party risks are managed, with annual reviews and clear accountability. Use the Vendor Risk Management Policy Template in this chapter to create a VRM policy.
- A budget that reflects organizational priorities and includes contingencies for unanticipated expenses.
- Key Risk and Performance Indicators (KRIs/KPIs) to facilitate data-driven decision-making and track program effectiveness.
- A risk register to capture and track risks identified during the TPRM review process.
- Generative AI and other technologies to help scan contracts for required terms and compliance to improve oversight and risk management.
- Data access controls which are essential for protecting sensitive information, especially with the use of advanced technologies.

Chapter 2

Required Resources

Introduction

In Chapter 2, we discuss the essential resources required for effective vendor, third-party, and supply chain risk management. Bill starts by tracing the evolution of vendor risk management (VRM) within organizations, using his own experiences to illustrate how VRM matures from reactive, department-driven oversight to a formalized, cross-functional program as businesses grow and face new risks. He describes how these early failures led to the discovery of core competencies and essential skills for successful vendor risk management. Besides people skills, Bill also articulates critical process and technical capabilities.

Matt emphasizes that effective third-party risk management (TPRM) depends on a combination of robust governance, clear roles and responsibilities, and well-defined processes and tools. He establishes that the foundation of any TPRM program is its governance model, which aligns risk tolerances with resource allocation—ensuring that budgets, staff, and technology are directed where they matter most.

In discussing supply chain risk management, Chris argues that in today's volatile business environment, effective organizational alignment is crucial for success, but many companies remain functionally siloed—a legacy approach that hinders performance, agility, and innovation. Chris draws on his decades of experience to outline common organizational dysfunctions, their impacts, and practical strategies for improvement.

The underlying theme of Chapter 2 is that well-defined operating models, with clear roles, lines of authority, and systems of accountability, help organizations of all sizes marshal the right combination of people, process, and technology to effectively manage their third-party relationships.

Immediately following Chris' essay is a list of publications he references throughout.

Required Resources for Vendor Risk Management

Bill Bonney

As organizations grow, VRM must evolve from a simple cost-control function to a comprehensive, cross-functional program that addresses a wide range of risks and supports strategic business objectives.

Vendor Risk Management, and more broadly, Vendor Management, is one of those functions that grows organically as businesses grow and mature until something happens to force a change. Picking up the story from my essay for Chapter 1, I mentioned three times that I was required to clean up a third-party mess. To make this essay more concise, I have blended these three instances into a single journey to more mature vendor risk management. I'll start by defining the core competencies and describing how they apply to our fledgling vendor management function. After that, I will discuss the skills that we identified that enabled those core competencies. I will finish the essay's first half by describing the roles we eventually recruited into our function. After the people-based discussion, I will review some of the tools we began to rely on as our third-party footprint grew and market pressures and regulatory scrutiny forced our due diligence efforts to operate at scale.

When I got involved, vendor management responsibility fell across multiple departments, typically vested in the person with budgetary control. As a direct outcome of those telephony challenges, periodic reviews became de rigueur, with understandable encouragement from the finance function. Over time, these reviews began to consistently focus on six areas: cost control, relationship building, contract negotiation, performance monitoring, strategic sourcing, and risk management. I unpack these six areas below.

Core Competencies

I have stacked these in the rough order we implemented them with the relationship managers.

In effect, the telephony cost overruns were the first risk they encountered. Still, their business acumen was not mature enough to categorize these as risks to manage rather than costs to control. Also, performance monitoring initially mainly focused on contract terms. Supply chain disruption was managed exclusively as a relationship management function, while alternate suppliers were readily available.

- **Cost Control**: Controlling costs through price negotiation and inventory control. Forecasting became an important addition in the medium term as wastage became more costly. Routine accounting governance, such as budget versus actual (AKA budget-to-variance) analysis, can help spot trends managers should address promptly to help manage costs, the relationship with the vendor, and the appropriateness of the material consumed.

- **Relationship Building**: Building and maintaining solid relationships with vendors. This also indicates that our relationships with partners are critical in transforming processes.

- **Contract Negotiation**: Negotiating terms and conditions, recognizing that to build long-term partnerships, both parties must get what they need from the contract.

- **Performance Monitoring**: Enforcing the contract terms while looking for opportunities to improve for the vendor and the customer.

- **Strategic Sourcing**: Identifying and selecting vendors that fit the company's plans, recognizing that "fit" has both a current and future tense – can the vendor grow with you?

- **Risk Management:** Managing supply chain disruption risk and cost overruns as early-stage risks, and then looking at more factors as we become more dependent on the partner and data sharing and system access become more prevalent.

When relationships with suppliers became more important to developing the customer base than funding bespoke development, this became strategic to the organization. When some of these relationships ended abruptly due to financial difficulties or a change in the direction of the suppliers, risk management became a focus for leadership.

As the organization matured, each of these core competencies matured. For example, cost control started as a function of contract negotiations and then evolved to include designing products to consume supplies differently and outsourcing final assembly to the supplier. As the supply chain matured across the industry, certain supplies became commodities, no longer requiring specialized knowledge to source them. At that point, procurement offloaded some of the relationship manager's activities. The relationships between the firm and its suppliers continued to mature (increasing trust), while technology changes allowed more firms to integrate directly with suppliers (driving efficiencies and augmenting capabilities). The increased trust, efficiency, and capability created explosive growth opportunities, while the integration exposed the firm to new risks.

Essential Skills

This growth and maturity led to formalizing the skills, helped by consulting from a Big Four accounting firm as the company prepared for a public offering. We listed out the following skills, which I have modified slightly to reflect current realities and add skills necessary for risk management:

- **Risk Assessment and Analysis Skills:** The ability to evaluate the potential risks posed by vendors, including financial stability, cybersecurity threats, compliance issues, and operational risks.

- **Due Diligence and Research Skills:** Proficiency in conducting thorough due diligence on vendors to uncover potential issues or risks.
- **Communication and Negotiation Skills:** The ability to clearly communicate with vendors and stakeholders and negotiate contracts.
- **Regulatory Knowledge:** Understanding the relevant laws, regulations, and industry standards that apply to vendor relationships, such as GDPR, HIPAA, or specific industry regulations.
- **Project Management:** Skills in managing projects and initiatives related to vendor risk management, including coordinating various tasks and multiple stakeholders.
- **Cybersecurity Knowledge:** Understanding of cybersecurity principles, especially if the vendor handles sensitive data or has access to critical systems.
- **Financial Acumen:** Understanding and assessing vendors' financial health and stability.
- **Problem-Solving Skills:** The capacity to identify potential issues and develop practical solutions.
- **Technology Proficiency:** Familiarity with vendor risk management software and tools.

Roles and Responsibilities

As the organization grows in size and complexity, the number of vendor relationships often explodes. Vendor Risk Management becomes a governance function to ensure the company's vendors perform to expectations and requirements and that the company understands and manages the associated risks. A cross-functional vendor risk management program can then help the company achieve these goals by defining and recruiting the following roles:

- **Vendor Risk/Program Manager:** Leads the vendor risk management program, overseeing risk assessments, due diligence, and mitigation strategies.
- **Compliance Officer:** Ensures vendor compliance with laws, regulations, and organizational policies.
- **IT Security Analyst:** Focuses on the cybersecurity aspects of vendor relationships, assessing and mitigating related risks.
- **Procurement Specialist:** Works on the acquisition side, ensuring vendor selection processes incorporate risk management principles.
- **Legal Counsel:** Provides legal expertise, especially in contract negotiations, and help in understanding regulatory requirements.
- **Auditor:** Regularly reviews and audits vendor relationships to ensure compliance and effective risk management.
- **Data Analyst:** Analyzes vendor performance and related risk data, providing decision-making insights.
- **Contract Manager:** Manages vendor contracts, ensuring they include necessary clauses and terms for risk mitigation.
- **Business Continuity Specialist:** Ensures vendor relationships align with the organization's business continuity and disaster recovery plans.
- **Quality Assurance Specialist:** Monitors and evaluates vendor performance to ensure vendors meet quality standards.

To recap this part of the journey, as the changes in vendor management requirements unfolded, we identified two changes that nudged the leadership team to make changes to the function. The first was cost overruns coupled with the poor quality of the telephone system, and the second was the preparation required to become a publicly traded company. In the first case, management desired to manage costs and outcomes. In the second case, management needed to formalize governance to achieve an outcome of transparent oversight.

SIGs and Other Tools

Returning now to our journey. The number of vendors that added to our information security, data privacy, and compliance risks grew faster than our ability to expand our due diligence. Like many others in the finance and technology industries, we began to adopt Standard Information Gathering (SIG) questionnaires.

Shared Assessments, a member-driven organization for delivering secure and resilient third-party partnerships, created the SIG questionnaire.[1] Shared Assessments started in regulatory and compliance-driven financial services but grew to include other industries and tools.

The SIG Questionnaire is a vendor assessment tool that maps to the requirements of multiple cyber regulations and frameworks. It is used to manage operational risks, business resiliency, security policies, cybersecurity risks, and third-party risks as part of a broader Third-Party Risk Management (TPRM) program and covers 21 different risk domains.[2] This is the original and probably the most widely recognized SIG questionnaire. It offers a comprehensive set of questions for third-party risk management, covering areas like information security, IT, privacy, data security, and business continuity.

The SIG Core questionnaire is a library of 855 control questions that help provide a comprehensive, risk-based service provider

1 Shared Assessments – "The Trusted Source in Third-Party Risk Management" – available here: https://sharedassessments.org/.

2 The 21 risk domains include Access Control, Application Security, Artificial Intelligence (AI), Asset and Information Management, Cloud Hosting Services, Compliance Management, Cybersecurity Incident Management, Endpoint Security, Enterprise Risk Management, Environmental, Social, Governance (ESG), Human Resources Security, Information Assurance, IT Operations Management, Network Security, Nth Party Management, Operational Resilience, Physical and Environmental Security, Privacy Management, Server Security, Supply Chain Risk Management (SCRM), and Threat Management.

assessment. SIG Lite is a shorter version of the SIG Core questionnaire, with 126 questions that cover the most critical risk domains.

SIG questionnaires are vital tools for conducting third-party risk assessments, particularly cybersecurity, compliance, and information security. Because the SIG Questionnaire from Shared Assessments is only available to member organizations, we had to rely on our own questionnaire with most vendors. However, the SIG Questionnaire was a step in the right direction, and as adoption has increased, so has its utility. It's worth noting, though, that even the "light" version can be quite extensive, and depending on the complexity and circumstances of the services being provided, can be quite lengthy. Recognize that you may require a task that takes several days to complete. Be sure to plan ahead and set expectations.

In addition to the original questionnaire, there are several others. The most notable are two from the Cloud Security Alliance: the Cloud Security Alliance (CSA) Questionnaire and an extension called the Consensus Assessments Initiative Questionnaire (CAIQ). Other prominent SIGs are the Vendor Security Alliance (VSA) Questionnaire, the Health Insurance Portability and Accountability Act (HIPAA) Compliance Questionnaire, and a favorite of mine, the Cybersecurity Framework (CSF) Questionnaires from the National Institute of Standards and Technology (NIST) and other organizations.

In addition to creating a standardized way of assessing a vendor's security and risk posture, we also required tools to organize our efforts and the data we collected and then to help us organize and automate workflow. Here, too, our needs never seemed entirely in sync with what the market could provide or, later on, what we could afford. Initially, vendor profiles were a combination of the contract (maintained by the relationship owner), purchase agreement (held by the accounting department), and spending history. The Corporate Controller provided the governance function, injecting price and performance discipline into the relationship.

As time passed, we outgrew file folders and manual processes and added a vendor tracking module to the requirements list for our Enterprise Business System (EBS). Rather than provide a late twentieth-century business automation history lesson, I'll skip ahead and say that we used three different toolsets to automate our vendor management data collection and organize records management and workflow: a module in our EBS system, a (mostly) home-grown record-keeping and workflow system, and a purpose-built governance application.

Key Components of a Third-Party Risk Management (TPRM) System

Again, I have stacked these in the rough order we implemented them:

- **Contract Management:** Managing contracts with third-party vendors, including tracking terms, conditions, and renewal dates, ensuring service level agreements (SLAs) are met, and managing contractual risks.

- **Vendor Information Management:** A centralized repository for storing and managing all vendor-related information, such as contracts, risk assessments, performance metrics, and audit results.

- **Due Diligence and Continuous Monitoring:** Workflow to perform due diligence before onboarding vendors and continuously monitor their performance and risk profile. This includes tracking changes in the vendor's business environment, compliance status, or security posture. Be prepared for flexible interpretations of red or yellow flags generated by this process. The importance of the vendor to the business will inform how much risk the company will tolerate. In my experience, due diligence rarely results in a hard "no." The more common outcome is a set of additional steps parties agree to that will mitigate the identified risks to an acceptable level.

- **Compliance Management:** Workflow to ensure third-party vendors comply with relevant industry regulations and standards (like GDPR, HIPAA, PCI-DSS). They may include features to track changes in regulatory requirements and assess vendors' adherence to these changes.

- **Reporting and Analytics:** Reporting tools and dashboards to provide insights into the overall risk landscape of the organization's third-party ecosystem. This can include analytics on vendor performance, risk levels, and compliance statuses.

- **Risk Assessment and Analysis**: Provide tools to conduct in-depth risk assessments of third-party vendors. This includes evaluating their security practices, compliance with relevant regulations, financial stability, and overall operational health.

Though we had separate systems for the following two functions, for very large or complex organizations it might be helpful to include:

- **Incident Management and Remediation:** Facilitate the incident response process and track remediation efforts.

- **Integration with Other Systems:** Integrate with enterprise systems like Enterprise Resource Planning (ERP), Governance, Risk Management, and Compliance (GRC) systems, and cybersecurity tools, to provide a comprehensive view of organizational risk.

I took this narrative approach in Chapters 1 and 2 because I think the evolution of vendor management and then vendor risk management is an integral part of the story that adds useful context. I hope you found this approach helpful.

Required Resources for Third-Party Risk Management

Matt Stamper

The foundation of any TPRM program is its governance model, which aligns risk tolerances with resource allocation—ensuring that budgets, staff, and technology are directed where they matter most.

Third-party risk management (TPRM) programs require an effective mix of procedures, tooling, administrative oversight, and governance to be effective. The governance model is ultimately the most critical resource for the TPRM. It will align organizational risk tolerances and ensure that more tactical and functional resources—be they budgets, tooling, staffing levels, and competencies—are allocated based on those risk tolerances.

Good governance is founded on clear roles and responsibilities and their associated authorizations. It's critical that the TPRM program clearly identifies participants in the program and their various roles and responsibilities for key TPRM functions. A responsible, accountable, consulted, and informed (RACI) matrix is critical to the program. As we're all aware, a key challenge with TPRM is that multiple departments and stakeholders are part of the process—legal, finance and accounting, lines of business, IT, security, and privacy—resulting in mixed priorities and overlapping responsibilities. The RACI matrix will help clarify these understandings. Critically, it's imperative that the accountable parties for given TPRM functions be identified and ultimately agreed to by the participants.

Ensure that your TPRM program starts with the basics and that participants are aware of their respective roles in the process, including their authorizations. A key goal of the RACI matrix is to ensure material risk decisions are not made in isolation. As an important example, if a material finding is discovered as part of the due diligence of a third party, who is authorized (accountable) to accept or reject that risk consideration? As highlighted throughout this book, these key TPRM functions should not be left to chance. Validate these functions across the lifecycle as shown below:

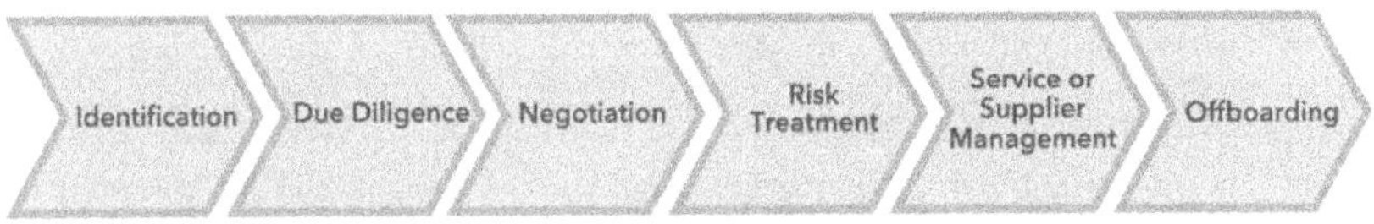

Figure 2.1 – TPRM Functional Lifecycle

Each organization will have unique activities associated with each phase of this high-level lifecycle. Delve into these with members of your team to understand who is responsible for the actual work, who is accountable for the results and outcomes of the function (including risk treatment decisions), who should be consulted, and who should be informed. Keep the RACI matrix handy to document these understandings. For each phase, identify specific tools and resources that may be required. For example, specialized questionnaires may be developed during the due diligence phase to support analysis and negotiations with prospective providers.

Since few of us have the luxury of building a TPRM program before onboarding vendors, the program will inevitably have two points of reference: onboarding new vendors and managing existing relationships. It's critical that existing relationships, especially those with inherently high-risk profiles, be front and center in the program, as ongoing oversight is just as important as initial onboarding. Monitoring existing relationships may require administrative resources, such as conducting stewardship reviews, and more technical measures, including monitoring the uptime of a service or evaluating product quality based on pre-defined criteria.

Determining a third party's inherent risk to the organization is a key first step in defining the materiality of that relationship. Determining materiality does not need to be overly complicated. This determination is about filtering signals from noise in the TPRM program (quickly categorizing material versus non-material providers). This filtering and materiality analysis can be loosely aligned to enterprise risk management considerations, namely the following:

- **Financial Considerations** – This is a bifurcated factor. The first element is whether the vendor or supplier is material to the organization's ability to derive revenue or enterprise value. Effectively, is the third party required for the organization to generate revenue? The second element of the financial review is the overall size of the relationship. Are the contemplated goods and services and their associated costs financially significant for the organization? There is an important "gotcha" with the second factor. It's not uncommon to have a non-financially material relationship that brings material risks to the organization. For example, an organization may use a small SaaS service for marketing purposes and load client data into that service. While the costs of the SaaS services may be nominal to the organization, the value of its client data is inherently high and should be managed accordingly.

- **Operational Considerations** – Assessing whether the third party's goods or services are necessary for the organization's operations is important. As we've witnessed during the COVID pandemic, our supply chains can be brittle, and the absence of a given component can shut down operations. Here, too, the financial metrics need to be validated. An inexpensive component or low-cost provider can have a disproportionately large impact if their product or service is unavailable. We also witness geopolitical risks that challenge the availability of supplies and raw materials. The basic question to help quickly determine the materiality of the relationship is whether an interruption in the provider's goods and services would materially impact your organization's operations.

- **Data Processing and Access** – Security and privacy factors should also be weighed as you evaluate the vendor's impact on your organization. Does the third party process sensitive data (e.g., personal data, sensitive personal data, protected health information, consumer financial data, controlled unclassified data), or does the provider have access to your internal applications and systems where this data is stored? Third parties accessing this information and data should be considered material and warrant initial security and privacy due diligence and continued oversight.
- **Regulatory or Contractual Considerations** – Does the relationship bring material regulatory requirements or contractual obligations? This determination is straightforward for certain industries—think healthcare and business associate relationships. For other industries, this analysis may require additional investigation, notably where contracts may have provisions for vendor oversight. Still, these provisions have not been widely conveyed to other stakeholders in the organization. Flow-down provisions and specific contractual requirements should be identified and communicated to the affected stakeholders.

Your organization must determine its unique mix of factors to help quickly identify material or high-impact providers and services. Once these factors have been agreed to, you'll need to use these considerations when identifying and onboarding new third parties and, equally important, when evaluating existing relationships. You'll likely find existing third-party relationships with inherently high-risk profiles that have not been evaluated in quite some time. Be sure to calendar these reviews and assign a "responsible" party to perform them. There should be zero ambiguity regarding the timing and assignment, including the time required to perform a review. A calendar of required reviews is foundational to your TPRM program. Ensure that the calendar is also aligned with any reporting obligations that your organization may have, including regulatory and year-end disclosures.

This filtering and materiality analysis is foundational to your TPRM program and will underpin all subsequent activities. Spend the necessary time with key stakeholders in legal, finance and accounting, operations, IT, cybersecurity, and other areas to ensure that the definition of materiality is unambiguous and widely understood throughout the organization. Where possible, start applying this materiality threshold and label existing relationships within your vendor master file or other system of record where third-party details are maintained. Many of the TPRM applications in the market today include this capability and have already pre-filtered vendors in their database according to the services that they offer.

Quantifying how many third parties are considered material to the organization is essential. This information will help inform the metrics needed to evaluate the cost and effectiveness of the TPRM program. For example, if conducting comprehensive due diligence on an existing third party requires two to four hours to complete, and 800 third parties have been classified as material or inherently high risk to the organization, you must plan for the 1,600 to 3,200 labor hours accordingly. If only 1,000 hours are available for this diligence, the organization will need to determine how to prioritize which third parties are selected for that year's analysis. For public companies facing increased disclosure obligations, there may be a need to indicate that not all third parties are adequately reviewed annually. Metrics should be tied to coverage considerations (e.g., X of Y providers were reviewed), operational risk reduction, and personnel requirements, including labor hours and required competencies. These metrics are integral to resourcing your TPRM program and providing status to key stakeholders, including the executive leadership team.

With the criteria for materiality established, the organization must define how it identifies and onboards new vendors. Larger organizations generally benefit from established procurement procedures. In many cases, the procedures focus on financial considerations related to the dollar value of the contract, payment terms, and the legal terms and conditions found in the master services agreement. Members of the TPRM program team should evaluate whether the identification and onboarding processes evaluate the risk criteria noted above or custom factors and considerations that are unique to the organization. Industry context may weigh especially strongly in this regard. As an example, companies in the defense industrial base (DIB) may be subject to specific requirements such as the International Traffic in Arms Regulations (ITAR) or the Defense Federal Acquisition Regulation Supplement (DFARS) that require special controls over controlled unclassified information (CUI) and validating the controls outlined in NIST 800-171 (as updated). Different organizational stakeholders have different priorities and requirements as part of the onboarding process. Ensure that your TPRM program effectively captures and documents these expectations and establishes a governance model to adjudicate the differing perspectives of risk that will invariably arise between stakeholders. You should validate whether your organization's ERP or accounting software and its vendor master file can be tailored to capture these nuanced requirements. Minimally, validate if vendors can be labeled or classified as material.

An integral part of onboarding is identifying prospective providers and evaluating their capabilities vis-à-vis your organization's specific requirements. Here, too, is an area where the RACI matrix can be useful. While lines of business typically focus on specific business requirements, these considerations are only part of the picture and may omit critical financial, legal, security, and privacy considerations. Your TPRM program needs to take a comprehensive view of the prospective provider to validate if their goods and services are fit for purpose and that other considerations are incorporated into the decision to either onboard or deselect the provider. Authorizations in this context are essential. As we have seen with shadow IT, it's common for stakeholders to either unwittingly bypass procurement procedures and onboard vendors with no due diligence or, worse, knowingly attempt to circumvent controls. Chapter 4 addresses some of the dynamics of onboarding third parties.

Your TPRM governance model, however, should clearly outline procurement guidelines and the level of due diligence that should be conducted based on the prospective supplier's inherent risk factors and considerations. As part of the broader governance model, clarify the workflows related to the due diligence and the applications and tools that may be used in the due diligence process (e.g., third-party rating services and standardized information gathering (SIG) questionnaires). Coordinating with the legal team ensures that contracts have the necessary language. We address some of the legal requirements associated with TPRM programs in Chapter 11 and some of the many regulations that mandate this diligence in Chapter 12.

Some additional governance tools are foundational to your program. For material service providers, validating the authorized personnel and emergency contact (APEC) status for key participants is critical. APEC details, similar to RACI matrices, should be validated to ensure that stakeholders are authorized to make changes when necessary to a given service. These changes could cover a gamut of issues ranging from technical configurations to billing terms to contract renewals.

Working through the governance requirements of your TPRM program will highlight the resources required to minimize risk and facilitate more predictable services and supplies. Minimally, validate the status of the following resources as part of the TPRM lifecycle.

Core Resources

These resources and capabilities should be considered integral to the overall TPRM program.

- **TPRM Charter** – The charter authorizes the TPRM program and outlines governance requirements, including risk management functions and how disparate perspectives of risk should be adjudicated by stakeholders.

- **TPRM Policy** – The TPRM policy should identify the criteria used to categorize material providers, authorization requirements for procuring new vendors and suppliers, expectations for stewardship, and other key parameters for the TPRM program. A critical element of the TPRM policy is to indicate the scope of the TPRM program and identify an accountable party (or committee) to oversee the program. Good policies will identify criteria where additional reviews and due diligence are necessary based on the materiality of the relationship.

- **RACI Matrix** – The RACI matrix should outline the TPRM program's core functions, who is involved with each function, and the corresponding roles and responsibilities.
- **Vendor Master File** – The vendor master file is a core component of any ERP or accounting package and ideally should allow customizable labels to be added to specific vendors. As noted above, labeling material vendors will help members of the TPRM team focus their due diligence and stewardship activities on vendors with the most impact on the organization.
- **TPRM Personnel and Requisite Competencies** – TPRM requires the right staffing level with the requisite competencies to minimize third-party risks to organizationally defined tolerances. Chapter 3 outlines some of the key competencies required of the TPRM team.
- **Contract Management Program or Procedures** – Depending upon the accounting software or ERP system in use, a contract management program is advisable to track terms and conditions, including addendums that are now frequently used where services may involve personal data, expiry dates, and other contract terms. Since many of the terms and conditions may be confidential or proprietary, access controls should be used for these applications, and access to contracts and related materials should be logged for accountability.

Identification

The identification phase centers on capturing requirements and filtering options for desired products or services.

- **Identification Criteria (Service or Supplier Specifications)** – Larger organizations typically benefit from mature procurement procedures that provide a structured approach to documenting product or service criteria. Ensure that your organization takes the time to define these criteria, including validating whether existing products or services may already be fit for purpose and are currently being used in the organization. Too frequently, products and services are duplicated, undermining potential economies for the procuring organization and adding to the administrative overhead of managing multiple supplier or vendor relationships. Ideally, the criteria are detailed enough to identify service metrics (e.g., service level agreements, service level objectives, and ticketing systems) or product-specific metrics (e.g., delivery times and quantities and procedures to address quality issues that may surface).

- **Request for Information (RFI) Template** – RFIs should be used to evaluate service and product options available in the market. They should ideally be constructed to be readily converted into a request for proposal (RFP) where circumstances warrant. The RFI should note potential legal requirements and other variables that the organization requires. Companies in highly regulated industries will have their counsel review RFIs and RFPs for requisite clauses (e.g., corporate responsibility agreements, ESG requirements, and jurisdictions).

- **Service Definitions and Service Demarcation** – During the identification phase, it's critical that services are defined in appropriate detail and demarcation points are highlighted. Too frequently, ambiguity at this phase results in costly contract renegotiation during the due diligence and onboarding phases.

- **Analyst Services** – Depending on the materiality and expense of the contemplated product or service, consider having a neutral analyst firm identify potential suppliers. These firms can help provide market context, review prospective suppliers' strengths and weaknesses, and provide illustrative market pricing.

Due Diligence and Negotiation

Negotiation and due diligence frequently occur concurrently for many organizations. The quality of these phases is predicated on how well service and product criteria have been developed. If an organization is not completely sure of its specific requirements, that ambiguity may impact the quality of the due diligence phase, and requirements may change or vary from department to department. The following resources will aid in the due diligence phase.

- **Independent Vendor Reviews** – Where available, having a neutral third party assess the prospective vendor or supplier is ideal. Where procurement practices may be subject to regulatory oversight, ensure criteria are defined, the due diligence process is transparent, and decisions are made with input from multiple stakeholders. As part of this function, consider the use of testimonials, recognizing the obvious fact that supplier-provided testimonials are cherry-picked relationships. If the materiality of the relationship warrants this level of scrutiny, ask to speak with previous/former clients to learn from their experiences.

- **Request for Proposal (RFP) Template** – The RFP template should reflect desired contract terms, SLA/SLO expectations, and other pertinent details. It's important to focus on the contract requirements and payment terms contemplated between the parties. It's also important to validate whether desired contract terms are actually tied to the requested services. This highlights a key dynamic in many TPRM programs—key program functions and requirements can occur in isolation, notably for legal clauses. For example, I've worked in the managed services sector, where service demarcation is critical to successful engagements. In certain engagements, there's no access to the client's data. Yet, the contracting party will require a data protection addendum (DPA), which is odd, given that there's no logical or physical access to client data. Whether to try and eliminate that requirement or to execute the DPA is a judgment call in these scenarios. The former approach introduces delay and potential legal fees, while the latter introduces legal exposure for the firm, recognizing that operationally, the risk is *de minimis*. This is one of the dynamics highlighting the value of close collaboration between counsel and the TPRM team. Knowing which terms and conditions are must-haves versus nice-to-haves can streamline the due diligence and negotiation phases. For services involving data (be it corporate or personal), be sure to validate requirements related to breach notification, the timeframes for these notifications, and the ever-present right-to-audit clause.

- **Authorized Budget** – The functions related to TPRM have costs, be they personnel hours and salaries, the opportunity costs of people's time, or the tooling related to overseeing and governing TPRM functions. Projects should have approved budgets where possible. Few things are worse for both parties than spending time and energy on a contemplated product or service only to have the budget denied.

Risk Treatment

Managing risks is integral to the TPRM program. Some important resources are needed to help oversee risk management, but most critically, it's defining the organization's methodology to identify, triage, and assess risk systematically.

- **Risk Adjudication Model** – Managing vendors and suppliers comes with risk, and frequently, tradeoffs are required for identified risks that surface during the due diligence and negotiation phase. As the TPRM charter outlines, procedures should be established to adjudicate these risks. The process needs to be as transparent as possible so that stakeholders who disagree with the proposed risk treatment at least know the rationale.

- **Risk Register** – Draft a basic risk register to document and track risk factors in the TPRM process. Ensure that the risk register is reviewed by key stakeholders and accountable parties who oversee and govern the TPRM program. The risk register should document the preferred risk treatment (e.g., transfer, insure, mitigate, or accept) and identify the risk owner within the organization. The risk register should also capture the estimated costs of risk treatment.

- **Ticketing and/or Service Management System** – There's value in tracking identified risks and, depending upon the organization's broader enterprise risk management program, opening tickets for identified risks. Using a ticketing system to track risks provides important data points and metrics that can inform TPRM activities. Traceability of risk management decisions is also valuable and may be required for organizations in highly regulated industries.

Service or Supplier Management

While justifiable attention is focused on the identification, due diligence, and negotiation phases, managing the ongoing relationship is also critical. A number of resources will help make this phase more effective.

- **Accurate and Complete Vendor Inventory** – The organization's vendor master file must be up-to-date and accurate. As noted above, ideally the vendor inventory can be readily filtered based on defined criteria (e.g., the nature and extent of the services provided, the expiry dates of the contracts, and the data that's shared among the parties). This detail underpins the broader TPRM program. The inventory informs metrics and workloads.

- **Authorized Personnel and Emergency Contact (APEC) List** – Where services warrant this level of detail, ensure that respective roles, responsibilities, and contact details are fully documented. Important roles must be validated, including administrative or legal contacts who can modify, request new, and/or cancel services. It's also important to capture billing contacts in the APEC. I've witnessed service interruptions because invoices were not paid on time. The invoices were sent to an individual no longer associated with the organization, and their email was not monitored. Up-to-date APEC lists minimize these types of risks. Multi-recipient email distribution lists are advisable. Ensure that these lists are actively monitored and updated when changes are made to roles or participants are departing the process.

- **Stewardship Meeting Standing Agenda** – Where the value of the relationship warrants extra attention and ongoing diligence, I strongly recommend scheduling stewardship meetings between the parties. Draft and maintain a standing agenda that can be tailored to the circumstances of the engagement. Topics to consider include forthcoming changes, service issues, and personnel status. Make sure that communication protocols and the desired media are identified. These protocols should be captured in the APEC.

- **Incident Response Procedures** – Where the contracted services require this level of diligence, validating the organization's incident response practices and how the two organizations are expected to collaborate when incidents do occur is valuable. Stakeholders who should validate incident response procedures include the organization's cybersecurity team, operations, and counsel. Counsel plays an especially important role given the sensitive nature of incidents and the potential requirement to have communication under privilege.

- **Service and Vendor Monitoring Services** – As described elsewhere in this book, a number of new services and applications provide scalable monitoring services over third parties. These services may alert to known security issues, audit and certification, changes to ESG practices, the status of key personnel, and other variables that may indicate changes to the risk profile of the relationship and its service. Some of these applications also work to quantify risk factors.

Off-Boarding

Relationships end. Your TPRM must have the resources to govern when products and services are canceled or discontinued.

- **Data Destruction** – Where services involve sharing data that may be governed by confidentiality, security, and retention requirements, IT and security staff must help validate data deletion and destruction activities. Ideally, these stakeholders can pre-identify and document the requirements for the appropriate return, deletion, or destruction of data shared with the service provider or vendor.
- **Transition and Migration Plans** – Members of the TPRM team should pre-establish migration and transition plans for services that have an important operational impact on the organization. These plans should be rigorously reviewed and validated by stakeholders outside the TPRM team where competencies and operational insights warrant. Validations should be related to potential evergreen clauses in a service agreement, data portability, and IP addresses, among other variables. A great question the team can ask is, "What is it that we don't know that we should know about this service, and how will canceling or migrating to another provider impact our operations or requirements?" Contemplating the exit of the engagement and the many implications should help inform the onboarding of the next engagement or service provider.

The resources and capabilities noted above, coupled with the broader governance model for the TPRM program, will help ensure that vendor and supplier risks are managed effectively throughout the TPRM life cycle. Remember that resources are never static, and an organization's requirements will evolve. Resources and capabilities warrant ongoing validation by the TPRM team. Should there be notable gaps in required resources or capabilities, these should be captured in the risk register and escalated to organizational stakeholders for their assessment and evaluation.

Your Organizational Model Is the Weakest Link

Chris Forbes

The organizational model is the foundation of enterprise agility, culture, and potential. Poor structure is a silent killer of execution, while great structure enables growth, responsiveness, and enduring excellence.

1.0 Essay Overview

In today's turbulent and chaotic business environment, aligning organizational strategies and goals has become a critical determinant of success. However, organizational misalignment can lead to issues that undermine performance across multiple business dimensions. Most companies have organized their supply chain management (SCM) and supply chain risk management (SCRM) functions, trading off effectiveness and efficiency in favor of managerial simplicity. It is common to see organizational models aligned by functional discipline. This approach separates the supply chain resources into different teams, primarily based on the function they perform or their primary skill set. Pooling resources based on functional skills allows those teams to centralize knowledge capture, transfer, and training by harvesting the experience and wisdom from more senior workers and making it available to less experienced workers.

These functionally aligned resource pools almost certainly have different strategies, priorities, resources, budgets, and performance measurements. This approach may have originated in the construction industry, where junior tradespeople, such as carpenters, plumbers, and electricians, would join their local guild and apprentice under master tradespeople for many years to learn the required skills. Trade unions promised innovation potential and accelerated practice advancement by consolidating all trade practitioners' collective experience and insights.

While skills-based resource pools may have fueled the early years of the Industrial Revolution, I would argue that knowledge workers, like those involved in supply chain management, material sourcing, procurement, vendor management, delivery logistics, quality management, and risk management, are, by their very nature, hybrid roles that require cross-functional skills and interdisciplinary knowledge to be highly effective and efficient.

In Chapter 1, the other authors and I highlighted many factors and considerations for companies in defining their supply chains, third parties, and vendor relationships, including their respective visions, missions, and goals. In Chapter 2, I will review some of the most common issues companies encounter with their organizational models and the tell-tale signs of misalignment. I will propose alternative approaches to designing an optimal organizational model and provide ideas and suggestions for improving your target operating model (TOM). I will explore how the TOM influences the organizational model and the crucial role that an organizational model plays in building a successful business. I will highlight the critical decisions when choosing which organizational model is best for a given situation.

2.0 Organizational Model Issues

Throughout my 42-year career, across the dozens of companies I have worked for and hundreds of executives I have spoken with, I have noticed many consistent patterns and symptoms of poorly aligned organizations. At first, I thought the root causes of those problems were the individuals who misunderstood their situation or made poor management decisions. However, I later realized that every organization faces the fundamental challenge of designing, building, nurturing, and evolving the organization they need to succeed.

I love the phrase "We the people..., to form a more perfect union..." which, in a way, exemplifies the highest priority and most important consideration of nation-forming: designing how the collective citizenry will cohabitate and self-govern. Companies, like civilizations, are meant to learn from their past mistakes and improve themselves. Sadly, most organizations fail to recognize the early warning signs of organizational dysfunction or choose incomplete or ineffective solutions to solve managerial problems. With a deeper understanding of the symptoms, the root cause, and possible cures, companies can avoid repeating their past mistakes and those of countless other organizations. Here are the most common themes of organizational dysfunction that I have come across.

2.1 Organizations Have Too Many Cooks in the Kitchen

Highly distributed organizations can experience significant inefficiencies and delays from overly complex decision-making spread across numerous specialized teams. When a supply chain manager seeks to implement a change, such as selecting a new supplier, they may require approvals from multiple departments, such as operations, procurement, legal, supply chain risk management, finance, and compliance. This approach slows decision-making and introduces fragmented and disconnected problem-solving, as each department might prioritize its agenda or risk profile over the broader organizational goals. This situation is further exacerbated by the need to present and gain approval from various operating committees and risk oversight councils, each with its own schedules, rule-making criteria, and concerns. As a result, the supply chain manager spends more time coordinating and reconciling conflicting interests than focusing on the supply chain's strategic objectives.

The inefficiency stems from the excessive effort required to manage inter-departmental coordination. Each department may have its processes, metrics, and priorities, leading to disagreement on what constitutes success for the organization. The need for compromise across departments can result in watered-down decisions that fail to address the core issues or take risks necessary for innovation. This can also lead to "decision fatigue," where the volume of inputs and the need to satisfy multiple stakeholders reduce decision quality and timeliness. Organizations must streamline decision-making processes, clarify roles and responsibilities, and ensure that strategic objectives precede departmental agendas.

2.2 Organizations Have Too Many Disparate Teams

Specialization is essential, but when overdone, it fragments the enterprise. The splintering of the organization into highly specialized, autonomous departments often results in silos. While these units may achieve internal goals, their efforts can easily misalign with enterprise-level objectives.

Silos increase complexity, delay decision-making, and slow down responsiveness during crises. Each department tends to optimize for its metrics, creating obstacles when swift, unified action is required. Silos also impede knowledge sharing, reducing the organization's ability to benefit from innovations, efficiencies, or insights gained elsewhere.

Furthermore, excessive fragmentation complicates oversight and weakens adherence to enterprise policies. Duplication of efforts, inconsistent standards, and wasted resources are the norm. To counter these risks, organizations must set shared goals and cultivate cross-functional collaboration across silos.

2.3 Organizations Assume Teams Will Collectively Optimize

Many organizations believe individual teams will naturally optimize for the enterprise's best interest. In reality, local optimizations often produce global inefficiencies. For example, a procurement team might negotiate cost reductions that delay logistics or create quality issues, ultimately hurting the business.

Even well-intended improvements can introduce friction elsewhere due to conflicting metrics, resource constraints, or disconnected workflows. Not all departments have equal tools, skills, or mandates, creating uneven performance and system-wide bottlenecks. Real optimization requires strategic coordination across all teams and partners. Leadership must foster cross-functional alignment, ensure communication, and oversee value chain performance with a system-wide view. Optimizing only at the micro level will not produce macro success.

2.4 Organizations Assume Teams Define and Measure Success Equally

Teams often use different success metrics, leading to internal conflict. A supply chain team may value delivery speed and customer satisfaction, while an IT team might prioritize system uptime and cost reduction. Both sets of KPIs are valid but create friction and confusion without alignment. Misaligned KPIs cause teams to pull in different directions. One team may delay maintenance to support operations, risking system failures. Another may push output over quality. These cross-purposes undermine strategy execution. Organizations must establish shared success definitions and KPIs that align with strategic goals. Transparency in measurement and cross-functional feedback are essential to building a cohesive performance culture.

2.5 Organizations Are Biased Based on Past Successes

Comfort with past successes often prevents organizations from adapting to change. Familiar strategies, technologies, and vendors can outlive their relevance. For instance, IT leaders may stay loyal to historical providers like IBM or Microsoft even when newer options offer superior value.

This legacy bias delays innovation adoption and causes firms to overlook shifting market dynamics. Companies trapped in yesterday's success formula will fall behind as competitors modernize. Strategic vigilance is required to guard against this form of institutional inertia.

2.6 Organizations Favor Consensus Decision-Making

Consensus-building promotes inclusivity but can paralyze progress. Organizations that require broad agreement for all decisions often delay action, especially in fast-moving markets.

Consensus also dilutes decision quality. Compromises tend to favor the lowest common denominator, not the optimal path. The loudest voices, not the most informed, can dominate discussions. To be effective, consensus must be balanced with leadership clarity. Define decision rights, timelines, and escalation paths. Encourage constructive dissent but empower decision-makers to act decisively.

2.7 Organizations Are Biased Toward Short-Term Profits

A short-term focus can undermine long-term competitiveness. Cost-cutting that sacrifices R&D, quality, or training may boost quarterly earnings but damage innovation and customer loyalty. Strategic missteps, such as market misalignment, often result. Classic examples include Kodak, Sears, GM, and Nokia, each suffering from underinvestment in change. Ethical lapses like Volkswagen's emissions scandal show how short-term gains can inflict lasting damage. Sustainable success requires balancing immediate profitability with long-term investments in people, innovation, and customer experience.

2.8 Organizations Are More Prone to Unilateral Actions

Budget freezes and process restrictions may seem prudent in uncertain times, but overuse creates paralysis. These measures disrupt operations, stall initiatives, and erode morale. They are often reactive, not strategic, and rarely address root causes. Instead of knee-jerk controls, organizations should assess broader impacts and explore alternatives. They should also empower local leaders, focus on long-term priorities, and avoid bureaucratic overload that suffocates progress.

2.9 Organizations Invest Resources Based on Prior Year Budgets

Rolling over last year's budget ignores evolving needs and opportunities. Legacy-based budgeting locks in inefficiencies and discourages innovation. Teams are incentivized to spend everything just to preserve allocations. This approach misallocates resources and leaves little room for strategic pivots. To fix this, flexible frameworks like zero-based budgeting or priority-based planning should be adopted. Realign spending with current goals, not outdated habits.

2.10 Organizations Follow the Lead of Their Competition

Reacting to competitors is not a strategy. Following industry trends without understanding context dilutes identity and derails priorities. Mimicking others without reflection can waste resources and divert focus from core strengths.

Strong organizations trust their strategies. They monitor competitors but do not mimic them without rationalizing. Strategy should be proactive, not reactive.

3.0 Impacts of Organizational Dysfunction

Organizational misalignment is an internal inconvenience and a costly, system-wide risk that erodes competitiveness over time. While some leaders may dismiss signs of dysfunction as inevitable or minor, waiting for problems to escalate before responding leads to long-term inefficiencies and missed opportunities. Proactive leadership is essential to maintaining organizational health, whereas reactive cultures incur hidden taxes in delays, confusion, resource waste, and low morale. These issues rarely surface as headline-grabbing crises. Instead, they accumulate across departments, degrading performance slowly but relentlessly. Good and great organizations often differ in their ability to recognize and correct misalignment before it becomes catastrophic. Here are ten specific and observable impacts of organizational dysfunction.

3.1 Lower Production Output

Misalignment across sales, procurement, and production creates bottlenecks and delays that reduce overall output. Forecasting errors, missed signals, and poor team communication can lead to resource shortages or overproduction.

For example, sales may overestimate demand without informing production planners, leading to shortages of raw materials and manufacturing delays. If procurement is unaware of upcoming promotions or product launches, it may under-order, triggering stockouts and unmet demand. These mismatches undermine operational efficiency, increase costs per unit, and reduce a company's ability to meet customer expectations. In competitive markets, the inability to deliver on time and at scale results in lost business and damaged reputation.

3.2 Higher Costs

Dysfunction inflates costs through duplication, inefficiency, and poor coordination. Independent decision-making across silos can cause multiple departments to purchase the same services, negotiate separately with suppliers, or invest in redundant technologies. Rushed production changes driven by misaligned marketing campaigns might require expedited shipping, overtime, or premium-priced materials. Poor communication can result in errors that require rework or damage control. Strategic misalignment also prevents organizations from achieving economies of scale. For instance, if two business units independently contract with logistics providers, they may pay higher rates than if their needs were aggregated into a single negotiation.

3.3 Lower Quality

Quality suffers when teams do not share a unified understanding of standards, timelines, or priorities. A cost-focused procurement team may select low-quality vendors, unaware that their choices compromise production specifications. Human error increases if product managers do not adequately train operational staff on new systems or workflows.

Misaligned incentives between departments, such as sales pushing aggressive timelines while engineering focuses on precision, often lead to defective products or inconsistent service. External partners may exacerbate the issue if they make uncoordinated changes, such as altering materials or packaging, without informing upstream stakeholders. The result is increased rework, returns, and customer dissatisfaction, all eating into profit margins and eroding brand loyalty.

3.4 More Management Indecision

When teams are not aligned, decision-makers are pulled in multiple directions, often with conflicting data, priorities, and expectations. For example, a sales department may push for expansion, while operations advocates for cost control. Without shared strategic direction, decisions stall. Indecision is further exacerbated by siloed data, which prevents leaders from seeing the whole picture. A lack of trust across departments can create resistance to change or skepticism toward proposed solutions. Over time, this indecision leads to delays in critical initiatives, missed market windows, and a general culture of hesitancy. Management becomes reactive, not strategic, constantly negotiating internal politics instead of driving innovation.

3.5 Slower Speed to Market

Agility is a competitive necessity, yet misalignment slows the product lifecycle from concept to customer. When departments operate with conflicting schedules and separate priorities, coordination breaks down. For example, a product may be ready for launch, but legal or finance teams might still be reviewing contracts or budgets. Marketing might begin promotions before production is prepared. Each disconnect delays release and weakens market momentum.

Outdated tools and incompatible systems further contribute to inefficiency. If departments use siloed platforms that cannot share real-time data, order processing, inventory updates, and logistics timelines, all lag behind demand. The result is a sluggish organization outpaced by nimbler competitors who can react faster and capitalize on emerging opportunities.

3.6 Missed Opportunities

Poor communication and limited collaboration prevent teams from recognizing valuable market trends, customer feedback, or innovation opportunities. Insights from sales, service, or partner networks are often trapped in departmental silos and never reach decision-makers. When marketing is unaware of successful regional campaigns or product managers miss customer requests for features, the organization fails to adapt to changing demands. Poorly executed expansion plans or late product introductions are common symptoms. Cross-functional misalignment can delay strategic initiatives like entering new markets, launching new services, or forming partnerships. Opportunities pass by while the organization tries to coordinate the basics.

3.7 Inconsistent Financial Performance

Inconsistent alignment between strategic goals and resource allocation causes unpredictable financial outcomes. The company may overspend or under-deliver if revenue teams grow top-line results without operations or supply chain coordination. Forecasting becomes less reliable when departments fail to align assumptions, priorities, and data inputs. Missed forecasts affect planning, budgeting, and external credibility. Surprise expenses from poor coordination, such as emergency orders or redundant software purchases, further distort financial results. This variability undermines investor confidence and makes it challenging to maintain a substantial valuation. Over time, repeated misses or irregular performance can lead to reputational damage, shareholder dissatisfaction, and weakened access to capital.

3.8 Reduced Customer Retention

The customer experience suffers when teams are not working toward the same outcomes. Promises made by marketing or sales may not align with delivery capabilities, creating a gap between expectations and reality. Customer service teams often bear the brunt of these misalignments, dealing with frustrated clients who encounter delays, inconsistencies, or confusion. When internal teams do not share data or updates, frontline staff may provide outdated or incorrect information. Over time, customers lose confidence and seek more reliable providers. High turnover increases acquisition costs and drains revenue. Brand loyalty erodes when a company cannot deliver a coherent and consistent experience.

3.9 Less Innovation

Innovation requires collaboration. Misalignment chokes creativity by isolating departments and blocking knowledge exchange. Without shared goals and open dialogue, ideas wither before they gain traction. Cross-functional teams that lack trust or shared language struggle to co-develop solutions. Misaligned priorities result in projects that stall or fail due to miscommunication or competing incentives. Innovation efforts miss the mark when R&D lacks market insight, or IT launches tools without business input. The organization becomes reactive instead of visionary, falling behind more integrated and adaptive competitors.

3.10 Lower Staff Loyalty

Misalignment causes confusion, stress, and dissatisfaction. When directives are inconsistent or priorities shift frequently, employees lose sight of how their efforts contribute to meaningful goals Frustration grows when collaboration is complex or internal politics override logic. Talented staff who feel unheard or underutilized will leave for organizations with greater clarity and purpose. Turnover disrupts team cohesion, increases costs, and diminishes morale. The organization becomes stuck in a cycle of recruitment and retraining while institutional knowledge erodes and momentum is lost.

4.0 Ideas for Improvement

If your organization is ready to escape the gravitational pull of legacy thinking and commit to systemic optimization, the following strategies offer a practical foundation. These ideas are not theoretical; they are grounded in decades of industry experience and are meant to help operationalize excellence.

4.1 Aggregate Success Measures Across All Activities

Many companies draft vision and mission statements early in their formation and rarely revisit them. Yet these foundational declarations should evolve as the organization grows. One way to re-anchor alignment is to conduct an annual "re-vision" and "re-mission" survey, gathering feedback from employees, customers, partners, and shareholders. This process revalidates the company's core purpose and ensures strategic coherence. Regardless, the survey's real value lies in management's willingness to listen and change. Results should inform a recalibrated set of observable outcomes and quantifiable performance measures, much like the Balanced Scorecard model. However, these metrics should emerge organically from stakeholder-defined success criteria rather than being limited to four quadrants.

4.2 Architect the Perfect Optimization Model

Claiming to be optimized is easy; proving it is not. Organizations need a transparent, repeatable framework that defines optimization and measures it against clearly articulated targets. All participants should understand optimization models, not just data scientists or executives. Success criteria must include weighted priorities, defined thresholds, constraints, and limits. Metrics should be traceable to business outcomes. As Patrick Lencioni notes, "If everything is important, nothing is." Prioritization is critical, and optimization must be translated into language employees can act on and align with.

4.3 Analyze Often and Reengineer Everything

Time and Motion Studies (TMS) are powerful tools for capturing how work is performed. This data fuels Business Process Reengineering (BPR), enabling organizations to redesign workflows to reduce waste, improve efficiency, and enhance quality. Organizations should go further by embracing Business Organization Reengineering (BOR), which focuses on transforming structures and roles, not just processes. Just as companies routinely revisit budgets and forecasts, they should institutionalize organizational reengineering as a recurring exercise.

4.4 Reorganize Based on Collective Goals

Organizing teams by function is efficient for skill development but inefficient for cross-functional execution. Reconfiguring around shared goals enhances performance. Imagine a football team composed of only specialist consultants with no shared practice or purpose. It would never win the Super Bowl. Similarly, true collaboration comes from consistent, co-located, goal-driven teams in business. In supply chain management, this might mean forming teams composed of procurement, logistics, finance, IT, and legal representatives. These teams work together daily, prioritizing collective success over departmental interests, not just when issues arise.

4.5 Focus on Core Competencies and Capabilities

There's an enduring debate between hiring generalists and specialists. The correct answer depends on your strategic priorities. Specialists tend to execute faster and with higher quality. Generalists are often better suited to ambiguous, complex, or evolving problems. If speed-to-market is your edge, prioritize specialization. If complexity and adaptability are your main concerns, value generalists. Either way, match your workforce model to your competitive needs, not just hiring trends.

4.6 Hone Your Competitive Advantage

Too many companies settle for being adequate across the board. However, competitive advantage often stems from being exceptional at one or two things. For an AI chip manufacturer, it might be design and fabrication. For a logistics provider, it might be delivery precision and routing. Excellence requires relentless focus and continual investment. History does not remember mediocre companies. As William Arthur Ward said, "The price of excellence is discipline. The cost of mediocrity is disappointment."

4.7 Master Orchestration

When restructuring is not feasible, orchestration is a powerful alternative. Performance depends on expertise and synchronization in orchestras, sports teams, and Michelin-starred kitchens. In hospital emergency rooms, studies have shown that better coordination, supported by dashboards, simulation models, and improved communication, can reduce patient wait times and improve outcomes. The same principles apply in business. Organizations should train and hire for orchestration skills: people who can manage timing, synchronize actions, and keep teams moving in unison, even when they're not directly executing the work themselves.

4.8 Let Go of the Need to Control

Control is necessary, but it need not always be internal. Many industries have adopted shared quality oversight models through third-party labs, regulatory cooperatives, or industry collectives. These arrangements ensure that each organization has full ownership. Before assuming that control equals in-house responsibility, consider whether a neutral third party can provide the same oversight more efficiently. Explore shared services or co-created consortia to reduce costs and increase standardization.

4.9 Education, Training, and a Learning Culture

Every successful transformation begins with people. Despite the rise of automation, most organizations are still human-centric in decision-making and innovation. Therefore, learning must be a core cultural value. Organizations should benchmark practices across industries, geographies, and technologies. They should also develop their people through continuous learning, challenge existing mental models, and create space for creative problem-solving.

Strategic expertise in a few key domains is essential. It drives innovation, anticipates change, and recovers from disruptions faster. For areas beyond your core focus, seek expertise via partners, consortia, or open innovation platforms.

4.10 Continuous Improvement and Innovation

The supply chain is ripe for innovation through IoT sensors, machine learning, blockchain, robotics, and collaborative planning systems. Companies like Amazon, Dell, and Carvana have revolutionized fulfillment using technology and direct-to-consumer models. Blockchain increases transparency, advanced analytics improve forecasting, and automation enhances throughput. But innovation is not just about tools. It's about rethinking how people and systems interact across ecosystems. As Winston Churchill said, "To improve is to change; to be perfect is to change often."

5.0 Recommendations and Strategic Actions

Leaders must continuously question their structures, priorities, and assumptions to become a high-performing organization. Misalignment is not a one-time fix but a recurring challenge that requires vigilance and adaptability.

Here is a strategic checklist to move forward:

- Reassess Mission, Vision, and Metrics Annually

  Treat your core identity as a living concept, revisited yearly through broad feedback.

- Design a Transparent Optimization Framework

  Define what "optimized" means for your organization and make it measurable, visible, and actionable.

- Embed Reengineering into Culture

  Treat organizational design as dynamic and regularly reconfigure teams, workflows, and responsibilities.

- Build Cross-Functional Work Teams

  Organize people by outcomes, not by disciplines. Reward collaboration that drives enterprise goals.

- Double Down on What You Do Best

  Identify your true competitive differentiator and invest heavily. Be world-class in a few areas, not average in all.

- Train for Coordination and Orchestration

  Hire and develop professionals skilled in aligning and synchronizing complex workflows.

- Decentralized Oversight When Strategic

  Use external validators and shared services to offload functions that do not differentiate you.

- Invest in People-Centric Innovation

  Build internal learning networks. Encourage bold ideas. Benchmark relentlessly.

- Leverage Emerging Technologies

Integrate digital tools into your supply chain to reduce costs and increase responsiveness.

- Stay Agile and Anticipatory

  Do not just react to competitors; define the future on your terms.

Conclusion

The organizational model is more than a chart of boxes and lines; it is the scaffolding that shapes your enterprise's agility, culture, and potential. Poor structure is the silent killer of execution. Great structure, on the other hand, enables growth, responsiveness, and enduring excellence. Treat your operating model as a strategic asset. Rebuild it, test it, measure it, and evolve it. Because in the end, your organizational model is either your greatest strength or your weakest link.

REFERENCES

- Burns, Tom, and G. M. Stalker. The Management of Innovation. London: Tavistock, 1961.
- Chandler, Alfred D. Strategy and Structure: Chapters in the History of the Industrial Enterprise. Cambridge, MA: MIT Press, 1962.
- Lawrence, Paul R., and Jay W. Lorsch. Organization and Environment: Managing Differentiation and Integration. Boston: Harvard Business School Press, 1967.
- Galbraith, Jay R. "Matrix Organization Designs." Business Horizons 14, no. 1 (1971): 29–40.
- Galbraith, Jay R. Designing Complex Organizations. Reading, MA: Addison-Wesley, 1973.
- Galbraith, Jay R. Organization Design. Reading, MA: Addison-Wesley, 1977.
- Chandler, Alfred D. Strategy and Structure: Chapters in the History of the American Industrial Enterprise. Cambridge, MA: MIT Press, 1962.

- Chandler, Alfred D. Scale and Scope: The Dynamics of Industrial Capitalism. Cambridge, MA: Harvard University Press, 1990.
- Lawrence, Paul R., and Jay W. Lorsch. Organization and Environment: Managing Differentiation and Integration. Boston, MA: Harvard Business School Press, 1967.
- Galbraith, Jay R. Organization Design. Reading, MA: Addison-Wesley, 1977.
- Mintzberg, Henry. The Structuring of Organizations: A Synthesis of the Research. Englewood Cliffs, NJ: Prentice-Hall, 1979.
- Porter, Michael E. Competitive Strategy: Techniques for Analyzing Industries and Competitors. New York: Free Press, 1980.
- Porter, Michael E. Competitive Advantage: Creating and Sustaining Superior Performance. New York: Free Press, 1985.
- Deming, W. Edwards. Out of the Crisis. Cambridge, MA: MIT Center for Advanced Engineering Study, 1986.
- Hammer, Michael, and James Champy. Reengineering the Corporation: A Manifesto for Business Revolution. New York: HarperCollins Publishers, 1993.
- McKinsey & Company. "Enduring Ideas: The 7-S Framework." McKinsey Quarterly, March 2008.
- Campbell, Andrew, Mikel Gutierrez, and Mark Lancelott. Operating Model Canvas. Van Haren Publishing, 2017.
- Ulrich, Dave. "Shared Services: From Vogue to Value." Human Resource Planning 18, no. 3 (1995): 12–23.
- Schein, Edgar H. Process Consultation Revisited: Building the Helping Relationship. Reading, MA: Addison-Wesley, 1999.
- Goldratt, Eliyahu M. The Goal: A Process of Ongoing Improvement. Croton-on-Hudson, NY: North River Press, 1984.
- Simatupang, Togar M., Alan C. Wright, and Ramaswami Sridharan. "Applying the Theory of Constraints to Supply

Chain Collaboration." Supply Chain Management: An International Journal 9, no. 1 (2004): 57–70.

- Kaplan, Robert S., and David P. Norton. The Balanced Scorecard: Translating Strategy into Action. Boston, MA: Harvard Business School Press, 1996.
- Ulrich, Dave. "Shared Services: From Vogue to Value." Harvard Business Review 73, no. 3 (1995): 172–188.
- Deming, W. Edwards. Out of the Crisis. Cambridge, MA: MIT Press, 1986.
- Schwaber, Ken, and Jeff Sutherland. The Scrum Guide: The Definitive Guide to Scrum. ScrumGuides.org, 2017.
- Womack, James P., and Daniel T. Jones. Lean Thinking: Banish Waste and Create Wealth in Your Corporation. New York: Simon & Schuster, 1996.
- Collins, James C., and Jerry I. Porras. "Building Your Company's Vision." Harvard Business Review 74, no. 5 (1996): 65–77.
- Norton, David P., and Robert S. Kaplan. "Using the Balanced Scorecard as a Strategic Management System." Harvard Business Review 74, no. 1 (1996): 75–85.
- Ulrich, Dave. "A New Mandate for Human Resources." Harvard Business Review 76, no. 1 (1998): 124–134.
- Ross, Jeanne W., Peter Weill, and David C. Robertson. 2006. Enterprise Architecture as Strategy: Creating a Foundation for Business Execution. Boston, MA: Harvard Business School Press.

Insights and Actions

This chapter traces the evolution of vendor risk management (VRM) within organizations, using one author's own experiences to illustrate how VRM matures from reactive, department-driven oversight to a formalized, cross-functional program as businesses grow and face new risks. Effective VRM requires a combination of core competencies, essential skills, dedicated roles, and robust tools.

A successful TPRM program requires a clear governance model, well-defined roles and responsibilities, and a suite of tools and resources to manage third-party risks throughout the vendor lifecycle. Materiality analysis is foundational, helping organizations focus on the most critical vendors and risks. Continuous validation and adaptation of resources are necessary as organizational needs and risk landscapes evolve.

Organizations that assume individual teams will naturally optimize for enterprise success often create local efficiencies that produce global inefficiencies. For instance, procurement teams may negotiate cost reductions that lead to downstream quality issues or logistics delays, ultimately damaging overall business performance.

Organizational misalignment is a strategic liability that hampers competitive advantage. Functional silos and misaligned teams create systemic inefficiencies that manifest as lower production output, higher costs, reduced quality, slower speed to market, and decreased customer retention. Organizations with "too many cooks in the kitchen" experience decision paralysis, where supply chain managers spend more time coordinating conflicting departmental interests than executing strategic objectives, ultimately resulting in watered-down decisions that fail to address core issues or enable necessary innovation risks.

Success requires reorganizing around shared outcomes rather than functional disciplines, implementing measurable optimization models that all participants understand, and continuously reengineering both processes and organizational structures to drive improvement. Companies must establish unified success metrics aligned with strategic goals, invest in orchestration capabilities that synchronize complex workflows, and treat organizational design as a dynamic strategic asset that requires annual reassessment of mission, vision, and performance measures to maintain competitive excellence.

The organizational model is the foundation of enterprise agility, culture, and potential. Poor structure is a silent killer of execution, while great structure enables growth, responsiveness, and enduring excellence. Treat your organizational model as a strategic asset: rebuild, test, measure, and evolve it continuously. The organizational model is either your greatest strength or your weakest link.

Core Competencies in VRM

- Cost Control: Managing vendor costs through negotiation, inventory control, forecasting, and routine budget analysis to spot trends and manage relationships.
- Relationship Building: Developing and maintaining strong, trust-based relationships with vendors, which becomes increasingly strategic as dependencies grow.
- Contract Negotiation: Negotiating terms that benefit both parties and support long-term partnerships.
- Performance Monitoring: Enforcing contract terms while seeking ways to improve vendor and customer outcomes.
- Strategic Sourcing: Selecting vendors that fit current and future business needs, ensuring they can grow with the company.
- Risk Management: Initially focused on supply chain disruption and cost overruns, then expanding to address risks from data sharing, system access, and vendor instability as reliance on suppliers deepens.

Essential Skills for VRM

Risk assessment and analysis
Communication and negotiation
Project management
Financial acumen
Technology proficiency
Due diligence and research
Regulatory knowledge
Cybersecurity awareness
Problem-solving

Roles and Responsibilities in VRM

Vendor Risk/Program Manager	Leads the VRM program
Compliance Officer	Ensures regulatory and policy compliance
IT Security Analyst	Addresses cybersecurity risks
Procurement Specialist	Manages vendor selection and risk integration
Legal Counsel	Provides expertise on contracts and regulations
Auditor	Reviews vendor relationships for compliance
Data Analyst	Analyzes performance and risk data
Contract Manager	Manages contract terms and risk clauses
Business Continuity Specialist	Ensures alignment with continuity plans
Quality Assurance Specialist	Monitors vendor performance and quality

Actions to Take

Materiality and Risk Prioritization

- Assess whether the vendor is critical to revenue generation or if the relationship is financially significant. Note that even small-cost vendors can pose material risks if they handle sensitive data.

- Determine if disruption of the vendor's goods or services would materially impact operations. Even low-cost providers can be critical if their products are essential.

- Vendors handling sensitive data or with access to internal systems require heightened scrutiny and ongoing oversight.
- Identify vendors subject to regulatory requirements or contractual obligations, especially in regulated industries.

Establish Core Resources and Tools

- TPRM Charter and Policy: Authorize the program, outline governance, and define risk management functions.
- Vendor Master File: Maintain an up-to-date inventory of vendors, ideally with customizable labels for materiality and risk.
- Personnel and Competencies: Ensure the TPRM team has the necessary skills and staffing levels to manage third-party risks.
- Contract Management: Track contract terms, SLAs, and access controls for sensitive documents.
- Identification and Due Diligence: Use RFIs, RFPs, and independent vendor reviews to assess prospective vendors. Service definitions and demarcation points should be clear to avoid contract ambiguity.
- Risk Treatment: Maintain a risk register and use a risk adjudication model to document and manage identified risks. Ticketing systems can help track risk management activities.
- Ongoing Management: Keep vendor inventories accurate, maintain authorized personnel and emergency contact (APEC) lists, and schedule stewardship meetings for high-value relationships.
- Incident Response and Monitoring: Validate incident response procedures and use monitoring services to track changes in vendor risk profiles.

- Offboarding: Ensure data destruction and transition plans are in place for ending vendor relationships.
- Stay Agile and Anticipatory: Define the future on your terms, not just in reaction to competitors.

Chapter 3

Roles and Responsibilities

Introduction

In Chapter 3, we outline the roles and responsibilities essential for effective vendor and third-party risk management. Bill starts by introducing the DACI and RACI frameworks to help organizations assign well-defined roles for decision-making and task execution, fostering efficient and accountable program management. He emphasizes that vendor risk management is inherently cross-functional, requiring leadership, input, and oversight from multiple organizational roles. He points out that as vendor relationships grow in cost, complexity, and risk, organizations are typically compelled to formalize risk management processes to address these challenges.

Matt stresses and adds important context to the cross-functional nature of TPRM, showing how each function has different priorities. He notes, for example, that the legal and security functions focus on risk, while business executives prioritize performance and expediency. He goes on to argue that without a clear governance model and an accountable party, TPRM processes can suffer from conflicting priorities and inadequate risk mitigation. The key to overcoming this is understanding each role's incentives and motivations, establishing effective governance, and assigning an arbiter to resolve disagreements over risk treatment.

Chris then elevates the discussion and posits that while companies in a free market have access to similar resources (e.g., raw materials, labor, and distribution), it is their organizational models and people that truly differentiate them and drive success. He demonstrates how to begin by laying a foundation for design, and dissecting the company's vision, mission, strategies, and goals in terms of people dependencies. He introduces two key tools: the Theory of Constraints (TOC) is used to identify and manage bottlenecks, and the Target Operating Model (TOM) is employed to align operational capabilities with strategic goals.

The chapter identifies key contributors—such as risk analysts, procurement specialists, financial analysts, IT infrastructure managers, legal counsel, security architects, security analysts, compliance specialists, contract managers, and auditors—each with distinct responsibilities critical to mitigating vendor risk. Additional roles, such as data analysts, business continuity managers and communications managers, are also discussed as vital to a robust VRM program.

Our discussions on organizational models highlight the importance of aligning VRM structures with strategic goals, whether through centralized, federated, distributed, or multi-local approaches, to enhance adaptability and resilience. Ultimately, the chapter concludes that effective VRM depends on strong leadership, clear communication, and ongoing process refinement to address the evolving risks and complexities of vendor relationships.

Many Contributors to the Cause

Bill Bonney

Vendor risk management is inherently cross-functional, requiring leadership, input, and oversight from multiple organizational roles.

In Chapter 2, I listed the core competencies, essential skills, and primary roles and responsibilities of the vendor risk management program. In this chapter, I'll expand on those contributions using tools I've relied on to identify stakeholders and contributors for cross-functional programs. As I mentioned, the vendor management function grows organically within an organization. As cost, complexity, and risk increase, the organization typically imposes a risk management discipline to deal with the identified risks. Vendor risk management requires leadership, input, and oversight from various functions. This is especially true under a formal enterprise risk management program.

Two tools I've often used when establishing and managing a cross-functional program are DACI and RACI matrices. DACI stands for Driver, Approver, Contributor, and Informed. For those unfamiliar with this tool, these roles have the following responsibilities:

- **Driver**: The person responsible for driving the decision-making process forward, ensuring deadlines are met and discussions happen.

- **Approver**: The person with the final decision-making authority. They review all inputs and make the ultimate decision.

- **Contributor**: Individuals who provide input and expertise to inform the decision. Their insights and information are crucial, but they do not make the final decision.

- **Informed**: Those who need to be kept in the loop about the decision and its outcomes. They are updated on progress and the final decision but do not actively contribute to the decision-making process.

Key characteristics of the DACI are that it:

- Focuses on decision-making processes rather than task completion.
- Emphasizes the role of a Driver to ensure the process moves forward and meets deadlines.
- Clearly distinguishes between those who contribute input and those with the final approval authority.

The DACI matrix is a close cousin to the more well-known RACI (Responsible, Accountable, Consulted, Informed). Even though the RACI is more well-known than the DACI, it's worth reviewing as well:

- **Responsible**: The person or people who do the work to complete the task. They are responsible for the action/implementation.

- **Accountable**: The person who is ultimately answerable for the correct and thorough task completion. They ensure the task is done and sign off on it.

- **Consulted**: People who provide input and advice before the work is done and decisions are made. They are typically subject matter experts.

- **Informed**: Those who need to be kept updated on progress and decisions but do not contribute directly to the task.

The RACI's key characteristics are that it:

- Focuses on assigning clear responsibilities for tasks within a project.
- Emphasizes accountability and ensures there is one person ultimately answerable for each task.

- Clearly defines who needs to be consulted and informed, helping to streamline communication.

These pair well together to drive programs because the DACI helps you make sound, crisp decisions, and the RACI enables you to drive tasks to completion.

For the DACI to work well, delegation from the Approver (think executive sponsor) to the Driver is essential. However, in some organizations (often but not always driven by size), these are the same person. The Driver keeps things moving and is best served by having a diverse set of Contributors so they make well-informed decisions. The Approver acts as executive sponsor, evaluates and approves the decision once made, and is the escalation point when needed.

For the RACI to be a potent tool for driving execution, it's crucial that the executive sponsor, in the Accountable role, delegates action to those in the Responsible role, ensures adequate budget and staffing, and defines a clear escalation path. The same applies to the DACI. Clear role definitions and sufficient executive sponsorship are essential for both models to clear budget hurdles and make decisive decisions that management supports.

The DACI for the program should be set up with the program charter and revisited as frequently as you review the charter. Initiatives might require or benefit from a delegated DACI. In these cases, consider using a different Driver and adding or subtracting to the group of Contributors, but try to keep the same Approver and Informed group. As organizations mature, executive sponsorship can shift. An executive who excels at implementation may not be the best long-term owner of the day-to-day operations. This is fine if the executive team respects the process and prioritizes risk management objectives.

The RACI is a tool that should be used situationally. While you might rarely change your RACI for the vendor risk management program's day-to-day operations, you can quickly draft a RACI that pulls in various implementation teams for initiatives as needed. The key is to let the situation dictate the tool, not the other way around. Don't become a servant of your tools.

Competencies and Roles and Responsibilities

Vendor risk management is the quintessential model of a cross-functional program. It requires operational input from every corner of the organization. Significant inherent risks require risk management skills across myriad disciplines, and the consequences of failures can be severe reputational, financial, and operational impacts. These factors then point to the need for significant board participation, achieved by partnering with executive leadership to manage the most critical relationships and relying on the audit committee to contribute diligent oversight. In addition to the board and executive leadership, procurement, legal, security, IT, finance, compliance, and, of course, risk management will all need to play significant roles in the program routinely.

To help visualize this, here are sample DACI and RACI charts for key program decision-making and key tasks for vendor risk management:

Decision	Driver	Approver	Contributor	Informed
Vendor Selection Criteria	Procurement Manager	Head of Procurement	Risk Management Team, IT Department	Finance Team, Legal Team
Risk Assessment Methodology	Risk Manager	Chief Risk Officer	IT Security Team, Legal Team	Procurement Team, Compliance Team
Vendor Onboarding Process	Procurement Manager	COO	Legal Team, Risk Management Team	Finance Team, IT Department
Contract Review and Approval	Legal Counsel	General Counsel	Procurement Team, Risk Management Team	Finance Team, Compliance Team
Continuous Monitoring Process	IT Security Lead	CISO	Risk Management Team, Procurement Team	Legal Team, Compliance Team
Incident Response Plan	Risk Manager	Chief Risk Officer	IT Security Team, Legal Team	Procurement Team, Finance Team
Vendor Performance Evaluation	Procurement Manager	Head of Procurement	Risk Management Team, IT Department	Finance Team, Legal Team
Audit and Compliance Checks	Compliance Officer	Chief Compliance Officer	Risk Management Team, IT Department	Procurement Team, Legal Team, Finance Team
Vendor Offboarding Process	Procurement Manager	COO	Legal Team, Risk Management Team	Finance Team, IT Department

Figure 3.1 – Sample DACI Chart for Vendor Risk Management

Task	Responsible	Accountable	Consulted	Informed
Conducting Vendor Risk Assessments	Risk Management Team	Risk Manager	IT Security Team, Legal Team	Procurement Team, Compliance Team
Reviewing and Approving Vendor Contracts	Legal Team	General Counsel	Risk Management Team, Procurement	Finance Team, Compliance Team
Monitoring Vendor Compliance	Compliance Officer	Chief Compliance Officer	Risk Management IT Team, Department	Procurement Team, Legal Team
Updating Vendor Risk Profiles	Risk Management Team	Risk Manager	IT Security Team, Legal Team	Procurement Team, Compliance Team
Handling Vendor-related Incidents	IT Security Team	CISO	Risk Management Team, Legal Team	Procurement Team, Compliance Team
Performing Vendor Performance Reviews	Procurement Team	Head of Procurement	Risk Management Team, IT Department	Finance Team, Legal Team
Conducting Audits of Vendor Operations	Compliance Officer	Chief Compliance Officer	Risk Management IT Team, Department	Procurement Team, Legal Team, Finance
Managing Vendor Offboarding	Procurement Team	Procurement Manager	Legal Team, Risk Management Team	Finance Team, IT Department
Updating Vendor Management Policies	Risk Management Team	Chief Risk Officer	IT Security Team, Legal Team	Procurement Team, Compliance Team
Reporting on Vendor Risk Status	Risk Management Team	Risk Manager	IT Security Team, Legal Team	Procurement Team, Compliance Team, Executives

Figure 3.2 - Sample RACI Chart for Vendor Risk Management

It's important to note the use of a single individual in the accountable cell of the DACI chart. This is because the DACI chart is designed to drive decisions, not to reach a consensus. A consensus, being the least controversial decision, often fails to bring about meaningful change when needed. By allowing contributors to research, state, and defend their positions, the driver can tap into their operational experience and trust that they will represent the collective input from their constituencies. It's also crucial to strike the right balance between contributors and informed individuals. Many decision-making processes fail to reach clear decisions because they listen to too many opinions from minor stakeholders in the process.

It's tempting to think of this as a large company problem, and indeed, larger organizations often have entrenched individuals who demand a voice in decisions that are best made elsewhere. However, this can be an even more challenging issue in smaller companies that are still in the process of maturing. In Chapter 1, I mentioned the HR department's role in Telephony. Their experience with the current state was relevant, and the reliance other groups had on that team gave them a role they otherwise would never have in decisions in the near term. Initially, they could play a contributor role, and eventually, they had to become an informed stakeholder. Maintaining the status quo with that group was not an effective long-term strategy. Fortunately, they understood that. However, if you are new to the organization, be prepared to have what could be difficult conversations, take care to have an executive sponsor who can champion the process, and get as much background as you can before wading in. If parties continue to disagree, it will ultimately fall to the process owner or executive sponsor to make the call, which is another reason that having the right level of authority with the appropriate responsibilities and experience is critical to the program's success.

Key Contributors

These two sample matrices are not exhaustive. Repeating the exercise, depending on the product or service the vendor provides and the subsequent risk assessment of the business processes will identify other roles you'll need to include. In smaller organizations, many of these roles will collapse to a single individual. IT infrastructure, security analyst, and security architect may be one person. The contract manager may be responsible for most of the legal counsel tasks, save periodic check-ins with outside counsel. The procurement specialist may well be the data analyst as well. Where there are not departments or individuals that can take each individual role, you'll need to get creative to ensure the outcomes are met. As the company grows, some team members will appreciate the help, while others might feel inclined to defend their turf. It'll be the program manager and executive sponsors who will help steer the program through the changes.

Besides the various functions' managers and the listed teams' generic members, some roles are essential to the vendor risk program. These descriptions expand upon the bulleted list I provided in Chapter 2.

Risk Analyst

The Risk Analyst identifies and evaluates the risks associated with the vendor and the affected business processes. They'll work closely with security, compliance, legal, and IT. They may keep the risk profile current and provide regular reports, or these tasks may fall to others if they are part of a larger risk management team.

Procurement Specialist

The Procurement Specialist manages the vendor selection, performance reviews, and onboarding/offboarding processes. They also evaluate vendor performance, ensure procurement activities meet organizational standards, and maintain vendor performance and compliance records. They work closely with the risk management and legal teams to ensure all procurement activities are aligned with risk and legal requirements.

Financial Analyst

The Financial Analyst provides detailed financial oversight for vendor-related activities. They monitor vendor costs, assess financial performance, and ensure budgetary compliance. They also consult on the financial aspects of vendor contracts and performance evaluations. The Financial Analyst keeps the organization informed about the financial status and implications of vendor relationships, contributing to sound financial decision-making.

IT Infrastructure Manager

The IT Infrastructure Manager ensures that IT systems and infrastructure support process integration and data flow with the vendor. They also ensure that business processes supporting the risk management function are fully supported. They work with the risk management and procurement teams to support IT-related strategies and provide critical input on IT capabilities and constraints.

Legal Counsel

Legal Counsel provides legal advice on all aspects of vendor contracts and risk assessments. They review and approve vendor contracts, ensuring compliance with legal and regulatory requirements. They draft and review contract clauses related to risk management, especially data security (privacy), and collaborate with the risk management team to address any legal concerns during risk assessments. Legal Counsel also keeps the organization updated on legal and regulatory changes and implications, ensuring that all vendor agreements remain legally sound.

Security Architect

The Security Architect designs and implements security measures to protect against vendor-related risks. They drive security assessments and work with the Security Analyst and other IT security team members to develop and enforce security measures. The security architect keeps the organization informed about the security posture and potential threats related to vendors, playing a crucial role in maintaining robust security defenses.

Security Analyst

The Security Analyst participates in security risk assessments, manages security incidents, and ensures compliance with security policies. They work closely with the CISO to develop and enforce security protocols and provide critical input during risk assessments conducted by the risk management team.

Compliance Specialist

The Compliance Specialist focuses on monitoring and ensuring vendor compliance with organizational policies and regulatory requirements. They conduct compliance audits, update compliance policies, and provide guidance on regulatory issues. They consult with the risk management and IT security team to ensure all vendor activities align with compliance standards. The Compliance Specialist communicates compliance status and issues to the organization, helping to maintain high standards of regulatory adherence.

Contract Manager

The Contract Manager oversees the creation, negotiation, and administration of vendor contracts to ensure they meet organizational standards and regulatory requirements. They draft and review contract terms, ensuring compliance with legal and risk management policies, and coordinating with the legal and procurement teams to address issues. The Contract Manager also ensures that all contracts align with organizational goals and mitigate potential risks, providing ongoing support throughout the contract lifecycle. They play a crucial role in maintaining the integrity and enforceability of vendor agreements.

Auditor

The Auditor conducts thorough reviews and assessments of vendor-related activities to ensure compliance with internal policies and regulatory requirements. This role involves examining vendors' financial records, performance metrics, and operational practices. The Auditor works closely with the compliance officer, risk management team, and IT security team to identify any discrepancies or areas of concern. They provide detailed audit reports with recommendations for improvement, ensuring transparency and accountability in vendor relationships. Audit reports often go directly to the board of directors to assist them in their oversight duties.

Additional Contributors

As the organization continues to grow, so will the vendor footprint, the use of and reliance on operational and program data, the dependence on vendors that play a more prominent and more integrated role within the organization, and the need to communicate effectively across a potentially vast organization. Here are three more roles that can significantly help your program.

Data Analyst

The Data Analyst collects, analyzes, and interprets vendor performance and risk management data. This expert uses statistical tools and techniques to identify trends, assess risk levels, and generate reports that support decision-making processes. The Data Analyst collaborates with the risk management, IT security, and procurement teams to ensure data accuracy and relevance. By providing actionable insights and data-driven recommendations, the Data Analyst helps the organization understand and mitigate vendor-related risks, thereby enhancing the effectiveness of the vendor risk management program.

Business Continuity Manager

The Business Continuity Manager is responsible for developing and implementing strategies to ensure that the organization can maintain operations in the event of a disruption involving vendors. This role involves creating and testing business continuity plans, assessing vendors' resilience, and coordinating with the risk management and IT security teams to address potential vulnerabilities. The Business Continuity Manager ensures that critical functions can continue without interruption.

Communications Manager

I have found that messaging is often one of the most overlooked areas for any cross-functional program, and vendor risk management is no exception. Like any program that requires broad organizational participation, ensuring that people know what to do and where to go for help is critical to the program's success. If I know I can't get a lot of help crafting the various messages, I can at least befriend someone in the communications department and pick their brain over lunch to help keep my messaging on point. If I can get a larger resource commitment from communications, the Communications Manager can oversee internal and external vendor risk management communications. They can develop and implement communication strategies to inform all stakeholders about vendor risk policies, procedures, and any incidents or changes. The Communications Manager could work closely with the risk management, legal, and compliance teams to create clear and compelling messaging. This could ensure timely dissemination of information through various channels, help with crisis communication in the event of vendor-related issues, and help me maintain open lines of communication with vendors.

Conclusion

In conclusion, effective vendor risk management requires a structured and disciplined approach that integrates input from multiple organizational functions. As demonstrated in this chapter, tools like DACI and RACI matrices are essential for establishing clear roles, responsibilities, and decision-making processes that drive strategic and operational success. The DACI framework ensures decisive, informed decision-making by distinguishing between Drivers, Approvers, Contributors, and Informed stakeholders, while the RACI model clarifies accountability and execution in day-to-day operations.

Successful vendor risk management also relies on strong executive sponsorship and well-defined escalation pathways to maintain efficiency and organizational alignment. As vendor risk management programs evolve, role definitions and responsibilities must be revisited regularly to reflect organizational maturity, shifting executive priorities, and changes in vendor dependencies. The involvement of key functions—including procurement, legal, security, IT, compliance, and finance—underscores the cross-functional nature of vendor risk management, reinforcing the need for a well-structured governance framework.

By leveraging these tools and frameworks, organizations can enhance their ability to mitigate vendor risks, ensure regulatory compliance, and safeguard their financial and reputational standing. Ultimately, the effectiveness of a vendor risk management program depends on strong leadership, clear communication, and a commitment to continuously refining processes to meet the evolving demands of the business.

Know the Team and Clarify Roles and Responsibilities

Matt Stamper

A successful TPRM program is built on understanding the diverse perspectives and incentives of all involved stakeholders, proactive engagement, and clear governance.

One of the unique dynamics of both third-party and supply-chain risk management is that neither discipline belongs to one specific department or corporate function. Unlike finance and accounting, which is the purview of the CFO, or human resources, which belongs to the Vice President of HR (or a similar title), determining who is ultimately accountable for third-party risk management (TPRM) is not so clear. In this chapter, I want to explore some of the challenges that result from this ambiguity and offer some approaches that can help clarify core responsibilities and ultimate accountability for this critical organizational function. Use these insights to think about who should be part of your organization's TPRM program and who should ultimately own this function.

Tackle Ambiguity

TPRM is a corporate function that spans multiple departments within an organization. Below, I'll highlight some of these functions and the role that each plays in the TPRM process, including how these departments view risk and some of their specific priorities and motivations. Let's understand why there are so many proverbial cooks in the kitchen. We'd love to think of our companies as well-oiled machines where every function, role, decision, and action is planned and well-governed. The reality is that organizations are chaotic, and the efforts to implement governance over key functions are frequently met with strong resistance from stakeholders with directives, incentives, and requirements that likely differ from ours. Knowing how different roles think of the TPRM process is a critical step in clarifying what appears to be a conflicting goal of the process. There's a reason why legal and security stakeholders are laser-focused on risk. It's their job. Similarly, there's a reason why business executives and operations are focused on performance and expediency. They need to meet demanding top-line goals to push the organization forward. Other roles, such as procurement, are more perfunctory but still play an important role in the TPRM process. Collectively, these perspectives balance out and ideally make our organizations more resilient when confronting different forms of supplier and vendor risk.

Absent a clear governing model and an accountable party, the TPRM process will consistently confront disparate expectations and conflicting priorities that can result in TPRM risk not being adequately addressed and mitigated. To help navigate through these dynamics, knowing how different roles think about vendor and supply chain risk is foundational. Once each respective role's core incentives and motivations are outlined, this context can help establish a governance model over TPRM that may not completely eliminate conflicting priorities but can ensure that these issues are addressed proactively and prescriptively. Ultimately, each organization needs to parameterize its TPRM efforts (e.g., what level of discretion is permitted by role or department) and to assign an arbiter to adjudicate legitimate disagreements on risk treatment and risk tolerances. This arbiter is effectively the accountable party over the TPRM program.

As with any effort to categorize and generalize organizational functions, some assumptions about different roles may be exaggerated for effect. Here are the key roles (players) in the TPRM process. For each, I'll highlight what I believe to be their perspectives on risk and some of their departmental dynamics, motivations, and incentives.

Legal

An organization's legal counsel is inherently risk-focused and looks to reduce legal, regulatory, and business risks. Reviewing master service agreements and other contracts takes time, and many legal departments are frankly overwhelmed with contract review. The consequence is that the legal team may have significant backlogs that slow down the TPRM process regardless of the legal guidance that is ultimately offered. Beyond the obvious considerations of the workload, the legal team needs to track the organization's contractual obligations and maintain currency on new privacy and security laws that could be in scope while also addressing a multitude of business and contractual risks on an individual case basis. Effectively, the legal team is pulled in multiple directions as they work to keep pace with the business, mitigate risks, and make informed judgments on which risks are acceptable and which risks should be eliminated contractually.

When the legal team is confronted with certain contractual clauses that are not in their organization's favor, they instinctively will attempt to modify contract terms to favor their organization. These changes require time and attention to address with the other party, who also has counsel focused on minimizing risks. Contract negotiations take time and resources. This process adds costs and delays onboarding new vendors and suppliers. This diligence, however, is necessary. For better or worse, we live in litigious societies, so negotiating contracts proactively to reduce risk is necessary. Stakeholders who collaborate with the legal team would be well-served to understand which legal risks are effectively a "no go" from the legal team and work to address these proactively with prospective business partners. Timing is also an integral part of working with the legal team. Validate how long it will take to have contracts reviewed and, if required, what's needed to expedite contracts that may be more pressing and significant to the organization.

Legal risks can also be hypothetical in nature. Many contracts model risk considerations that are actually not part of the contemplated services or engagement. Effectively, the legal risk associated with the contract or clause may be high, but the operational risk is *de minimis*. We frequently see this when data protection agreements are executed even when data sharing does not occur. However, striking these clauses may cause more delay and costly negotiation than accepting the "legal risk," knowing that the actual or operational risk is immaterial. Use your judgment when confronting these scenarios.

Another challenge with legal review is that the costs of the legal review can materially change the financial model of the contemplated services. While working in the colocation and data center industry, we had a standard master services agreement for all client engagements. Certain clients wanted to make extensive and material changes to the agreement that would require extensive legal expenses. In these cases, the legal fees changed the profitability of the engagement. Spending $5,000 in legal fees for a $12,000 service doesn't make financial sense, but the legal considerations remain—draft service agreements to address and anticipate common issues proactively.

There are also asymmetries that need to be considered. Large organizations will undoubtedly have contracts written to their benefit. Smaller prospective customers may want to negotiate specific clauses (e.g., limitations of liability, indemnification) that the larger provider will not agree to. Conversely, larger customers may request terms and conditions of their smaller vendors that present significant risks for the provider and request service commitments that the smaller provider may not be operationally able to comply with but accepts to land a marquee client. While not common, there can be scenarios where a large customer can effectively take a small provider to the brink, as with GT Advanced Technologies and Apple.[3] When confronting notable asymmetries between the parties, take a moment to ensure that new risks are not introduced beyond the inherent risks of the actual service or product.

There's value in meeting frequently with counsel to review and validate their perspectives on which legal, regulatory, and business

3 https://www.nhbr.com/apple-agrees-to-3-5m-settlement-in-gtat-lawsuit/.

risks are key to their reviews of service agreements. Ensure you understand their workloads and timeframes for legal review and incorporate this into your onboarding activities.

While the challenges with legal review at scale cannot be overstated, a glimmer of hope is on the horizon. The advent of generative AI (GenAI) legal tools may be useful in scanning contracts for desired clauses and making recommendations where those clauses are absent. While the fidelity of these tools is a bit challenged today, we can anticipate improvements over time that may assist with managing the legal side of TPRM.

Privacy / Chief Privacy Officer (CPO) – There is likely overlap between the organization's legal counsel and those stakeholders who focus on privacy matters. Where privacy is managed separately from the legal team, the CPO will want to determine which vendors will have access to organizational data that is in-scope with privacy regulations, including the General Data Protection Regulation (GDPR) in Europe, the California Privacy Rights Act (CPRA), and the Health Insurance Portability and Accountability Act (HIPAA), among numerous other state and sector-specific laws. Many of these regulations have specific requirements related to vendor risk management. As a case in point, Article 28 of the GDPR outlines the obligations of a "data processor," including notably that the processing activities follow the data controller's explicit instructions and no derivative processing activities or alternative uses of the data are permitted. The CPO and/or their team must remain vigilant for third parties that may come into the organization's operations that process employee and consumer data (if in scope). These could be applications and services focusing on wellness programs and other HR services. Security monitoring services that address insider risk also warrant diligence and review by the CPO, notably in jurisdictions where employee privacy rights differ from those in the U.S.

Like counsel, CPOs are risk averse and want to obtain adequate assurances that consumer and employee data are treated consistently with agreements and applicable regulations. The CPO will generally rely upon the assurances from the CISO team's review of the third party. When this diligence occurs after the fact, obvious challenges arise. Security and privacy teams should collaborate to identify services, applications, and technologies with access to personal data and proactively manage these through their respective TPRM lifecycle. Minimally, these services should be inventoried, including the data elements they process, and their basic data flows documented. I believe the CPO should be accountable for maintaining this detail with strong support from the CIO and CISO as needed.

Corporate Security / Chief Information Security Officer (CISO)

The role of the CISO is inextricably linked to risk management. For CISOs, risk can arise from any number of sources, be it third-party or open-source code in applications, unsanctioned devices connected to the network, independently procured cloud services and SaaS applications, and non-vetted third parties and suppliers. Effectively, the CISO is charged with discovering and categorizing a near-infinite universe of risk. While legal colleagues are typically part of the onboarding process with third parties since they review contracts and agreements, security reviews have an unfortunate tendency to be after the fact. As a result, the diligence performed by the security team and overseen by the CISO may be sub-optimal—too little too late. As a CISO, I can state emphatically that being brought in after the fact to address risks that could have been addressed reasonably with some forethought and planning does not engender goodwill. Moreover, the broader context of the services, products, or engagements is rarely conveyed, undermining the CISO team's efforts to provide thorough diligence and risk analysis.

CISOs want to be proactively engaged to look at the risk considerations of prospective vendors and suppliers. CISOs are well served to ensure that their diligence also captures the business context of the contemplated application, service, product, or technology to help contextualize their analysis and ensure that recommendations are business-focused and address valid cybersecurity concerns. Frequently, CISOs are kept in the dark about material factors that could influence how they evaluate providers. This could result from need-to-know considerations or when CISOs are seen as too risk-averse and slow down business functions. This undermines the CISO's ability to provide detailed guidance. Engage CISOs and their teams early in the process and provide them with the necessary context to benefit from their analysis and diligence. Leverage these insights over the term of the engagement with the vendor or supplier.

Infrastructure & Operations (I&O) and the Chief Information Officer (CIO)

Organizations run on technology. More frequently than not, this technology is not under the company's direct control, and I&O teams do not directly manage large portions of the technology stack employed by the organization as it is delivered via either a software-, platform-, or infrastructure-as-a-service model. Like the CISO, the CIO should be proactively engaged regarding applications and services with IT context that connect to the organization's operations. Specifically, the CIO oversees a portfolio of services and their underpinning applications and IT infrastructure throughout their lifecycle. In that vein, the CIO oversees budgeting related to these services, including application licensing. This portfolio for larger organizations may result in something akin to a company store of sanctioned applications and services accessed via a single sign-on (SSO) portfolio. Part of the CIO's remit is rationalizing this portfolio of services and applications and reducing service and application overlap to minimize the administrative costs of overseeing multiple providers or services that effectively do the same thing.

While more and more of the technology we use is no longer under the direct physical control of the organization, there is still a requirement to ensure good governance over its use (e.g., authorizations, licensing, budgeting). The CIO, or an authorized designee, must ensure this governance occurs. CIOs are keenly focused on the availability of services and the impacts on the business when service interruptions occur. The CIO, accordingly, is a key player in the TPRM process, focusing on service-level agreement management.

Business Unit Executives / Lines of Business

In most organizations, business unit executives are focused on the top line, namely sales and marketing activities and the corresponding underlying operational functions. These stakeholders are typically less risk-averse than other participants in the TPRM process. Their focus is on meeting corporate operational, sales, and marketing objectives. The vendors or suppliers who help them achieve these are simply tools used to accomplish the goal. In other words, the focus is transactional. These stakeholders don't focus on the nuance that surfaces from legal and security reviews that may be necessitated based on the scope of the relationship with the third party and applicable regulations that may mandate detailed assessments and reviews. These "delays" muddy the waters and keep them from meeting their objectives. The creativity employed to bypass internal onboarding procedures and vetting activity by less senior staff cannot be underestimated. There is a reason why "shadow IT" and other forms of risk-taking occur: expediency. Business unit executives work at the speed of the business and react to changing market conditions. Ultimately, the TPRM process must keep this pace or risk being bypassed.

Other stakeholders in the TPRM process must understand business unit executives' pressures to meet quarterly objectives and other metrics. As a common theme, there's value in being proactive when collaborating with business unit executives. Work to understand their specific metrics, how they are judged, upcoming projects and renewals for key clients, and other contexts that could inform the TPRM process. These stakeholders are results-oriented and will focus on creative solutions to the challenges that they confront. When this creativity and initiative are harnessed and focused, business unit executives can be great allies in the TPRM process, notably in obtaining resources necessary to support an expedited and efficient TPRM program that helps them meet their business objectives.

Procurement

Larger organizations have formalized procurement departments that have myriad responsibilities as part of their remit, including interfacing with the Accounts Payable department to ensure that billing terms and conditions are established correctly, that tax tracking documents such as a W-9 in the U.S. are accurate and complete, and that pricing terms are favorable to the contracting organization. Many procurement departments will be charged with obtaining multiple bids and overseeing formal procurement functions such as requests for information (RFIs) and requests for proposals (RFPs). As a rule, procurement departments do not have much discretionary authority, though they can function as a gating mechanism for the onboarding process.

Leverage the organization's procurement function to help ensure that requisite documentation for onboarding is obtained, that negotiations on terms and conditions and pricing are consistent with organizational policy, and that onboarding decisions are generally free from undue bias. This may be an especially important consideration for multinational corporations subject to the Foreign Corrupt Practices Act (FCPA) or those conducting business with government agencies. In that context, and at the direction of Corporate Counsel, the procurement function can help ensure that regulatorily-mandated documentation related to the process or transaction is collected, validated, and maintained. The procurement function also brings strong project management capabilities to the broader TPRM process.

Internal Audit (IA) and Compliance

The IA and compliance teams are frequently overlooked in the TPRM process in all but the most highly regulated industries. In industries such as pharmaceuticals, which are subject to various validations, these teams oversee quality environments and audits of contract research organizations (CROs), contract manufacturing organizations (CMOs), and other validated contract providers. Similarly, financial service organizations leverage internal audit functions to review the TPRM process. As described in Chapter 12, the role of regulations in the TPRM process continues to expand.

Depending on the scope of the compliance and IA functions, these teams can bring impartiality and diligence to the broader TPRM program. There's value in determining if they are available to support TPRM efforts.

Subject Matter Experts (SMEs)

Complex projects, engagements, and supply chains frequently require expertise in multiple subjects, ranging from technology and sciences to international customs and practices. The SMEs' role will be highly contextualized to the unique circumstances of the contemplated engagement. Members of the extended TPRM team should know when and where SMEs should be brought into the TPRM process and ensure adequate resources to support their role.

Executive Leadership Team (ELT) / Board of Directors (BOD)

These senior roles ultimately inform and control the TPRM process, be it informally with the tone at the top to more overt accountability over budgeting and resourcing for services required to support the TPRM process. The ELT may engage in strategic projects with vendors and suppliers that are material to their organization's operations. It's incumbent upon the TPRM program to keep these two critical stakeholders adequately informed of materials risks presented by the organization's use of vendors and suppliers.

Stakeholders within the TPRM program would be well-served to understand which risk factors warrant executive attention, not based on their perspective but on direct guidance from the ELT and the BOD (if and where applicable). Moreover, how these risk factors are communicated and their frequency and timing should not be left to any vagaries. Ensure that the TPRM program does not happen in a vacuum from executive oversight and directives.

Key Team Dynamics

Knowing how different roles view TPRM is integral to establishing a program that manages vendor and supply chain risk in a manner consistent with broader organizational risk tolerances and equally important business initiatives. There is a balancing act between inherently risk-averse roles such as those of legal counsel and the CISO and those focused on top-line business priorities. There is no substitute for proactive engagement and collaboration among these participants. The differing perspectives among these participants are not "right" or "wrong." They simply reflect the incentives and priorities associated with that role or corporate function. There's nothing wrong with putting these issues and dynamics on the table when bringing the TPRM team together. For example, if you were speaking with counsel, you may want to pose some questions to ensure that interactions between the TPRM program and counsel are productive and efficient. Some basic framing questions would include the following:

- Which legal or contractual risks are front and center for your team?
- What is your guidance on proactively addressing these risks as part of our TPRM program?
- How do you recommend we address scenarios or risks contemplated in contracts that are not part of the services or products that are contemplated?
- How much time does your team require to complete a contract review?
- What should the TPRM team understand about legal reviews that could impact the TPRM program and its effectiveness?

These open-ended questions will start the dialogue that will ultimately underpin an effective TPRM program in your organization. As the adage goes, "Seek first to understand, then to be understood." Further, there is great value in having diverse perspectives looking at topics as challenging as TPRM. As you build your TPRM team, ensure that you have these diverse perspectives by design and have a team that helps bring a holistic view of vendor and supply chain risk management to your organization. Ultimately, the success of the TPRM program translates into a resilient and effective organization.

The Crucial Role of Organizational Models

Chris Forbes

Organizations that continuously optimize their structures will be best positioned to thrive in volatile and complex environments.

1.0 Introduction

In a free and open economy, all companies should have similar access to the same corporate building blocks, such as raw materials, intellectual property, labor pools, distribution avenues, sales platforms, and marketing channels. If companies had equal access, wouldn't all companies eventually achieve the same level of success or begin to look the same? For example, gas stations have evolved to the point that they all offer the same products and services at very similar price points. I would also say they all purchase their raw materials on the same global market at the same price. The primary distinction or differentiating factor would appear to be their organization and, by extension, the inherent intellectual property people bring with them.

In reality, most companies have a different mix of access to raw materials, sources of energy, size of the labor pool, access to talent with advanced skills, and depth and maturity of their intellectual property. It is precisely this mix of strengths and weaknesses that makes Organizational Design so important. I am a firm believer that everything begins and ends with people. Walt Disney famously said, "You can design, create, and build the most wonderful place in the world, but it takes people to make the dream a reality."

To answer the question, "Is my organization designed and aligned to optimize our goals and strategies?" we must first acknowledge that companies and agencies exist for many reasons and must operate in vastly different situations and environments. The core difference that separates good companies from great companies is their ability to assess their situation and focus their efforts and investments on solving the most pressing challenges that offer the highest strategic rewards and return on investment. In other words, what separates the best companies from the rest is their ability to assemble a team capable of developing and delivering strategies and optimizing outcomes.

1.1 The Primary Factors Driving the Choice of Organizational Models

If you asked thousands of CEOs and business executives how they came up with their organizational model, the top five answers would look something like this:

1. The CEO and/or founder decided on the current organizational model.
2. The employees prefer the current model. This statement implies that some thought went into analyzing various models, and the employees chose this one. Examples could include charities, co-ops, and sole practitioners.
3. The industry has evolved to prefer this organizational model.
4. Humanity has proven that this model is the best way to do things. In other words, we do not dare mess with it.
5. The company designed the organization before I arrived, so I do not know how much thought went into it.

I have yet to hear management say it has rigorously analyzed the current organizational model and repeatedly realigned it to ensure it is the most conducive to our overall success. In my 42 years of business experience, I have encountered very few companies that recognized the importance and potential benefits of radically realigning an organization with an apparent aim to maximize a particular outcome. Let us dissect the critical steps involved in analyzing an organizational model.

- Lay the foundations for organizational design.
- Dissect the Company's Vision, Mission, Strategies, and Goals into People Dependencies.
- Identify the biggest Challenges and Constraints in terms of people and organizational competencies.
- Analyze the potential benefits and drawbacks of various organizational structures.

1.2 Target Operating Model (TOM)

Supply Chain Management (SCM) is the integrated planning, coordination, and control of all business processes and activities in sourcing, procurement, conversion, and logistics management. It encompasses the flow of materials, information, and finances as they move from supplier to manufacturer to wholesaler to retailer to consumer. SCM aims to optimize and streamline these processes to achieve efficient and effective operations, reduce costs, and enhance customer satisfaction. In essence, SCM integrates supply and demand management within and across companies, focusing on creating value for stakeholders by efficiently and effectively managing people and processes.

SCM encompasses discovering and overseeing all externally required components and services in a company's value chain, including financial resources, intellectual property, creativity and novelty, data and information, raw materials, processing and transformation, external manufacturing, delivery and distribution, and logistical support.

The Target Operating Model (TOM) originated from the intersection of strategic management and organizational design research (Ross 2006). It has gained prominence as businesses seek structured approaches to aligning their operational capabilities with strategic goals. The concept evolved from traditional business process reengineering and enterprise architecture frameworks, becoming a standard tool in strategic planning and transformation initiatives.

1.3 Lay the Foundations for Organizational Design

Lee Iacocca, the former CEO of Chrysler, said, "In the end, all business operations can be reduced to three words: people, product, and profits. People come first." Steve Jobs, former CEO of Apple, said, "Great things in business are never done by one person; they are done by a team of people." Many leaders have discussed the importance of people and organizational structures in achieving success. Pioneering research in organizational design has provided some basic foundations and tenets, such as mechanistic structures suited for stable environments. In contrast, organic structures are better for dynamic, rapidly changing environments (Burns, 1961). "Structure follows strategy," meaning corporate strategy changes necessitate corresponding organizational structure changes (Chandler, 1962).

Optimal organizational structure depends on the environment in which an organization operates and requires management to adjust based on the degree of uncertainty and complexity (Lawrence, 1967). Effective organizational design aligns strategy, structure, processes, rewards, and people to ensure success and adaptability (Galbraith, 1977). Different organizational structures, such as simple, mechanical, professional, divisionalized, and ad hoc, are better suited to different environments and types of work (Mintzberg, 1979).

Companies should structure themselves to effectively implement their chosen competitive strategies, whether they are focusing on cost leadership, product differentiation, or customer satisfaction (Porter, 1980). To create and sustain superior performance, companies should identify primary and support activities that create customer value and competitive advantage as part of their value chain (Porter, 1985). Companies should reevaluate legacy processes by involving all stakeholders, empowering employees, providing continuous training and development, and demonstrating leadership commitment to improve the quality of products and services (Deming, 1986). To achieve dramatic performance improvements, companies must fundamentally rethink and radically redesign themselves using business process reengineering (BPR) (Hammer and Champy 1993). Leading companies can be studied using the 7S framework of Strategy, Structure, Systems, Shared Values, Style, Staff, and Skills (McKinsey, 2008).

Ensuring that operating models align with business strategy requires analysis across six dimensions: processes, organization, locations, information, suppliers, and management systems (Campbell, 2017).

Many leading business luminaries agree that organizational design has the potential to significantly enhance a company's long-term success. Multiple approaches are available, and most highlight the need to identify a company's dependencies on people. The evidence further suggests that the critical factor separating great companies from the competition is management's willingness to let go of historical precedents, challenge the status quo, and experiment with new organizational structures. Given the rapid pace of technological innovation, the fast-moving geopolitical landscape, and the growing list of environmental challenges, I would go so far as to say that the most successful companies in the future will be those that can completely transform themselves over and over again.

1.4 Dissect the Company's Vision, Mission, Strategies, and Goals in Terms of People Dependencies

J. C. Collins (HBR 1996) outlined the importance of a well-defined vision and mission to guide organizational direction. It highlighted the critical need to understand the dependencies on people to achieve optimal alignment. Norton and Kaplan (HBR 1996) developed the Balanced Scorecard for Translating Strategy into Action, emphasizing the importance of aligning people and their roles with the organization's strategic goals to ensure effective execution. D. Ulrich (HBR 1997) discussed the strategic role of human resources in achieving business objectives. Ulrich believed effective HR practices ensure alignment of people with the business strategy. We can gain additional insights by digging below the surface to understand the general nature of work and the level of skills, physical prowess, and mental abilities needed to complete those tasks.

Early in my career, I was fortunate to participate in a "Time and Motion Study" as part of a Business Process Reengineering (BPR) exercise. The project team documented and analyzed hundreds of tasks in terms of temporal factors (e.g., time required per task, the volume of tasks, frequency of tasks, pace/throughput over time), physical factors (e.g., size, strength, stamina, speed, dexterity, agility, visual acuity), adaptability factors (e.g., task predictability, depth and breadth of task variation), knowledge factors (e.g., complexity of tasks, pre-task analysis required, memory required), wisdom factors (e.g., ability to rationalize, ethical judgment, capable of balancing competing goals). I profoundly appreciated the value of seeing how reengineering experts used the data to identify activity-based costing, value creation, and net return on energy invested. The BPR specialists also used this information to determine the people profiles needed to complete tasks, including the relative scarcity of that particular skill or talent.

1.5 Identify the Biggest Challenges and Constraints in Terms of People

Those Time and Motion studies identified the ten most common business constraints: Employee Attraction/Retention, Knowledge/Physical Skills, Leadership Skills, Customer Access, Legal/Regulatory, Financial, Resources/Materials, Technology, Process Stability/Maturity, and Competitive Force. Over half the constraints are dependent on people.

The Theory of Constraints (TOC) is a management practice published by Goldratt in the 1984 book *The Goal: A Process of Ongoing Improvement*. TOC's primary focus is identifying and managing the constraints (bottlenecks) preventing an organization from achieving its goals and improving its performance. TOC is widely used in manufacturing to improve production processes, reduce inventory levels, and increase throughput. Techniques such as Drum-Buffer-Rope (DBR) are employed to synchronize production flow. The book *Applying the Theory of Constraints to Supply Chain Collaboration* (Simatupang, 2004) suggested using TOC to optimize supply chain operations by identifying and managing constraints, reducing lead times, and improving customer satisfaction. The core principles of the Theory of Constraints are:

- Identify the Constraint: Determine the most significant limiting factor (bottleneck) that prevents the organization from achieving its highest performance.
- Exploit the Constraint: Optimize the use of the constraint without significant investments or changes. Focus on making quick improvements to the bottleneck to increase its efficiency.
- Subordinate Everything Else: Align the entire system or organization to support the constraint's maximum capacity. Ensure that all other processes are adjusted to meet the constraint's needs.
- Elevate the Constraint: If the constraint is still a bottleneck after optimization, take additional actions such as investing in new resources or making significant changes.
- Repeat the Process: Once a constraint is resolved, move on to the next constraint and repeat the process. This continuous improvement cycle ensures that the organization's performance is continuously enhanced.

1.6 Analyze Potential Benefits and Drawbacks of Various Organizational Structures

Warren Bennis said, "The factory of the future will have only two employees, a man and a dog. The man will be there to feed the dog, and the dog will be there to keep the man from touching the equipment." While this statement is partially in jest, it raises an interesting question: "Who is working for whom?" I will extrapolate this question to cover the hierarchical and inter-relationships between all employees, contractors, and temporary workers involved in the company's supply chain. Management must consider the organizational structure's effects and impacts on overall company success and competitiveness. In addition, management needs to be mindful of and possibly design around the people-centric constraints listed above.

Organizational structures vary widely, including flat hierarchy, tiered hierarchy, matrixed reporting, agile or temporary assignments, project teams, shared service teams, and internal consulting teams. Here is a brief comparison of the advantages and disadvantages of the most common organizational models:

Flat Hierarchy Structure

Flat organizations have minimal levels of management between staff and executives. Roles have a broad span of control with fewer hierarchical levels. Flat organizations exhibit faster decision-making, improved communication and collaboration, and greater employee autonomy and empowerment. However, flat organizations can be challenging to manage as they grow. This structure may lead to role ambiguity, overload on managers, and decreased employee oversight and discipline (Hempel, 2004).

Tiered Hierarchy Structure (Divisional)

Tiered organizations typically have multiple layers of management with a well-defined chain of command, defined roles and responsibilities at each level, and well-defined career progression paths. They emphasize simplified job functions and accountability. Tiered structures are easier to manage in large organizations with complex operations. However, due to multiple approval levels, tiered organizations exhibit slower decision-making, have a higher risk of communication breakdowns, and can create a rigid and bureaucratic environment (Mintzberg, 1979).

Matrixed Reporting Structure

Matrixed organizations have employees reporting to multiple managers, such as a cost center, functional group, project, or geography. Matrix structures combine elements of both functional and divisional structures and offer flexible resource allocation across long-lived initiatives. Matrixes attempt to balance technical expertise across assignments and encourage collaboration across departments. However, matrices have a higher chance of conflicting priorities, increased complexity in performance management, and employee confusion from having multiple leaders. Matrixes require strong communication and conflict-resolution skills. (Galbraith, 1971).

Agile or Temporary Reporting Structure

Agile structures are dynamic teams that form and dissolve based on project needs. They emphasize flexibility, speed, and adaptability. Agile is highly responsive to changes in market or project requirements, fosters innovation and cross-functional collaboration, and shortens product development cycles. However, Agile structures can lead to role ambiguity, employee confusion, workforce instability, and a lack of consistency/continuity, requiring a high degree of coordination and communication (Schwaber, 2017).

Shared Service Teams Structure

Shared service team structures create centralized pools of workers performing similar functions across departments. Shared services are formed around scarce or limited skill sets, expensive tooling, or the requirement for particular legal or regulatory oversight (e.g., IT, HR, Legal, Finance). Shared service teams provide economies of scale, cost savings, increased service efficiency, and greater consistency and standardization in service delivery. They also remove commodity work from other departments, allowing them to focus on their core activities and customers. However, shared service teams risk becoming disconnected from the needs of individual departments, which may lead to bureaucratic inefficiencies and require strong governance and service-level agreements. (Ulrich, 1995).

Internal Consulting Teams Structure

Internal consulting teams provide specialized expertise and support on a task or assignment basis. Examples include regulatory compliance, information security, and business continuity planning. Consulting teams leverage internal subject matter expert knowledge and capability and typically provide targeted, high-impact support to business units. However, consultants can be seen as external or disconnected from core operations, leading to integration issues. Consultants require strong project management skills, client-relationship finesse, and problem-solving abilities to work effectively across many departments and managers (Schein, 1999).

Understanding these organizational models helps organizations choose the best structure for their strategic goals and operational needs. Companies can optimize efficiency, adaptability, and overall performance by leveraging each model's strengths.

1.7 SCM Program Core Business Functions

SCM is the process that oversees the entire flow of goods and services, from the initial raw materials to the final delivery to consumers. SCM optimizes the supply chain to ensure efficiency, reduce costs, and deliver high-quality products and services. SCM covers a broad range of activities, including:

- Procurement of raw materials
- Manufacturing and production processes
- Logistics and transportation
- Inventory management
- Forecasting supply and demand
- Coordination and collaboration with various partners and stakeholders
- Understanding government regulations and geopolitical volatility
- Anticipating atmospheric and environmental conditions and extreme changes in those conditions

Companies can divide their organization by product, service, legal entity (parent/affiliates/subsidiaries), or geographic location. Mid and large-sized companies tend to fragment and distribute design, operations, and oversight responsibility to geographic operating centers. Regardless of the number of divisions and departments involved in a company's supply chain management practice, all teams must perform essential or core business functions. I would classify these core professional and managerial functions as follows:

Strategic Planning:

- Supply and Demand Forecasting: Accurate prediction of customer demand to inform production planning and inventory management.
- Supply Chain Strategy: Develop and implement a strategic plan that aligns with business goals and market conditions.
- Supplier Relationship Management: Establish and maintain solid relationships with key suppliers to ensure reliable supply and quality.
- Supply Chain Risk Management: Identify potential risks in the supply chain and develop mitigation strategies.

Procurement:

- Sourcing and Procurement: Identifying, evaluating, and selecting suppliers to procure goods and services.
- Contract Management: Managing supplier contracts and agreements to ensure compliance and optimal terms.
- Supply Cost Management: Controlling purchasing and supply chain operations costs.

Operations:

- Inventory Management: Maintaining optimal inventory levels to meet demand without excessive stock.
- Production Planning and Scheduling: Coordinating production activities to meet demand efficiently.
- Quality Control: Ensuring products meet specified quality targets through rigorous quality control processes.

Logistics:

- Transportation Management: Planning and optimizing transportation to ensure the timely delivery of goods.
- Warehouse Management: Efficiently managing warehousing operations, including storage, retrieval, and order fulfillment.
- Distribution Management: Coordinating the distribution of finished products to customers or retailers.

Information Technology:

- Information Systems: Implementing and maintaining systems for tracking and managing supply chain activities.
- Data Analytics: Leverage data, information, and associated signals to gain insights and drive decision-making in supply chain operations.
- Automation and Integration: Utilizing automation technologies and integrating systems to streamline operations and improve efficiency.

Financial Management:

- Budgeting and Cost Control: Developing budgets and controlling costs associated with supply chain activities.
- Financial Reporting and Analysis: Analyze financial performance and report on key metrics related to supply chain operations.

Compliance and Sustainability:

- Regulatory Compliance: Ensuring compliance with local, national, and international regulations related to supply chain operations.
- Sustainability Initiatives: Implement sustainable practices and reduce the environmental impact of supply chain activities.

Customer Relationship Management:

- Order Management: Efficiently managing customer orders from receipt to delivery.
- Customer Service and Support: Providing exceptional customer service and support throughout the fulfillment of orders.

Collaboration and Coordination:

- Cross-functional Collaboration: Ensuring effective communication and collaboration across different departments involved in the supply chain.
- Supplier Collaboration: Working closely with suppliers to improve processes and achieve mutual benefits.

Continuous Improvement and Innovation:

- Performance Monitoring: Monitoring key performance indicators (KPIs) and metrics to assess supply chain performance.
- Process Improvement: Continuously identify and implement improvements in supply chain processes.
- Research and Development: Investing in R&D to innovate and improve supply chain processes and technologies.
- Market Adaptation: Adapting supply chain strategies to changing market conditions and customer preferences.

1.8 Supply Chain Risk Management (SCRM)

Supply Chain Risk Management (SCRM) is a critical organizational function designed to identify, assess, and mitigate supply chain risks, ensuring operational continuity and safeguarding a company's reputation and financial stability. In today's globalized economy, supply chains are increasingly complex, often involving multiple tiers of suppliers across various geographical regions. This complexity exposes organizations to a broad spectrum of risks, including geopolitical instability, natural disasters, supplier insolvency, cybersecurity threats, and more. Effective SCRM aims to minimize these risks by implementing proactive strategies that address potential vulnerabilities before they disrupt the supply chain.

Organizational Purpose of SCRM

The primary purpose of SCRM is to enhance the resilience and robustness of the supply chain. By identifying potential risks early, organizations can develop mitigation strategies that reduce the likelihood of disruptions and minimize their impact if they do occur. SCRM involves close monitoring of the supply chain environment, ongoing risk assessments, and the development of contingency plans to ensure that the supply chain can adapt to unexpected challenges. This function is essential for maintaining operational continuity, meeting customer expectations, and protecting the company's competitive position in the market.

Organizational Structures for SCRM

Organizations typically adopt one of several structures to manage their SCRM functions, each with its advantages and challenges. These structures include centralized, federated, distributed, and multi-local models.

Centralized Structure

In a centralized SCRM structure, all risk management activities are consolidated within a single central unit. This structure allows for consistent risk assessment methodologies and streamlined decision-making processes. It is particularly effective in organizations where risk management practices are essential, and supply chain operations are relatively uniform across regions. However, the centralized model can be less responsive to local risks and may struggle to adapt to the unique challenges faced by different parts of the supply chain.

Example: Many large multinational corporations, such as automotive manufacturers, use centralized SCRM structures to maintain consistent risk management practices across their global supply chains. This approach ensures that all regions adhere to the same standards and protocols, which is critical in industries with stringent regulatory requirements.

Federated Structure

A federated SCRM structure balances central oversight with local autonomy. In this model, the central SCRM unit sets overarching policies and guidelines, while regional or business unit-specific teams are responsible for implementing these policies and managing risks relevant to their specific contexts. The federated structure allows for greater flexibility and responsiveness to local risks while maintaining consistency and control from the central unit.

Example: Companies in the pharmaceutical industry often adopt a federated SCRM structure. The central risk management team develops global policies and standards, while local teams adapt these guidelines to address region-specific regulatory requirements and supply chain risks.

Distributed Structure

Risk management responsibilities are decentralized in a distributed SCRM structure, with each business unit or regional office managing its risks independently. This structure offers maximum flexibility and allows teams to respond quickly to local risks. However, it can lead to inconsistencies in risk management practices, making achieving a cohesive, organization-wide risk management strategy difficult.

Example: A global retail chain might use a distributed SCRM model, where each regional office manages its supply chain risks. Federated management models allow the company to tailor its strategies to the specific challenges of its local markets.

Multi-Local Structure

The multi-local SCRM structure is similar to the distributed model but strongly emphasizes localization. In this model, risk management is deeply embedded in the local context, with local teams having significant autonomy to develop and implement risk management strategies highly tailored to their specific environment. This structure is particularly effective in regions with highly diverse risk profiles but can lead to a lack of coordination and difficulties sharing best practices across the organization.

Example: A company operating in a diverse geographical landscape, such as a global food and beverage company, might adopt a multi-local SCRM structure to ensure local teams can address region-specific risks such as varying agricultural conditions, local regulations, or supply chain disruptions due to political instability.

Case Studies and Statistics

Recent studies indicate that about 60% of companies with global supply chains prefer a federated SCRM structure, which balances centralized control and local flexibility. For instance, a leading technology company successfully implemented a federated SCRM model, which allowed its regional teams to address region-specific cyber threats while adhering to the overarching cybersecurity policies set by the central office. This approach significantly reduced the company's overall exposure to supply chain disruptions and helped maintain a stable operational flow. In contrast, companies that operate in highly regulated industries, such as pharmaceuticals or aerospace, often opt for a centralized SCRM structure to ensure strict compliance with global standards and regulations. These companies prioritize consistency and control, making the centralized model ideal for maintaining uniform risk management practices.

The choice of organizational structure for SCRM should align with the company's overall strategic goals, the complexity of its supply chain, and the specific risks it faces. Whether centralized, federated, distributed, or multi-local, the effectiveness of SCRM depends on the organization's ability to integrate risk management into its broader operational strategy and to ensure that all parts of the supply chain are prepared to respond to potential disruptions. By carefully selecting and optimizing the appropriate SCRM structure, organizations can better protect themselves from supply chain risks and enhance their overall resilience.

1.9 Third-Party Risk Management (TPRM)

TPRM identifies, assesses, and oversees risk mitigation associated with third-party products and services. These third parties could include vendors, suppliers, contractors, and partners. TPRM aims to protect the organization from hazards such as data breaches, financial losses, operational disruptions, and reputational damage that can arise from third-party relationships and typically includes:

- Risk assessment: Evaluating the potential risks posed by third parties.
- Due diligence: Conducting thorough checks before entering into agreements with third parties.
- Monitoring: Continuously overseeing third-party activities to ensure compliance with standards and manage emerging risks.
- Mitigation: Implementing strategies to minimize the impact of identified risks.

1.10 Vendor Risk Management (VRM)

Vendor Risk Management is closely tied to Third-Party Risk Management and focuses explicitly on managing risks associated with vendors or suppliers. VRM ensures that vendors deliver the required quality of goods or services, meet delivery timelines, and do not pose undue risk to the organization. VRM typically involves:

- Vendor selection: Evaluating and choosing vendors based on risk profiles and capabilities.
- Contract management: Establishing clear terms and conditions to mitigate potential risks.
- Performance monitoring: Regularly assessing vendor performance against agreed-upon standards and metrics.
- Compliance checks: Ensuring that vendors comply with regulatory requirements and internal policies.

Conclusion

The strategic alignment of organizational models with corporate vision, mission, and operational realities is no longer optional, it is imperative. While organizations may share access to similar resources, the differentiating factor that enables sustainable success lies in the deliberate design and continual refinement of a company's organizational models. From foundational principles of organizational theory to modern constructs such as the Target Operating Model (TOM), and from strategic supply chain management to nuanced structures for third-party and vendor risk oversight, agility, clarity of purpose, and people-centered design remain central to high-performing organizations. The ability to dissect dependencies, anticipate constraints, and apply appropriate structural models—whether centralized, federated, or agile, defines those enterprises that thrive amid volatility and transformation. Ultimately, organizations that continuously assess, realign, and optimize their operational architecture will be best positioned to convert strategy into superior execution, resilience, and long-term value creation.

Insights and Actions

Understand the organizational structures and their impact.

This chapter reviewed various structures (flat, tiered, matrix, agile, shared services, internal consulting) and their suitability for different environments and strategic goals. The choice of structure should reflect the company's need for flexibility, control, and responsiveness.

While companies may have similar access to raw materials, labor pools, and distribution channels, the critical differentiating factor is how they organize and align their people to execute strategy.

Organizations must deliberately choose between centralized, federated, distributed, or multi-local structures for Supply Chain Risk Management (SCRM) and Third-Party Risk Management (TPRM) based on their operational complexity, regulatory requirements, and geographic diversity. Approximately 60% of global companies prefer federated SCRM structures that balance centralized control with local flexibility. At the same time, highly regulated industries, such as pharmaceuticals and aerospace, require centralized models to ensure uniform compliance and risk management practices.

Time and Motion Studies reveal that over half of business constraints are people-dependent, including employee attraction and retention, knowledge and physical skills, and leadership capabilities. Organizations must move beyond traditional functional silos to create structures that optimize the ten core SCM business functions—from strategic planning and procurement to logistics and continuous improvement—while applying Theory of Constraints principles to identify and systematically address organizational bottlenecks that prevent optimal supply chain performance and resilience.

Supply Chain Management (SCM) and Risk Management

- SCM encompasses procurement, manufacturing, logistics, inventory, forecasting, and collaboration with partners.

- Supply Chain Risk Management (SCRM) is crucial for identifying and mitigating risks such as geopolitical instability, supplier insolvency, and cyber threats.
- Different organizational structures for SCRM include centralized, federated, distributed, and multi-local models, each with advantages and drawbacks depending on industry and risk profile.

Third-Party and Vendor Risk Management

- Third-Party Risk Management (TPRM) and Vendor Risk Management (VRM) are specialized functions within SCRM, focusing on assessing and mitigating risks from external partners and suppliers.
- These functions involve risk assessment, due diligence, ongoing monitoring, and mitigation strategies.

Actions to Take

Use These Key Tools and Frameworks

- DACI Matrix: The DACI focuses on decision-making, not just task completion, and is especially useful for driving clear, informed decisions.
- RACI Matrix: The RACI clarifies who is responsible and accountable for tasks, streamlining project execution and communication.
- Target Operating Model (TOM): Aligns operational capabilities with strategic goals, originating from strategic management and organizational design research.

Adopt Program Governance and Best Practices

- Executive Sponsorship: Strong leadership is essential for delegating authority, securing resources, and defining escalation paths.

- Regular Review: Role definitions and responsibilities should be revisited as organizations mature and priorities shift.
- Communication: Clear, consistent messaging is crucial for cross-functional programs.
- Flexibility: Tools like DACI and RACI should be used situationally, not rigidly.

Acknowledge the Cross-Functional Nature of TPRM

- TPRM spans legal, security, operations, procurement, and more. Each function has different priorities—legal and security focus on risk, while business executives prioritize performance and expediency.
- Without a clear governance model and an accountable party, TPRM processes can suffer from conflicting priorities and inadequate risk mitigation.
- Understanding each role's incentives and motivations is crucial for establishing effective governance and assigning an arbiter to resolve disagreements over risk treatment.

Recognize Important Team Dynamics

- TPRM requires balancing risk-averse roles (legal, security) with business-focused ones (executives, operations).
- Proactive engagement, open communication, and understanding each function's pressures are essential.
- Diverse perspectives contribute to a more holistic and resilient approach to vendor and supply chain risk.

Use Organizational Models as Differentiators

- Companies with similar resources can achieve vastly different outcomes depending on their organizational design and the talent they attract.

- The most successful organizations continually assess and realign their models to maximize performance and adaptability.

Appreciate these Foundations of Organizational Design

- The process begins by laying a foundation for design, dissecting the company's vision, mission, strategies, and goals in terms of people dependencies.
- Organizations must identify their biggest challenges and constraints, especially those related to people—such as employee attraction/retention, skills, leadership, and regulatory compliance.
- The Theory of Constraints (TOC) is highlighted as a method to identify and manage bottlenecks, with a focus on continuous improvement.

Section 2

Operational Considerations for Third-Party Risk Management Programs

What we hope ever to do with ease, we must first learn to do with diligence.

~ Samuel Johnson, 19th Century English Writer

Preamble

Aristotle famously said: "We are what we repeatedly do. Excellence, then, is not an act, but a habit." In Section 2, authors Bill Bonney, Chris Forbes, Gary Hayslip, and Matt Stamper introduce you to the habits we must form to address our third-party risks appropriately. We, as a group, are steeped in process. We don't view process as a yoke, but rather as a harness. It doesn't bind our movement but instead gives us a structure and a platform from which to channel our effort toward the best chance for success. You'll start to see the value as we progress through this section.

We identified the foundational elements of third-party risk management programs in Section 1, and beginning with Chapter 4, "Onboarding," we'll see that foundation start to pay off. During the onboarding phase, we begin the relationship with specific third parties while also adding to the solid foundation of third-party risk management. Each third party has an impact on business processes and interacts with the people and technology the organization relies on. How we onboard each third party impacts how we manage and monitor that third party, as we'll discuss in Chapter 5.

In Chapter 6, "Incident Response," and Chapter 7, "Offboarding," we'll see how the diligence we preach throughout this book can make the risks associated with third-party incidents and the removal of a third party from a particular business process (or processes) easier to anticipate and manage. As in Section 1, we'll present these topics from the perspective of managing vendor risk, third-party risk, and supply chain risk. This will again enable us to introduce topics in less complex settings and gradually increase complexity in a measured and understandable way.

Chapter 4

Onboarding

Introduction

In Chapter 4 we look at the essential steps for onboarding a new third party so that it may be integrated into the appropriate business processes. Bill begins by framing vendor management as a structured lifecycle, emphasizing that successful outsourcing depends on clear expectations and robust governance, especially when organizations and vendors differ in size, sophistication, and experience. He goes on to stress the importance of precise requirements and flexible contracts, noting that anything not explicitly specified in a contract often leads to additional costs or unmet expectations. Bill describes the vendor management lifecycle in broad strokes: planning, engaging, implementing, managing, and terminating relationships, while focusing on the first three stages in this chapter.

Chris then presents a detailed and rigorous approach to onboarding mission-critical suppliers, particularly those involved in software supply chains. This methodology is designed for organizations that require an extra level of due diligence and preparation, typically large corporations or government agencies where the risks are significant and justify the additional investment of time and resources. The approach is modeled after NIST 800-18 and serves as a checkpoint in the onboarding process, ensuring that all necessary documentation and controls are in place before transitioning the supplier into ongoing operations. He provides an instructive narrative for implementing a systematic threat assessment across ten asset groups to provide an essential understanding of supplier risk exposure.

Jointly, Bill and Chris advocate for continuous improvement, proactive risk management, and the integration of structured oversight. The overarching message is that meticulous planning, clear governance, and ongoing collaboration are the keys to building and sustaining successful vendor and supplier relationships.

Immediately following Chris' essay is a list of publications he references throughout.

Vendor Onboarding Process

Bill Bonney

A well-governed vendor onboarding process, underpinned by clear expectations, comprehensive risk assessment, and proactive stakeholder engagement, is essential for minimizing risk and ensuring long-term success in outsourcing relationships.

Regardless of the purpose for outsourcing, the premise is always the same—a third party agrees to supply you with widgets or workflow for a price. As each party gains experience in the marketplace, they tend to get better at defining exactly what they want (or will provide) and how much they are willing to pay (or should charge). For equally sophisticated and experienced participants, there is little difference in expectations. However, when there is a mismatch in sophistication and experience, the resulting difference in expectations can be expensive.

Very early in my outsourcing journey, I learned a critical maxim for aligning those expectations—if it's not in the contract, it either won't get done or it'll cost extra. Accepting this maxim leads to prioritizing crisp requirements definitions. The experience of lacking the ability to be perfectly precise and the result of defining requirements too narrowly lead to building flexibility into our contracting and budgeting.

Before diving into the onboarding activities, I think it's important to put them in the context of a vendor management lifecycle. For simplicity, let's keep the lifecycle high-level:

Figure 4.1 – Vendor Management Lifecycle

- Plan – Requirements definition and initial research.
- Engage – Vendor selection and contract negotiation.
- Implement – Onboarding and integration.
- Manage – Monitoring and management.
- Terminate – Terminate and offboard.

This chapter focuses on the first three stages of the lifecycle: plan, engage, and implement. Chapter 5 focuses on monitor and manage, and Chapter 7 focuses on terminate and offboard.

We're concerned with risk management and for me, that means paying attention to governance. With that in mind, here are some aspects of governance as applied to the first three stages of the Vendor Management Lifecycle that I believe warrant special attention.

Requirements Definition and Initial Research

Knowing our requirements, performing appropriate market research, and negotiating a comprehensive yet flexible contract are the essential prerequisites for a successful implementation. I associate these three high-level activities with stage 1:

- Define the business needs and objectives.
- Define requirements for the products or services.
- Conduct initial market research and create a short list for vendor selection.

Here I focus on ensuring alignment with organizational objectives, compliance with regulations and standards, and establishing clear frameworks for decision-making and accountability. This is where you'll put the tools discussed in Chapter 2, the RACI and DACI matrices, to work. Key governance concerns for this stage include:

- **Stakeholder Engagement:** It is essential to engage all relevant stakeholders when defining requirements. For core business processes and processes subject to data protection laws, there are often well-defined criteria or tacit agreements already in place. For other processes, rely on the experience of your core VRM team and the business process owner.
- **Performance Metrics and Objectives:** Define clear performance metrics, service level agreements (SLAs), and objectives for vendor engagements. These should be aligned with the organization's goals with an eye toward monitoring and evaluating vendor performance. I recommend documenting a rough draft of how you will measure performance at this stage.
- **Risk Assessment:** Identify, assess, and develop appropriate mitigations and monitoring strategies for the risks associated with this relationship. This includes financial risks, cybersecurity risks, supply chain disruptions, and reputational risks. One of the outputs of this step should provide guidelines for risk assessment throughout the vendor lifecycle.
- **Compliance and Regulations:** Identify and understand the compliance requirements and regulatory standards that affect the vendor selection, onboarding, and management for this project. This would include data protection laws, industry-specific regulations, and internal compliance standards.
- **Data Governance:** Beyond compliance and regulations, this includes considerations for data handling, storage, and processing.
- **Sourcing Strategy:** Develop a selection process that considers the mix of vendors, the geographic location of vendors (to manage geopolitical risks and supply chain considerations), and the approach to competitive bidding or direct negotiations.

- **Budget and Financial Planning:** Develop a clear understanding of the budgetary constraints and financial implications of this relationship. This includes considering the total cost of ownership (TCO) of engaging with the vendor and ensuring that the vendor's costs align with the organization's financial planning and budgeting processes.
- **Communications:** Define the roles and responsibilities for managing the vendor selection, negotiation, onboarding, and integration processes to keep stakeholders informed and involved.

With the planning stage complete, you have a blueprint for the next stage where you enter a third-party relationship.

Vendor Selection and Contract Negotiation

It is common to have a short list of potential vendors based on past relationships and general awareness of industry players. But there are several reasons you should still conduct an assessment. You want to avoid choosing a vendor based on undue influence from an interested party, making a hasty decision based on information that is out of date, or failing to account for new players that may offer a better solution for your organization. Use the rankings published by the major consulting firms to add potential candidates to your short list. Here are the high-level vendor selection activities for stage 2:

- Research and identify potential vendors.
- Issue Requests for Proposal (RFPs) or Requests for Information (RFIs).
- Evaluate proposals and conduct due diligence.
- Select the vendor(s) that best meet the organization's needs.

During the vendor selection and contract negotiation stage of the vendor management lifecycle, governance plays a critical role in ensuring that the selection process is fair, transparent, and aligned with organizational goals and regulatory requirements. Key governance concerns for vendor selection include:

- **Transparency and Fairness:** Establish a transparent and fair process for evaluating and selecting vendors. This involves clear criteria for selection, unbiased evaluation of proposals, and ensuring that all potential vendors have an equal opportunity to compete.

- **Due Diligence and Vendor Evaluation:** Perform thorough due diligence on potential vendors to assess their financial stability, reputation, compliance with relevant laws and regulations, and ability to meet the organization's needs. This includes evaluating the vendor's track record, references, and capabilities. I cannot emphasize enough how important references are. The best references are those you identify on your own; limit how much you rely on vendor-supplied references as they are often picked for their glowing admiration for the vendor.

- **Conflict of Interest:** Identify and manage any potential conflicts of interest that may affect the vendor selection process. This requires policies to disclose and address conflicts of interest among those involved in the selection process. It's important not to over correct. It's perfectly acceptable to entertain a recommendation from someone with a potential vested interest as long as there is a process for an unbiased evaluation.

- **Compliance and Regulatory Requirements:** Ensure that the vendor and the products or services they provide comply with all relevant laws, regulations, and industry standards. This is particularly important for data protection, privacy regulations, and specific industry compliance standards.

- **Security and Data Privacy:** Evaluate the vendors' security measures and data privacy policies to ensure they meet the organization's standards and regulatory requirements. This includes assessing the vendors' ability to protect sensitive or confidential information and their policies for data breach response and notification. I am a big believer in independent assessments over key data controls. The more detail you can examine, the better. High-level summaries are not as valuable as control testing results. It's likely these will not be available to you until you are evaluating the finalists.

- **Risk Assessment:** Conduct risk assessments to understand the potential risks associated with each vendor, including operational, financial, reputational, and cybersecurity risks. These assessments should inform the selection process and the development of mitigation strategies.

- **Stakeholder Involvement:** Ensure key stakeholders stay involved in the vendor selection process to ensure that the chosen vendor can meet the needs of different parts of the organization. This includes gathering input from departments such as IT, legal, finance, and the end users of the vendor's products or services. It's common for stakeholders' engagement to fluctuate depending on need, but make sure everyone knows when and how their participation is needed.

- **Ethical Considerations:** Ensure that the vendor operates in an ethical manner, including labor practices, environmental impact, and corporate social responsibility. Organizations increasingly consider these factors as part of their vendor selection criteria.

It's important to clearly identify a second choice because negotiations and vendor onboarding do sometimes fail. It can be tricky to keep a second-choice vendor engaged. Be transparent with their representative so they are clear why they were not selected and what your process is going forward but be careful not to lead them on.

Key governance concerns for contract negotiation include:

- Negotiating terms and conditions, including pricing, delivery schedules, and service levels.
- Establishing performance metrics and penalties for non-compliance.
- Finalizing and signing the contract.

During contract negotiations governance concerns are crucial to ensure that agreements protect the organization's interests, align with strategic objectives, and comply with relevant laws and regulations. Key governance concerns for contract negotiation include:

- **Alignment with Organizational Objectives:** Ensure the contract terms align with the organization's strategic goals, operational needs, and risk management framework. This includes service levels, deliverables, and performance metrics that support the organization's objectives.

- **Legal and Regulatory Compliance:** Confirm that the contract complies with all applicable laws, regulations, and industry standards. This is particularly important for data protection, privacy, intellectual property rights, and specific compliance requirements relevant to the organization's sector.

- **Risk Management and Mitigation:** Include provisions in the contract to identify, allocate, and mitigate risks associated with the vendor relationship. This involves defining responsibilities for data security and incident response and ensuring adequate insurance coverage.

- **Cost Management and Financial Terms:** Establish clear financial terms, including pricing, payment schedules, and penalties for non-performance. Also ensure that the contract provides for cost predictability and transparency.

- **Confidentiality and Data Protection:** Ensure the contract includes strong confidentiality clauses and data protection measures to safeguard sensitive information and comply with data privacy regulations.

- **Service Levels and Performance Metrics:** Defining specific service level agreements (SLAs) and performance metrics in the contract to ensure the vendor meets expected performance standards. This includes mechanisms for monitoring performance and addressing service failures.

Again, if it's not in the contract, it won't get done or it'll cost more. Sometimes a lot more.

- **Dispute Resolution:** Establish clear processes for resolving disputes, including escalation procedures, mediation, arbitration, and jurisdiction. This aims to resolve conflicts efficiently and minimize disruption to the organization.
- **Termination Clauses and Exit Strategies:** Include clear termination clauses that allow for the orderly conclusion or transition of services at the end of the contract or in case of significant issues. This includes conditions under which the contract can be terminated, notice periods, and the handling of transition responsibilities. It is essential to give offboarding the vendor and transitioning to in-house or an alternate vendor due consideration at this stage. Getting married is a lot easier than getting divorced.
- **Intellectual Property Rights:** Clearly define the ownership and use of intellectual property (IP) created or used during the vendor relationship. This is critical to protect the organization's and the vendor's IP rights.
- **Change Management:** Incorporate mechanisms for managing changes to the contract or scope of work, including processes for requesting, reviewing, and approving changes. This ensures flexibility and adaptability over the contract term. Ensure that the change management process is fair to your organization. Thinking back to the point I made and then emphasized regarding activities not adequately described in the contract, poorly defined or onerous change management terms compound that problem.
- **Audit and Compliance Monitoring:** Include the right to audit the vendor's compliance with the terms of the contract, especially in areas related to financial reporting, security measures, and regulatory compliance.

Addressing these governance concerns during contract negotiation is vital to ensuring that the contract serves the organization's best interests, minimizes risks, and establishes a clear framework for the vendor relationship.

Now that we've got a contract in place, it's time for the final stage of the onboarding process.

Onboarding and Integration

These are the high-level onboarding and integration activities in stage 3:

- Set up accounts, access, and systems for the vendor.
- Communicate expectations and integrate vendor processes with internal processes.
- Train staff on new systems or processes related to the vendor's products or services.

The onboarding and integration stage of the vendor management lifecycle is critical for setting the foundation of a successful vendor relationship. Proper governance during this stage ensures smooth transition and integration of the vendor's services or products into the organization's operations. Key governance concerns during this stage include:

- **Clear Communication and Documentation:** Establish clear channels of communication and ensure that all necessary documentation is shared between the organization and the vendor. This includes service level agreements (SLAs), contact points, and process guides. I recommend establishing and maintaining an Authorized Personnel and Emergency Contact (APEC) list that is validated by both the organization and the vendor.

- **Compliance and Security Protocols:** Ensure that the vendor understands and complies with the organization's compliance requirements and security protocols from the outset. This is crucial for protecting sensitive data and adhering to regulatory standards.

- **Access Control and Data Security:** Set up appropriate access controls to ensure that the vendor has only the necessary level of access to the organization's systems and data. Implement strong data security measures to protect against unauthorized access or data breaches. A data flow diagram that depicts the expected data flow is helpful here, and any deviations from the expected data flow must be approved and then properly documented.
- **Training and Support:** Provide training for both the organization's staff and the vendor's team on the processes, tools, and systems that will be used during the engagement. This includes any necessary support structures to address issues promptly.
- **Integration with Existing Systems:** Ensure that the vendor's products or services are fully compatible with and can be seamlessly integrated into the organization's existing systems and processes. This may involve technical adjustments, compatibility testing, and sometimes customization.
- **Performance Monitoring Setup:** Implement mechanisms for monitoring and reporting on the vendor's performance against agreed-upon metrics and SLAs from the start. This includes setting up dashboards, reporting tools, and regular review meetings.
- **Risk Management Measures:** Integrate risk management measures specific to the vendor engagement into the organization's broader risk management framework. This includes identifying potential risks related to the vendor relationship and establishing mitigation strategies.
- **Change Management Processes:** Establish clear change management processes for handling any changes in the vendor's services, scope of work, or contractual terms during the engagement. This ensures that changes are managed systematically and with minimal disruption.

- **Business Continuity and Disaster Recovery:** Ensure that the vendor has robust business continuity, incident response, and disaster recovery plans that align with the organization's requirements. This is critical to maintaining operations in case of disruptions. Integrate the organization's BCP and DRP with the vendor's plans.

- **Cultural Alignment:** Begin aligning the vendor's working culture and practices with those of the organization to foster a positive and productive working relationship. This includes understanding each party's values, communication styles, and working methods. This will be an ongoing process and it's important to revisit regularly to ensure cultures and values remain aligned.

- **Stakeholder Engagement:** Keep key stakeholders informed and engaged throughout the onboarding and integration process. This ensures that any concerns are addressed promptly and that there is broad support for the vendor relationship.

Addressing these governance concerns during the onboarding and integration stage is essential for ensuring a smooth start to the vendor relationship, minimizing risks, and setting the stage for long-term success. We'll cover the ongoing relationship in Chapter 5 when we provide several looks at stewardship.

Supply Chain Risk Management: Critical Supplier Onboarding Methodology (CSOM)

Chris Forbes

By systematically assessing and mitigating risks across all aspects of supplier operations—from technology and data to logistics and workforce—organizations can build resilient supply chains capable of withstanding disruptions and supporting long-term business success.

Essay Overview

This essay builds upon Bill Bonney's Vendor Onboarding Framework and describes the additional onboarding steps for mission-critical suppliers, including software supply chains. This essay provides an extra level of due diligence and preparation that goes above and beyond the preliminary requirements documented by the business. These additional activities are usually undertaken by large, well-funded corporations or government agencies where the severity of risks can justify the extra time and cost. The Critical Supplier Onboarding (CSO) methodology serves as a checkpoint and tollgate in the onboarding process to collect or create necessary documentation in preparation for a turnover to the SCRM teams for steady-state operations.

We modeled the CSO approach after the NIST 800-18 Rev. 1 Guide for Developing Security Plans for Federal Information Systems, and its primary objective is to oversee the assembly of comprehensive plans for supplier oversight of risk, security, continuity, and compliance. The importance of these plans lies in identifying the necessary technology, controls, and management practices required to supervise the company's critical suppliers effectively. The essay emphasizes the need for thorough due diligence and preparation that goes above and beyond the preliminary requirements documented by the business. It highlights the significance of collecting information about the supplier's organization, including financial stability, operational capabilities, and industry reputation. Additionally, it stresses the importance of conducting thorough risk assessments to identify potential vulnerabilities and implementing robust security measures to mitigate those risks.

Furthermore, this essay explores the unique considerations for onboarding suppliers within a Software Supply Chain. It discusses the need to evaluate the supplier's software development lifecycle (SSDLC) processes, including their security practices, version control systems, and testing procedures. It also emphasizes the importance of establishing clear expectations regarding intellectual property rights, data privacy, and compliance with relevant regulations.

1.0 Document Supplier Relationship Requirements

The Critical Supplier Onboarding and planning process lays the foundation of a successful supplier relationship. This entails mapping out the intricate patterns of interaction between the organization and the supplier, encompassing the flow of raw materials, the exchange of data, the integration of systems, and the establishment of communication protocols. The objective is to understand this critical supplier's potential vulnerabilities and risks.

A crucial aspect of this process is identifying and documenting the planned data exchanges between the two entities, including sensitive information such as personally identifiable information (PII), financial data, and intellectual property. By understanding the nature and volume of data shared, organizations can implement appropriate security measures to protect this information throughout its lifecycle.

Furthermore, the integration architecture assessment should cover the technical aspects of the supplier's systems and infrastructure. These additional onboarding steps involve evaluating the security posture of the supplier's networks, applications, and databases and their incident response capabilities. The goal is to ensure that the supplier's technology environment aligns with the organization's security standards and can withstand potential cyber threats.

In addition to technical considerations, the assessment should also encompass the supplier's business processes and operational practices. This assessment includes evaluating their supply chain management practices, quality control procedures, and risk management frameworks. The aim is to ensure that the supplier's operations are aligned with the organization's expectations and can support the seamless flow of goods and services.

The insights gained from this comprehensive assessment will inform the development of a robust integration plan that addresses potential risks and vulnerabilities. The plan should actively outline specific security controls, monitoring mechanisms, and communication protocols to safeguard the integrity and confidentiality of data exchanged between the two entities. It should also define the roles and responsibilities of both parties in managing the integration and responding to potential incidents.

By conducting a thorough and detailed vendor onboarding process that captures and validates business requirements and the specific risks associated with individual critical suppliers, organizations can lay a solid foundation for a successful and mutually beneficial relationship. This proactive approach to supply chain risk management will enable organizations to navigate the complexities of the modern business landscape with confidence and resilience.

1.1 Supplier Requirements – Business Integration Architecture

The first step in establishing a resilient and secure relationship with a critical supplier involves meticulously examining the supplier's integration into the existing business architecture. This step entails mapping out the intricate patterns of interaction between the organization, the supplier, any external business partners, and possibly direct client contacts. The objective is to understand this integration's potential vulnerabilities and risks.

Documenting the specific business processes that will be created or integrated with this new critical supplier is paramount. This analysis includes a detailed mapping of the business architecture and specific business process flows that interact between all parties. The goal is to visually represent the interdependencies and potential points of failure within the integrated system.

By documenting the business processes, organizations can identify potential bottlenecks, single points of failure, and areas where data integrity or confidentiality may be at risk. This information is crucial for developing mitigation strategies and ensuring the seamless flow of information and goods throughout the supply chain.

The documentation should also describe each party's roles and responsibilities in the business processes. This step will help establish clear lines of communication and accountability, ensuring that everyone understands their role in maintaining the integrity and security of the integrated system.

In addition to documenting the current state of the business processes, it is also essential to consider the future state. This step includes identifying potential areas for improvement and innovation and anticipating possible changes in the business environment that may impact the integration architecture.

Organizations can lay a solid foundation for a successful and resilient supplier relationship by taking a proactive and comprehensive approach to documenting business processes. This analysis will enable them to identify and mitigate risks, optimize performance, and ensure the long-term success of their supply chain operations.

1.2 Supplier Requirements – Raw Material Flows

The meticulous planning and management of raw material flows from critical suppliers to the organization's warehouses and storage depots constitute a pivotal facet of supply chain risk management. The efficacy of this process significantly influences the uninterrupted operation of production lines, the preservation of product quality, and the overall financial well-being of the enterprise. The focal point of this endeavor lies in formulating and documenting a comprehensive Materials Delivery Management Plan (MDMP), which meticulously addresses the multifaceted aspects of transportation, logistics, delivery, handling, and the requisite care during the transit of specific raw materials.

The MDMP serves as a strategic blueprint that orchestrates the seamless movement of raw materials across the supply chain. It encompasses a range of critical considerations, including selecting optimal transportation modes, identifying reliable logistics partners, establishing efficient delivery schedules, and implementing stringent handling and care protocols tailored to the raw materials' specific attributes. The plan also incorporates contingency measures to address unforeseen disruptions, such as natural disasters, geopolitical events, or transportation bottlenecks, ensuring the supply chain's resilience in the face of adversity.

The transportation component of the plan actively evaluates various modes of transport, including road, rail, sea, and air, based on factors such as cost-effectiveness, transit time, and the nature of the raw materials. The selection of logistics partners necessitates a rigorous assessment of their capabilities, track record, and adherence to industry best practices. Establishing delivery schedules requires careful synchronization between the supplier's production capabilities, the organization's inventory requirements, and the logistics partners' capacity. The handling and care protocols encompass a range of measures, such as temperature control, humidity management, and specialized packaging, to ensure the preservation of the raw materials' integrity and quality throughout the transit process.

The MDMP also plays a pivotal role in mitigating supply chain risks. It incorporates risk assessment methodologies to identify potential vulnerabilities and develop proactive mitigation strategies. These may include diversifying transportation routes, establishing buffer stocks, and implementing real-time tracking and monitoring systems to enhance visibility and control over the movement of raw materials. The plan also emphasizes the importance of collaboration and communication among all stakeholders, including suppliers, logistics partners, and internal teams, to ensure the seamless execution of the plan and the timely resolution of any issues that may arise.

1.3 Supplier Requirements – Intellectual Property and Trade Secrets

Sharing intellectual property (IP) and trade secrets with critical suppliers is necessary in today's interconnected business landscape. However, it also presents inherent risks necessitating meticulous planning and management to safeguard these valuable assets. The cornerstone of this endeavor lies in creating and documenting a robust Intellectual Property and Trade Secrets Management (IPTSM) Plan. This plan is a comprehensive framework that governs the identification, protection, transfer, and oversight of IP and trade secrets throughout the supplier relationship.

In the plan's initial phase, we thoroughly identify and document the exact IP and trade secrets to be shared with the supplier. This step includes patents, trademarks, copyrights, proprietary algorithms, formulas, customer lists, and confidential information that confers a competitive advantage. The documentation should clearly define the scope and limitations of the supplier's access to and use of these assets.

The subsequent step entails establishing prerequisite security and handling requirements the supplier must adhere to. This step encompasses a range of measures, such as implementing robust access controls, encryption protocols, data loss prevention mechanisms, watermarking for traceability, mechanisms for data consistency, non-repudiation, and employee training programs. The objective is to create a secure environment that minimizes the risk of unauthorized access, disclosure, or misuse of the shared IP and trade secrets.

The transfer process necessitates careful orchestration to ensure the confidentiality and integrity of the assets. This step may involve using secure file transfer protocols, digital rights management solutions, or even physical handoffs under controlled conditions. The plan should also stipulate that the supplier must acknowledge receipt of the assets and confirm their understanding of the associated security and handling requirements.

The final and ongoing phase of the plan focuses on establishing a mechanism for continuous oversight and monitoring of the supplier's handling of the shared IP and trade secrets. This step may include periodic audits, reviews of the supplier's security practices, periodic reviews of compliance with laws and regulations, and implementing incident response protocols to address potential breaches or unauthorized disclosures. The plan should also outline the consequences of non-compliance with the established requirements, including termination of the supplier relationship and legal action.

1.4 Supplier Requirements – Identity and Access Management

Planning for and implementing safe and secure access to internal systems is crucial in onboarding and integrating critical suppliers. The exchange of credentials, authorization, authentication, and implementing multi-factor authentication (MFA) mechanisms are paramount in establishing a trusted and resilient relationship with critical suppliers. The Supplier Identity and Access Management Plan (SIAMP) is the cornerstone of this endeavor, providing a structured framework for managing the complexities of access control in the supply chain ecosystem. A good example of the criticality of SIAMP can be seen in the growing number of cell phone SIM-swapping incidents where bad actors can impersonate the legitimate owner and exploit weak authentication procedures.

The SIAMP begins by identifying and documenting the specific systems and resources to which the organization and the supplier will require access. In this step, conduct a comprehensive inventory of applications, databases, networks, and other relevant digital assets. When documenting access boundaries, grant privileges based on need-to-know and the principle of least privilege.

The subsequent phase involves establishing robust authentication and authorization protocols. This step encompasses implementing strong password policies, multi-factor authentication mechanisms, and role-based access controls. The objective is to create a layered defense that verifies users' identities, validates their access rights, and prevents unauthorized access or actions.

The exchange of credentials necessitates the utilization of secure channels and protocols. This exchange may involve encrypted communication channels, secure file transfer mechanisms, or even physical handoffs under controlled conditions. The SIAMP should also stipulate that both parties must acknowledge receipt of the credentials and confirm their understanding of the associated security and handling requirements.

The plan also emphasizes the importance of ongoing access rights monitoring and review. This task includes periodic audits, reviews of user activity logs, and the implementation of incident response protocols to address any potential breaches or unauthorized access attempts. The SIAMP should also outline the consequences of non-compliance with the established requirements, including revocation of access privileges and termination of the supplier relationship.

1.5 Supplier Requirements – Data Exchange

Secure and efficient data exchange between an organization and its critical suppliers is paramount for seamless operations and effective risk management. The Critical Supplier Data Exchange Plan (CSDEP) serves as a blueprint for orchestrating the intricate dance of information across the supply chain, ensuring that data is transmitted securely, accurately, and in compliance with regulatory requirements. The success of the CSDEP depends on establishing well-defined policies for data ownership, accountability, retention, data governance, and compliance.

The organization begins the CSDEP plan by identifying and documenting the specific data elements that the suppliers, external business partners, clients, and regulators will share. This step includes a comprehensive inventory of data types, formats, and transmission protocols, encompassing bulk data transfers, Electronic Data Interchange (EDI), data definitions, software code exchanges, and interactions with Application Programming Interfaces (APIs). The documentation should clearly define each data flow's purpose, frequency, and volume, ensuring that data exchanges are aligned with business needs and optimized for efficiency.

The subsequent phase involves establishing robust data protection, encryption, and privacy protocols tailored to the specific attributes of each data type. This step may include implementing encryption algorithms, access controls, data masking techniques, anonymization and de-identification procedures, watermarking, and Cyclical Redundancy Checks (CRCs). The objective is to create a multi-layered defense that safeguards data's confidentiality, integrity, and availability throughout its lifecycle, mitigating the risk of unauthorized access, disclosure, or modification.

The SCRM team ensures supplier data management policies comply with regulatory obligations and industry standards. The CSDEP plan should also outline data breach notification and incident response procedures, enabling swift and effective action during a data security incident.

1.6 Supplier Requirements – Products and Goods Flows

The Critical Supplier Product Lifecycle Plan (CSPLP) documentation between the supplier, the company, any external business partners, clients, and communities is a crucial building block for ensuring adequate monitoring, supervision, business continuity, and incident response related to the critical supplier. The CSPLP should carefully detail the entire product and service lifecycle, directly dependent on the individual critical supplier.

The CSPLP should identify and document the products and services the critical supplier will provide. This step includes a comprehensive inventory of product specifications, service level agreements, delivery schedules, and other relevant contractual obligations. The documentation should clearly define the scope and limitations of the supplier's responsibilities to ensure aligned expectations and objectively measurable performance.

The subsequent phase involves mapping out the intricate flow of products and services from the supplier to the organization and, ultimately, to the end customers or clients. This task includes documenting the transportation and logistics processes, inventory management practices, and any value-added services the supplier provides. The objective is to visually represent the supply chain, highlighting potential bottlenecks, dependencies, and areas where disruptions could occur.

The plan should also address the critical aspects of quality assurance and control throughout the product and service lifecycle. This step includes documenting the supplier's quality management system, inspection and testing procedures, and any certifications or accreditations they hold. The objective is to ensure that the products and services delivered by the supplier consistently meet or exceed the organization's quality standards.

Furthermore, the CSPLP should incorporate contingency measures to address potential disruptions in the supply chain. This activity includes identifying alternative suppliers, establishing buffer stocks, and developing robust communication protocols to ensure timely notification and resolution of any issues that may arise. The objective is to create a resilient supply chain that can withstand unforeseen events and minimize the impact on the organization's operations.

1.7 Supplier Requirements – Service Delivery Management

In the intricate tapestry of supply chain management, the effective delivery and tracking of services rendered by critical suppliers are central to the process. The Supplier Service Delivery Management Plan (SSDMP) emerges as a strategic instrument to orchestrate this process, ensuring that services are delivered seamlessly and adhere to stringent quality, compliance, and performance benchmarks.

At the inception of the SSDMP, the SCRM team should document specific supplier services in detail. This step encompasses a detailed breakdown of service level agreements (SLAs), service level objectives (SLOs), key performance indicators (KPIs), and other pertinent contractual obligations. The documentation should delineate each service's scope, deliverables, and expected outcomes, fostering clarity and alignment between the organization and the supplier.

Subsequently, the plan should elucidate the precise methodologies through which the supplier will furnish these services. This activity encompasses a comprehensive exposition of service delivery models, communication channels, escalation procedures, and any specialized tools or technologies employed. The aim is to establish a transparent and well-defined framework that facilitates effective service delivery and management.

A pivotal facet of the SSDMP is incorporating stringent quality control and compliance mechanisms. This step entails outlining the quality standards and regulatory requirements the supplier must adhere to and implementing robust monitoring and auditing procedures to ensure adherence. The objective is to uphold the highest service quality and integrity levels, mitigating the risk of non-compliance and its associated repercussions.

The plan should also delineate how the organization tracks and monitors the supplier's service delivery performance. This task may encompass the utilization of performance dashboards, regular service reviews, and establishing clear communication channels for feedback and issue resolution. The goal is to maintain proactive oversight of the supplier's performance, enabling timely identification and rectification of deviations from the agreed-upon standards.

In essence, the Supplier Service Delivery Management Plan functions as a strategic compass, guiding the effective delivery and management of services provided by critical suppliers. It furnishes a structured framework that fosters transparency, accountability, and continuous improvement, ensuring that services are rendered seamlessly and aligned with the organization's strategic objectives and risk management imperatives.

1.8 Supplier Requirements – Performance and Control Communications

In the dynamic supply chain management landscape, real-time monitoring and adjusting the flow of goods and services is vital. The Supplier Controls Communications Management Plan (SCCMP) functions as the "control plane" to ensure the supplier and the company function synchronously, enabling organizations to maintain proactive oversight and respond swiftly to deviations or disruptions.

At its core, the SCCMP entails accurate documentation of the communication protocols and channels utilized for interaction between the organization and the supplier. This step encompasses a detailed specification of communication modes, contact points, escalation procedures, and response time expectations. The objective is to establish a clear and efficient communication framework that facilitates seamless information exchange and enables rapid decision-making.

The plan should also outline the specific instructions and directives the organization may issue to the supplier to regulate the flow of goods and services. This task may include adjustments to delivery schedules, modifications to product specifications, or requests for additional information or documentation. The documentation should clearly define the format, content, and authorization protocols for such instructions, ensuring they are unambiguous, actionable, and auditable.

Furthermore, the SCCMP should detail the performance metrics, alerts, and incident communications the supplier expects to provide to the organization. This activity may include real-time updates on production status, inventory levels, shipment tracking information, and notifications of any potential delays or disruptions. The documentation should specify the frequency, format, and delivery mechanisms for these communications, ensuring that the organization receives timely and actionable information to maintain visibility and control over the supply chain.

The SCCMP is vital for orchestrating the dynamic interplay between the organization and its critical suppliers. It provides a structured framework for communication, control, and collaboration, enabling the organization to proactively manage the flow of goods and services, respond effectively to disruptions, and optimize supply chain performance.

1.9 Supplier Requirements – Incident Response

Supply chain management and planning for disruptions and incidents are foundational for keeping relationships healthy and mutually beneficial. The Supplier Disruption Incidents and Compliance Plan (SDICP) emerges as a critical safeguard, outlining the coordinated response strategies to navigate such challenges effectively.

The SDICP's foundation lies in the identification and documentation of potential incidents and compliance violation scenarios. This step encompasses many possibilities, from cyberattacks and data breaches to product recalls and regulatory non-compliance. The documentation should describe each scenario, including potential triggers, impact assessments, and escalation procedures.

A cornerstone of the SDICP plan is the development of incident response playbooks tailored to specific use cases. These playbooks outline the step-by-step procedures for incident identification, containment, eradication, recovery, and lessons learned. They delineate the organization's and supplier's roles and responsibilities in managing the incident, ensuring a coordinated and efficient response.

The plan should also address communication and information sharing during an incident or compliance violation. This step includes establishing clear protocols for notifying relevant stakeholders, such as internal teams, external business partners, clients, regulators, and even the media, if necessary. The documentation should specify such communications' content, format, and timing, ensuring transparency and accountability throughout the incident response process.

Furthermore, the SDICP plan should emphasize the importance of continuous improvement and learn from incidents and compliance violations. This task includes conducting post-incident reviews to identify root causes, assess the effectiveness of the response, and implement corrective actions to prevent future occurrences. The objective is to foster a proactive risk management and resilience culture, enabling the organization to learn from its experiences and strengthen its supply chain defenses.

1.10 Supplier Requirements – Business Continuity Plans (BCP)

Supply chain risk management must oversee the creation of the Supplier Business Continuity Plan (SBCP) and ensure it has been defined and deployed before going live with a critical supplier. This plan necessitates particular foresight and collaboration to define the triggers for contingency arrangements and the concrete assurances of supplier continuity.

The SBCP relies on identifying and documenting potential disruptions that could affect the supplier's operations. This step includes various scenarios such as natural disasters, cyberattacks, labor strikes, and financial insolvency. The documentation should include a detailed analysis of each scenario, including its potential impact on the supplier's ability to deliver goods or services, the estimated duration of the disruption, and the potential cascading effects on the organization's operations.

An essential part of the SBCP is setting clear triggers for enacting contingency plans. This step involves defining specific measurements and limits that, when exceeded, indicate the need to start predefined recovery or failover procedures. These measurements could include delivery delays, production shortages, or indicators of financial problems. The goal is to enable a proactive and timely response to potential risks, reducing the impact on the supply chain.

The SBCP should also provide specific details on the supplier disruption contingency arrangements. This step may include activating backup suppliers, rerouting shipments, or utilizing alternative production facilities. SBCPs can also cover non-material suppliers who perform critical functions such as quality inspections, delivery logistics, legal work required to deliver products and services, or external technology services. The documentation should outline the organization's and supplier's roles and responsibilities in executing these arrangements, ensuring a coordinated and efficient response.

Furthermore, the SBCP should address the critical aspect of communication and coordination during a disruption. This step includes establishing clear protocols for notifying relevant stakeholders, such as internal teams, external business partners, and clients, about the disruption and the anticipated impact on their operations. The documentation should specify the communications' content, format, timing, labeling requirements, and discoverability, foster transparency, and manage expectations.

Finally, the SBCP should emphasize the importance of regular testing and review to ensure its effectiveness. This step includes conducting tabletop exercises, simulations, and drills to validate the plan's feasibility and identify areas for improvement. The objective is to maintain a state of preparedness and ensure that the plan remains aligned with the evolving risk landscape.

2.0 Supplier Threats by Asset Group

The optimal time to identify and plan for threats related to critical suppliers is before you integrate them into your supply chain. It is imperative to identify all possible hazards and threat scenarios that are relevant to this new relationship. Critical supplier onboarding warrants additional care and attention to reviewing and analyzing the specifics of this new supplier relationship, acknowledging that hazards and threats may not be unique to an individual supplier.

The onboarding of a new critical supplier necessitates a comprehensive Supplier Risk Assessment (SRA) to identify and evaluate potential hazards and threat scenarios proactively. This assessment serves as a crucial foundation for establishing a baseline understanding of the supplier's risk profile, enabling informed decision-making and the implementation of appropriate risk mitigation strategies. Companies should not assume that existing controls and practices are adequate without conducting an initial SRA and controls analysis to ensure legacy controls are up to the task.

The SRA process systematically examines various facets of the supplier's operations, including financial stability, operational capabilities, cybersecurity posture, compliance adherence, and resilience to disruptions. This evaluation may encompass a range of activities, such as reviewing financial statements, conducting site visits, assessing security controls, and analyzing incident response capabilities. The objective is to better understand the supplier's strengths, weaknesses, and potential vulnerabilities.

A key benefit of documenting the supplier risk assessment is the establishment of a baseline for future comparison and trending. By capturing the initial risk profile, organizations can track changes, identify emerging risks, and proactively adjust their risk mitigation strategies. This step enables a dynamic and adaptive approach to supplier risk management, ensuring that the organization remains vigilant and responsive to the evolving threat landscape.

The SRA's documentation ensures the identification of all required controls and the development of a plan for their deployment and testing. This plan specifies the technical, operational, and managerial controls necessary to mitigate the identified risks and outlines their implementation, monitoring, and evaluation procedures. The objective is to create a comprehensive supplier risk management framework that safeguards the organization's interests and ensures the continuity of critical supplier relationships.

2.1 Threats to Supplier's Facilities from Physical and Environmental Hazards

A supplier's facilities' physical and environmental security is a cornerstone of supplier operational resilience. Identifying and mitigating potential hazards that could disrupt or damage these facilities is vital in ensuring the continuity of the supply chain. The supplier risk assessment should carefully evaluate all vital supplier locations, even those not directly involved in producing the resources the company will consume. The rationale behind this extensive approach is to ensure a holistic understanding of the supplier's risk landscape, recognizing that disruptions in any part of their operations could have cascading effects on their ability to fulfill their obligations.

The Business Continuity Institute's 2023 Supply Chain Resilience Report revealed that 55% of organizations experienced at least one supply chain disruption in the past year, with 25% attributing these disruptions to natural disasters or extreme weather events. The World Economic Forum's 2023 Global Risks Report also highlighted the increasing frequency and severity of climate-related events, posing a significant threat to supply chain stability.

A practical methodology for identifying and qualifying these hazards and threat sources is to utilize an all-hazards catalog. This catalog provides a structured framework for systematically evaluating a wide range of potential threats, including natural disasters (e.g., earthquakes, floods, hurricanes), man-made incidents (e.g., fires, explosions, chemical spills), and even socio-political events (e.g., civil unrest, terrorism). By applying this catalog to each supplier's facilities, organizations can comprehensively understand their exposure to various risks.

The supplier's physical and environmental hazards analysis can also be instrumental in identifying supplier concentration risks. This analysis refers to situations where multiple critical suppliers are located in the same geographic region or rely on the same scarce resources. Such concentration can amplify the impact of disruptions, as a single event could affect multiple suppliers simultaneously. By identifying these concentration risks, organizations can take proactive measures to diversify their supplier base or implement contingency plans to mitigate the potential impact of disruptions.

2.2 Threats to Supplier's Raw Materials

Identifying and mitigating risks associated with raw materials is essential in ensuring the integrity and continuity of the supply chain. The ability to quickly identify and respond to potential disruptions in the availability or quality of raw materials can be the difference between maintaining smooth operations and facing costly delays or production shutdowns. A comprehensive risk assessment necessitates thoroughly examining potential threats that could compromise the viability and usability of critical raw materials. These threats may stem from various sources, including environmental factors, transportation and storage conditions, and inherent material properties.

The BCI 2023 Supply Chain Resilience Report indicated that vendor and raw material problems caused 37% of the supply chain disruptions. The volatility of raw material prices and availability can also have a significant financial impact; a McKinsey study highlights that companies can lose up to 40% of their annual profits in a single year due to supply chain disruptions.

Extreme temperatures, humidity, and exposure to contaminants are environmental factors that can significantly impact the quality and usability of raw materials. For example, perishable goods may spoil if exposed to excessive heat or cold, while certain chemicals may degrade or become unstable under high humidity conditions. The risk assessment should identify vulnerabilities and outline preventive measures, such as temperature-controlled transportation and storage facilities.

Transportation and storage conditions also play a crucial role in preserving the integrity of raw materials. Delays in transit, improper handling, or inadequate storage facilities can lead to damage, contamination, or even theft. The assessment should evaluate the robustness of the supplier's transportation and logistics network and the security and environmental controls in place at their storage facilities. This evaluation will inform the development of appropriate safeguards, such as real-time tracking systems, tamper-evident packaging, and stringent access controls.

Inherent material properties, such as flammability, reactivity, or toxicity, can pose significant risks. The mishandling of such materials can result in accidents, injuries, or environmental damage, leading to supply chain disruptions and reputational harm. The assessment should identify any hazardous materials in the supply chain and outline the necessary safety and handling protocols, including specialized training for personnel, appropriate protective equipment, and emergency response procedures.

2.3 Threats to Supplier's Material Fourth Parties

Identifying and evaluating potential threats to the supplier and its material third parties constitutes a crucial facet of a comprehensive supplier risk assessment. The term "fourth parties" encompasses a wide range of entities that play a pivotal role in the supplier's operations, including subcontractors, vendors, logistics providers, and even the supplier's suppliers. Identifying and assessing threats to these fourth parties is essential to understanding the supplier's risk exposure and potential vulnerabilities within its extended network. Modern supply chains' growing complexity and interconnectedness have amplified the importance of scrutinizing fourth-party risks.

The BCI 2023 Supply Chain Resilience Report revealed that 17% of disruptions originated from fourth parties, underscoring the potential for cascading effects from disruptions further upstream in the supply chain. The BlueVoyant 2021 Third-Party Cyber Risk Management Report also highlighted that 60% of organizations had experienced a data breach caused by a third party.

A rigorous supplier threat documentation process should be followed, meticulously examining the supplier's locations and facilities, including headquarters, mines, wells, oceanographic installations, and other critical infrastructure. This process should also extend to the fourth parties, scrutinizing their locations, facilities, and operational practices. The goal is to build confidence that all hazards and threats unique to this new supplier relationship, both direct and indirect, have been identified and thoroughly assessed.

Documenting these threats provides various benefits. It creates a central knowledge repository for continuous risk monitoring and mitigation. This step allows for informed decision-making in supplier selection, contract negotiation, and the implementation of appropriate controls. Additionally, it promotes transparency and accountability by ensuring that all stakeholders know the potential risks and the measures taken to address them.

2.4 Threats to Supplier's Transportation and Logistics

Critical suppliers' transportation and logistics networks act as vital arteries in the supply chain, ensuring the timely and secure delivery of goods and services. Identifying and assessing potential threats that could disrupt or compromise this network is crucial to any comprehensive risk assessment, as such disruptions may cause delays, damage, or complete breakdowns in material flow. The 2023 BCI Supply Chain Resilience Report revealed that 31 percent of disruptions originated from logistics or transportation issues, and the Allianz Risk Barometer 2023 ranked supply chain disruption as the top business risk globally.

The assessment should commence with a detailed mapping of the supplier's logistics and transportation infrastructure, encompassing the modes of transport utilized, the routes traversed, and the key hubs and facilities involved. This mapping exercise will visually represent the network's complexities and interdependencies, highlighting potential vulnerabilities and chokepoints.

The assessment must identify and evaluate potential threats to the various components of the mapped network. This analysis will encompass threats to transportation infrastructure, including roads, railways, cargo ships, and air transport, as well as critical facilities such as tunnels, bridges, shipping ports, airports, and railway depots. Natural disasters, accidents, sabotage, or geopolitical events may trigger these threats. Additionally, the assessment should consider the potential impact of disruptions to the supplier's logistics partners (e.g., trucking companies, freight forwarders, customs brokers), whose interruptions can have cascading effects across the entire network.

Finally, the assessment should consider both external threats and internal vulnerabilities within the supplier's logistics operations by evaluating fleet management practices, driver training programs, and cargo security measures. The goal is to identify any weaknesses that malicious actors could exploit or that could lead to accidental losses or damage.

2.5 Threats to Supplier's Technology

Identifying and assessing threats to a supplier's technology infrastructure is paramount in ensuring the resilience and continuity of the supply chain. The intricate reliance on technology in modern business operations necessitates a proactive approach to safeguarding these critical assets. The supplier risk assessment should thoroughly examine the supplier's technology landscape, hardware, software, networks, and data centers to identify potential vulnerabilities that could disrupt the supplier's delivery of goods or services.

The 2023 Cost of a Data Breach Report by IBM and the Ponemon Institute revealed that the average cost of a data breach reached a record high of $4.45 million. The report also highlighted that supply chain attacks were among the most expensive breaches, costing an average of $4.55 million. While this dollar figure may seem small for some suppliers, it may cause financial hardship or severely hinder small to mid-sized suppliers from sustaining their operations.

The assessment should commence with a comprehensive inventory of the supplier's technology assets, including their core systems, applications, databases, and network infrastructure. This inventory should also encompass any third-party technologies or services the supplier relies upon, as vulnerabilities in these external dependencies can pose significant risks. The company must recognize and understand the core supplier systems that could cause a supply chain disruption or incident. The goal is to gain a holistic understanding of the supplier's technology ecosystem and its potential points of failure.

Using the supplier's technology inventory allows the SCRM team to identify and assess potential threats to those assets. This analysis includes threats such as cyberattacks, data breaches, system outages, and hardware failures. The assessment should consider external threats, such as those posed by hackers or malicious software, and internal vulnerabilities, such as inadequate security controls or outdated software. Identifying critical infrastructure and platforms that could lead to a supplier outage can benefit concentration risk analysis.

The assessment should actively evaluate the supplier's technology risk management practices, including security policies, incident response procedures, and disaster recovery plans. The supplier technology assessment should measure their preparedness to prevent, detect, and respond to technology-related incidents. When supplier concentration risks exist, the SCRM team should consider diversification strategies.

2.6 Threats to Supplier's Digital Data

Identifying and assessing threats to a critical supplier's digital data is vital in ensuring the resilience and continuity of your supply chain. The increasing reliance on data-driven decision-making and the pervasive digitization of business processes necessitate a proactive approach to safeguarding this critical asset. The SRA should actively examine the supplier's data landscape, assessing the types of data they collect, store, process, and transmit, and evaluate the systems and infrastructure they utilize to manage this data. The objective is to identify potential vulnerabilities that malicious actors can exploit or that could lead to accidental data loss, impacting the supplier's ability to fulfill its obligations. The possible consequences of data threats are substantial. The 2023 Cost of a Data Breach Report by IBM and the Ponemon Institute revealed that the average cost of a data breach reached a record high of $4.45 million.

The assessment should commence with a comprehensive inventory of the supplier's data assets, including customer, financial, intellectual property, operational, and other sensitive or critical information. The inventory should also encompass the various data repositories, such as databases, file servers, and cloud storage platforms, where this data is stored. The goal is to gain a holistic understanding of the supplier's data ecosystem and its potential points of vulnerability. After compiling the inventory, the assessment should proceed to identify and evaluate potential threats to the integrity and security of the data, including:

- **Cyberattacks:** Unauthorized access, modification, or data destruction by external actors.
- **Data Breaches:** The accidental or intentional release of sensitive information to unauthorized parties.
- **Ransomware Attacks:** Malicious software that encrypts data and demands payment for its release.
- **Accidental Data Loss or Corruption:** Data loss due to hardware failures, software glitches, or human error.
- **Loss of Confidentiality:** Unauthorized disclosure of sensitive information impacts privacy and trust.
- **Loss of Non-Repudiation:** The inability to prove the authenticity and integrity of data transactions, leading to disputes and legal challenges.

The assessment should consider external threats, such as those posed by hackers or malicious software, and internal vulnerabilities, such as inadequate access controls or poor data management practices. Acknowledging the growing threat of misinformation, disinformation, and human error in essential data that could lead to a supply chain disruption or incident is important. The assessment should evaluate the supplier's data security measures, including access controls, encryption protocols, data backup and recovery procedures, and incident response plans. The objective is to gauge the supplier's preparedness to prevent, detect, and respond to data-related incidents, minimizing their impact on the supply chain.

2.7 Threats to Supplier's Labor and Workforce

The human element within a supplier's operations is often the most unpredictable yet crucial. Identifying and assessing threats to a supplier's labor and workforce is essential in ensuring the resilience and continuity of the supply chain. The supplier risk assessment should meticulously examine the supplier's workforce dynamics, encompassing labor relations, skill levels, workforce availability, and succession planning. The objective is to identify potential vulnerabilities that could impact the supplier's ability to maintain consistent operations and deliver goods or services, thus disrupting the supply chain.

The assessment should commence with a comprehensive understanding of the supplier's workforce demographics, including the size of their workforce, skill sets, and any reliance on specialized expertise. It should also consider the labor relations environment, including the presence of unions, any history of labor disputes, and the overall stability of the workforce. The goal is to gain insights into potential disruptions arising from labor-related issues.

Specific examples of threats to a local labor pool include:

- **Pandemics:** The COVID-19 pandemic highlighted the vulnerability of global supply chains to widespread illness and quarantine measures, leading to workforce shortages and operational disruptions.
- **Union Strikes:** Labor disputes and strikes can significantly impact a supplier's ability to meet production targets and delivery schedules.
- **Workforce Shortages:** A lack of skilled workers in specific industries or regions can hinder a supplier's ability to scale operations or respond to increased demand.
- **Attrition of Key Individuals:** The loss of key personnel, particularly those with specialized knowledge or expertise, can create operational bottlenecks and impact the quality of goods or services.

- **Weaknesses in Supplier Management or Technical Expertise:** Ineffective management practices or a lack of technical expertise within the supplier's workforce can lead to inefficiencies, errors, and quality issues.

According to a 2022 Deloitte survey, 77% of procurement leaders reported experiencing supply chain disruptions due to labor shortages in the preceding year. The World Economic Forum's 2023 Global Risks Report also highlighted the potential for social and economic instability arising from workforce challenges, including skills gaps and income inequality. In essence, a thorough assessment of threats to the supplier's labor and workforce is crucial in ensuring the resilience and continuity of the supply chain. By proactively identifying and addressing potential vulnerabilities, organizations can mitigate the risk of disruptions, maintain operational stability, and protect their bottom line.

2.8 Threats to Supplier's Other Customers

Identifying and assessing threats that a supplier's other customers face is a crucial yet often overlooked aspect of a comprehensive supplier risk assessment. The rationale behind this evaluation lies in the understanding that disruptions or attacks targeting the supplier's other customers can have indirect yet significant repercussions on your company's supply chain. Your company could become collateral damage from events impacting other clients of your critical supplier.

For instance, if a cyberattack cripples a significant customer of your supplier, it could lead to a sudden surge in demand for the supplier's resources as they strive to support the affected customer's recovery efforts. This could strain the supplier's capacity and potentially delay or disrupt their ability to fulfill your company's orders. Similarly, if your supplier's customer faces financial difficulties or even bankruptcy, it could impact their cash flow and economic stability, potentially hindering their ability to invest in maintaining or expanding their operations to meet your company's growing needs.

Therefore, the supplier risk assessment should include an evaluation of the supplier's customer base, identifying any significant customers that could pose a potential risk due to their size, industry, geographic location, or any other relevant factors. The assessment should also consider the nature of the supplier's relationships with these customers, including any dependencies or interdependencies that could amplify the impact of disruptions.

Suppliers should quantify and factor attacks or threats to other customers into their overall risk assessment (SRA) to prevent them directly. This analysis will ensure that suppliers with a high degree of customer concentration risk or exposure to volatile customer segments are subject to appropriate levels of supervision, diversification strategies, and robust backup plans. The goal is to proactively manage the potential indirect risks arising from the supplier's other customers, ensuring the resilience and continuity of your company's supply chain.

2.9 Threats to Supplier's Operations from Economic and Financial Sources

Identifying and assessing threats from economic and financial sources constitutes an indispensable facet of a comprehensive supplier risk assessment. The intricate interplay between global markets, financial institutions, and macroeconomic trends can profoundly influence a supplier's operational stability and financial health. The potential repercussions of economic downturns, financial crises, or fluctuations in commodity prices can reverberate throughout the supply chain, disrupting the flow of goods and services and jeopardizing the organization's ability to meet its objectives. The supplier risk assessment should meticulously scrutinize the supplier's financial standing, market exposure, and resilience to economic shocks. The aim is to identify potential vulnerabilities that could impair the supplier's ability to fulfill its contractual obligations, thus disrupting the supply chain.

The assessment should thoroughly evaluate the supplier's financial health, encompassing a review of their financial statements, credit ratings, and any outstanding debt obligations. It should also consider the supplier's exposure to market volatility, mainly if they operate in industries susceptible to fluctuations in commodity prices or currency exchange rates. The goal is to gauge the supplier's financial resilience and ability to withstand economic downturns or unforeseen financial challenges. The Allianz Risk Barometer 2023 ranked macroeconomic developments as the third top business risk globally, highlighting the potential for economic downturns, inflation, and financial market volatility to disrupt supply chains. The report also noted that 45% of companies surveyed had experienced a supply chain disruption due to financial instability in the preceding year.

The assessment should also consider the broader economic and financial landscape, including macroeconomic trends, geopolitical developments, and potential regulatory changes that could impact the supplier's operations. The objective is to identify any systemic risks that could affect the supplier's industry or market segment, potentially leading to disruptions in the supply chain. The World Economic Forum's 2023 Global Risks Report emphasized the interconnectedness of economic and geopolitical risks, highlighting the potential for cascading effects from trade wars, sanctions, or political instability. The report also noted that 52% of companies surveyed had experienced a supply chain disruption due to geopolitical events in the preceding year.

In essence, a conscientious assessment of threats to the supplier's operations from economic and financial sources is crucial in ensuring the resilience and continuity of the supply chain. By proactively identifying and addressing potential vulnerabilities, organizations can mitigate the risk of disruptions, maintain operational stability, and safeguard their financial interests.

2.10 Threats to Supplier's Operations from Government and Geopolitical Sources

Identifying and assessing threats emanating from government and geopolitical sources is integral to a comprehensive supplier risk assessment. The dynamic landscape of international relations, regulatory frameworks, and political events can significantly impact a supplier's operational stability and ability to fulfill its contractual obligations. The potential repercussions of trade wars, sanctions, political instability, or changes in government policies can disrupt supply chains, leading to delays, shortages, or even complete breakdowns in the flow of goods and services. The supplier risk assessment should meticulously examine the supplier's exposure to geopolitical risks, compliance with relevant regulations, and ability to navigate potential political or regulatory changes. The objective is to identify potential vulnerabilities that could impair the supplier's ability to maintain consistent operations and deliver goods or services, thus disrupting the supply chain.

The assessment should thoroughly evaluate the supplier's geographic footprint, including the countries where they operate, source materials, or have significant business relationships. It should also consider these regions' political stability, ongoing conflicts or tensions, and potential for future geopolitical events that could impact the supplier's operations. The goal is to gauge the supplier's exposure to geopolitical risks and ability to navigate potential disruptions.

The assessment should also consider the regulatory landscape in the regions where the supplier operates, including any trade restrictions, sanctions, or import/export controls that could affect their ability to conduct business. It should also evaluate the supplier's compliance with relevant regulations, such as environmental standards, labor laws, and data privacy regulations. The objective is to ensure the supplier operates ethically and responsibly, minimizing the risk of legal or reputational damage that could impact the supply chain.

The World Economic Forum's 2023 Global Risks Report ranked geopolitical fragmentation as the second top business risk globally, highlighting the potential for increased trade tensions, sanctions, and political instability to disrupt supply chains. The report also noted that 52% of companies surveyed had experienced a supply chain disruption due to geopolitical events in the preceding year. The assessment should also consider the potential impact of changes in government policies or regulations, such as tariffs, import quotas, or environmental restrictions, on the supplier's operations. The objective is to anticipate potential challenges and develop contingency plans to mitigate their impact on the supply chain.

3.0 Supplier Risk Assessment (SRA) Baseline

The initial Supplier Risk Assessment (SRA) is essential for several reasons: it establishes a baseline set of measures to track and monitor over time for variances and significant changes, to help identify necessary controls needed to protect supplier integration, and to prioritize investments in missing or insufficient controls. It is important to note that most organizations conduct individual risk assessments when onboarding critical vendors and conducting enterprise-wide supplier risk assessments annually or semi-annually. These two exercises are complementary, with the crucial difference being that the scope of an individual SRA is limited to the specific threats that apply to this single supplier. The enterprise-wide supplier risk assessment looks at the entire inventory of suppliers and the aggregate of all threats that apply across the portfolio. Another key difference to highlight is that SRAs for critical suppliers will go into a much more detailed analysis commensurate with the increased level of risk and exposure.

Building upon the Threat Identification by Asset group outlined in sections 2.0 through 2.10 above, the SCRM team can organize and prioritize all identified risk scenarios that apply to the new critical supplier. One essential step is identifying the specific supplier vulnerabilities and weaknesses that increase the supplier's susceptibility to threats. For each identified threat, the SCRM team needs to qualify the likelihood and frequency of that threat affecting the new supplier. It is also essential to qualify the potential business impacts that could result from a disruption in this individual supplier's flow of goods and services. The SCRM team can use the individual supplier vulnerabilities, the likelihood of occurrence, and the magnitude of impacts to estimate the Inherent Risks, which represent the worst-case risk scenario before we consider how specific controls and safeguards reduce that risk.

Building from the Inherent Risks, the SCRM team can identify and map individual threats to the specific enterprise or local controls that can prevent, deter, detect, mitigate, compensate, or reduce the recovery time or impact. In addition to the mapped controls, SCRM teams can also consider the benefits of safeguards outside of the company's direct control, such as those provided by industry or governmental agencies, that offer additional assurances or protections.

3.1 SRA – Enumerate and Prioritize Risk Scenarios

The first step in the SRA process involves the systematic enumeration and prioritization of potential risk scenarios that could impact the critical supplier's ability to fulfill its contractual obligations. This process entails meticulously consolidating threat events into distinct groupings based on their shared impact on specific assets, facilities, business processes, business partners, or end clients. The prioritization of these threat groupings is contingent upon a preliminary assessment of their potential impact and probability of occurrence. The objective is to establish a hierarchical framework that guides allocating resources and implementing targeted risk mitigation strategies.

For each identified risk scenario, the SCRM team should craft a concise yet comprehensive risk statement that encapsulates the potential consequences of the threat event. This statement should articulate the specific assets, facilities, business processes, business partners, or end-clients that could be affected, along with a qualitative or quantitative estimation of the potential impact. The risk statement should also consider the cascading effects that could ripple through the supply chain, potentially impacting other suppliers or the organization's operations. I provide in-depth examples of risk statements in Chapter 13.

Consolidating threat events into cohesive groupings streamlines the risk assessment and facilitates a more focused analysis. By identifying commonalities in the impact and probability of various threat events, the SCRM team can develop a more targeted and efficient risk mitigation strategy. This approach also enables the identification of potential synergies between different risk mitigation measures, optimizing resource allocation and maximizing the overall effectiveness of the risk management framework.

The prioritization of threat groupings is a critical step in the SRA process as it guides the allocation of resources and the sequencing of risk mitigation efforts. The prioritization should be based on a preliminary assessment of the potential impact and probability of each threat grouping. High-impact, high-probability threats should be accorded the highest priority, followed by high-impact, low-probability threats, and so forth. This hierarchical approach ensures that the most critical risks are addressed first, minimizing the potential for disruptions and safeguarding the continuity of the supply chain.

Prioritizing supplier threats based on preliminary impact sizing is dynamic and iterative. As the SRA progresses and more information becomes available, the prioritization may be refined and adjusted to reflect the evolving risk landscape. This adaptive approach ensures that the risk management framework remains agile and responsive to emerging threats, enabling the organization to proactively manage supplier risks and safeguard its supply chain operations.

3.2 SRA – Existing Vulnerabilities and Weaknesses

The second step in the SRA process delves into identifying and documenting existing vulnerabilities and weaknesses that could amplify the supplier's susceptibility to the identified threat scenarios. This process entails meticulously examining the supplier's operations, infrastructure, and risk management practices to uncover any inherent flaws or deficiencies that could be exploited by threat actors or exacerbate the impact of disruptive events. The objective is to comprehensively understand the supplier's risk profile, enabling the SCRM team to develop targeted mitigation strategies and prioritize risk treatment efforts.

Identifying vulnerabilities and weaknesses necessitates a multi-faceted approach encompassing various dimensions of the supplier's operations, including:

- **Physical Security Assessments:** Evaluating the adequacy of physical security controls at the supplier's facilities, such as access controls, perimeter security, and surveillance systems, to identify potential weaknesses that could facilitate unauthorized access or sabotage.
- **Cybersecurity Audits:** Assessing the robustness of the supplier's cybersecurity posture, including their network security, application security, and data protection measures, to identify potential vulnerabilities that cybercriminals could exploit.
- **Operational Reviews:** Examining the supplier's operational processes and procedures, such as quality control mechanisms, inventory management practices, and logistics protocols, to identify potential weaknesses that could lead to disruptions or inefficiencies.
- **Financial Analysis:** Scrutinizing the supplier's financial statements and credit ratings to identify any financial weaknesses or vulnerabilities that could impact their ability to fulfill their contractual obligations.
- **Compliance Reviews:** Evaluating the supplier's adherence to relevant regulations and industry standards to identify any compliance gaps or weaknesses that could expose the organization to legal or reputational risks.

The SCRM team should describe each identified vulnerability or weakness, including its potential impact on the supplier's operations and the specific threat scenarios it could exacerbate. The team should also assess the severity of each vulnerability or weakness, considering factors such as its exploitability, potential impact, and the existing controls in place to mitigate it. The objective is to create a prioritized list of vulnerabilities and weaknesses that guides the development of targeted risk treatment plans.

Documenting existing vulnerabilities and weaknesses is a critical input for the subsequent phases of the SRA. It informs the estimation of threat likelihood and impact, identifies control gaps, and calculates residual risk. It also provides a valuable reference for ongoing supplier risk monitoring and management, enabling the organization to track its progress in addressing identified weaknesses and proactively adjust its risk mitigation strategies.

3.3 SRA – Threat Likelihood of Occurrence and Frequency

The third step in the SRA process estimates the threat likelihood and frequency for the previously identified threat scenarios. This process necessitates a comprehensive analysis of diverse threat intelligence sources, encompassing historical data, industry benchmarks, expert opinions, and real-time threat feeds. The objective is to quantify the probability of each threat event materializing and its potential recurrence rate, enabling the SCRM team to gauge the supplier's exposure to various risks and prioritize mitigation efforts accordingly.

The estimation of threat likelihood and frequency necessitates a multi-faceted approach that leverages a variety of information sources. This estimation may include:

- **Historical Data Analysis:** Examining past occurrences of similar threat events within the supplier's industry or geographic region to discern patterns and trends that could inform the estimation of future likelihood and frequency.
- **Industry Benchmarking:** Comparing the supplier's risk profile against industry averages and best practices to identify areas where they may be more or less susceptible to specific threats.
- **Expert Consultations:** Engaging subject matter experts, such as security consultants, risk analysts, or industry specialists, to elicit their insights and opinions on the likelihood and frequency of specific threat scenarios.

- **Real-Time Threat Monitoring:** Utilizing threat intelligence feeds and monitoring tools to track emerging threats and vulnerabilities that could impact the supplier's operations.

The SCRM team should assign a likelihood rating for each identified threat scenario, typically expressed as a qualitative assessment (e.g., low, medium, high) or a quantitative probability (e.g., 10%, 50%, 90%). The team should also estimate the frequency of occurrence, typically expressed as the expected number of times the threat event could materialize within a given timeframe (e.g., annually, quarterly, monthly). The determination of likelihood and frequency should be based on a careful analysis of the available threat intelligence, considering factors such as the supplier's industry, geographic location, operational practices, and any existing vulnerabilities or weaknesses.

The documentation of threat likelihood and frequency serves as a crucial input for the subsequent phases of the SRA, informing the estimation of the magnitude of impact, the calculation of inherent risk, and the prioritization of risk treatment efforts. It also provides a valuable reference for ongoing supplier risk monitoring and management, enabling the organization to track changes in the threat landscape and proactively adjust its risk mitigation strategies.

3.4 SRA – Magnitude of Impact Over Time

The fourth step in the SRA process estimates the potential magnitude of impact associated with each identified threat scenario. This process necessitates a comprehensive analysis of the supplier's business impact assessments (BIAs) and other relevant data sources to quantify the operational and financial ramifications that could ensue if a threat event materializes. The objective is to gauge the severity of potential disruptions, enabling the SCRM team to prioritize risk treatment efforts and develop contingency plans to mitigate the impact on the organization's operations.

Estimating the magnitude of impact necessitates a multi-faceted approach that considers various dimensions of the supplier's operations and their connection with the company's business processes. This estimation may include:

- **Operational Impact Analysis (OIA):** The OIA evaluates the potential impact of a threat event on the supplier's ability to deliver goods or services, considering factors such as production downtime, inventory shortages, and logistical bottlenecks. This analysis should also consider the cascading effects that could ripple through the supply chain, potentially impacting other suppliers or the organization's operations.
- **Financial Impact Analysis (FIA):** The FIA involves calculating the potential financial losses that could occur in the event of a threat. These losses may include lost revenue, increased costs, and possible penalties or fines. This analysis should also consider the long-term financial implications, such as the impact on the organization's reputation or market share.
- **Customer Impact Analysis (CIA):** The CIA assesses the potential impact of a threat event on the organization's customers, considering factors such as service disruptions, product delays, and possible reputational damage. This analysis should also consider the potential for customer churn or loss of business opportunities.
- **Regulatory Impact Analysis (RIA):** The RIA evaluates the potential impact of a threat event on the organization's compliance with relevant regulations and industry standards. This analysis should also consider the potential for fines, penalties, or legal action.

The SCRM team should assign an impact rating for each identified threat scenario, typically expressed as a qualitative assessment (e.g., low, medium, high) or a quantitative estimate (e.g., financial loss in dollars, production downtime in hours). The impact determination should be based on a careful analysis of the available data, considering the specific attributes of the threat event, the supplier's vulnerabilities, and the organization's risk tolerance.

The documentation of the magnitude of impact serves as a critical input for the subsequent phases of the SRA, informing the calculation of inherent risk, identifying control gaps, and prioritizing risk treatment efforts. It also provides a valuable reference for ongoing supplier risk monitoring and management, enabling the organization to track changes in the supplier's risk profile and proactively adjust its mitigation strategies as needed.

3.5 SRA – Supplier Inherent Risk

The culmination of the first half of the SRA process involves aggregating and quantifying the inherent risk associated with this new critical supplier. This pivotal step entails consolidating the previously assessed threat scenarios, their likelihood of occurrence, and their potential magnitude of impact into a cohesive risk profile. The resultant inherent risk profile encapsulates the supplier's overall risk exposure before considering the mitigating effects of existing or planned controls. It is a crucial benchmark for evaluating the supplier's risk posture and informing subsequent risk treatment decisions.

The calculation of inherent risk typically involves assigning a risk score or rating to each identified threat scenario based on its likelihood and impact. These scores are then aggregated to derive the supplier's inherent risk rating. Various risk-scoring methodologies can be employed, such as qualitative scales (e.g., low, medium, high) or quantitative models that utilize numerical values or risk matrices. The choice of methodology depends on the organization's risk appetite, the supply chain's complexity, and the availability. The inherent risk profile provides valuable insights into the supplier's risk landscape, enabling the SCRM team to:

- **Prioritize risk treatment efforts:** By identifying the most critical risks, the team can allocate resources and implement mitigation strategies in a targeted and efficient manner.
- **Develop contingency plans:** The inherent risk profile informs the development of contingency plans to address

potential disruptions, ensuring the continuity of the supply chain.

- **Negotiate contractual terms:** The inherent risk profile is helpful during contract negotiations to establish clear expectations regarding risk mitigation and allocate responsibilities between the organization and the supplier.
- **Make informed decisions about the supplier relationship:** The inherent risk profile serves as a crucial input for evaluating the overall viability and desirability of the supplier relationship, enabling the organization to make informed decisions about supplier selection, onboarding, and ongoing management.

Estimating supplier-related inherent risk represents a pivotal juncture in the SRA process. It provides a comprehensive and quantifiable assessment of the supplier's risk exposure, enabling the organization to make informed decisions about risk treatment, contingency planning, and overall supplier relationship management. By proactively addressing inherent risks, organizations can enhance the resilience of their supply chains and safeguard their operations against potential disruptions.

3.6 SRA – Map Supplier Threats to Enterprise and Common Controls

The sixth step in the SRA process entails methodically mapping individual supplier threats to the enterprise's existing or planned controls. This process necessitates a comprehensive inventory and analysis of the organization's control framework, encompassing technical, operational, and managerial safeguards designed to prevent, deter, detect, mitigate, or compensate for the identified threats. The objective is to ascertain the extent to which the existing controls address the specific risks associated with the critical supplier, thereby facilitating the identification of control gaps and informing the development of targeted risk treatment plans. The SCRM team should meticulously document the mapping of supplier threats to enterprise controls, creating a visual representation or matrix that illustrates the relationships between specific threats and the corresponding controls designed to address them. This documentation serves as a valuable reference for evaluating the effectiveness of the control framework and identifying areas where additional controls or enhancements may be necessary. The mapping process should also consider the potential for control overlaps or redundancies, ensuring the control framework is optimized for efficiency and effectiveness.

The analysis of enterprise controls should encompass a wide range of safeguards, including:

- **Technical Controls:** These controls leverage technology to prevent, detect, or mitigate threats. Examples include firewalls, intrusion detection systems, antivirus software, data encryption, and access controls. The SCRM team should evaluate the adequacy of these controls in addressing the specific supplier threats, considering factors such as their configuration, effectiveness, and ongoing maintenance.

- **Operational Controls:** These controls involve processes and procedures designed to manage and mitigate risks. Examples include security policies, incident response plans, change management processes, and employee training programs. The SCRM team should assess the effectiveness of these controls in addressing the supplier threats, considering factors such as their clarity, adherence, and enforcement.

- **Managerial Controls:** The SCRM team should assess the effectiveness of these controls in overseeing the supplier relationship and ensuring the prompt identification and resolution of risks. These controls, such as risk assessments, internal audits, and performance monitoring, are designed to manage risks effectively through oversight and governance mechanisms.

The SCRM team should identify the specific enterprise controls that directly or indirectly address the risk for each identified supplier threat. The team should also estimate the degree of risk reduction or benefit each control provides, considering its effectiveness, reliability, and implementation status. This estimation may be expressed qualitatively (e.g., low, medium, high) or quantitatively (e.g., percentage reduction in risk). The team should also determine whether the control benefits or protects an individual asset, an asset group, or the entire enterprise. This information is crucial for prioritizing risk treatment efforts and allocating resources effectively.

In addition to enterprise controls, the SCRM team should consider the potential applicability of entity-level or local controls. These controls are shared across multiple systems or processes within the organization and can provide a baseline level of protection against various threats. Examples of standard controls include password policies, access controls, and data backup procedures. The team should evaluate the relevance of these controls to the specific supplier threats and assess their effectiveness in mitigating risks.

Mapping supplier threats to enterprise and standard controls is dynamic and iterative. As the SRA progresses and more information becomes available, the mapping may be refined and adjusted to reflect the evolving risk landscape. This adaptive approach ensures that the control framework remains aligned with the organization's risk appetite and can address the risks associated with the critical supplier.

3.7 SRA – Compensating and Mitigating Factors

In the seventh step of the SRA process, the SCRM team should actively identify and document compensating controls and mitigating factors that can lessen the impact or likelihood of the identified supplier risk scenarios. This phase aims to recognize and evaluate existing or potential measures that can reduce the severity or probability of disruptions, thereby enhancing the supply chain's resilience. The team should carefully document these measures, creating a comprehensive repository of risk treatment options to develop targeted risk mitigation strategies. The identification process should encompass a wide range of potential measures, including:

- **Insurance and Financial Instruments:** Insurance policies, surety bonds, or other instruments can provide a financial safety net during disruptions, offsetting potential losses and facilitating recovery efforts. The SCRM team should evaluate the adequacy of existing insurance coverage and explore additional options that could provide further protection against specific supplier risks.
- **Contingency Plans and Redundancies:** The development and implementation of robust contingency plans, such as backup suppliers, alternative transportation routes, or diversified sourcing strategies, can enhance the organization's ability to respond to disruptions and maintain continuity of operations. The SCRM team should assess the feasibility and effectiveness of these contingency plans in addressing the identified supplier risks.
- **Supplier Collaboration and Communication:** Establishing strong communication channels and collaborative relationships with suppliers can facilitate the early identification of potential risks and enable proactive mitigation efforts. The SCRM team should evaluate the effectiveness of existing communication protocols and explore opportunities to enhance collaboration and information sharing with critical suppliers.
- **Technology Solutions:** Deploying technology solutions, such as real-time monitoring systems, predictive analytics tools, or blockchain-based traceability platforms, can enhance visibility and control over the supply chain, enabling early detection of disruptions and facilitating rapid response. The SCRM team should assess the potential benefits of these technology solutions in addressing the identified supplier risks and evaluate their feasibility and cost-effectiveness.
- **Industry Best Practices and Standards:** Adopting industry best practices and standards, such as ISO 28000 (supply chain security management) or ISO 22301 (business continuity management), can enhance the organization's

overall risk management capabilities and demonstrate a commitment to supply chain resilience. The SCRM team should evaluate the relevance and applicability of these standards to the specific supplier risks and assess their potential benefits in mitigating disruptions.

For each supplier risk scenario, the SCRM team should identify the compensating controls and mitigating factors that could reduce its impact or likelihood. The team should also estimate the degree of risk reduction or benefit each measure provides, considering its effectiveness, reliability, and implementation cost. This estimation may be expressed qualitatively (e.g., low, medium, high) or quantitatively (e.g., percentage reduction in risk or financial impact). The team should also determine whether the control or mitigating factor benefits or protects an individual asset, an asset group, or the entire enterprise. This information is crucial for prioritizing risk treatment efforts and allocating resources effectively.

Identifying and documenting compensating controls and mitigating factors is an ongoing process that should be revisited periodically as the supplier relationship evolves and the risk landscape changes. By proactively identifying and implementing these measures, organizations can enhance the resilience of their supply chains and safeguard their operations against potential disruptions.

3.8 SRA – Control Gaps and Issues

The eighth step in the SRA process involves meticulously identifying and documenting control gaps and issues that could undermine the enterprise's risk mitigation efforts. This phase necessitates a comprehensive review of existing control test results, audit findings, regulatory examinations, and incident reports to pinpoint specific weaknesses or deficiencies in the control framework. The objective is to gain a granular understanding of the control environment's shortcomings, enabling the SCRM team to develop targeted remediation plans and enhance the overall resilience of the supply chain.

For each control mapped to a specific supplier threat or risk scenario, the SCRM team should thoroughly analyze its performance and effectiveness. This analysis may involve:

- **Reviewing control test results:** Examining the outcomes of recent control tests or assessments to identify instances where the control failed to operate as intended or did not adequately mitigate the associated risk.
- **Analyzing audit findings:** Scrutinizing internal or external audit reports to identify any observations or recommendations related to the control's design, implementation, or effectiveness.
- **Examining regulatory examinations:** Reviewing any findings or citations from regulatory bodies or industry oversight organizations that pertain to the control's compliance with relevant standards or regulations.
- **Investigating incident reports:** Analyzing past incidents or near-misses to identify any instances where the control failed to prevent or mitigate the impact of a threat event.

The SCRM team should document each identified control gap or issue, describing the weakness, its potential impact on the control's effectiveness, and the specific supplier threat or risk scenario it could exacerbate. The team should also estimate the degree to which the control's effectiveness is reduced due to the gap or issue, typically expressed as a percentage or a qualitative assessment (e.g., minor, moderate, significant). This estimation will inform the calculation of residual risk and the prioritization of remediation efforts.

Furthermore, the SCRM team should determine the scope of impact of each control gap or issue, assessing whether it affects an individual asset, a more significant asset group, or the entire enterprise. This determination is crucial for understanding the potential cascading effects of control weaknesses and prioritizing remediation efforts based on their possible impact on the organization's operations.

Identifying and documenting control gaps and issues is an ongoing process that should be integrated into the organization's continuous monitoring and improvement efforts. By proactively addressing these weaknesses, organizations can enhance the effectiveness of their control framework, strengthen their supply chain resilience, and safeguard their operations against potential disruptions.

3.9 SRA – Aggregate Residual Risk

The ninth step in the SRA process involves calculating the aggregate supplier residual risk, representing the cumulative risk profile derived from each identified supplier threat and risk scenario. The aggregate supplier residual risk represents the level of risk that remains after accounting for the cumulative risk reduction or benefit provided by the existing controls. The objective of this phase is to quantify the net risk exposure, enabling the SCRM team to make informed decisions about the acceptability of the residual risk and the need for additional risk treatment measures. The SCRM team should carefully document the residual risk calculations for each threat scenario, creating a comprehensive risk register that captures the net risk exposure and informs subsequent risk management decisions. The calculation process should consider the following factors:

- **Inherent Risk:** The intrinsic risk represents the level of risk before considering the mitigating effects of controls. It is typically calculated by combining each threat scenario's estimated likelihood and impact.

- **Control Effectiveness:** The control effectiveness represents the degree to which the existing or planned controls reduce the likelihood or impact of the threat scenario. It is typically expressed as a percentage or a qualitative assessment (e.g., low, medium, high).

- **Control Gaps and Issues:** Control gaps and issues represent weaknesses or deficiencies in the control framework that could undermine its effectiveness. Their impact on control effectiveness should be factored into the residual risk calculation.

The residual risk can be calculated using the following formula:

Residual Risk = Inherent Risk * (1 - Control Effectiveness)

The SCRM team should also consider the scope of impact of each control gap or issue when calculating the residual risk. If a control gap or issue affects an individual asset, the residual risk calculation should be applied specifically to that asset. If the gap or issue affects a larger asset group or the entire enterprise, the residual risk calculation should be applied accordingly. The residual risk documentation should include a clear and concise risk statement for each threat scenario, the calculated residual risk value, and any relevant assumptions or considerations. The risk register should also highlight any threat scenarios where residual risk exceeds the organization's risk tolerance, indicating additional risk treatment measures are needed. The residual risk profile serves as a crucial input for the final phase of the SRA, where the SCRM team will make risk acceptance or treatment decisions based on the organization's risk appetite and the available risk mitigation options.

3.10 SRA – Risk Disposition and Acceptance

The tenth and final step in the SRA process involves the presentation of the aggregate supplier residual risk profile to executive management and, potentially, the Board of Directors. This critical step serves as a foundation for informed decision-making regarding the acceptability of the residual risk and the necessity for further risk treatment measures. The SCRM team should prepare a comprehensive report articulating the aggregate supplier residual risk profile, highlighting key findings, potential impacts, and recommended courses of action. The report should be presented clearly and concisely, comparing new risks to existing ones, reviewing how other companies address the risks, and utilizing visual aids and executive summaries to facilitate understanding and engagement.

The presentation to management and the Board should emphasize the following key points:

- The inherent risks associated with the critical supplier, including their potential impact on the organization's operations, financial performance, and reputation
- The effectiveness of existing or planned controls in mitigating these risks, highlighting any control gaps or issues that could undermine their efficacy
- The calculated residual risk for each threat scenario, emphasizing any instances where the residual risk exceeds the organization's risk tolerance
- The recommended risk treatment options, including risk acceptance, risk avoidance, risk transfer, and risk mitigation, and the associated costs and benefits

The objective of the presentation is to ensure that management and the Board have a thorough understanding of the residual risk profile and its potential implications. The discussion should focus on the following key questions:

- Is the residual risk within the organization's risk appetite? (I cover risk appetites in more detail in Chapter 13)
- Are there any specific threat scenarios that require further risk treatment?
- What are the most cost-effective and feasible risk treatment options?
- What are the potential consequences of accepting the residual risk?

Based on the discussion and the organization's risk appetite, management and the Board will decide on risk disposition for each identified threat scenario. This decision may involve:

- **Risk Acceptance:** Acknowledging the residual risk and taking no further action, typically for low-impact, low-likelihood threats.

- **Risk Avoidance:** Terminating or altering the supplier relationship to eliminate the risk, typically for high-impact, high-likelihood threats that cannot be adequately mitigated.
- **Risk Transfer:** Shifting the financial burden of the risk to a third party, such as an insurance provider, typically for high-impact, low-likelihood threats.
- **Risk Mitigation:** Implementing additional controls or enhancing existing ones to reduce the likelihood or impact of the threat, typically for high-likelihood threats where the residual risk exceeds the organization's risk tolerance.

The SCRM team should capture the risk disposition decisions in the organization's risk register, ensuring they align with the organization's overall risk management strategy. The team should also initiate control improvement projects to address identified control gaps or implement additional risk treatment measures. The risk register and control improvement projects should be subject to ongoing monitoring and review to ensure that the residual risk remains within acceptable levels and that the organization's supply chain resilience is continuously enhanced.

Conclusion

The Critical Supplier Onboarding Methodology detailed in this essay underscores the essential role of meticulous planning and proactive risk management to ensure supply chain resilience and operational continuity. Key themes emerging from this analysis highlight the necessity of comprehensive supplier assessments, diligent mapping of vulnerabilities to enterprise controls, and robust oversight mechanisms to address a broad spectrum of risks—including technology vulnerabilities, geopolitical instability, financial health, and workforce reliability. A standout lesson learned is that supply chain disruptions are significantly amplified when organizations underestimate or inadequately address the complex interdependencies involving critical suppliers and their extended networks.

To strengthen the supply chain against these challenges, I strongly recommend that organizations integrate a structured Supplier Management and Oversight Plan (SMOP), enhanced by specialized controls tailored for critical suppliers and software supply chains. This includes proactive practices like regular financial health checks, rigorous security and privacy evaluations, transparent intellectual property protections, and continuous software vulnerability management. Executives should ensure that supplier risk mitigation is not only a compliance task but an integral part of strategic business operations—enabling better decision-making, more agile responses to disruptions, and sustained competitive advantage.

REFERENCES

- Allianz Risk Barometer. 2023. Allianz Risk Barometer 2023: Top Global Business Risks. Allianz.
- BlueVoyant. 2021. Third-Party Cyber Risk Management Report 2021. BlueVoyant.
- Business Continuity Institute. 2023. Supply Chain Resilience Report 2023. Business Continuity Institute.
- Deloitte. 2022. Deloitte Global Procurement Leadership Survey 2022. Deloitte.
- Deloitte. 2023. Third-Party Risk Management Survey 2023. Deloitte.
- Deloitte. 2023. Reputation Risk Management Study 2023. Deloitte.
- Dun & Bradstreet. 2023. Global Supply Chain Risk Report 2023. Dun & Bradstreet.
- ENISA. 2023. Threat Landscape for Supply Chain Attacks. European Union Agency for Cybersecurity (ENISA).
- IBM & Ponemon Institute. 2023. Cost of a Data Breach Report 2023. IBM & Ponemon Institute.
- International Labour Organization (ILO). 2023. World Statistics on Occupational Safety and Health. ILO.
- KPMG. 2023. Global Supply Chain Fraud and Misconduct Report 2023. KPMG.

- Liberty Mutual Insurance. 2023. Workplace Safety Index 2023. Liberty Mutual Insurance.
- McKinsey & Company. 2023. Supply Chain Risk Management Insights 2023. McKinsey & Company.
- Resilinc. 2023. Supply Chain Disruption Annual Report 2023. Resilinc.

Insights and Actions

A well-governed vendor onboarding process, underpinned by clear expectations, comprehensive risk assessment, and proactive stakeholder engagement, is essential for minimizing risk and ensuring long-term success in outsourcing relationships. By addressing governance concerns at every stage, from planning and selection through onboarding and integration, organizations can build strong, resilient partnerships with their vendors.

The vendor management lifecycle consists of five key stages:

1. Plan: Define business needs and requirements and conduct market research.
2. Engage: Select vendors, negotiate contracts, and ensure alignment with organizational goals.
3. Implement: Onboard and integrate vendors, set up systems, and train staff.
4. Manage: Monitor and manage vendor performance and risks.
5. Terminate: Offboard vendors and manage transitions.

Key Governance and Activities

The following bulleted lists represent the key actions that should be integrated into your vendor onboarding process.

Requirements Definition and Initial Research:

- Clearly define business needs and product/service requirements and conduct market research.
- Engage all relevant stakeholders, establish performance metrics and SLAs, and assess risks (financial, cybersecurity, supply chain, reputational).
- Ensure compliance with regulations and data governance standards.
- Develop a sourcing strategy, budget, and communication plan.

Vendor Selection and Contract Negotiation:

- Research and identify potential vendors; issue RFPs/RFIs.
- Evaluate proposals, conduct due diligence, and select vendors based on fair, transparent criteria.
- Address conflicts of interest, ensure compliance and security, and involve key stakeholders.
- Set performance metrics and include dispute resolution and termination clauses.
- Finalize contracts with clear expectations for both parties.

Onboarding and Integration:

- Set up accounts, access, and systems for the vendor.
- Communicate expectations, integrate processes, and train staff.
- Implement compliance and security protocols, access controls, and data security measures.
- Monitor performance, manage risks, and establish business continuity and disaster recovery plans.
- Foster cultural alignment and maintain stakeholder engagement.

Critical Supplier Onboarding Methodology

The Critical Supplier Onboarding Methodology emphasizes the importance of thorough planning, proactive risk management, and robust oversight for mission-critical supplier relationships. By systematically assessing and mitigating risks across all aspects of supplier operations—from technology and data to logistics and workforce—organizations can build resilient supply chains capable of withstanding disruptions and supporting long-term business success. This structured approach should be integrated into broader supplier management and oversight plans, ensuring that risk mitigation is a strategic priority rather than just a compliance exercise.

Key Insights for Onboarding Suppliers

Organizations must meticulously document ten core supplier relationship requirements—including business integration architecture, raw material flows, intellectual property exchanges, identity and access management, data exchanges, product flows, service delivery, performance communications, incident response, and business continuity plans. This comprehensive approach goes beyond traditional vendor onboarding to create detailed blueprints that map intricate patterns of interaction, data flows, system integrations, and communication protocols, enabling organizations to identify potential vulnerabilities and single points of failure before they become operational risks.

Effective supplier risk management demands thorough analysis of threats across ten critical asset categories: supplier facilities, raw materials, fourth-party dependencies, transportation/logistics, technology infrastructure, digital data, labor/workforce, other customers, economic/financial sources, and government/geopolitical factors.

Organizations must establish baseline Supplier Risk Assessments (SRA) that enumerate and prioritize risk scenarios, identify existing vulnerabilities, estimate threat likelihood and impact magnitude, calculate inherent risk, map threats to enterprise controls, identify compensating factors, document control gaps, and calculate aggregate residual risk for executive decision-making. This ten-step methodology enables informed risk disposition decisions—including risk acceptance, avoidance, transfer, or mitigation—and ensures that residual risks remain within organizational risk tolerance levels while providing precise accountability mechanisms for ongoing supplier oversight and continuous improvement initiatives.

Due Diligence for Mission-Critical Suppliers

- Supplier Relationship Requirements: Map business processes, data flows, and integration architecture to identify vulnerabilities and risks.

- Raw Material Flows: Develop a Materials Delivery Management Plan (MDMP) to manage transportation, logistics, and contingencies.
- Intellectual Property and Trade Secrets: Create a robust management plan to protect and monitor shared IP.
- Identity and Access Management: Implement strict access controls and authentication protocols.
- Data Exchange: Develop a plan for secure, compliant data sharing.
- Products and Goods Flows: Map and manage the product lifecycle with quality assurance and contingency measures.
- Service Delivery Management: Define SLAs, KPIs, and quality controls for service delivery.
- Performance and Control Communications: Establish communication protocols and real-time monitoring.
- Incident Response: Prepare playbooks for incident management and communication.
- Business Continuity Plans (BCP): Develop and test continuity plans for supplier disruptions.

Supplier Risk Assessment (SRA) and Threat Management

- Threat Identification: Systematically identify threats across all asset groups (facilities, raw materials, technology, data, labor, customers, economic, geopolitical).
- Risk Assessment: Enumerate and prioritize risk scenarios, identify vulnerabilities, estimate likelihood and impact, and calculate inherent risk.

- Control Mapping: Map threats to enterprise and common controls, identify compensating controls and mitigating factors, and document control gaps.
- Residual Risk Calculation: Calculate residual risk after applying controls and present findings to management and the board for risk disposition decisions (accept, avoid, transfer, mitigate).

Chapter 5

Operating and Stewardship

Introduction

In Chapter 5, we focus on integrating the newly onboarded third party into ongoing operations and managing the relationship to ensure the organization obtains the results it needs. Bill begins by exploring the fourth phase of the vendor management lifecycle—monitoring and managing vendor relationships—emphasizing the critical role that risk management and governance play throughout the process. Bill underscores that effective oversight of vendor performance is essential to ensure alignment with organizational expectations and contractual commitments, noting that regular reviews and audits, while often neglected, are indispensable for maintaining accountability and driving continuous improvement.

Matt dives into the stewardship of third-party risk management (TPRM), specifically how organizational culture shapes the approach to relationships with vendors and suppliers. Matt focuses on two prevailing mindsets: one that treats vendor relationships as adversarial and zero-sum, focusing on extracting the most favorable terms and cost savings, and another that values collaboration, recognizing the mutual dependence between organizations and their providers for long-term success. While he believes that both approaches have their place, Matt advocates for the collaborative model that still safeguards the organization from undue risk or unfavorable pricing.

Chris then provides a comprehensive exploration of supply chain management (SCM), focusing on the critical importance of reliability, resilience, and responsive operations. He begins by establishing SCM as the backbone of organizational efficiency, emphasizing the role of business-as-usual teams in managing daily activities such as supplier due diligence, onboarding, integration, and offboarding to ensure smooth and compliant operations. Chris then delves into the integration of technology and automation, highlighting how connecting suppliers through digital platforms and automating core processes like order processing and inventory management leads to greater efficiency and real-time visibility across the supply chain.

Collectively, Bill, Matt, and Chris make the point that people, process, and technology, tempered with continued diligence and a cooperative ongoing investment of management attention, are critical for the success of vendor, third-party, and supply chain risk management.

Immediately following Chris' essay is a list of publications he references throughout.

Managing and Monitoring Your Vendors

Bill Bonney

Effective monitoring and management of vendors require a proactive, governance-driven approach that emphasizes risk identification, compliance, open communication, quality assurance, and alignment with organizational strategy and culture.

In Chapter 4, I scoped out the governance issues for the onboarding process, covering planning, engaging, and implementing. It involves determining your needs, who can meet them, and contracting with that vendor. This chapter covers the fourth stage of the vendor management lifecycle: Monitor and Manage. Then, in Chapter 7, I'll finish the discussion by addressing Termination and Offboarding.

As a quick refresher of the five stages of the vendor management lifecycle, here again is the lifecycle diagram introduced in Chapter 4:

Figure 5.1 – Vendor Management Lifecycle

- Plan – Requirements definition and initial research.
- Engage – Vendor selection and contract negotiation.
- Implement – Onboarding and integration.
- Manage – Monitoring and management.
- Terminate – Terminate and offboard.

I want to reiterate that risk management and, therefore, governance are the lenses through which I view this process. With that in mind, here are some aspects of the Monitor and Manage stage of the vendor lifecycle that deserve our attention.

Here, the focus shifts to overseeing the vendor's performance to ensure it aligns with the organization's expectations and contractual agreements. And while regular reviews and audits are essential and often overlooked, audits only look to the past. To get the most from reviews, we must start with a complete agreement of expectations.

Performance Management

The most essential vendor risk management principle is ongoing due diligence. To facilitate the due diligence, I look to these fundamental activities:

- Identify, assess, and mitigate risks associated with the vendor relationship.
- Ensure compliance with legal, regulatory, and security requirements.
- Provide feedback and address any issues or concerns.
- Manage data privacy and intellectual property concerns.

I then consider the following topics of concern to performance management:

- **Risk Identification:** Systematically identify all potential risks associated with the vendor relationship that you uncovered as you developed your initial risk assessment. Include operational, financial, legal, reputational, and cybersecurity risks. Consult your RACI chart to make this a joint effort and pay special attention to the hand-offs from client to vendor and vendor to client. These hand-offs create potential seams in your security.
    - **Compliance and Regulatory Risks:** Ensure the vendor complies with all relevant laws (this should be part of your contract terms), regulations, and industry standards, minimizing legal and regulatory risks. This includes data protection laws (such as GDPR and

CCPA), industry-specific regulations, and internal policies.

- **Cybersecurity and Data Privacy:** Manage risks related to data breaches, cyberattacks, and data privacy violations. This includes ensuring the vendor adheres to robust cybersecurity practices and data encryption standards and that you integrate your incident response plans where appropriate.
- **Financial Stability and Continuity Risks:** Assess and monitor the vendor's financial health to mitigate risks related to vendor failure, bankruptcy, or significant service disruptions. This may involve periodic financial reviews or setting up escrow arrangements for critical services.
- **Operational Risks:** Address risks that could affect the organization's operations, such as supply chain disruptions, quality issues, or failure to meet service level agreements (SLAs). This includes developing contingency plans and closely monitoring vendor performance.
- **Reputational Risks:** Consider the potential impact of the vendor's actions or failures on the organization's reputation. This involves monitoring the vendor's compliance with ethical standards, labor practices, and environmental regulations.
- **Contractual and Legal Risks:** Manage risks related to contract enforceability, intellectual property rights, and liabilities. This includes ensuring clear contractual terms, indemnities, and warranties.

- **Risk Assessment:** Evaluate the identified risks in terms of their likelihood and potential impact on the organization. This assessment should consider both quantitative and qualitative factors to prioritize risks effectively.

- **Risk Mitigation Strategies:** Develop and implement strategies to mitigate the identified risks. This may involve contractual safeguards, insurance, enhanced security measures, compliance audits, or establishing alternative suppliers to reduce dependency on a single vendor.
- **Review and Adaptation:** Regularly review the risk management strategies and adapt them as necessary based on changes in the vendor relationship, organizational priorities, or the external environment.
- **Contract Management:** Ensure both parties adhere to the contract terms, including deliverables, timelines, and payment schedules. It is easy to blame the vendor, but organizations must live up to their commitments, including deliverables and payment. When proposing contract modifications, be aware of how far you are from the original parameters and resist using disproportional economic power and hardball tactics. You may receive what appear to be small near-term concessions, but ultimately you build fear, distrust, and resentment into your ongoing relationship and few relationships can flourish in that dynamic.
- **Feedback and Communication:** Facilitate open and effective communication between the organization and the vendor. Provide constructive feedback to the vendor about performance and work collaboratively to address any issues or areas for improvement. To develop these concepts a bit, being open means being honest and transparent. Be direct; this is no place for an indirect communication style. Also, I emphasize constructive feedback. Feedback should unpack what went wrong and what needs to be different. Stick to facts. In my experience, speculating on motive or cause tends to be counterproductive.
- **Quality Control:** Implement quality control measures to ensure that the products or services provided by the vendor meet the organization's standards and requirements. This may involve regular quality audits, testing, and validation

processes. Again, audits look to the past; agree with the vendor on what quality control steps each party will take and how each will report the results.

- **Continuous Improvement:** Work with the vendor to identify opportunities for continuous improvement in service delivery, efficiency, and innovation. Encourage the vendor to suggest improvements or new solutions that benefit the organization. Note that this is not the same as quality control. Quality can be perfect and perfectly inefficient.
- **Data and Intellectual Property Protection:** Ensure that the vendor continues to protect any sensitive data and intellectual property rights as per the agreements, including adherence to data handling, storage, and sharing policies. At the risk of repeating myself, here is another place where we do not want to rely on audits to "catch" problems. Put proactive measures in place to verify that the vendor is meeting your data handling standards.
- **Dispute Resolution:** Use the conflict resolution protocol you established during contract negotiation. Try to start informally and avoid using threats of escalation as a bullying tactic. Escalation is most effective as a way to sharpen decision-making and impact change rather than as a flog to enforce the terms of the contract.

Monitoring

Having established the expectations, activities, and measurements, we can now look to prudent monitoring steps to keep the process and the relationship on track. Key governance concerns during the risk management stage include:

- Monitoring and measuring vendor performance against agreed-upon metrics and service level agreements (SLAs).
- Conducting regular reviews and audits.

I then consider the following topics of concern to monitoring:

- **Performance and SLA Monitoring:** Continuously monitor the vendor's performance against agreed-upon service level agreements (SLAs) and performance metrics. This includes addressing any performance issues, conducting regular performance reviews, and working collaboratively with the vendor to identify areas for improvement. There are two sides to the tolerance coin here. On one side of the coin, you don't want to have so little tolerance for process variability that you make the job difficult to staff. This includes policing your own ranks for toxic employees that might poison the relationship. On the other side of the coin, be on the lookout for the vendor working so tightly to the letter of the contract that they may be having difficulty servicing your contract and have not yet found an effective way to communicate the issue.

- **Compliance Monitoring:** Ensure the vendor consistently complies with legal, regulatory, and contractual obligations. This includes regular audits and assessments to verify adherence to data protection laws, industry regulations, and security standards. Don't rely on audits alone to ensure the vendor complies with regulatory obligations; have them proactively report status through the relationship manager. Depending on the scale and the process layers between the vendor's data handling procedures and your own, you may also need to rely on third-party attestations or audits to ensure the vendor continues to meet their compliance obligations.

- **Strategic Alignment:** Continually validate that the vendor relationship remains aligned with the organization's strategic goals and objectives. This may involve adjusting the scope of work, renegotiating terms, or exploring new opportunities for collaboration that support the organization's strategic direction.

- **Cultural and Ethical Alignment:** Ensure that the vendor's corporate culture, values, and business practices remain compatible with your organization's corporate culture, values, and business practices. This includes monitoring the vendor's adherence to ethical standards, labor practices, and environmental responsibilities.

- **Vendor Dependency and Diversification:** Manage the level of dependency on the vendor to avoid over-reliance on a single source for critical products or services. This may involve developing a diversification strategy or contingency plans in case of vendor failure.

- **Exit Strategy Planning:** Prepare for the potential end of the vendor relationship by regularly evaluating the vendor's performance and the organization's ongoing needs. This includes considering the implications of contract termination and planning for a smooth transition if vendor changes are needed. All relationships eventually end, and being prepared for that eventuality will help you mitigate downside risk during the transition.

Addressing these governance concerns is essential for effective relationship management, facilitated by the Monitoring and Managing stage of the vendor management lifecycle. This ensures that the organization can maximize the value of its vendor relationships, achieve its strategic objectives, and mitigate potential risks.

TPRM Stewardship

Matt Stamper

By leveraging clear documentation, regular oversight, and robust governance tools (such as R&R and RACI matrices, escalation protocols, and stewardship meetings), organizations can reduce risk, clarify expectations, and ensure that third-party services are fit for purpose.

How we approach our relationships with third parties and suppliers is frequently the product of organizational culture. From my experience, there are two approaches. One approach is to view relationships with vendors and third parties as intrinsically zero-sum and adversarial. Every dollar (or penny) of savings and each favorable contract term must be won for that relationship to be deemed successful. We see these dynamics with suppliers, especially in the manufacturing and retail industries, where pricing terms reflect asymmetries between the larger organization and its suppliers.

The other approach consists of firms that take a more collaborative approach with their suppliers and vendors, recognizing that the contracting firm depends on these relationships. Absent these providers, the contracting firm's ability to execute would be stifled. Moreover, these firms understand that having financially viable and stable providers is ultimately in their best interests.

While each approach has its merits and unique operational context, I have personally attempted to seek collaborative, positive-sum engagements with third parties. This does not mean accepting contractual terms that would put my organization at risk (see Chapter 11) or being gouged with out-of-market pricing.

Regardless of your firm's approach, tools and techniques should be used to ensure that the relationship meets its objectives and is well governed. This chapter will focus more on service-provider relationships, but the concepts will apply to product-based supply chains. Some basic tools and validations underpin successful stewardship relationships. First among these is ensuring that the services contemplated are unambiguously documented. Let's highlight some core validations necessary to underpin your TPRM program.

Service Definition and Service Demarcation – Services should be clearly defined with details outlined for deliverables and reporting, their cadences, and descriptions of key functions and services. The definitions should also clearly define service demarcation points. I have found that service demarcation is an underutilized element in TPRM programs. The provider and the service consumer must understand where services start and stop. To accomplish this, it's important for key stakeholders, notably in operations, to document and clarify which services and deliverables are contemplated and to ensure that the supporting agreements accurately reflect these understandings. In Chapter 11, I offer an illustrative example.

Coming from the security industry, we see challenges concerning managed security service providers (MSSPs) and providers of extensible detect and response services (XDR). Too frequently, there's ambiguity about "response" and "response actions" by the providers. The provider may assume that they've completed their requirements when they notify the client of a security incident. The client may assume that the MSSP or XDR provider will manage the incident. While some providers take an active role in the response, many do not, and when services are contracted, how security responses will be addressed may be nebulous. This ambiguity serves no one and should be clarified proactively. Based on the materiality of the relationship, take the time to ensure that services are adequately defined and that service demarcation points are clear. As another example, who is responsible for the rulesets if firewall administration is outsourced to an MSSP? Many providers will implement the rules the client requests, even if these rules introduce insecure configurations. For a subset of MSSPs, firewall management (administration) may only be hardware administration (the firewall is up and responding, and which rules are in play are irrelevant). It's important to walk through scenarios and "what ifs" with the provider for more critical engagements. Important word of caution: even if consensus is reached verbally during a scenario review, ensure that this understanding is consistently conveyed in the statement of work (SOW) or master services agreement (MSA).

Roles and Responsibilities (R&R) – I've used and advocated for roles and responsibilities matrices throughout my career. As with a RACI matrix, the time invested in developing comprehensive roles and responsibilities documentation is time well spent. Not all R&R matrices are the same. A common error I see with R&R documentation is that there are two sections in the matrix. One section highlights the provider's roles and responsibilities, while another indicates the client's responsibilities. They are similar to the complementary user entity controls (CUECs) in SOC 2 audit reports.[4] I strongly recommend developing R&R matrices that show functions with distinct columns for the service provider's and client's obligations next to each other. The effect is that each party's respective responsibilities and role in the process are noted for a given service or activity. Having side-by-side detail facilitates a deeper understanding of the contemplated activity and its role in the engagement. While many service providers have a roles and responsibilities matrix that they provide by default, consider drafting a standard template for your organization that can be used to clarify understandings. When I worked in the managed services, managed security, and data center space, we drafted a detailed roles and responsibilities matrix for each service layer, starting with functions related to the application and then detailing roles and responsibilities deeper into the technology stack, specifically, the database, the underlying operating system, virtualization services, the front-end network, and the back-end networks for monitoring and backup services. Each layer contemplated what our firm would provide and what the client would need to know or perform to use the service

[4] The American Institute of Certified Public Accountants (AICPA) and the Chartered Institute of Management Accountants (CIMA) oversee the standards for these structured audits and provide guidance on the reasonable assurance to be provided by these audit reports. To learn more, please reference:
https://www.aicpa-cima.com/topic/audit-assurance/audit-and-assurance-greater-than-soc-2.

correctly. Our matrices became pretty granular depending on the engagement at hand. Your firm will have specific requirements and context, but these R&R matrices are foundational to good TPRM stewardship and governance.

Cadence of Activities – Where warranted, draft a calendar of activities and functions and capture key deliverables associated with the engagement or service. If the service contemplates monthly reports, clarify when they are due, schedule them on the calendar, and ensure that adequate time is made available to review the status of the reports. Obviously, ensure that desired reports are reviewed and acted upon where recommendations are applicable. There's a tendency to allow dates and commitments to slip over time. Having these key functions calendared and agreed to among the parties will reduce the risk of missed expectations and obligations.

Stewardship Meetings – Similarly, I strongly advocate stewardship meetings with key providers. These, too, should be scheduled. To facilitate these meetings, establish a standing agenda. Use these meetings to look at the past quarter's (or whichever period is appropriate) services, the status of service level agreements, any issues that may have occurred, service-impacting maintenance, forthcoming changes, etc. These stewardship meetings keep the engagement professional and should be used to clarify understandings that may not have been adequately captured in SOWs and MSAs. Good stewardship practices will also address metrics, training, SLAs/SLOs, and other context-specific variables germane to the relationship. If not captured on the meeting agenda, draft a checklist to ensure that key items are not overlooked during the meeting. As noted below regarding RACI matrices, ensure that participants in stewardship meetings know what's required of them as part of this governance model.

Responsible, Accountable, Consulted, and Informed (RACI) Matrices – To complement the R&R matrix noted above, ensure that your firm establishes an appropriately detailed RACI matrix for key services and functions. You may want to consider having two matrices developed. One RACI matrix would be used internally to clarify key stakeholders and their respective roles with respect to the service, while another would be used to validate requirements with the service provider. Having a solid RACI matrix developed for service provider governance is advisable and is an extensible tool for your TPRM program. Adjust your RACI matrix to your firm's specific operational considerations and ensure that the details and understandings are maintained current.

Escalation Matrices and Authorized Personnel and Emergency Contact (APEC) Detail – In the theme that all governance seems to be built on matrices, I highly recommend developing and, most importantly, maintaining escalation matrices. Both organizations should know whom they should communicate with when issues arise. Managed service providers typically maintain an APEC form of key stakeholders. Certain stakeholders may be contacted for administrative functions such as billing or adding or removing contacts to the APEC form. In contrast, others may be contacted for service-impacting issues. Keeping escalation protocols documented with accurate and up-to-date contact details for providers is foundational. Email distribution lists should be used for scenarios where service-impacting issues may be more acute or impactful. For example, if the provider only has Jane or John Doe's contact details and they've left the organization, there's a risk that if issues surface the provider cannot reach the appropriate party. I've seen firms' websites go down because the Certificate Authority's attempt to renew the certificate is sent to a former employee, and that mailbox is not monitored. Don't leave escalation and APEC matrices to chance. These matrices should be reviewed, ideally quarterly, for more mission-critical services.

Disclosure and Communication Protocols – Similar to the service demarcation points noted above, communication protocols and mandated disclosures should not be overlooked. If your organization wants certain service-related details to be maintained confidential and only available to specific designated stakeholders, these expectations should be codified. Communication protocols should reflect the materiality of the relationship between the two parties. As services and requirements become more important, formalizing the entities' communication protocols should reflect the same.

Communication protocols can be interwoven into the APEC and R&R matrices. To reduce litigation risk, I advise getting counsel's perspective on how sensitive matters should be communicated between the parties. Be sure to validate expectations for how privileged communication should be handled.

Disclosure obligations are part of the communication protocols between the two entities. These should be validated and reviewed with legal counsel. Key topics to review with your TPRM team include least privilege, separation of duties, and need-to-know principles. If your firm has engaged a third party to provide mission-essential functions for your organization, that provider should understand the gravitas of the relationship and ensure that their personnel (and contractors) are operating under appropriate confidentiality requirements and that service details are only shared with staff with a legitimate business need-to-know. Verify how the provider maintains confidentiality and communication protocols within its environment. You may also want to explore more nuanced technical topics impacting disclosure and communication protocols. Specifically, how are multi-tenant ticketing systems configured? Are service details filtered by assigned teams? Could one team see the confidential details of another team's interactions with other clients?

As discussed in Chapter 6 regarding incident response practices with third parties, validate the provider's obligations to notify your organization if a data breach or service-impacting incident occurs. As part of this review, validate expectations related to how and to whom these disclosures would be made, your firm's expectations about disclosures to federal or regulatory authorities, or other expectations that counsel and the TPRM team may have.

Certifications and Audits – As part of the stewardship relationship with material third parties, if your organization requires that these providers maintain certifications such as those from the International Standards Organization or audits such as SOC 2 or SSAE 18 audits, ensure that the certifications and audits are current and valid. For audit reports, validate complementary user entity controls (CUECs) and whether any exceptions are noted. There's a tendency among many SaaS firms to provide their cloud service provider's audit report in lieu of actually performing their own. For smaller-sized SaaS providers, the costs of SOC 2 audits may be material financially. Your team will need to determine how it will address providers who are not in a position to provide the desired certifications or audits. Chapter 4 discusses approaches for onboarding due diligence. Where relationships have been established and desired certifications and audits are absent, look for alternative ways to increase assurance. The aforementioned stewardship meetings with various service validations can help in this regard. If a provider has committed to obtaining a desired certification or completing a specific audit at some point, ensure that the expected date is placed into the vendor governance calendar.

Record Keeping and Document Management – TPRM requires service agreements, service matrices, reports, and other service-related documentation to be well-managed and access-controlled. Spend time with your TPRM team to determine and validate which documents should be managed and where they should be maintained. Service-related documents frequently contain sensitive information, so effective security controls must be implemented for the environment where these materials are stored. Validate access controls, logging procedures, and data loss prevention controls over these materials. This documentation should be part of your organization's broader data retention policy and will likely have mandated retention periods.

Ultimately, stewardship and governance with third parties should be filtered through the lens of materiality. Critical relationships and services require diligence, documentation, and active management. Commonsensical tools like R&R and escalation matrices, service demarcation documentation, calendars for oversight activities, and stewardship meetings with key providers will help reduce risk and ensure that services are fit for purpose. Use these techniques and those noted in Chapter 4 as integral elements of your TPRM program.

Supply Chain Operations – Managing Reliability, Resilience, and Response

Chris Forbes

Continuous monitoring and logistical oversight are essential for maintaining supply chain integrity, with teams tasked to track flows, manage unexpected changes, and foster open communication among stakeholders to swiftly address disruptions.

1.0 SCM Operations Overview

Supply Chain Management (SCM) is the backbone of any organization's ability to deliver products and services efficiently and effectively. As global markets grow increasingly complex, businesses must develop and maintain robust SCM operations to ensure their supply chains are resilient, agile, and aligned with their strategic objectives.

Business-as-usual (BAU) teams are responsible for the day-to-day management of supply chain activities, and their primary goal is to ensure that the supply chain operates smoothly, efficiently, and in alignment with the organization's strategic objectives. These teams typically consist of supply chain managers, inventory analysts, procurement specialists, and change management professionals, all working together to manage these critical operations. Core SCM operational activities include supplier due diligence and onboarding, building supplier integrations, running and monitoring the supply chains, building supply chain inventories and managing changes, building supply chain resilience and business continuity planning, deploying and tracking controls, performing maintenance and upgrades, producing management and stakeholder reports, and conducting governance and oversight activities. The following sections provide a comprehensive overview of key SCM operations, detailing the critical functions and processes of managing modern supply chains.

1.1 SCM Supplier Due Diligence, Onboarding, and Offboarding

SCM starts with Supplier Due Diligence, which includes selecting, evaluating, and onboarding suppliers to ensure they meet organizational standards. Day-to-day tasks involve maintaining a list of approved suppliers, sending RFPs, evaluating proposals, conducting audits, negotiating contracts, and managing supplier performance.

Onboarding integrates suppliers into the supply chain, ensuring they understand requirements and metrics. BAU teams create onboarding procedures, provide training, and monitor supplier performance.

Offboarding is disengaging with a supplier due to poor performance, non-compliance, or changing needs. BAU teams develop offboarding procedures, communicate the decision, and manage the transition.

Contract management oversees supplier contracts, ensuring they are up-to-date, accurate, and compliant. BAU teams develop contract management procedures, negotiate contracts, track expirations and renewals, and manage disputes.

These operational activities are critical for BAU teams to ensure a resilient, efficient, and compliant supply chain.

1.2 SCM Building Technology, Integrations, Instrumentation, and Automation

After onboarding, BAU teams integrate suppliers into the supply chain infrastructure, creating seamless connections between components. This integration may involve developing custom technologies or configuring ERP platforms to optimize resource allocation. Automation is key in areas such as order processing, inventory management, and quality control to streamline operations and enhance efficiency. Additionally, data flow integration with partners enables real-time visibility and collaboration, while instrumentation monitors supply flow and identifies bottlenecks.

1.3 SCM Logistical Operations and Continuous Monitoring

SCM Logistical Operations and Continuous Monitoring are essential for maintaining supply chain integrity and performance. BAU teams oversee the movement and delivery of materials, goods, and services, supervising inbound, outbound, internal, and reverse logistics to optimize supply chain flows. By collecting and analyzing real-time data, BAU teams track KPIs, identify potential issues, and ensure the supply chain operates within predefined parameters, enabling early detection of anomalies and swift corrective actions. Daily operational tasks include:

- **Monitoring Supply Chain Flows:** Continuously track the movement of goods, identify bottlenecks, and address delays or disruptions using real-time tracking, data analytics, and collaboration with logistics partners.
- **Managing Unexpected Changes:** Manage fluctuations in demand or supply by adjusting production, inventory, and transportation plans. Monitor product quality and implement quality control measures.
- **Maintaining Communication and Collaboration:** Maintain open communication with all stakeholders to ensure alignment and information sharing.

1.4 SCM Inventory Management

In inventory management, BAU teams maintain optimal stock levels, reduce costs, and meet customer demand. They use inventory management systems, demand forecasting tools, audits, and cycle counting. They are also responsible for change management, identifying the need for change, planning and executing it, and evaluating its success. They collaborate with other departments to implement changes effectively with minimal disruption.

Inventory management ensures the right products are available at the right time to meet customer demand while minimizing excess inventory costs. Key activities include:

- **Demand Forecasting:** Analyzing historical sales data and market trends to predict future product demand, informing inventory ordering decisions.
- **Inventory Replenishment:** Maintaining stock levels to meet demand without overstocking, by setting reorder points and safety stock levels.
- **Stock Level Monitoring:** Tracking stock levels in real time to identify discrepancies and take corrective actions, using inventory management systems and regular audits.
- **Inventory Turnover Optimization:** Analyzing sales data and adjusting pricing strategies to optimize inventory turnover, improve cash flow, and reduce holding costs.

1.5 SCM Resilience and Business Continuity Planning (BCP)

Building a resilient supply chain is a strategic imperative. Business Continuity Planning (BCP) involves identifying potential risks, assessing their likelihood and impact, and developing strategies to ensure the supply chain can withstand and quickly recover from disruptions. This element includes contingency planning, redundancy strategies, and maintaining critical reserves to ensure business operations can continue with minimal interruption.

A fundamental challenge to improving risk management is the inability to identify potential threats or the probability (likelihood) that those hazards will occur near a business asset or supply chain. To increase certainty, you must better predict when and where threats will happen and when they will surpass or exceed your ability to withstand or absorb them.

All disruptions and incidents should be reviewed to see if they were just "bad luck" or "once in a blue moon" occurrences that will likely never happen again. This critical analysis helps avoid investing and consuming precious resources to build controls for improbable scenarios. This analysis should be considered for situations that have not previously occurred or where the precursors and compounding factors may never occur again (like the planets aligning or an airplane falling out of the sky onto your data center).

In these situations, businesses should consider Risk Pooling (e.g., relying on community or industry services), Risk Transfers to partners and suppliers better prepared to handle those scenarios, Risk Avoidance by staying away from the behaviors that result in the disruption, and Risk Acceptance.

1.6 SCM Controls: Design, Deployment, Monitoring, and Testing

Adequate controls are essential for a secure and compliant supply chain. BAU teams design, develop, deploy, and test operational controls to collect metrics, measure quality, monitor risks, and alert on deviations. Key activities related to SCM controls are:

- **Controls Design:** Collaborate with stakeholders to design controls that address risks and align with objectives.
- **Controls Development:** Implement controls within the supply chain, configure systems, or establish procedures.
- **Controls Deployment:** Oversee deployment, ensuring integration into processes and systems.
- **Monitoring:** Collect and monitor operational and quality metrics and key risk indicators (KRIs).
- **Alerting:** Trigger alerts for unexpected deviations and investigate to restore normal operations.
- **Ongoing Testing:** Regularly test controls using various methods to verify effectiveness and identify weaknesses.

1.7 SCM Maintenance, Repairs, and Change Management

The longevity and reliability of supply chain infrastructure depend on regular maintenance, timely repairs, and well-managed changes. BAU teams are responsible for the upkeep of physical assets and digital systems. Daily operational tasks related to maintenance and repairs include:

- **Preventive Maintenance:** BAU teams implement routine maintenance schedules to inspect and service equipment, identify potential issues before they cause disruptions, and extend the lifespan of assets.

- **Minor Repairs:** BAU teams promptly address minor repairs to prevent them from escalating into more significant, costly problems.

- **Overseeing and Coordinating Changes:** BAU teams are critical in managing and coordinating all requested and required changes to the supply chain.

Change management ensures that modifications to processes, technologies, or supplier relationships are implemented smoothly and without disrupting the flow of goods and services. BAU teams are responsible for:

- **Rigorous Change Request Review Processes:** BAU teams follow established procedures to evaluate, approve, and implement changes.

- **Change Approval Processes:** BAU teams ensure that all changes undergo a rigorous approval process involving relevant stakeholders and decision-makers.

- **Change Implementation and Monitoring:** BAU teams oversee the implementation of approved changes, ensuring that they are executed according to the plan and that any issues are addressed promptly. They also monitor the impact of changes to verify their effectiveness and identify any unintended consequences. Finally, teams must monitor for unplanned or unauthorized modifications.

1.8 SCM Training, Disruption Drills, and Tabletop Exercises

Proper training is essential for supply chain personnel to handle their roles and potential disruptions. Training should include:

- **Daily Operations:** Personnel should be trained on day-to-day tasks and standard operating procedures.
- **Disruption Response Training:** Uses simulations of disruptions, such as natural disasters or supplier failures, to practice response plans and minimize disruptions.
- **BCP Training:** Training on the Business Continuity Plan (BCP), roles, and transferring operations during disruptions.
- **Tabletop Exercises:** Simulated scenarios to practice response to disruptions, test the BCP, and improve coordination.
- **Executive Training:** Specialized training for executives on risk management, BCP, crisis management, and communication.
- **External Partner Training:** Training suppliers and logistics providers to align with the organization's BCP and collaboration during disruptions.

1.9 SCM Operational and Stakeholder Reporting

Transparency and communication are vital for effective supply chain management. BAU teams keep stakeholders informed and engaged by producing various reports that provide insights into the supply chain's current state, identify trends, and highlight areas for intervention.

- **Operational Reports** provide detailed insights into supply chain operations, including metrics such as on-time delivery rates, order fulfillment rates, inventory turnover, and production efficiency. They help management monitor performance, identify bottlenecks, and optimize operations.

- **Compliance Reports** ensure the supply chain adheres to regulations and internal policies. They may include audits of supplier practices, documentation of compliance with industry standards, and tracking of corrective actions.
- **Risk Monitoring Reports** assess and communicate potential risks within the supply chain. They may include supplier risk assessments, analyses of geopolitical events, and monitoring of key risk indicators (KRIs).
- **Specialty Reports** are tailored to the needs of external partners, clients, or regulatory groups. They may focus on specific aspects of the supply chain, such as sustainability metrics, supplier diversity statistics, or financial performance data.

1.10 SCM Governance and Oversight

Effective governance and oversight are essential to ensure SCM operations align with strategic goals, comply with regulations, and maintain high performance standards. A strong governance framework defines policies, procedures, and accountability structures to manage risks, drive performance, and uphold ethical and legal compliance. Regular audits and reviews sustain the program's integrity and effectiveness.

BAU teams play a vital role by executing the following tasks:

- **Gathering and Presenting Operational Metrics:**

  BAU teams collect and analyze data on key metrics, such as on-time delivery, order fulfillment rates, inventory turnover, and production efficiency. Clear presentation of these metrics enables informed, data-driven decisions.

- **Calculating Key Performance Indicators (KPIs):**

  BAU teams calculate KPIs tied to strategic objectives and industry benchmarks, such as cash-to-cash cycle time, perfect order rate, and total supply chain cost, to highlight performance trends and areas for improvement.

- **Assembling Status Reports for Change Requests:**

  BAU teams track and report on change request progress, noting challenges and estimated completion dates to ensure smooth, proactive initiative management.

- **Updating on Projects and Transformation Initiatives:**

  BAU teams stay current on supply chain initiatives through regular communication with project managers and meeting participation, helping anticipate operational impacts.

- **Collecting Root-Cause Analysis (RCA) and Remediation Status:**

  BAU teams document supply chain incidents and remediation efforts, using these insights to spot trends, evaluate response effectiveness, and strengthen future resilience.

- **Reviewing and Approving New Project Requests:**

  BAU teams assess new project proposals for strategic alignment, risk, benefits, and resource needs, ensuring initiatives contribute meaningfully to supply chain success.

2.0 SCM Problem Management

Supply Chain Problem Management encompasses a range of processes and practices designed to identify, assess, and resolve disruptions that can impact the flow of goods and services. Effective problem management is essential for maintaining operational continuity, minimizing financial losses, and upholding the organization's reputation. Problem Management covers a vast array of operational activities, including:

- Issues management and remediation tracking
- Problems discovered in audits, contractual reviews, and regulatory examinations
- Problems related to technology obsolescence and replacements
- Problems associated with SCM alert investigations and incident response
- Problems requiring SCM crisis management and business continuity coordination
- Problems requiring root-cause analysis (RCA) and break-fix
- Problems involving law enforcement and criminal investigations
- Problems involving records retention and requests for legal discovery
- Problems involving supplier deficiencies and supplier replacements
- Problems requiring supply chain insurance claims

2.1 SCM Issues Management

Issues management is a proactive approach to identifying, assessing, and resolving supply chain problems. It is vital for maintaining operational continuity, minimizing disruptions, and ensuring supply chain efficiency. According to the Aberdeen Group, best-in-class organizations are 50% more likely to have a formal issues management process, underscoring its importance in supply chain excellence.

Key issues management activities include:

- **Issue Identification and Reporting:**
  Establish clear channels for employees, suppliers, and customers to report problems promptly. Use centralized systems to capture and organize reports.

- **Issue Assessment and Prioritization:**
  Evaluate reported issues based on impact and urgency, helping prioritize resources effectively.

- **Issue Resolution and Tracking:**
  Assign ownership for issue resolution and track progress to ensure timely outcomes. Regular updates keep stakeholders informed.

- **Remediation Tracking:**
  Implement systems to track corrective actions, verifying completion to prevent recurrence. Gartner reports that mature remediation tracking reduces disruptions by 60%.

2.2 SCM Contractual Reviews, Audits, and Regulatory Examinations

Supply chain audits, contractual reviews, and regulatory examinations are critical components of Supply Chain Problem Management. According to Deloitte, strong audit programs significantly reduce disruptions by up to 60% by identifying vulnerabilities, non-compliance, and potential risks early.

- **Supply Chain Audits:** Systematic, independent reviews ensure compliance with internal policies, standards, and regulations. Audits assess supplier relationships, inventory management, logistics, and quality controls and may be conducted internally or by third parties.

- **Contractual Reviews:** These evaluations ensure contracts with suppliers and vendors are current, accurate, and aligned with organizational needs. Reviews help uncover legal or financial risks and verify that all parties meet obligations.

- **Regulatory Examinations:** Conducted by government or industry bodies, these reviews ensure compliance with laws regarding environmental practices, labor standards, and product safety.

Executive and board oversight is crucial. KPMG reports that 82% of executives stress the importance of supply chain risk management. Leadership must review audit reports, ensure timely corrective actions, and allocate proper resources to support audit improvements. Robust audits, contractual reviews, and regulatory examinations enhance supply chain visibility, reduce risk, and drive overall performance. Executive involvement is key to ensuring that findings are effectively addressed.

2.3 SCM Technology Obsolescence, Vulnerability Patches, and Replacements

Managing technology obsolescence and replacements is essential in modern supply chain operations. Regular assessments identify aging components or vulnerabilities, allowing proactive upgrades before failures occur. Staying ahead with new technologies enhances efficiency, reduces costs, and strengthens resilience.

- **Technology Obsolescence:** Outdated technologies can cause:
    - Decreased Performance: Older systems may create bottlenecks or expose vulnerabilities due to unsupported software.
    - Compatibility Issues: Integration with newer systems becomes complicated.
    - Higher Maintenance Costs: Specialized expertise and scarce parts increase operational costs.

- **Vulnerabilities and Patches:** Patches address exploitable software or hardware weaknesses. Prompt patching is critical to maintaining security and avoiding regulatory non-compliance. Organizations must deploy compensating controls, such as isolation or heightened monitoring, if patching is delayed.

- **Technology Replacement:** Replacement becomes necessary when existing systems no longer meet performance, security, or compliance standards due to obsolescence, vulnerabilities, or evolving business needs.

Proactive technology management safeguards the supply chain, ensuring reliability, security, and operational efficiency.

2.4 SCM Event Research and Incident Response

Unified supply chain operations centers are increasingly necessary to monitor metrics and respond to disruptions across complex, global supply chains. Traditional, siloed centers for procurement, manufacturing, transportation, and finance delay recognition and response, creating inefficiencies. Key benefits of unified operations centers include:

- **Enhanced Visibility and Real-Time Decisions:** Integrating systems into a single platform enables faster, data-driven decisions. AI and machine learning improve disruption prediction and management.

- **Collaboration and Data Integration:** Centralized platforms streamline communication between internal teams and external partners, reducing errors and enhancing efficiency.

- **Risk Management and Resilience:** Continuous monitoring of supply chain metrics supports early risk detection, which is critical for building resilience against disruptions like those seen during the COVID-19 pandemic.

- **Efficiency and Cost Reduction:** Automating manual tasks reduces operational inefficiencies and mitigates the costs associated with fragmented systems.

- **Comprehensive Incident Response:** Unified centers systematically investigate supply chain events like delivery delays or security breaches. Root cause analysis, impact assessments, and response plans (including alternate suppliers, disaster recovery sites, and fallback logistics) are coordinated across all stakeholders to minimize downtime and maintain trust.

2.5 SCM Crisis Management and Business Continuity

Supply chain crisis management requires preparing for large-scale disruptions through Command, Control, Communication, and Coordination. Command sets the leadership structure; Control ensures plan execution; Communication aligns stakeholders; and Coordination manages resource deployment. A strong crisis management plan enables fast, effective responses, minimizing operational impacts.

ISO 22361:2022 Crisis Management — Guidelines

This standard outlines a structured approach to crisis management, encouraging integration with business continuity (ISO 22301) and risk management (ISO 31000) frameworks. Key components include:

- **Crisis Management Structure:** Defining clear roles and leadership for quick decision-making.
- **Preparation and Planning:** Conduct regular training and develop crisis scenarios and pre-defined plans.
- **Response and Communication:** Establishing internal and external communication strategies to manage crises and reputation.
- **Stakeholder Engagement:** Maintaining open communication with suppliers, partners, and customers during crises.
- **Continuous Improvement:** Conducting post-crisis reviews to refine plans.

ISO 22301:2019 Business Continuity Management System (BCMS)

ISO 22301 provides a framework for resilience:

- **Context Analysis:** Understanding internal and external challenges.

- **Leadership and Resources:** Top management ensures BCMS integration and resource support.
- **Risk Assessment and Planning:** Identifying threats and developing continuity strategies.
- **Operational Execution:** Maintaining practical and updated continuity plans.
- **Performance and Improvement:** Regular audits, tests, and corrective actions drive ongoing resilience.

2.6 Root Cause Analysis (RCA) and Break-Fix

Root cause analysis (RCA) is essential for identifying the true causes of supply chain disruptions. It is a structured problem-solving approach widely applied across industries, notably emphasized in ISO 9001:2015 and central to Six Sigma methodologies aimed at minimizing defects and improving efficiency. Key steps in the RCA process are:

- **Problem Definition:** Clearly describe the issue, its symptoms, and impacts.
- **Data Collection:** Gather evidence, timelines, and contributing factors.
- **Causal Analysis:** Use techniques like the 5 Whys, Fishbone Diagrams, and Fault Tree Analysis to trace root causes.
- **Solution Implementation:** Develop corrective actions to prevent recurrence.
- **Break-Fix Strategies:** Address immediate operational disruptions while implementing corrective actions to avoid future incidents.

RCA and break-fix approaches help maintain stability, improve quality, reduce costs, and boost customer satisfaction.

2.7 Law Enforcement and Investigations

Supply chain disruptions involving theft, fraud, or counterfeit goods require clear engagement protocols with law enforcement. Organizations must create operational playbooks that define when to engage law enforcement, assign liaisons, protect sensitive data, and maintain evidence integrity. Handling external requests involves verifying legitimacy, consulting legal counsel, and documenting all interactions. Organizations must preserve evidence, cooperate with investigations, and maintain thorough case management to protect legal interests.

2.8 Records Retention and Legal Discovery

Strong records retention and legal discovery practices ensure compliance and readiness for litigation. Organizations must categorize records, define retention periods, secure storage, and establish compliant disposal methods. During legal discovery, they must verify subpoena legitimacy, manage digital evidence under FRCP Rules, and protect privileged information. Legal holds require notifying custodians, maintaining preserved records, and monitoring compliance to prevent spoliation risks. Effective management of records protects against regulatory and legal vulnerabilities.

2.9 Supplier Deficiencies, Replacements, and Legal Recourse

Supplier deficiencies must be identified, documented, and addressed promptly. Organizations should set clear performance metrics, engage suppliers for remediation, and replace non-compliant vendors when necessary, based on severity, willingness to improve, availability of alternatives, and cost considerations. If significant losses occur, legal action through penalties or contract termination may be warranted to protect operations.

2.10 Insurance Claims

Insurance helps mitigate the financial impact of supply chain disruptions. Managing claims involves documenting incidents such as natural disasters, accidents, theft, or supplier failures, and filing for recovery.

Best Practices for Managing Insurance Claims:

- Timely Reporting: Promptly notify insurers to avoid disputes.
- Accurate Documentation: Maintain thorough records of incidents and financial losses.
- Collaboration with Insurers: Work closely to assess losses and negotiate settlements.
- Legal Counsel: Involve legal advisors to ensure compliance and protect interests.
- Risk Mitigation: Strengthen preventive measures to minimize future claims.

Substantiating Insurance Claims:

- Collect evidence (photos, reports) and quantify direct and indirect financial losses.

3.0 Supply Chain Operating Metrics

Supply Chain Operating Metrics are essential for evaluating a supply chain's efficiency, effectiveness, and overall performance. These metrics provide the data needed to make informed decisions, identify areas of improvement, and align supply chain operations with organizational objectives. Peter Drucker, a noted expert on Business Management, is quoted as saying, "You can't improve what you don't measure," and W. Edwards Deming, another business luminary, said, "If you can't measure it, you can't manage it." Dr. Deming recognized the value of using data to improve organizational management, but also acknowledged that many things cannot be measured and must still be managed and decisions made.

Reliable metrics support critical decision-making, proactive risk management, and efficient response and recovery planning. This section will examine the key operating metrics for supply chain management across various dimensions, providing insights into how these metrics can enhance performance and ensure resilience in supply chain operations.

3.1 Supplier Performance Metrics

Supplier performance is a critical aspect of supply chain management, as it directly impacts the quality, cost, and timeliness of the products and services delivered. The following metrics are essential for evaluating supplier performance:

- **Supplier Lead Time:** This metric measures suppliers' time to deliver orders after placing them. Shorter lead times increase supply chain flexibility and responsiveness.
- **Supplier On-Time Delivery Rate:** This metric tracks the percentage of orders that suppliers deliver within the agreed-upon timeframe. High on-time delivery rates indicate reliable suppliers and contribute to smooth supply chain operations.
- **Supplier Quality Metrics:** These metrics assess the quality of suppliers' products or services, including defect rates and compliance with specifications. High-quality suppliers contribute to fewer disruptions and higher customer satisfaction.

These metrics allow organizations to evaluate their suppliers, make informed decisions about supplier relationships, and identify areas for improvement or renegotiation.

3.2 Manufacturing and Production Metrics

Manufacturing and production metrics help organizations assess how effectively they utilize their production resources and manage costs. The top metrics in this category include:

- **Capacity Utilization:** This metric indicates how effectively an organization uses its production capacity. It helps determine whether the company is over- or under-utilizing its resources, impacting cost efficiency and production schedules.
- **Total Supply Chain Management Cost:** This comprehensive metric includes all costs associated with the supply chain, from procurement to manufacturing to delivery. Understanding these costs is crucial for optimizing budget allocations and reducing inefficiencies.
- **Manufacturing Cycle Time:** This metric measures the total time to produce a product, from receiving raw materials to the final product. Shorter cycle times can lead to quicker customer delivery and reduced inventory costs.

By monitoring these metrics, organizations can optimize production processes, reduce costs, and improve overall supply chain efficiency.

3.3 Inventory Metrics

Effective inventory management ensures that the right products are available at the right time while minimizing holding costs. Key metrics in this area include:

- **Inventory Turnover:** This metric measures how often inventory is sold and replaced over a specific period. A higher turnover rate typically indicates efficient inventory management and strong sales.
- **Inventory Accuracy:** This metric refers to the match between the physical inventory and the records in the management system. High accuracy minimizes issues such as stockouts or overstocking, ensuring that inventory levels are managed effectively.
- **Days of Inventory on Hand (DOH):** This metric measures the average number of days inventory is held before being

sold. Lower DOH indicates a leaner inventory, which can reduce carrying costs and free up capital.

Monitoring these metrics helps organizations maintain optimal inventory levels, reduce excess stock, and improve cash flow.

3.4 Warehouse Operations Metrics

Warehouse operations are a crucial component of the supply chain, impacting both cost efficiency and customer satisfaction. The following metrics are vital for assessing warehouse performance:

- **Warehouse Capacity Utilization:** This metric measures how much available warehouse space is utilized. High utilization rates indicate efficient use of space, while low rates suggest opportunities to consolidate operations or reduce costs.
- **Order Picking Accuracy:** This metric tracks the percentage of orders picked correctly. High accuracy in order picking is essential for minimizing errors, reducing returns, and ensuring customer satisfaction.
- **Order Cycle Time:** This metric measures the time taken to complete an order from its placement until it is ready for shipment. Shorter cycle times contribute to faster delivery and improved customer service.

Organizations can enhance warehouse efficiency, reduce operational costs, and improve service levels by focusing on these metrics.

3.5 Customer Demand Metrics

Understanding and forecasting customer demand is critical for aligning supply chain operations with market needs. Key metrics in this area include:

- **Customer Order Cycle Time:** This metric measures the time elapsed from when a customer places an order to when they receive it. A shorter cycle time is crucial for customer satisfaction and competitive advantage.

- **Demand Forecast Accuracy:** This metric assesses how close the forecasted demand is to actual sales. Accurate demand forecasting helps maintain optimal inventory levels and avoid stockouts or excess inventory.
- **Demand Variability:** This metric measures fluctuations in customer demand over time. Understanding demand variability helps adjust production schedules and inventory levels to meet changing market conditions.

These metrics provide insights into customer behavior and help organizations optimize their supply chains to meet customer expectations efficiently.

3.6 Order Fulfillment Metrics

Order fulfillment metrics are essential for evaluating the efficiency and effectiveness of the process, from receiving orders to delivering products to customers. The top metrics in this area include:

- **Order Fulfillment Rate:** This metric measures the percentage of orders fulfilled within the agreed-upon time frame. High fulfillment rates are critical for customer satisfaction and loyalty.
- **Perfect Order Rate:** This composite metric assesses the percentage of error-free orders with regard to delivery time, condition, documentation, and quantity. A high ideal order rate indicates a fulfillment process that is functioning well.
- **Backorder Rate:** This metric measures the percentage of orders that cannot be filled when they are placed due to inventory shortages. Lower backorder rates indicate adequate inventory and demand management.

Monitoring these metrics helps organizations streamline order fulfillment processes, reduce errors, and enhance customer satisfaction.

3.7 Transportation Operating Metrics

Transportation metrics are crucial for managing the costs and efficiency of moving goods through the supply chain. The key metrics in this area include:

- **Freight Cost per Unit:** This metric tracks the cost of transportation per unit of goods shipped. Monitoring freight costs is essential for maintaining cost efficiency in the supply chain.
- **On-Time Delivery (OTD):** This metric measures the percentage of shipments delivered on time to customers. High OTD rates are critical for customer satisfaction and maintaining service quality.
- **Transportation Time:** This metric tracks the total time transporting goods from the warehouse to the customer. Reducing transportation time can lead to faster deliveries and improved customer satisfaction.

These metrics help organizations optimize transportation strategies, reduce costs, and improve delivery performance.

3.8 Supply Chain Productivity and Efficiency Metrics

Productivity and efficiency metrics assess how resources are utilized in the supply chain. The top metrics in this area include:

- **Supply Chain Cycle Time:** This metric measures the total time taken to produce and deliver a product, from the procurement of raw materials to the final delivery. Reducing cycle time can lead to faster market response and increased customer satisfaction.
- **Cash-to-Cash Cycle Time:** This metric measures the time from paying for raw materials to receiving payment for the finished product. Shorter cash-to-cash cycles improve liquidity and reduce the need for working capital.

- **Cost of Goods Sold (COGS):** This metric represents the direct costs attributable to producing goods sold, including materials and labor. Understanding COGS is essential for managing cost structures and improving profitability.

Focusing on these metrics enables organizations to enhance productivity, reduce costs, and improve overall supply chain efficiency.

3.9 Supply Chain Quality Metrics

Quality metrics ensure the products meet customer expectations and regulatory standards. Key quality metrics include:

- **Return Rate:** This metric measures the rate at which customers return products. High return rates can indicate issues with product quality or fulfillment errors, requiring corrective action.

- **Defect Rate:** This metric tracks the percentage of products not meeting quality standards. Lower defect rates contribute to higher customer satisfaction and reduced costs associated with rework and returns.

- **Supplier Quality Assurance:** This metric evaluates suppliers' effectiveness in meeting quality standards. It includes assessments of defect rates, compliance with specifications, and adherence to quality certifications.

By monitoring these metrics, organizations can maintain high-quality standards, reduce waste, and enhance customer satisfaction.

3.10 Customer Service Metrics

Customer service metrics gauge how well the supply chain meets customer expectations. Key metrics include Customer Satisfaction Score (CSAT) for overall satisfaction, Net Promoter Score (NPS) for customer loyalty and advocacy, and Customer Order Cycle Time for delivery speed. These metrics provide critical insights into supply chain performance, enabling data-driven decisions and continuous improvement. Regular monitoring helps identify strengths, address weaknesses, and align operations with strategic goals. These metrics ensure resilience, efficiency, and superior customer experience, helping organizations maintain a competitive advantage and meet evolving market demands.

4.0 Key Performance Indicators (KPIs)

Key Performance Indicators (KPIs) in supply chain management (SCM) are crucial for evaluating supply chain operations' efficiency, effectiveness, and overall health. They provide strategic insights that guide management in making informed decisions, ensuring the supply chain aligns with organizational objectives, and enhancing resilience against disruptions. The KPIs discussed in this section focus on management-level and enterprise-level metrics, avoiding core operational metrics to concentrate on broader performance assessments.

4.1 Raw Material KPIs

Raw material management is a foundational element in the supply chain, directly impacting production quality, cost, and efficiency. Effective tracking of KPIs related to raw materials ensures that the supply chain remains robust and can respond flexibly to changes in demand or supply conditions. The Top 3 raw material KPIs are:

- **Material Cost Variance (MCV):** MCV measures the difference between the actual cost of raw materials and the standard cost expected by the organization. It helps identify cost overruns and opportunities for cost-saving. Calculation: MCV = (Actual Cost - Standard Cost) × Quantity Used
- **Supplier Lead Time Variability:** This KPI tracks the consistency of lead times from raw material suppliers. High variability can indicate supply chain risks and potential disruptions in production schedules. Calculation: Standard Deviation of Lead Times

- **Material Yield Variance (MYV):** MYV assesses the difference between the expected and actual material usage in production. It indicates the efficiency of raw material usage and highlights areas for process improvement. Calculation: Material Yield Variance = (Standard Quantity - Actual Quantity) × Standard Cost

4.2 Supplier and Vendor KPIs

Managing supplier relationships effectively is essential for maintaining a reliable, high-quality supply chain. KPIs in this category help organizations assess supplier performance, financial stability, and their impact on the supply chain. The Top 3 supplier and vendor KPIs are:

- **Supplier On-Time Delivery Rate:** This KPI measures the percentage of orders delivered by suppliers within the agreed timeframe, reflecting their reliability and the impact on supply chain efficiency. Calculation: On-Time Delivery Rate = (Number of On-Time Deliveries / Total Deliveries) × 100

- **Supplier Financial Stability Index:** This index assesses the financial health of suppliers, helping to anticipate potential risks of bankruptcy or failure, which could disrupt the supply chain. Calculation: A composite score based on financial ratios such as debt-to-equity ratio, current ratio, and profitability margins.

- **Supplier Defect Rate:** This KPI tracks the percentage of materials or products received from suppliers that do not meet quality standards, indicating supplier performance and its impact on production quality. Calculation: Supplier Defect Rate = (Defective Units / Total Units Received) × 100

4.3 Production Capacity and Warehousing KPIs

Production capacity and warehousing KPIs are critical for optimizing resource use and ensuring inventory levels align with demand. These

KPIs help manage space, inventory health, and overall warehousing efficiency. The Top 3 KPIs in this area are:

Inventory Health Index: This index evaluates the overall health of inventory, considering factors like safety stock levels, turnover rates, and obsolescence. It helps to balance supply and demand effectively. Calculation: A weighted composite score based on inventory turnover, safety stock, and obsolescence rates.

- **Warehouse Capacity Utilization:** This KPI measures the percentage of warehouse space being utilized, indicating how efficiently the space is managed and identifying opportunities for consolidation or expansion. Calculation: Capacity Utilization = (Used Space / Total Available Space) × 100

- **Order Picking Accuracy:** This KPI tracks the accuracy of order-picking processes within the warehouse, directly impacting customer satisfaction and fulfillment efficiency. Calculation: Order Picking Accuracy = (Correct Picks / Total Picks) × 100

4.4 Manufacturing Quality KPIs

Manufacturing quality KPIs are essential for maintaining high standards in production, reducing waste, and ensuring customer satisfaction. These KPIs focus on the quality outputs of the manufacturing process. The Top 3 manufacturing quality KPIs are:

- **First Pass Yield (FPY):** FPY measures the percentage of products that pass quality inspections without rework, indicating the efficiency of the production process and adherence to quality standards. Calculation: FPY = (Units Passed without Rework / Total Units Produced) × 100

- **Quality Reject Rate:** This KPI tracks the percentage of manufactured products rejected due to quality issues, highlighting areas where process improvements are needed.

Calculation: Reject Rate = (Rejected Units / Total Units Produced) × 100

- **Cost of Poor Quality (COPQ):** COPQ calculates the total costs associated with defects, including rework, scrap, and warranty claims, helping to quantify the financial impact of quality issues. Calculation: COPQ = Total Costs of Defects / Total Production Costs

4.5 Customer Demand KPIs

Understanding and predicting customer demand is crucial for aligning supply chain activities with market needs. KPIs in this category provide insights into customer behavior and help optimize inventory and production planning. The Top 3 customer demand KPIs are:

- **Demand Forecast Accuracy:** This KPI measures how closely forecasted demand matches actual sales, impacting inventory levels and production planning. Calculation: Forecast Accuracy = 100% - [(|Actual - Forecast| / Actual) × 100]
- **Customer Order Cycle Time:** This KPI tracks the time taken from when a customer places an order to when they receive it, which is critical for customer satisfaction and operational efficiency. Calculation: Order Cycle Time = Delivery Date - Order Date
- **Demand Variability:** This KPI measures the fluctuations in customer demand over time, helping to identify trends and adjust supply chain strategies accordingly. Calculation: Demand Variability = Standard Deviation of Demand over a Specific Period

4.6 Delivery and Transportation KPIs

Delivery and transportation KPIs are vital for managing the cost, efficiency, and reliability of moving goods through the supply chain.

They directly impact customer satisfaction and overall supply chain performance. The Top 3 KPIs in this area are:

- **On-Time Delivery (OTD):** This KPI measures the percentage of shipments delivered on time to customers, which is critical for maintaining service quality and customer satisfaction. Calculation: OTD = (Number of On-Time Deliveries / Total Deliveries) × 100

- **Freight Cost per Unit:** This KPI tracks the transportation cost per unit of goods shipped, helping to optimize shipping strategies and control logistics costs. Calculation: Freight Cost per Unit = Total Freight Costs / Total Units Shipped

- **Transportation Time:** This KPI tracks the total time to transport goods from the warehouse to the customer, aiming to reduce delivery times and improve service levels. Calculation: Transportation Time = Delivery Date - Shipping Date

4.7 Customer Satisfaction KPIs

Customer satisfaction KPIs gauge the effectiveness of the supply chain in meeting customer expectations, which is crucial for maintaining loyalty and enhancing brand reputation. The Top 3 customer satisfaction KPIs are:

- **Net Promoter Score (NPS):** NPS measures customer loyalty by assessing the likelihood that customers will recommend the company to others, reflecting overall satisfaction with the supply chain. Calculation: NPS = % Promoters - % Detractors

- **Customer Satisfaction Score (CSAT):** CSAT measures customer satisfaction with the products and services received, providing direct feedback on supply chain performance. Calculation: CSAT = (Number of Satisfied Customers / Total Customers Surveyed) × 100

- **Customer Order Fill Rate:** This KPI measures the percentage of customer orders that are entirely fulfilled without backorders, directly impacting customer satisfaction. Calculation: Fill Rate = (Orders Fulfilled Completely / Total Orders) × 100

4.8 Audit, Legal, and Regulatory Compliance KPIs

Compliance KPIs ensure the supply chain adheres to legal and regulatory requirements, minimizing risks and avoiding costly penalties. The Top 3 KPIs in this area are:

- **Policy Compliance Rate:** This KPI measures the degree to which supply chain activities adhere to established risk management policies and procedures, ensuring regulatory compliance. Calculation: Compliance Rate = (Compliant Activities / Total Activities Audited) × 100
- **Audit Findings Closure Rate:** This KPI tracks the percentage of audit findings resolved within the designated timeframe, reflecting the efficiency of the compliance management process. Calculation: Closure Rate = (Closed Findings / Total Findings) × 100
- **Regulatory Compliance Score:** This KPI evaluates the supply chain's adherence to relevant regulations, helping to identify and mitigate legal risks. It is calculated as a composite score based on compliance audits and regulatory assessments.

4.9 Financial Profitability KPIs

Financial KPIs in SCM assess the profitability and cost-effectiveness of supply chain operations, which are critical for overall business success. The Top 3 financial KPIs are:

- **Cost of Goods Sold (COGS):** COGS represents the direct costs attributable to producing goods sold, which are essential for managing cost structures and improving profitability. Calculation: COGS = Direct Material Costs + Direct Labor Costs + Manufacturing Overheads. Costs can be presented as a cost per unit or overall costs related to all goods sold over time.

- **Return on Supply Chain Assets (ROSCA):** ROSCA measures the efficiency of the supply chain in generating profit relative to its assets, indicating how well the supply chain contributes to the company's financial performance. Calculation: ROSCA = (Supply Chain-Related Earnings / Supply Chain Assets) × 100
- **Total Supply Chain Cost:** This KPI tracks the total costs associated with the supply chain, including procurement, production, warehousing, and transportation, helping to identify cost-saving opportunities. Calculation: Total Supply Chain Cost = Sum of all supply chain-related costs

4.10 Supply Chain BCP Resilience, Response, and Recovery KPIs

Resilience and recovery KPIs measure the supply chain's ability to withstand and recover from disruptions, ensuring continuity and minimizing the impact of adverse events. The Top 3 KPIs in this area are:

- **Supply Chain Resilience Index:** This composite metric assesses the supply chain's ability to recover from disruptions, considering the flexibility of supply sources and alternate logistic options. Calculation: A composite score based on recovery time, alternate sourcing, and supply chain redundancy metrics.
- **Incident Response Time:** This KPI measures the time taken to respond to supply chain disruptions, reflecting the agility and responsiveness of the supply chain management system. Calculation: Response Time = Incident Resolution Time - Incident Occurrence Time

- **Recovery Time Objective (RTO):** RTO measures the timeframe within which a business process must be restored after a disruption to avoid unacceptable consequences. Calculation: RTO = Maximum Acceptable Downtime before Significant Impact Occurs

These KPIs provide a comprehensive framework for assessing and improving supply chain management performance at the management and enterprise levels. By regularly monitoring these indicators, organizations can ensure that their supply chains remain resilient, efficient, and aligned with strategic objectives.

5.0 SCM Critical Success Factors (CSFs)

Critical Success Factors (CSFs) identify the essential outcomes companies must achieve for long-term success. CSFs provide a roadmap for aligning strategies, improving decision-making, and tracking operational performance. Organizations should review CSFs annually or after major strategic shifts. Below are the top ten SCM CSFs.

5.1 SCM Is in Alignment with Company Mission and Goals

Supply chains must align with the organization's strategic goals. As company strategies evolve, SCM processes must adapt. Tools like SWOT and PEST analysis help identify external and internal drivers of change.

Alignment Measures include:

- Time and cost to build or retool supply chains
- Responsiveness to market shifts
- Operational defects and their impact
- Strategic change volume and pace

Frequent misalignments indicate the need to reevaluate supply chain strategy.

5.2 SCM Is Adaptive to Industry Trends and Competition

SCM must quickly respond to emerging industry shifts. Adaptation measures track the company's flexibility and the cost of adjusting to external changes.

Adaptation Metrics include:

- Detection rate of market surprises
- Time and cost to reconfigure supply chains
- Competitive gap analysis
- Agility in contract negotiation and technology adoption

Continuous improvement and risk-taking are vital to survive evolving markets.

5.3 SCM Is in Compliance with Government Laws and Regulations

Effective SCM compliance minimizes regulatory risks and costs. Regulatory overhead should be monitored separately from operational costs.

Compliance Metrics include:

- Financial and human resource investment in compliance
- Costs of regulatory changes and penalties
- Regulatory feedback integration
- Opportunities for revenue from compliance leadership

Proactive regulatory engagement provides both risk reduction and competitive advantage.

5.4 SCM Communicates Effectively with Stakeholders

Transparent, timely stakeholder communication supports seamless operations and coordination across business units.

Communication Measures include:

- Stakeholder identification and their SCM roles
- Information delivery, subscriptions, and reporting
- Communication channel efficiency and feedback mechanisms

Effective communication ensures all participants are aligned and informed.

5.5 SCM Coordinates Successfully with Suppliers

Strong supplier coordination ensures reliable deliveries and quality control, which is vital for competitiveness.

Supplier Coordination Metrics include:

- Supplier performance monitoring and issue tracking
- Supplier governance capacity and due diligence
- Cost and time of supplier remediation or replacement

Building collaborative supplier partnerships strengthens resilience and market agility.

5.6 SCM Is Profitable and Predictable

Profitability must be measured at the supply chain level using practices like Activity-Based Costing (ABC).

Profitability Metrics include:

- Gross and Net Profit Margins
- Supply Chain Cost as a percentage of sales
- ROA, ROI, and risk-adjusted return metrics (Sharpe, Sortino)
- Inventory turnover, fulfillment times, and defect rates

Organizations must quantify supply chain-driven costs to optimize profitability.

5.7 SCM Threats and Risks Are Managed and Mitigated

Identifying and mitigating supply chain risks are essential to operational resilience.

Risk Management Metrics include:

- Comprehensive threat and risk catalogs
- Likelihood and impact modeling
- Implementation of threat controls and mitigations
- Supplier risk management
- Capital reserves and insurance coverage levels

Regular review of threats and control effectiveness maintains supply chain security.

5.8 SCM Customer Demands Are Analyzed and Understood

Accurately anticipating and fulfilling customer demand sustains supply chain relevance and profitability.

Customer Demand Metrics include:

- Forecast Accuracy (MAPE, MAD, Bias)
- Demand Variability (Coefficient of Variation, Standard Deviation)
- Customer Order Cycle Time
- Order Fill Rate, Line Fill Rate, and Backorder Levels
- Lost Sales and Net Promoter Score (NPS)

Data-driven demand analysis improves service quality, inventory management, and customer loyalty.

5.9 SCM Community and Environmental Impacts Considered

Supply chains must track environmental and community impacts to meet ESG goals and regulations.

Environmental Metrics include:

- Carbon footprint and CO2 emissions per unit
- Energy use and energy intensity
- Waste generation and diversion rates
- Water use efficiency
- Hazardous emissions and chemical usage

Social Metrics include:

- Labor standards compliance (wages, working conditions)
- Supplier diversity spending
- Human rights protections (anti-child labor, anti-forced labor)
- Community development investment
- Health and safety incident rates

Monitoring these metrics enhances brand reputation and risk management.

5.10 SCM Employee Satisfaction and Loyalty Are High

Employee satisfaction directly impacts supply chain performance, productivity, and innovation.

Satisfaction Metrics include:

- Overall Satisfaction and Engagement Index scores
- Work-Life Balance and Career Development Satisfaction
- Workplace Culture and Physical Environment Ratings

Loyalty Metrics include:

- Retention and voluntary turnover rates
- Average tenure and absenteeism rates
- Internal promotion and employee referral rates
- Engagement and participation in company initiatives
- Advocacy scores and recognition satisfaction

Tracking these indicators helps create an engaged, high-performing workforce.

Conclusion

By systematically measuring and optimizing these Critical Success Factors, companies can ensure their supply chain remains agile, efficient, resilient, and aligned with business goals and customer expectations.

6.0 Critical Supplier Controls Plan

After evaluating supplier threats, risks, and management approval, the SCRM team initiates the development of Critical Supplier Control Plans (CSCPs). While prior control plans may be leveraged, most require updates to address specific critical supplier risks. Recent studies show rising supply chain disruptions, with control failures and human error contributing significantly. Resilinc reported over 8,000 disruptions in early 2023, while McKinsey found that only 2% of companies have complete visibility into their multi-tier suppliers, increasing vulnerability.

Most disruptions are tied to fragmented control, ownership, and oversight. To address this, organizations should document CSCPs in line with NIST 800-18 standards, capturing control selection, ownership, operation, and oversight. Each CSCP must:

- Document the rationale for control selection.
- Assign clear ownership for implementation, operation, and monitoring.
- Detail operational processes, maintenance, testing, and escalation.
- Serve as a living document, regularly updated as risks evolve.

Maintaining dynamic CSCPs helps organizations proactively manage supplier risks and ensure long-term resilience. Industry standards like ISO 9001:2015 and IATF 16949 offer frameworks for structuring these controls, emphasizing quality and reaction planning.

6.1 Critical Supplier Control of Standardized Information Gathering

The first step in CSCP development is collecting and validating supplier information. The SCRM team identifies the required data—questionnaires, documentation, or interviews—typically using Standardized Information Gathering (SIG) tools, shared assessments, or trusted intermediaries.

Responsibilities are assigned to subject matter experts, and the collection frequency depends on supplier criticality (e.g., annual financials, more frequent security certifications).

Clear criteria are established to evaluate supplier responses, with pass/fail thresholds and red flag identification. A cross-functional team (legal, operations, security) assesses supplier risk profiles, documenting findings and any control gaps into a centralized repository for ongoing risk management.

The SCRM team provides guidance and ensures suppliers understand the requirements by maintaining open communication. This foundation of proper information gathering is essential for designing adequate targeted controls in the later CSCP phases.

6.2 Critical Supplier Control of Materials Quality Tests

The second stage of CSCP development documents the methods for ensuring supplier material quality. The SCRM team assigns specific teams or external partners to conduct material tests, outlining test frequency, procedures, equipment, and acceptance criteria. The CSCP oversees reviewing test results, ensuring assigned individuals have the expertise to objectively determine pass/fail outcomes. It also defines protocols for corrective actions, retesting, and escalation where quality issues persist. By documenting these procedures, the SCRM team ensures that material quality consistently meets standards, strengthening supply chain reliability and customer trust.

6.3 Critical Supplier Control of Physical Site Inspections

The third CSCP stage details controlling supplier site inspections. The SCRM team identifies responsible inspection teams and outlines inspection frequency, aligned with regulatory standards and supplier criticality. A comprehensive checklist specifies areas to assess, including security, safety, and operational controls. The CSCP assigns review responsibilities for inspection results and defines procedures for remediation, retesting, and escalation of serious issues.

This framework helps maintain supplier facility standards, minimizes operational risks, and reinforces supply chain resilience and reputation.

6.4 Critical Supplier Control of Interactions with External Stakeholders

In the fourth CSCP stage, the SCRM team documents methods to control supplier interactions with external stakeholders like regulators, customers, and partners. A designated team or partner reviews interactions regularly, following a checklist covering contracts, communications, and compliance. The CSCP outlines responsibilities for evaluating results, implementing corrective actions, retesting, and escalating persistent risks. Prompt escalation protects supply chain integrity and reputation.

Studies from Deloitte, McKinsey, PwC, and Capgemini highlight that companies with strong oversight of supplier interactions experience better operational reliability, reduced disruptions, and improved profitability, particularly in regulated industries like healthcare and manufacturing.

6.5 Critical Supplier Control of Financial Health Checks

The fifth CSCP stage details financial health controls for suppliers. A designated internal or external team conducts regular financial assessments, reviewing balance sheets, credit reports, and insurance coverage against documented benchmarks. The CSCP specifies who reviews financial data, oversees remediation efforts, and escalates critical financial risks. Rapid escalation ensures protective action when a supplier's financial health deteriorates.

A 2023 Dun & Bradstreet report found that 55% of disruptions stemmed from supplier financial failures, emphasizing the importance of proactive monitoring for supply chain resilience.

6.6 Critical Supplier Control of Security and Privacy Checks

The sixth CSCP stage focuses on documenting security and privacy checks for suppliers. The SCRM team must assign responsibility to internal experts or third-party auditors to verify compliance with industry standards (e.g., GDPR, HIPAA, CCPA). The security checklist covers certifications (ISO 27001, SOC 2), privacy policies, incident response plans, breach history, and vulnerability assessments. The CSCP details responsibilities for reviewing supplier information, remediation actions, and escalation for high-risk findings.

A 2023 IBM report showed that third-party breaches accounted for 19% of incidents, reinforcing the need for robust supplier security and privacy checks to protect organizational assets.

6.7 Critical Supplier Control of Criminal Background and Security Clearances

The seventh CSCP stage addresses background checks and security clearance verification. The SCRM team assigns specialists or third-party providers to perform reviews, documenting the scope, databases consulted (e.g., criminal records, debarred lists), and acceptance criteria. The CSCP defines responsibility for reviewing results, overseeing remediation, and escalating significant risks. Escalation ensures that critical security or legal concerns are addressed swiftly.

Industry research shows 40% of companies suffered disruptions from supplier fraud (KPMG, 2023), and reputational damage is cited as the top risk associated with third-party relationships (Deloitte, 2023).

6.8 Critical Supplier Control of Technology Standards

The eighth CSCP stage focuses on documenting technology checks for suppliers. The SCRM team assigns IT or cybersecurity experts to assess supplier infrastructure security, vulnerability management, data protection, and incident response. Key documentation includes network diagrams, software inventories, vulnerability reports, and recovery plans.

The CSCP defines review responsibilities, remediation procedures, and escalation for high-risk findings. Prompt escalation ensures critical risks are addressed. A 2023 ENISA report noted a 74% rise in supply chain attacks, with the average breach costing €1.23 million, underscoring the urgency of robust technology checks.

6.9 Critical Supplier Control of Workforce Health and Safety Checks

The ninth stage of CSCP details how to confirm that a supplier's health and safety practices are being followed. The SCRM team assigns specialists to assess policies, training records, incident investigations, and emergency preparedness plans, ensuring alignment with regulations (e.g., OSHA). The CSCP designates roles for reviewing health and safety data, remediation actions, and escalation procedures when serious risks emerge. Prompt escalation helps protect workers and the organizational reputation. According to the ILO (2023), 2.3 million deaths occur annually from workplace incidents, costing 3.94% of global GDP, emphasizing the need for strong safety oversight.

6.10 Critical Supplier Control of Reputation and Public Image

The final CSCP stage documents how to monitor and manage supplier reputation. The SCRM team assigns public relations or reputation management experts to review media coverage, social media sentiment, customer feedback, employee reviews, and legal records. Documentation specifies checklists, sources, and review frequencies based on risk appetite and supplier criticality. The CSCP outlines roles for analyzing reputational data, setting remediation protocols, and escalating serious concerns. Prompt escalation protects the organization's brand and supply chain stability. A 2023 Deloitte study found 87% of consumers would stop buying from companies linked to unethical practices, highlighting the critical nature of reputation management.

7.0 Supplier Management and Oversight Plan (SMOP)

The SMOP is a strategic framework for managing critical supplier relationships, detailing responsibilities for deliveries, services, quality, financial transactions, compliance, health and safety, incident response, and risk management. It is especially vital for large organizations where multiple teams engage suppliers. The SMOP fosters proactive oversight, transparency, and continuous improvement, aligning supplier performance with strategic goals. It supports collaboration by defining clear expectations and escalation procedures. As a living document, the SMOP must be regularly updated to address evolving risks and supplier changes, ensuring resilient and efficient supply chain operations.

7.1 Supplier Management and Oversight Plan for Deliveries

SMOP-Deliveries standardizes procedures for placing, tracking, and verifying supplier orders. It defines communication channels, order formats, and stakeholder roles, minimizing errors and ensuring transparency.

Tracking mechanisms like shipment tracking and EDI provide real-time visibility. Procedures require inspections, documentation of discrepancies, and defined acceptance criteria upon delivery. Regular performance monitoring via KPIs—such as delivery timeliness and order accuracy—supports continuous improvement and operational excellence.

7.2 Supplier Management and Oversight Plan for Services

SMOP-Services defines how to request, monitor, and inspect services from critical suppliers. It specifies communication channels, formats, and stakeholder roles for initiating service requests, ensuring clarity and minimizing errors.

Tracking tools like service management platforms monitor progress, address bottlenecks, and maintain schedules. Upon service completion, outcomes are reviewed against specifications and SLAs, with deviations documented and corrected. KPIs such as service quality and responsiveness are tracked to drive continuous improvement and optimize service delivery.

7.3 Supplier Management and Oversight Plan for Quality

SMOP-Quality defines steps for maintaining rigorous quality standards for materials from critical suppliers. It outlines collaboration on setting precise specifications, performance benchmarks, and compliance expectations.

Monitoring mechanisms include supplier-led inspections, independent audits, and periodic reviews. Deviations trigger corrective action protocols, including clear communication, escalation procedures, and root-cause analysis. This structured approach ensures suppliers meet quality standards, supports continuous improvement, and enhances supply chain resilience.

7.4 Supplier Management and Oversight Plan for Financial Transactions

SMOP-Financials outlines controls to manage financial obligations with suppliers transparently and accurately. It details payment terms, invoicing procedures, and dispute resolution channels. Invoice reconciliation involves verifying documentation against orders using technology platforms for efficiency. Strong internal controls—such as authorization hierarchies and audits—are emphasized to prevent errors and fraud. Transparent communication processes are maintained to address payment delays and foster trust, ensuring financial risks are proactively managed.

7.5 Supplier Management and Oversight Plan for Legal and Contracts

SMOP-Legal defines steps for managing contractual requirements with suppliers. It includes identifying, documenting, and reviewing contracts, SLAs, and regulatory obligations, ensuring clear articulation of rights, responsibilities, and terms such as delivery, quality, payments, and jurisdiction. Triggers for contract reviews include significant scope or pricing changes. Designated teams, such as legal counsel or procurement specialists, oversee legal matters to minimize disputes. Clear communication and escalation protocols are established to proactively handle legal or contractual concerns.

7.6 Supplier Management and Oversight Plan for Technology

SMOP-Technology governs the management and oversight of supplier technology operations. It specifies installation, integration, maintenance responsibilities, and compatibility standards to ensure seamless operations.

Roles for IT support and technical teams are clearly defined for issue management. The plan details handling repairs, upgrades, and end-of-life transitions for technology assets. Communication protocols ensure ongoing visibility into supplier technology performance, enabling proactive risk mitigation.

7.7 Supplier Management and Oversight Plan for Compliance

SMOP-Compliance outlines processes to ensure supplier adherence to laws, regulations, and internal standards. It includes identifying applicable compliance requirements and assigning roles to compliance officers, QA personnel, or legal teams. Procedures for conducting regular audits, documenting findings, and evaluating supplier compliance are established. Communication protocols for addressing violations and escalation paths for unresolved risks are emphasized, ensuring continuous ethical and legal compliance across the supply chain.

7.8 Supplier Management and Oversight Plan for Incident Response

SMOP-Incidents documents steps for preparing and responding to supplier disruptions, including natural disasters, cyberattacks, and equipment failures. It defines incident types, impacts, and escalation procedures. Internal teams, like crisis managers and procurement specialists, are assigned clear roles. Communication protocols for incident reporting, escalation to senior management, and stakeholder notification are established. Incident evidence must be preserved for investigations, insurance claims, and continuous improvement to strengthen resilience.

7.9 Supplier Management and Oversight Plan for Business Continuity

SMOP-Continuity ensures that critical suppliers have adequate business continuity plans (BCPs) to sustain operations during disruptions. It outlines reviewing suppliers' BCPs for completeness, alignment with organizational goals, and risk coverage. Assigned teams oversee supplier continuity plans and ensure clear communication during disruptions. Expectations for testing, reporting, and escalation protocols for critical incidents are established. Documenting business continuity events supports post-incident reviews and continuous resilience improvement.

7.10 Supplier Management and Oversight Plan for Risk

SMOP-Risk focuses on proactively identifying, assessing, and mitigating supplier-related risks. It specifies periodic risk assessments covering operations, financial health, and compliance. Responsibilities are assigned to risk managers and other stakeholders. The plan outlines communication, escalation for critical risks, and documentation of incidents and disruptions. Capturing and analyzing risk events enables continuous learning, strengthens risk management capabilities, and improves supply chain resilience.

8.0 Software Supply Chain Controls Plan

The Software Supply Chain Controls Plan (SSCP) provides a structured framework for managing interactions with software suppliers, covering delivery, patching, monitoring, integration, quality, security, and incident response. It fosters transparency, accountability, and continuous improvement, ensuring supplier software aligns with security, quality, and compliance standards. The SSCP is a living document, regularly updated to reflect evolving threats and supplier changes, helping organizations optimize supply chain resilience and manage software-related risks.

8.1 Software Bill of Materials (SBOM)

A Software Bill of Materials (SBOM) lists all components, libraries, and dependencies in software products, enabling:

- Vulnerability Management: Identifying risks early.
- License Compliance: Ensuring legal use of components.
- Incident Response: Quickly isolating affected components.

The SSCP-SBOM section specifies SBOM formats (e.g., SPDX, CycloneDX), assigns review responsibilities, and requires automation to manage SBOM updates. Clear communication protocols address discrepancies, ensuring continuous risk visibility and software integrity.

8.2 Software Composition Analysis (SCA)

Software Composition Analysis (SCA) scans software to detect:

- Vulnerabilities: Proactive risk management.

- License Compliance: Mitigating legal risks.
- Obsolete Components: Identifying unsupported software.
- Community Health: Assessing open-source project stability.

The SSCP-SCA section defines SCA tool requirements, assigns internal ownership for SCA reviews, and sets clear protocols for reporting and addressing vulnerabilities. A robust SCA process enhances supply chain security and operational resilience.

8.3 Software Provenance and Origin

Software Provenance and Origin analysis ensures components originate from trusted sources and their integrity is protected throughout development and delivery, mitigating supply chain attacks.

The SSCP-SPO section should require:

- Code Signing: Verification of trusted digital signatures.
- Secure Repositories: Use of protected distribution channels.
- Hash Verification: Validation against known-good cryptographic hashes.
- Provenance Tracking: Recording development and distribution history.

A designated team must perform these verifications, assess risks, and manage remediation. Communication protocols should define how discrepancies are addressed and escalated to protect software integrity and organizational resilience.

8.4 Software Licensing Requirements

Software Licensing compliance mitigates legal risks by ensuring software use aligns with licensing terms.

The SSCP-SLR section must cover:

- License Inventory: Tracking software licenses, terms, and expirations.

- Compliance Audits: Regularly checking usage against license terms.
- License Optimization and Renewals: Managing procurement and minimizing costs.

Assigned teams must oversee license management, audits, and discrepancy resolution. The plan should also address specific restrictions (e.g., deployment location, usage limits, export controls). Transparent processes prevent unauthorized use and protect against legal exposure.

8.5 Software Testing and Quality Assurance

Software Testing and Quality Assurance (STQA) verifies that supplier software meets functionality, performance, security, and reliability requirements.

The SSCP-STQA section should require:

- Functional, Performance, Stress, and Security Testing
- Compatibility and Usability Testing
- Error Handling Validation

Assigned QA teams must conduct and review testing, track issues, and collaborate with suppliers to resolve them. Communication protocols ensure that defects or delays are escalated appropriately. Frameworks like the OWASP Application Security Verification Standard (ASVS) can guide secure development practices.

8.6 Software Open Source Management

Software Open Source Management (SOSM) ensures open-source components are tracked, assessed for risks, and used responsibly.

The SSCP-SOSM section should define:

- Inventory and Tracking: Catalog components, versions, licenses, vulnerabilities.

- Risk Assessment and Policy Enforcement: Vet components and enforce selection standards.
- Trusted Sources: Verify authors, repositories, and integrity.
- Upgrade Management: Procedures for evaluating and deploying updates.

An internal team (e.g., software engineers, security analysts) should oversee SOSM, handle issues, and escalate critical vulnerabilities. Effective SOSM ensures license compliance, security, and supply chain transparency.

8.7 Software Vulnerability Management

Software Vulnerability Management (SVM) identifies, assesses, and remediates vulnerabilities across supplier software to maintain security and resilience.

The SSCP-SVM section must cover:

- Vulnerability Identification: Involves scans, penetration tests, and verification processes.
- Patching Oversight: Track remediation and validate patch effectiveness.
- Secure Configurations: Enforce hardened setups and monitor deviations.
- Communication Protocols: Clear internal and supplier coordination for vulnerabilities and escalations.

Security analysts or vulnerability managers must lead the SVM process, ensuring timely fixes and reducing the risks of cyberattacks.

8.8 Software End-of-Life (SEOL) Support and Code Escrow

SEOL management ensures business continuity after software support ends.

The SSCP-SEOL section should include:

- EOL Support Verification: Confirm the supplier's ongoing patching and support policies.
- Risk Mitigation Plans: Assess EOL risks and plan upgrades or compensating controls.
- Communication and Planning: Notification protocols for upcoming EOL transitions.

Organizations should also secure software escrow arrangements to protect against supplier insolvency. A robust SEOL strategy minimizes operational disruptions and strengthens resilience.

8.9 Software Architecture and Design Documentation

Software Architecture and Design Documentation (SADD) provides detailed blueprints of a system's structure, behavior, and data flows, supporting transparency, maintainability, and risk mitigation.

The SSCP-SADD section should include:

- Architecture Descriptions: High-level system structure.
- System Diagrams and Network Flows: Visuals for integration and communication paths.
- Data Dictionaries and Logging Specifications: Details of data formats and logging mechanisms.

An internal team (e.g., software architects, security analysts) should review the SADD for risks and design flaws. Clear communication protocols must be established to address any issues. A robust SADD review enhances software security, integration, and maintainability.

8.10 Software Performance Monitoring and Observability

Software Performance Monitoring and Observability (SPMO) involves real-time data collection to track application health, detect issues early, and optimize resource use.

The SSCP-SPMO section should define:

- Metrics and KPIs: Track performance (e.g., response times, error rates).
- Monitoring Tools: Specify APM tools and observability platforms.
- Alerting and Reporting: Set thresholds, generate alerts, and define escalation procedures.

A designated team (e.g., site reliability or DevOps engineers) should interpret metrics, address performance issues, and ensure SLA compliance. Clear communication channels must support fast incident resolution. Effective SPMO ensures supplier software remains reliable and efficient.

9.0 Capability Maturity Model (CMM)

Human error, limited training, siloed operations, and outdated processes often drive risks in supply chains. Capability Maturity Models (CMMs) offer a structured way to assess and improve processes, aiming for fewer errors and greater resilience. Originally developed at Carnegie Mellon's Software Engineering Institute, CMMs like Capability Maturity Model Integration (CMMI) have expanded across industries, helping businesses optimize efficiency, agility, and risk management.

A supply chain management (SCM) CMM assessment identifies gaps, sets benchmarks, and supports systematic improvement, which is critical for achieving supply chain excellence.

9.1 Supply Chain Maturity Models

The Supply Chain Operations Reference (SCOR) Model, developed by the Association for Supply Chain Management (APICS), is a leading framework for measuring supply chain performance across five core areas:

- Plan: Demand forecasting, inventory, and capacity planning.
- Source: Supplier management and procurement.
- Make: Manufacturing, quality control, and production.
- Deliver: Order fulfillment, warehousing, and distribution.
- Return: Managing product returns and recycling.

SCOR offers performance metrics such as Perfect Order Fulfillment, Order Fulfillment Lead Time, Total Supply Chain Management Cost, and Cash-to-Cash Cycle Time. Maturity levels under SCOR include:

- Level 1: High-level supply chain design.
- Level 2: Process categories (e.g., Make-to-Order).
- Level 3+: Detailed workflows and customized best practices.

Alternative models include Gartner's Supply Chain Maturity Model (SCMM) and the American Productivity & Quality Center's (APQC) Process Classification Framework (PCF), both of which offer frameworks for maturity progression and benchmarking.

9.2 Benefits of an SCM CMM Assessment

CMM assessments deliver several advantages:

- Comprehensive Evaluation: Holistic review of supply chain strengths and weaknesses.

- Standardization: Common process language enables better cross-functional collaboration.

- Strategic Alignment: Ensures supply chain initiatives support the overall business strategy.

- Enhanced Risk Management: Mature organizations can predict and mitigate disruptions better.

- Continuous Improvement: A CMM roadmap drives progress toward higher operational maturity.

- Informed Decision-Making: Baseline metrics reveal gaps and opportunities for targeted investment.

9.3 Approach to Conducting an SCM CMM Assessment

Conducting a CMM assessment follows these steps:

1. Define Scope and Objectives: Clarify the business goals and processes in focus.
2. Select a Relevant Model: SCOR is widely preferred for its depth.
3. Baseline Assessment: Gather data through surveys, interviews, and system reviews.
4. Gap Analysis: Compare current capabilities to desired future states.
5. Roadmap Creation: Define projects, allocate resources, and set KPIs.
6. Implement and Monitor: Launch improvements and measure progress consistently.

9.4 Developing a Roadmap to Achieve the Desired Target State

Key elements of a practical roadmap include:

- Clear Goals: Measurable targets aligned with business priorities.
- Prioritized Actions: Focus first on improvements with the most significant performance impact.
- Resource Planning: Allocate necessary staffing, tools, and budget.
- Stakeholder Engagement: Secure buy-in from leadership and frontline teams.
- Agility: Adjust the roadmap as challenges and opportunities evolve.

9.5 CMM Benchmarking and Best Practices

Benchmarking against industry standards highlights gaps and improvement opportunities. SCOR provides a vast repository of best practices that organizations can adopt to accelerate their maturity journey and ensure efficient and competitive supply chain operations.

9.6 Capability Maturity, Performance, and Profitability

Higher supply chain maturity correlates directly with better performance and profitability:

- 15% lower supply chain costs and 50% higher asset returns (Accenture).
- 2-3% higher profit margins among mature organizations (Deloitte).

Key metrics include:

- Total Supply Chain Management Cost
- Return on Supply Chain Assets (ROSCA)
- Cash-to-Cash Cycle Time

Mature supply chains use data-driven insights to optimize operations and sustain competitive advantage.

9.7 Capability Maturity, Market Share, and Competitive Advantage

Mature supply chains translate into superior market performance:

- 2-3% higher annual market share growth (McKinsey).
- 30% greater likelihood of outperforming competitors (Supply Chain Council).

Key enablers include:

- Cost Efficiency: Competitive pricing through lean operations.

- Agility: Rapid adaptation to market shifts.
- Supplier Collaboration: Driving innovation and quality.

9.8 Capability Maturity, Customer Satisfaction, and Brand Loyalty

With improved supply chain maturity, customer satisfaction scores increase by 20% (Bain) and customer loyalty by 35% (PwC).

Drivers include:

- Reliable Fulfillment: On-time, accurate, and high-quality deliveries.
- Responsive Service: Fast handling of inquiries and complaints.
- Visibility and Transparency: Order and inventory status are readily accessible.
- Proactive Resolution: Addressing problems before they reach the customer.

9.9 Capability Maturity, Improved Quality, and Lower Defect Costs

Mature supply chains improve product quality and lower defect costs:

- 20% reduction in defect rates (ASQ).
- 15% lower cost of poor quality (Aberdeen Group).

Maturity emphasizes process discipline, root cause analysis, and preventive measures, boosting product reliability and profitability.

9.10 Capability Maturity, Bolstering Image and Marketing Communications

Communicating supply chain maturity can enhance brand positioning and customer trust. According to the Reputation Institute, this practice can lead to a 15% increase in customer trust and a 20% improvement in brand perception. Additionally, the Global Supply Chain Institute reports that companies that effectively communicate their supply chain maturity are 25% more successful in attracting and retaining top talent.

Effective communication strategies include:

- Clear Messaging: Publicize achievements and maturity milestones.
- Engaging Content: Share case studies, whitepapers, and metrics.
- Thought Leadership: Publish insights and participate in industry events.
- Stakeholder Engagement: Maintain open channels with customers, suppliers, and investors.

Organizations build trust, strengthen their brand, and secure competitive advantage by promoting their maturity journey.

10.0 Resilience Maturity Model (RMM)

Operational resilience, contingency planning, and disaster recovery are fundamental to effective supply chain risk management. Resilient supply chains anticipate threats, prepare with resources and strategies, withstand various hazards, absorb impacts, and quickly recover operations and data. Resilience Maturity Models (RMMs) offer a structured method to assess current resilience levels, pinpoint vulnerabilities, and strengthen capabilities systematically across domains such as cybersecurity, disaster recovery, and business continuity.

10.1 CERT Resilience Management Model (CERT-RMM)

Developed by Carnegie Mellon's Software Engineering Institute, the CERT-RMM helps organizations build operational resilience against cyber threats, disasters, and crises. Widely used by U.S. government agencies like DHS, DoD, and FEMA, it covers four categories:

- Enterprise Management (EM): Process focus, definition, and staff training.
- Engineering (ENG): Asset management, configuration control, vulnerability resolution.
- Operations (OPS): Incident response, service continuity, and technology management.
- Process Management (PM): Measurement, process institutionalization, and compliance auditing.

This structured approach integrates resilience into daily operations and strategic planning.

10.2 DRI Resilience Risk Index

The Disaster Recovery Institute International (DRI) developed the Resilience Risk Index to help organizations prioritize resilience by identifying and ranking top operational, strategic, and emerging risks.

Based on global industry surveys, the index highlights threats like cyberattacks, IT failures, natural disasters, and supply chain disruptions. Trend analysis enables better long-term risk planning, while global insights make the tool especially valuable for multinational organizations. The index serves as a data-driven foundation for developing targeted resilience strategies.

10.3 Business Continuity Institute (BCI) Good Practice Guidelines (GPG)

The BCI GPG provides a global benchmark for Business Continuity Management (BCM). Its framework includes:

- Policy and Program Management: Establishing leadership commitment.

- Business continuity management (BCM) should be embedded into the organizational culture for successful implementation.
- The Analysis phase outlines steps for conducting Business Impact Analyses (BIA) and risk assessments.
- The design phase describes principles for crafting resource strategies and recovery plans.
- Operational Execution: This stage involves building and maintaining actionable business continuity plans.
- Validation: Regular exercises and testing.
- Organization and People: Defining roles and assembling BCM teams.

BCI emphasizes regular updates and continuous improvement to build adaptive, effective continuity programs.

10.4 ISO 22301 Business Continuity Management Systems

ISO 22301 is the internationally recognized Business Continuity Management Systems (BCMS) standard. It outlines:

- Scope and Objectives: Safeguarding operations against disruptions.
- Leadership Commitment: Embedding continuity across organizational practices.
- Risk Assessment and BIA: Identifying vulnerabilities and critical dependencies.
- Strategy Development: Creating mitigation strategies, such as supplier diversification.
- BCP Implementation: Detailed, actionable business continuity plans.

- Performance Monitoring: Regular evaluations and drills.
- Continuous Improvement: Adapting the BCMS to emerging threats.

ISO 22301 promotes a cycle of planning, testing, and enhancing organizational resilience.

10.5 Resilience Rising Maturity Model

The Resilience Rising Maturity Model focuses on adapting to global challenges such as climate change and geopolitical instability. Its progression includes:

- Foundational Resilience: Basic emergency response and risk awareness.
- Adaptive Resilience: Feedback loops, organizational learning, cultural integration.
- Proactive Resilience: Predictive analytics and scenario planning.
- Transformational Resilience: Full integration of resilience into strategic frameworks.

Organizations, particularly those in high-risk industries, can build antifragile systems that strengthen through adversity.

10.6 SMI Resilience Maturity Model (RMM)

Created by the Strategic Marketplace Initiative (SMI), this model helps healthcare organizations strengthen supply chain resilience with four maturity levels:

- Preparedness
- Responsiveness
- Resiliency
- Collaborative Immunity

It provides a scoring system to assess resilience and a playbook for advancing through the stages. Developed with diverse stakeholder input, the model emphasizes resilience alongside sustainability, which is crucial for industries with significant social and environmental impacts.

10.7 Gartner's Supply Chain Resilience Maturity Model

Gartner's framework tracks progression through:

- Foundational: Basic risk awareness.
- Visibility: Transparency with suppliers and customers
- Predictability: Scenario modeling and predictive tools.
- Resiliency: Embedding resilience considerations in decision-making processes.
- Sustainability: Integrating resilience into corporate governance.

The model stresses proactive preparation, not reactive response, and encourages the use of digital twins and real-time risk dashboards to anticipate disruptions.

10.8 Maturity and Resilience in Supply Chains – A Systematic Review

A 2022 Emerald study linked supply chain maturity and resilience, identifying 13 key factors:

- Agility: Ability to adapt quickly.
- Environments: External influences like regulations and sustainability.
- Capabilities and Resources: Financial strength, technological capacity, human capital.
- Customer Focus: Service quality and satisfaction.
- Collaboration: Internal and external cooperation.
- Cost Management: Efficient inventory and operational practices.

- Culture of Innovation: Fostering trust, learning, and continuous improvement.
- Strategic Focus: Risk management and internationalization.
- Flexibility: Managing demand variability.
- Leadership and Management: Strong governance practices.
- Metrics and KPIs: Measuring resilience progress.
- Process Optimization: Lean and agile methods.
- Technology and Tools: Advanced analytics and decision support systems.

Maturity and resilience are deeply interconnected, emphasizing the importance of strong management, innovation, and agility.

10.9 FEMA HAZUS

Hazus is FEMA's GIS-based modeling tool that estimates natural disasters' physical, social, and economic impacts (earthquakes, floods, hurricanes, tsunamis). It supports:

- Mitigation Planning: Identifying vulnerabilities.
- Preparedness Efforts: Scenario modeling.
- Response and Recovery: Estimating real-time impacts.

Hazus supports continuous assessment, measurement, and improvement, which are vital elements of a resilience maturity framework.

10.10 European Resilience Management Guideline (ERMG)

Developed through the Smart Mature Resilience (SMR) Project, the ERMG helps European cities strengthen resilience against risks like climate change and infrastructure failures. Key tools include:

- Resilience Maturity Model (RMM): Structured resilience assessment stages.

- Risk Systemicity Questionnaire (RSQ): Mapping interconnected risks.

- Resilience Information Portal (RIP): Sharing data and best practices.
- City Resilience Dynamics Tool (CRD): Modeling risk scenarios and responses.
- Resilience Building Policies Tool (RBPT): Embedding resilience in policy.

The ERMG promotes iterative, participatory resilience planning that strengthens city governance and emergency management.

Conclusion

This essay highlighted the importance of building resilience to help avoid and minimize business disruptions, ensure business continuity, and improve business recovery after a supply chain breakdown. Supply Chain Resilience can be measured and improved using Resilience Maturity Models. RMMs help organizations assess their current state, identify gaps, and prioritize improvements. I also discussed specific tools and guidelines for resilience management, such as Hazus and the European Resilience Management Guideline, emphasizing the role of continuous assessment, planning, implementation, measurement, and improvement. Embracing resilience management practices enables organizations to adapt to challenges, minimize disruptions, and enhance their long-term competitiveness.

REFERENCES

- The Business Continuity Institute. 2023. Supply Chain Resilience Report 2023. BCI.
- Thales. 2023. Data Threat Report 2023. Thales Group.
- Weber Shandwick. 2023. Global Reputation Risk and Opportunity Report 2023. Weber Shandwick.
- World Economic Forum. 2023. Global Risks Report 2023. World Economic Forum.

- Aberdeen Group. "Supply Chain Management Best Practices." Aberdeen Group Research, n.d.
- Gartner, Inc. "Supply Chain Management and Disruption Mitigation Practices." Gartner Research Reports, n.d.
- Deloitte. "Supply Chain Audit and Risk Management Survey." Deloitte Insights, n.d.
- KPMG. "Supply Chain Executive Survey." KPMG, n.d.
- International Organization for Standardization. "ISO 22361:2022 - Crisis Management Guidelines." Geneva: ISO, 2022. https://www.iso.org/standard/50267.html.
- International Organization for Standardization. "ISO 22301:2019 - Business Continuity Management Systems—Requirements." Geneva: ISO, 2019. https://www.iso.org/standard/75106.html.
- Zubulake v. UBS Warburg, 220 F.R.D. 212 (S.D.N.Y. 2003).
- Druker, Peter F. The Practice of Management. New York: Harper & Row, 1954.
- Deming, W. Edwards. "Out of the Crisis." Cambridge, MA: MIT Press, 1982.
- Accenture. "Supply Chain Capability Maturity Study." Accenture Reports, n.d.
- McKinsey & Company. "Supply Chain Maturity and Competitive Advantage." McKinsey Reports, n.d.
- Supply Chain Council. "Supply Chain Maturity and Performance Benchmarking Study." APICS/Supply Chain Council Reports, n.d.
- Bain & Company. "Supply Chain Maturity and Customer Satisfaction." Bain & Company Reports, n.d.
- PwC. "Supply Chain Capability Maturity and Customer Loyalty Survey." PricewaterhouseCoopers Reports, n.d.
- American Society for Quality (ASQ). "Supply Chain Capability Maturity and Quality Outcomes." ASQ Reports, n.d.

- Reputation Institute. "Supply Chain Excellence and Corporate Reputation." Reputation Institute Research Reports, n.d.
- Global Supply Chain Institute. "Communication of Supply Chain Capabilities and Talent Retention." University of Tennessee, n.d.
- Carnegie Mellon University Software Engineering Institute. "CERT Resilience Management Model (CERT-RMM)." Carnegie Mellon University, Software Engineering Institute, n.d.
- Disaster Recovery Institute International (DRI). "Global Risk and Resilience Trends Report." Disaster Recovery Institute International, 9th ed., 2022. https://drii.org/pressreleases/details/7515724014a6/dri-international-releases-9th-annual-global-risk-and-resilience-trends-report.
- Business Continuity Institute (BCI). "Good Practice Guidelines." The Business Continuity Institute, n.d. https://www.thebci.org/resource/good-practice-guidelines.html.
- Smart Mature Resilience (SMR) Project. "European Resilience Management Guideline." Smart Mature Resilience Project, European Union, n.d. https://smr-project.eu/tools/maturity-model-guide/.
- FEMA. "Hazus: FEMA's Methodology for Estimating Potential Losses from Disasters." Federal Emergency Management Agency, n.d. https://www.fema.gov/hazus.
- Software Engineering Institute, Carnegie Mellon University. "CERT Resilience Management Model (CERT-RMM)." Carnegie Mellon University, n.d.
- American Society for Quality (ASQ). "Quality Management Systems and Defect Rate Reduction through CMM." American Society for Quality Reports, n.d.
- Emerald Group Publishing. "Maturity and Resilience in Supply Chains: A Systematic Review." International Journal of Industrial Engineering and Operations Management, 2022. https://doi.org/10.1108/IJIEOM-08-2022-0035.

- SMR Project. "Resilience Rising Maturity Model." Smart Mature Resilience Project, European Union, n.d. https://smr-project.eu/tools/maturity-model-guide/.
- SMI Supply Chain. "Resilience Maturity Model (RMM)." SMI Supply Chain, n.d. https://www.smisupplychain.com/wp-content/uploads/2023/09/SMI-Resilience-Maturity-Model.pdf.

Insights and Actions

Chapter 5 focuses on the fourth stage of the vendor management lifecycle: monitoring and managing vendor relationships after onboarding, with a strong emphasis on risk management and governance as guiding principles throughout the process. Key insights for vendor risk management include:

- Effective oversight and ongoing due diligence of vendor performance are essential to maintain alignment with organizational expectations and contractual commitments. Regular reviews and audits are indispensable for maintaining accountability and driving continuous improvement.
- Collaborative efforts among stakeholders, guided by tools such as RACI charts to clarify responsibilities and manage hand-offs between client and vendor, are essential.
- Take a balanced approach to risk assessment, combining quantitative and qualitative methods to prioritize and address identified risks effectively. Review regularly and adapt risk management strategies in response to performance relationships or changes in the external environment.
- Contract management is a two-way street; both the organization and the vendor must uphold their commitments, including deliverables and payments.
- Guard against the use of disproportionate economic power or aggressive tactics, as such approaches ultimately erode trust and undermine long-term relationships.
- Open and constructive communication is vital to successful vendor management. Ground feedback in facts and be transparent. Focus on collaborative problem-solving rather than assigning blame or speculating on motives.
- Quality control is different from quality assurance. Quality control involves taking proactive measures such as regular

audits, testing, and validation processes to ensure that products and services meet organizational standards.

Effective TPRM stewardship requires a proactive and structured approach to managing third-party relationships. By leveraging clear documentation, regular oversight, and robust governance tools (such as R&R and RACI matrices, escalation protocols, and stewardship meetings), organizations can reduce risk, clarify expectations, and ensure that third-party services are fit for purpose. Materiality should guide the level of diligence applied to each relationship. Keep these principles in mind when managing your third-party risk management program:

- Organizational culture shapes the approach to relationships with vendors and suppliers. Aim for a collaborative model that still safeguards the organization from undue risk or unfavorable pricing.
- Clearly define and demark delivery of services. Ensure that all deliverables, reporting cadences, and responsibilities are explicitly documented. Use detailed roles and responsibilities (R&R) matrices to delineate provider and client obligations side by side.
- Establish a calendar of key activities and deliverables and institute regular stewardship meetings with providers to review service performance, address issues, and plan for upcoming changes.
- Document escalation protocols and maintain a current Authorized Personnel and Emergency Contact (APEC) list.
- Keep up-to-date and accurate notes of issues as they arise so that the organization may measure progress and provide appropriate feedback throughout the relationship, including at its potential termination.

Effective supply chain management requires a holistic, integrated approach that combines robust operations, risk management, resilience planning, governance, and continuous improvement. By leveraging structured frameworks, rigorous controls, clear metrics, and proactive oversight, organizations can achieve supply chains that are reliable, resilient, and responsive, supporting long-term business success. Here are three essential takeaways from our discussion on supply chain operations:

Business-as-usual operations require systematic integration of ten core operational functions with robust problem management capabilities. Effective SCM operations encompass supplier due diligence and onboarding, technology integration and automation, continuous monitoring, inventory management, resilience planning, controls deployment, maintenance and change management, training and exercises, stakeholder reporting, and governance oversight. Organizations must complement these with comprehensive problem management capabilities covering issues remediation, audits and regulatory examinations, technology obsolescence, incident response, crisis management, root-cause analysis, legal investigations, records retention, supplier deficiencies, and insurance claims—creating a unified operational framework that prevents disruptions and ensures rapid recovery when issues occur.

Comprehensive control plans must address traditional and software supply chain risks through structured documentation and monitoring. Organizations require two complementary control frameworks: Critical Supplier Control Plans (CSCPs) covering ten traditional areas including standardized information gathering, materials quality testing, physical site inspections, external stakeholder interactions, financial health checks, security and privacy verification, background checks, technology standards, workforce safety, and reputation monitoring; and Software Supply Chain Control Plans (SSCPs) addressing ten software-specific areas including Software Bill of Materials (SBOM), composition analysis, provenance verification, licensing compliance, testing and quality assurance, open source management, vulnerability management, end-of-life support, architecture documentation, and performance monitoring.

Maturity models drive measurable performance improvements with proven ROI across multiple business dimensions. Organizations implementing Capability Maturity Models (CMMs) and Resilience Maturity Models (RMMs) achieve quantifiable benefits, including:

- 15% lower supply chain costs
- 50% higher asset returns
- 2-3% higher profit margins
- 20% improvement in customer satisfaction
- 35% increase in customer loyalty
- 20% reduction in defect rates
- 2-3% higher annual market share growth

The structured assessment and improvement approach, utilizing frameworks such as SCOR, CERT-RMM, ISO 22301, and Gartner's models, enables organizations to systematically progress through maturity levels while building operational resilience, competitive advantage, and long-term sustainability through continuous measurement and improvement cycles.

Chapter 6

Incident Response

Introduction

In Chapter 6, Gary and Matt provide hard-won guidance about responding to incidents involving third parties, that is based on their many years spent in the trenches. Gary begins by exploring the complexities organizations face when a third-party vendor is compromised and outlines a structured approach to managing these incidents. He makes the essential point that a company's security depends not only on its internal controls but also on the security practices of its vendors and service providers. To overcome the lack of direct control over your vendor's security hygiene, Gary emphasizes the importance of preparedness, starting with the establishment of a robust vendor risk management (VRM) program. This program should involve thorough due diligence before onboarding vendors, continuous monitoring of their security posture, and the inclusion of explicit contract clauses regarding incident reporting and breach management.

Matt further explores the intricate relationship between third-party risk management (TPRM) and incident response, highlighting the growing prevalence and complexity of cyber incidents involving vendors and suppliers in today's business environment. He stresses the importance of establishing a clear operational context for every third-party relationship, utilizing tools such as dependency analysis, business impact assessments, data flow diagrams, and software bills of materials to understand the potential impacts a vendor's security incident could have on the organization's operations and data. Matt goes on to note that not all third parties are of equal importance, and organizations must identify and prioritize those vendors that are truly critical to their resilience, ensuring these relationships receive heightened diligence and oversight.

Together, they convey the criticality of preparedness to deal with the inevitable incidents as we are long past the cliché of "it's not if but when." Instead, it's a constant disruptive threat that firms must diligently prepare for.

Responding to a Vendor Compromise: A Guide for Companies

Gary Hayslip

Organizations lack direct control over their vendors' security hygiene and therefore it is critical to be prepared, beginning with the establishment of a robust vendor risk management (VRM) program.

In today's interconnected digital landscape, your business's security depends not just on your internal cybersecurity measures but also on the security posture of your vendors and third-party service providers. A breach or compromise at your vendor can directly affect your operations, data security, and reputation. This is one of the most challenging parts of managing a security program as you have no direct control of your vendors' security hygiene, so it's best to be prepared.

Thus, having a robust incident response plan that includes procedures for handling vendor compromises is critical. The following is a recommended process for managing this type of risk exposure in your organization and its business operations.

Establish a Vendor Risk Management Program

Before delving into the incident response for a vendor compromise, it's crucial to have a vendor risk management (VRM) program in place. This program should assess and manage the risks associated with third-party vendors and service providers. It includes conducting due diligence before onboarding new vendors, continuously monitoring their security posture, and having clear contract clauses related to incident reporting and data breach handling. Each business approaches establishing its VRM program differently. As the Chief Information Security Officer (CISO) for my organization, I have partnered with Procurement, IT, and Legal to review contract terms and conditions. One area I constantly review is the controls for protecting company data. I verify the process for reporting an incident and request the most current SOC2 audit report or other risk framework certification such as ISAE 3402 (Assurance Reports on Controls at a Service Organization), or ISO27001.

Immediate Steps Responding to a Vendor Compromise

So, as we begin, let's start with receiving news that a vendor you have partnered with has been compromised. My first step is to understand how bad my day is going to be.

Assess the Impact

Immediately upon learning of a vendor compromise, assess the impact on your company. Determine what data was exposed, which systems were affected, and the potential implications for your operations and customers. This step is critical because your organization may have regulatory reporting requirements if sensitive data is exposed. If this is the case, consult with in-house counsel to review and understand how this may influence current business operations. Alerting in-house counsel has the added benefit of allowing them to prepare for litigation down the road.

Start by identifying the specific data types and systems involved in the breach. Was sensitive customer information compromised? Were any internal systems infiltrated that could affect your broader network security? If not immediately known, I'd also circle back to understand how the breach occurred (e.g., API compromise, exploited vulnerability) to identify other corrective actions we need to take. Additionally, consider the potential repercussions for your customers and partners, and any regulatory obligations that the breach may trigger. For instance, in certain jurisdictions, the exposure of personally identifiable information (PII) may necessitate immediate notification to affected individuals and authorities.

To guide this process, consider the following questions:

1. **What is the scope of the incident?**
   Identify which customer information systems and types of customer information have been accessed or misused and which systems and equipment were compromised. Understanding the scope of the incident is critical to gauging the severity of the breach. Determining which customer information, systems, or equipment were compromised will directly influence the actions you need to take. For example, if a threat actor accessed sensitive customer data like social security numbers or credit card information, the breach could have significant financial and reputational consequences. Similarly, if essential systems or equipment were compromised, this could disrupt your business operations or expose other network vulnerabilities that could lead to secondary incidents. By precisely identifying what has been accessed or misused, you can prioritize your response efforts and allocate resources effectively.

2. **Which stakeholders are potentially affected?**
   Estimating the number of stakeholders affected is crucial in understanding the potential fallout from the breach. Stakeholders can include customers, employees, partners, and even regulatory bodies. The number of affected individuals or entities will dictate the scale of your response, including the need for communications, compensation, or remediation efforts. For example, if the breach impacts a large number of customers, you may need to prepare for widespread notifications and customer support inquiries. A clear estimate will also help you assess the potential damage to your organization's reputation and financial standing and understand if the costs are going to be significant enough to trigger the use of your corporate cyber-insurance policy to help pay for returning business to normal.

3. **Which of the vendor's services are potentially affected by the incident?**
   It's essential to determine which specific services provided by the vendor were impacted by the breach. This knowledge will help you assess how the incident could disrupt your operations. For example, if the vendor provides cloud services or critical software, a compromise could halt your business processes or expose sensitive data stored within these services. Understanding which services are affected allows you to evaluate the extent of the risk to your business and decide whether you need to suspend using the vendor's services temporarily, switch to an alternative provider, or take other mitigating actions.

4. **What steps do we need to take to fully understand the type and extent of the risk to the business, stakeholders, and employees? How quickly can that be done?**
   Assessing the risk to your business, stakeholders, and employees is vital in shaping your response strategy. This includes understanding how the breach could impact your organization's financial health, legal standing, and overall reputation. Consider the potential for legal liabilities, loss of customer trust, or disruptions to current and future operations. Additionally, the risk to employees, such as the exposure of their personal information or the potential for increased workload during the incident response, should be assessed. By thoroughly understanding these risks, you can prioritize your response efforts to protect your most critical assets and maintain business continuity.

5. **Which corporate-owned services and systems were affected by the incident?**
   The situation becomes even more critical if the vendor compromise extends to your corporate-owned services or systems. Identify which internal systems have been affected, as this could signify a broader security incident within your organization. For instance, if your email system, financial software, or other core business applications are

compromised, this could lead to significant operational disruptions or additional security vulnerabilities. Understanding the extent of the impact on your systems will guide your efforts in containing the breach, preventing further damage, and restoring normal operations as quickly as possible.

6. **Are there other third parties involved?**
   In today's interconnected business environment, it's common for vendors to work with multiple third parties. If the compromised vendor has relationships with other third parties, there could be a cascading effect, leading to further security risks. Identify if other third parties are involved or affected by the breach, as this could widen the scope of the incident and introduce additional complexities into your response efforts. If other third parties are involved, you may need to establish communication with them as well and assess the broader implications for your business and potentially negotiate restoration sequencing.

Contact the Vendor

Upon discovering a vendor compromise, it is imperative to promptly establish a direct line of communication with the affected vendor. The goal is to obtain a more comprehensive understanding of their incident's scope, including the specific data and systems that they believe have been compromised and the immediate actions the vendor is taking to mitigate the issue. This dialogue is crucial, as it enables your organization to stay informed about the evolving situation and adjust your response strategies accordingly.

To ensure continuous and effective communication, request regular updates from the vendor and designate a single point of contact who will be responsible for managing communications throughout the incident. This individual should be well-versed in the details of the breach and the ongoing remediation efforts. Given that the vendor may still be triaging the event, it's essential to remain patient yet persistent in your communications. Having a reliable point of contact ensures that your organization is kept up to date with the latest developments and can respond swiftly to any changes in the situation.

Regular updates from the vendor will also enable your internal teams to align their efforts with the vendor's remediation strategy, ensuring a coordinated and efficient response. By maintaining a close partnership with the vendor during this critical time, you can better safeguard your organization's interests and minimize the potential fallout from the incident.

Notify Internal Teams

Upon identifying a vendor compromise, it is crucial to promptly inform all relevant internal teams, including your incident response team, legal department, business continuity team, compliance team, and senior leadership. Each of these stakeholders plays a vital role in managing the incident and mitigating its effect on your organization. The incident response team will immediately begin implementing technical measures to assess, contain, and address a breach if applicable. The legal department will assess any regulatory implications and prepare for potential breach notifications. Meanwhile, the business continuity team will evaluate the impact on ongoing operations and activate contingency plans as needed. Finally, keep senior leadership (and the board when necessary) informed so they may make strategic decisions, guide public communications, communicate with critical stakeholders, and ensure alignment across the organization.

The success of your response hinges on the seamless coordination and communication among these teams. By working together, they can share insights, address challenges, and adapt quickly to the evolving situation, ensuring that your organization's response is both swift and effective. This coordinated effort is especially critical if the vendor event has the potential to disrupt business operations, as it allows for a unified approach to minimizing damage, maintaining customer trust, and preserving business continuity.

Communication and Legal Considerations

One of the most critical aspects of a vendor management program is how you and the business effectively manage communications.

Communicate with Stakeholders

Once you have thoroughly assessed the impact of the incident on your business, it becomes essential to develop a comprehensive communication strategy for all stakeholders. This includes employees, customers, partners, and regulatory bodies, each of whom may require different levels of information and reassurance. Crafting the right message is crucial to maintaining trust and credibility, but you must balance it with caution as more data becomes available from the vendor that could possibly endanger the organization from new risks.

To begin, clearly outline the key points you will communicate to each stakeholder group. Inform employees of any potential changes to their current work processes or security practices. Do not forget customers as they will need reassurance that their data and services are protected. Partners will also want to understand how the incident could affect their business with you, and regulators will require precise, timely updates to ensure compliance with all legal obligations.

However, before any communication is issued, it is imperative that all messages are meticulously vetted by your legal team—whether internal counsel or external advisors, depending on the complexity of the incident. This legal review process ensures that your communications are fully compliant with applicable regulations, thereby reducing the risk of regulatory penalties and safeguarding your organization from unnecessary exposure to legal action. This step is especially critical in today's stringent regulatory environment, where the repercussions of mishandling a breach can be severe.

By carefully considering both the content and delivery of your communications, you can navigate the delicate balance of being transparent while protecting your organization's interests.

Legal Compliance and Reporting

It is imperative to have a thorough understanding of your legal responsibilities regarding data breach notifications. In today's highly regulated landscape, many jurisdictions mandate that companies promptly report breaches to regulatory authorities and notify affected individuals within a strictly defined timeframe. Failure to comply with these requirements can result in severe penalties, legal actions, and lasting reputational damage.

As a CISO, you must be intimately familiar with these regulatory timeframes and the specific obligations that apply to your organization. This knowledge is not just a legal requirement but a critical component of your role in protecting the organization's interests and maintaining trust with stakeholders. Regularly review and update your understanding of these obligations, particularly when vetting new vendors or entering new markets. Each vendor relationship brings with it potential exposure to different regulatory regimes, and being proactive in understanding these risks will enable you to make informed decisions that safeguard your organization.

In today's regulatory environment, where scrutiny of security practices is more intense than ever, security executives are increasingly in the spotlight. The visibility of your role means that your actions, decisions, and preparedness are under constant examination—not just by your organization but by regulators, investors, and the public. Therefore, continuous education and awareness of the evolving regulatory landscape is essential. Equip yourself with the knowledge and tools necessary to navigate these complexities confidently, ensuring that your organization remains compliant and resilient in the face of any data breach.

Mitigation and Recovery

1. **Isolate Affected Systems**
   If a vendor compromise directly connects to your company's enterprise systems, take immediate steps to initiate incident response procedures and review, isolate, and secure those connections and systems to prevent further exposure.

2. **Implement Contingency Plans**
   Activate your business continuity plan to maintain business operations. This may involve switching to alternative systems or processes or temporarily suspending certain services, such as access to a SaaS application.

3. **Work on Remediation with the Vendor**
   If necessary, collaborate with the vendor to understand the compromise's root cause and assist in implementing remediation measures on your corporate networks. Remediation may involve enhancing security controls, updating software, and changing access credentials.

4. **Document the Incident**
   Throughout the entire process, it's essential to document every step taken from the moment you discover the vendor compromise. This documentation should include details of the impact assessment, communications with the vendor, notifications to internal teams, and any actions taken in response to the breach. This record will be invaluable for post-incident analysis, potential legal actions, and improving your organization's incident response protocols.

   Ensure that the documentation is thorough and accurate, capturing the timeline of events, key decisions made, and the rationale behind those decisions. This will aid in regulatory compliance and serve as a critical learning tool to enhance your organization's preparedness for future incidents.

Post-Incident Review and Lessons Learned

Conduct a post-incident review after the incident has been contained and normal operations have resumed. The affected vendor may initiate this process and involve all stakeholders, including other compromised vendors. The goal is to identify what went wrong, assess the effectiveness of the response, and update policies, procedures, and contracts to prevent future incidents.

Enhance Future Preparedness

1. **Update Incident Response and Business Continuity Plans**
   Based on the affected vendor's lessons learned and your organization's response to this incident, update the incident response and business continuity plans and runbooks to mature your vendor compromise response procedures.

2. **Strengthen Vendor Management**
   Using the information you learned from this event, review and strengthen your vendor risk management program. This may involve more rigorous security assessments, regular audits, and stronger communication and reporting protocols with vendors.

Conclusion

In today's "always on" interconnected digital landscape, vendor compromises represent a significant and ever-present risk to your organization. These incidents can have far-reaching consequences, impacting your operational integrity, reputation, and regulatory compliance. However, with the right preparation and response strategy, you can significantly mitigate the impact of such events and safeguard your organization's interests.

Establishing a comprehensive vendor risk management (VRM) program is the cornerstone of an effective defense against vendor-related risks. Design this program to assess, monitor, and manage the risks associated with each third-party relationship. By ensuring that your vendors adhere to the highest security standards and embedding robust incident response protocols into your contracts, you can proactively reduce the likelihood and severity of a breach.

Equally important is responding swiftly and effectively when an incident occurs. Clear, predefined protocols for incident response are crucial; they ensure that your organization can act decisively in the critical moments following a vendor compromise. Moreover, treat each incident as a learning opportunity to refine your strategies, update your VRM program, and strengthen your overall security posture. The dynamic nature of today's threat landscape demands this continuous improvement as cyber threats evolve in complexity and sophistication.

Collaboration within your organization and strong, transparent partnerships with your vendors form the backbone of a resilient security strategy. By fostering open communication and a shared commitment to security, you can work together to identify potential vulnerabilities and implement effective safeguards. This collaborative approach, combined with a dedication to ongoing improvement, will significantly enhance your organization's resilience against the myriad cybersecurity challenges that lie ahead.

TPRM and Incident Response

Matt Stamper

Incident response is a cornerstone of organizational resilience, and it is especially challenging when companies outsource business functions, as this reduces direct operational control and requires a high degree of trust in the security practices of third parties.

It's becoming increasingly common to see cyber incidents involving third parties in the news—those entities that handle data on our behalf or provide applications and services for corporate functions. When these third parties suffer a data breach, our organization's resilience and incident response programs are put to the ultimate test. In this chapter, I'll walk through some of the key considerations when integrating your third-party risk management and incident response programs.

Incident response is not just challenging; it's a critical discipline that underpins organizational resilience. It demands near real-time telemetry across disparate IT assets and infrastructure services and coordination among stakeholders who may not be available during the heat of the incident or able to agree on containment strategies and post-incident remediation. Managing incidents that involve third parties, and our supply chains takes the inherent challenges of successful incident response to a new level, underscoring the urgency and importance of your work as risk management professionals, cybersecurity experts, and business leaders responsible for third-party risk management.

One of the critical challenges in incident response involving third-party services is the absence of direct operational control. When an organization outsources a business function or relies on suppliers, it inherently relinquishes some degree of control. While outsourcing brings the benefits of service expertise and economies of scale, it also requires a significant level of trust that the third party is implementing adequate security measures. With incidents, your organization's response relies on the provider's incident response program and, potentially, the incident response programs of your third party's third parties—and their third parties. For many of us, relinquishing this control does not come easy.

Effective strategies can be implemented to navigate the complex dynamics of incident response with third parties, but they require a proactive approach. The first step is establishing a clear operational context related to the services, products, or support that the third party will provide. This operational context is the bedrock of TPRM and cybersecurity. Various tools, such as dependency analysis, business impact analyses, and technical documentation like data flow diagrams and software bill of materials (SBOMs), can help validate this operational context. Collectively, these tools should be used to understand the potential impacts that could occur should the provider have a security incident that impacts your organization's operations and data. If you oversee TPRM functions for your firm, it's imperative that this context and analysis remain front-and-center and are maintained current.

The role of materiality here should not be overlooked. Third parties and suppliers are not created equal. A meaningful subset of these entities will have a direct impact on your organization's resilience and well-being. These could be third parties that directly support operations, collect, process, or store information on your behalf, or who deliver unpinning technologies used by your company. Ensure that these critical third parties' security, privacy, and data governance practices are not left to chance. Here are some topics that require ongoing diligence.

Service Demarcation

When a third party delivers services to your organization, know explicitly where their services start and stop. Too frequently, these demarcation points are assumed, leaving both organizations flat-footed when issues arise. Demarcation points can also be critical to forensics, telemetry, and the availability of log data to support an investigation. Coordinate with your security team and the vendor to determine if there are gaps in monitoring and visibility or if certain logs that would support a forensic investigation are not collected. Where gaps exist, get them on the table to be resolved. Your review should also include procedural validations required to request logs and support when incidents occur. Assume the worst and work backward to confirm understandings and processes. Depending upon the services contemplated, consider drafting a detailed roles and responsibilities matrix that shows your organization's responsibilities side by side with the provider's responsibilities for critical functions or elements within the technology stack. An illustrative roles and responsibilities matrix is shown in Chapter 11. For managed services, as an example, detail roles and responsibilities across the following service layers:

- Application
- Database
- Operating System
- Hypervisor/Microservices
- Network
- Storage
- Backups
- Data Center/Facilities

Security services would apply to each layer and should be verified. There is a particular elegance to open-ended questions when it comes to validation. I particularly like simple questions like, "What is it that we don't know about [insert topic] that we should know, and how could that impact our use of this application, service, or product?" Each identified layer has its nuance, and subject matter experts may be required to examine the details thoroughly. This process is used strategically based on the degree of potential impact and materiality of the contemplated services. Delving into service demarcation will undoubtedly highlight risks that may have been overlooked during onboarding.

Get the Contract Right

Make sure that material third-party relationships are underpinned and supported by contracts that support your organization. Specific clauses should be incorporated into these agreements, including breach notification. Ensure the breach notification timescales are consistent with your organization's regulatory requirements and contractual obligations. If your organization must notify stakeholders and regulators within 24 hours and your vendors' obligations are to notify you within 48 hours, that's not an acceptable disconnect. Maintain an inventory of each material vendor's disclosure obligations with your firm. Confirm, as contracts are renewed with existing providers, that the required terms and conditions are brought current, incorporating any lessons learned from previous incidents.

Your contracts should also require that your vendors and suppliers meet minimum security standards. This could include providing SOC 2 / Type 2 audits, certification with ISO 27001, or reviewing the results of assessments that show the provider's security program has the coverage and maturity tied to cybersecurity frameworks such as the NIST Cybersecurity Framework (NIST CSF) or the Center for Internet Security's Critical Security Controls. Depending upon the criticality of the relationship, you may want to coordinate with your security colleagues to mandate specific security controls prescriptively. Cases in point could include phishing-resistant multi-factor authentication (MFA) when the provider can access your organization's IT infrastructure or data.

Beyond minimum security standards and breach notification, right-to-audit clauses should be considered. These allow the contracting entity to review more sensitive information to support their initial due diligence or specific issues that may surface during the engagement with the provider.

The topic of contracting asymmetries should not be underestimated during contract negotiations. Large providers may tell smaller clients they will not entertain contract provisions necessary for incident response requirements simply because they hold the proverbial cards.

Similarly, large clients may require services of their smaller contractors that are not operationally tenable but agreed to, undermining their ability to address security incidents. Don't let these dynamics go unassessed.

Authorized Personnel and Emergency Contact (APEC) List

While contracts define the relationship with the third party, how your organization uses the services or projects is where the rubber meets the road. Both organizations must know who to contact when issues arise and who is authorized to take specific actions if necessary. This is why an authorized personnel and emergency contact (APEC) list must be maintained with the provider. Service providers use APEC lists (or something similar) to ensure that requested changes from their clients are authorized. It's important, depending upon the level of authorizations, to stipulate the level of authentication required to verify the identities of these individuals. For high-impact requests, verification mechanisms should be more stringent.

There's value in using pre-defined distribution lists to ensure vendor communication is received. I've seen firsthand how a third party sends important service messages to an individual named by the contracting firm who left the organization. That email is either lost in a non-monitored inbox or overlooked by the recipient, who is overloaded with forwarded messages. Knowing and validating who should receive vendor-specific communication is foundational. Ensure that this contact detail is kept current, and ideally, use a distribution list of authorized personnel who can take actions based on the communique of the third party. There will be distinct roles in the APEC. Specific roles are technically focused. Others serve administrative and billing purposes. Ensure that billing contacts use a distribution list. There are cases where "incidents" were actually billing disconnects, literally and figuratively. I strongly recommend using a shared calendar to note the cadence of when APEC details should be re-validated. Basic governance can prevent potential risks from materializing.

Stewardship

I've never been a fan of zero-sum adversarial relationships with third parties and key vendors. While it's essential to convey your organization's requirements and negotiate what's ultimately in your organization's best interests, your vendors and suppliers are integral to your organization's success. The relationship should be more about complementarity than competition. As a CISO for a multinational data center and managed services firm, I routinely met with our clients to discuss their security requirements, service demarcation points for critical services, and any upcoming changes or maintenance issues that could impact our services. I wanted to "declare war on ambiguity" with my colleagues on the other side of the table. It was essential to build trust and clarify understandings as a matter of course. These stewardship meetings were invaluable. Both parties left the discussion with a more detailed understanding of current practices, shared risks, and procedures to address issues that surfaced. When issues surfaced, it was good to know I was not meeting that client for the first time. For your organization, determine which third-party relationships warrant this high-touch approach. If you are a security leader, this may be an excellent opportunity for your team members to develop these skills by interacting with their peers at the third party. Again, it's important to frame these discussions correctly. This is not a negotiating tactic. These discussions are about building a mutually beneficial relationship that will be stressed during incidents.

Tabletop Exercises

As part of your organization's incident response program, draft tabletop scenarios that contemplate data breaches and service interruptions that result from security incidents with your third-party vendors and suppliers. Initially, ask participants to think expansively about what information they would need to manage the incident. Depending upon the level of integration with the vendor, detection could be a shared responsibility as both organizations receive similar telemetry and alerting (think shared responsibilities with cloud services). More than likely, however, you'll learn of the third party's security incident from media reports (remember SolarWinds and Snowflake), from the vendor directly, or, based on the sensitivity of the incident at hand, from Federal law enforcement in the form of victim notification. Particularly challenging issues arise where the nature and extent of the exposure may be inadequately understood at the time of notification. I directly witnessed several companies trying to determine whether the Log4j vulnerability impacted their applications and code bases.

These tabletop exercises and workshops do not need to be facilitated by outside security advisory services, although they do bring a wealth of experience and knowledge to the exercise. Water cooler discussions, team meetings, and other informal venues will suffice to review how prepared your organization is to confront security incidents that are outside your direct control. Consider scenarios where sensitive data such as material, non-public information (MNPI), or personal data is compromised. Corporate counsel will be integral to overseeing the responses to these scenarios. As your team develops muscle memory addressing third-party security incidents, widen the circle of concern. For example, with your most material third parties, invite them to participate in the scenario. Most will reject the invitation, but certain forward-thinking providers will welcome this engagement to validate their specific goals and perspectives related to the response.

The SolarWinds Orion breach offered some critical insights into one particularly challenging scenario: software updates. Our organizations run on software, most of which is provided by third parties. Ensure that your incident response team rehearses how they would respond to "trusted" software suddenly found to be nefarious. Derivatives of this scenario highlight how "trust" can be a vulnerability and where validation and authentication should be front-and-center with our security practices and architecture.

We conduct tabletop exercises to learn and evaluate organizational preparedness. After each exercise, key stakeholders, notably the CISO and the organization's General Counsel, must draft and review a summary of observations, findings, and recommendations. This analysis is not the end game. If there were procedural challenges or gaps in telemetry, they should be evaluated, resourced, and remediated accordingly. Counsel and the executive leadership team may also be required to determine if the circumstances were "material" and what, if any, disclosure obligations may have been triggered based on the scenario. For public companies, the materiality determination cannot be unreasonably delayed and upon determination, the Securities and Exchange Commission's Cybersecurity Risk Management, Strategy, Governance, and Incident Disclosure Ruling requires registrants to disclose the incident publicly by filing a Current Report on Form 8-K within four business days.

As part of the post-exercise analysis, the linkages between continuity of operations and crisis management should be evaluated. Ideally, we never have to address a material business interruption or a crisis that envelops the organization. As leaders, however, we don't have the luxury of hoping these scenarios never occur. Ensure that the security team knows how and when to escalate incidents with broader implications for the firm. Ideally, the CISO liaises with crucial members of the business continuity and disaster recovery and crisis management teams if they are not already a member of these teams.

Corporate communications also play an essential role in addressing incidents and data breaches resulting from third-party security failures. Indeed, depending upon the service demarcation and the specific circumstances of the incident, your organization's security team may only have a limited, consultative role. The onus of the incident will fall on legal counsel and Corporate Communications to describe how a third party's security failure resulted in the impact on your company. Given that we live in a litigious society, how the third party was selected and the level of due diligence performed during the selection and onboarding processes will be in the crosshairs of plaintiffs' attorneys, especially if the incident resulted in a data breach. Be sure to bring Corporate Communications into your incident response process and model scenarios where their role will be tested.

Managing third-party incidents brings unique challenges and dynamics to our organizations. Chief among these is the lack of direct operational control and reliance on the quality of your supplier's or vendor's incident response program. This dynamic highlights the necessity of thorough pre-contracting due diligence and ongoing stewardship with that subset of vendors who are material to your organization's resilience, operations, and obligations to internal and external stakeholders. To minimize risks, you must take a proactive approach to validate the organizational context of the vendor's services or the supplier's components, keep APEC details current, and exercise responses with high-fidelity scenarios to ensure that your organization is prepared for the inevitable.

Insights and Actions

In today's interconnected digital landscape, a vendor's security incident can directly impact your organization's operations, data security, and reputation. Since you lack direct control over a vendor's security, preparedness is essential. Chapter 6 provides a practical guide to managing vendor compromises, emphasizing the need for a robust incident response plan integrated with your vendor risk management (VRM) program.

Key Steps in Responding to a Vendor Compromise

Establish a Vendor Risk Management (VRM) Program:

- Conduct due diligence before onboarding vendors, continuously monitor their security posture, and include clear contract clauses for incident reporting and breach handling.
- Regularly review controls for protecting company data and ensure vendors provide up-to-date security certifications (e.g., SOC 2, ISO 27001).

Immediate Steps After Discovering a Vendor Compromise:

- Assess the Impact: Determine what data was exposed, which systems were affected, and the potential implications for your operations and customers.
- Identify Stakeholders: Estimate the number and types of stakeholders impacted (e.g., customers, employees, partners, regulators).
- Determine Affected Services: Identify which vendor services are impacted and how this could disrupt your business.
- Evaluate Risk: Assess the risk to your business, stakeholders, and employees, including legal, financial, and reputational consequences.

- Check Internal Systems: Determine if corporate-owned systems were affected, which could indicate a broader security incident.
- Identify Other Third Parties: Assess if other third parties are involved or affected by the vendor's compromise.

Contact the Vendor:

- Establish direct communication with the vendor to understand the scope of the incident and their remediation actions.
- Designate a single point of contact for ongoing updates and ensure regular, reliable communication.

Notify Internal Teams:

- Inform the incident response team, legal, business continuity, compliance, and senior leadership.
- Ensure coordinated efforts across teams to assess, contain, and remediate the incident.

Communication and Legal Considerations:

- Develop a comprehensive communication strategy for all stakeholders (employees, customers, partners, regulators).
- Vet all communications through legal counsel to ensure compliance with regulations and to protect the organization from legal exposure.
- Understand and fulfill legal obligations for breach notifications to authorities and affected individuals.

Mitigation and Recovery:

- Isolate Affected Systems: Secure or disconnect affected systems to prevent further exposure.

- Activate Contingency Plans: Implement business continuity plans, such as switching to alternative providers or suspending affected services.
- Collaborate with the Vendor: Work with the vendor to understand the root cause and assist with remediation.
- Document the Incident: Maintain detailed records of all actions taken, communications, and decisions for post-incident review and legal purposes.

Post-Incident Review and Lessons Learned:

- Conduct a thorough review to identify what went wrong, assess the effectiveness of the response, and update policies and contracts to prevent future incidents.
- Strengthen your VRM program based on lessons learned, including more rigorous security assessments and improved communication protocols.

Integrating Third-Party Risk Management (TPRM) and Incident Response

- Operational Context: Clearly define the services, products, or support provided by each vendor to understand potential impacts of a security incident.
- Service Demarcation: Know where vendor responsibilities begin and end and ensure visibility and coordination for forensic investigations.
- Contracts: Include breach notification clauses, minimum security standards, and right-to-audit provisions. Align vendor notification timelines with your regulatory requirements.
- Authorized Personnel and Emergency Contact (APEC) List: Maintain up-to-date contact information for both your organization and the vendor to ensure effective communication during incidents.

- Stewardship: Foster collaborative, trust-based relationships with key vendors through regular meetings and open communication.
- Tabletop Exercises: Regularly test your incident response plan with scenarios involving vendor compromises to build readiness and identify gaps.
- Materiality: Focus on vendors that are critical to your organization's resilience, operations, and regulatory obligations.

Chapter 7

Offboarding

Introduction

In Chapter 7, we address the offboarding of third parties. Bill starts by making the point that this phase is not merely procedural but a critical governance function that demands thorough evaluation and planning. The heart of the offboarding process that Bill unpacks is a structured decision-making approach that begins with a comprehensive assessment of the vendor's performance throughout the contract period, focusing on whether service level agreements and performance metrics have been met. Once the decision to terminate has been made, Bill shifts his focus to transition planning, addressing knowledge transfer, data migration, and minimizing operational disruptions. This includes the ability to run parallel processes if necessary.

Gary then delves into the critical importance of safeguarding corporate data, maintaining operational integrity, and ensuring secure transitions when vendor relationships come to an end. He advocates for formal notification to establish clear expectations and a timeline for the offboarding activities. In his experience, a thorough review of contractual obligations is foundational, requiring careful examination of clauses related to data handling, confidentiality, and the final settlement of accounts while working closely with the legal and procurement teams to ensure that all legal and compliance requirements are met during the transition. Gary focuses a lot of attention on data handling and destruction to ensure the organization's needs and regulatory obligations are addressed.

Matt positions offboarding as a cornerstone of organizational risk management and operational resilience. He makes the point that offboarding should never come as a surprise to either party. Instead, it should be the culmination of a transparent process in which clear expectations around quality, service levels, and performance are established from the outset. When offboarding becomes necessary, organizations must be prepared with a well-developed exit checklist tailored to the specific products and services involved, ensuring a smooth transition with minimal disruption to business operations. As Matt emphasizes, the records you kept during the management of ongoing activities now become crucial documentation and a key resource in managing the inherent risks of offboarding your partner.

While organizations don't enter into relationships expecting them to end or end badly, thorough preparation, continued diligence, and transparent communication throughout the engagement lifecycle will reduce the likelihood of exposing the organization to insurmountable risks during the eventual termination.

Vendor Offboarding Process

Bill Bonney

Offboarding is not just an administrative step but a critical governance process requiring careful consideration of performance, alignment, risk, and transition planning.

In Chapter 4, I scoped out the governance issues for the vendor onboarding process, covering planning, engaging, and implementing. In Chapter 5, I looked at the governance issues associated with the monitor and manage stage. This chapter finishes the discussion by addressing the governance issues regarding termination and offboarding.

As a quick refresher on the five stages of the vendor management lifecycle, here is the lifecycle diagram introduced in Chapter 4:

Figure 7.1 – Vendor Management Lifecycle

- Plan – Requirements definition and initial research.
- Engage – Vendor selection and contract negotiation.
- Implement – Onboarding and integration.
- Manage – Monitoring and management.
- Terminate – Terminate and offboard.

We support a straightforward decision tree in the termination and offboarding stage. We're analyzing how well the vendor has performed and whether they will continue to perform well against our future requirements. We're deciding whether to continue with the current vendor and if not, engage another third party, bring the process in-house, or discontinue it. Finally, if we've decided to end this relationship in favor of a new approach, we support the exit by carefully considering and managing the risks associated with offboarding and potentially switching to another vendor. This stage requires careful evaluation of the vendor's performance, the alignment of their services with the organization's strategic needs, and the overall value delivered. To support the decision-making process, we have these three objectives:

- Evaluate the vendor's performance and the continued relevance of their services or products.
- Decide whether to renew, renegotiate, or terminate the contract.
- Determine the necessary steps (e.g., notification window) or impacts (e.g., termination fee) from terminating the contract.

Key governance concerns during the decision-making process include:

- **Performance Evaluation:** Conduct comprehensive reviews of the vendor's performance throughout the contract period, assessing whether they have met or exceeded the agreed-upon service level agreements (SLAs) and performance metrics. Referring to the monitoring and management stage, ideally, this has been happening on some periodic basis, balancing the need to stay current in the assessment with the burden that these place on the organization to conduct and document the assessment and the strain they put on the vendor by generating a cloud of uncertainty about the strength of the relationship.

- **Strategic Alignment:** Evaluate whether the vendor's services and capabilities, including their financial status and availability or turnover of key personnel, continue to align with the organization's strategic objectives and future direction. This includes considering changes in the organization's needs, market conditions, technological advancements, and shifting supply-chain constraints. See Chapter 13 for a deep dive into supply chain concerns.

- **Cost-Benefit Analysis:** Perform a cost-benefit analysis to assess the financial value delivered by the vendor, including an examination of the total cost of ownership (TCO) and return on investment (ROI) of the vendor's services or products. It could be beneficial to be well connected to the team driving mergers and acquisitions because the execution of this business process may be better or worse in the acquisition or merger target, and this can present a new opportunity for the broader organization to benefit.

- **Risk Assessment:** Reassess the risks associated with continuing, adjusting, or terminating the vendor relationship. This includes considering the impact on operational continuity, data security, compliance, and potential costs associated with transitioning to a new vendor. A potential yellow flag here is that if the result of this assessment is that transitioning this business process by changing vendors or bringing the process in-house poses a significant risk, you should consider developing a mitigation strategy so the organization is not held hostage to this risk.

- **Market Analysis and Vendor Comparison:** Analyze market trends and compare alternative vendors to ensure that the current vendor remains competitive in pricing, technology, service quality, and innovation. Innovation is essential today. Too much innovation can lead to excessive costs, but too little innovation can allow the competition to leapfrog you because they use a superior vendor to deliver this product or service.

- **Stakeholder Feedback:** Gather and analyze feedback from key stakeholders and end-users regarding their satisfaction with the vendor's services, support, and overall relationship management. The new hybrid workplaces that companies are embracing have introduced new sources of friction. Radically different approaches or management attitudes about support for remote work can have a toxic effect on morale if not managed appropriately.

- **Contract Terms Review:** Review the existing contract terms to identify any areas that may require renegotiation, such as pricing adjustments, changes in service scope, or updated SLAs, based on the organization's current and future needs. This is another issue that should rely on the continual feedback loop you and the vendor established as part of the monitoring and management stage. As you see changes in process requirements spurred by experience or innovation, capture these and work proactively with the vendor where possible. Where not possible, add them to the list of items to be renegotiated over some appropriate interval.
- **Negotiation Strategy:** Develop a negotiation strategy for contract renewal discussions, considering the organization's leverage and the importance of maintaining a positive relationship with the vendor. I need to offer a warning here about abusing your organization's potentially disproportionate leverage to drive lower prices or greater service commitments. Using hardball tactics to alter the relationship too much may place your vendor in a no-win scenario where they cannot successfully deliver their products or services to your firm. This may create new risks, leading to regulatory lapses or challenges to data protection controls. Proceed with caution.

And then the transition objective:

- Manage the transition if switching vendors or discontinuing the service.

Here, I consider these issues paramount to managing the risk associated with offboarding a vendor you are transitioning away from:

- **Transition and Exit Planning:** If terminating the relationship, begin planning as soon as possible for a smooth transition to a new vendor or the insourcing of services. This includes considerations for knowledge transfer, data migration, and minimizing disruption to business operations. Don't underestimate the need for a robust knowledge transfer, especially for a relationship that spans an extended period or involves a significant business process. There may be a lot of informal steps that don't appear in the documentation. Ideally, you've established contract terms that facilitate this eventuality. Data transfer is another area that warrants serious consideration. Hopefully the data flow diagrams are current, and along with a thorough review and migration, you've worked out a transfer of backups and a comprehensive data destruction process. Finally, running the processes you are beginning and ending in parallel is essential to minimizing disruptions to business operations.

- **Legal and Compliance Implications:** Understand the legal and compliance implications of renewing or terminating the contract, including any penalties for early termination, data retention requirements, and obligations under regulatory standards. Final payments should be structured to allow for inspection and signoff of mandatory attestations and audits by the respective stakeholders.
- **Documentation and Record-Keeping:** Ensure proper documentation of the renewal or termination process, including the rationale for the decision, negotiation records, and transition plans, for audit and governance purposes. Regardless of the contract terms and the closeness of the business relationship, there is often a tendency to view the relationship in terms of money owed and a strict (formal or informal) "work-to-rule" or "malicious compliance" approach.[5] Ensure you have contingency plans in place, use non-confrontational language, and foster respect for the outgoing workers throughout your organization. The extra

[5] "Work to Rule" or the "Italian Strike" ("Sciopero bianco" in Italian) is a form of striking when not allowed to strike. I am using the term here to mean a spiteful slowdown of work or introducing friction into a relationship that is ending.

documentation could prove helpful should either party be compelled to initiate litigation.

- **Communication Plan:** Develop a communication plan to inform internal stakeholders, employees, and possibly customers of the decision regarding the vendor contract, ensuring clarity on the reasons and the expected impact. Because of the possibility of litigation, vet the communication plan with your communications team and legal counsel. Words have the power to raise or lower the temperature. Choose them wisely.

Addressing these governance concerns is essential for making informed decisions at the contract renewal or termination stage, ensuring that vendor relationships continue to deliver value and align with the organization's strategic goals and operational needs. After reviewing the terminate and offboard stage, revise your processes for the first four stages with lessons learned from this review.

Effective vendor management is critical for organizations to ensure they receive the best possible value from their vendors, maintain service quality, and mitigate potential risks. It requires ongoing attention and management throughout the entire lifecycle of the vendor relationship. While I have viewed all five stages through the governance lens, other authors have unpacked a more process-oriented treatment. Together, I hope we have provided you with a complete reference for the vendor risk management lifecycle.

Offboarding Vendors: Safeguarding Corporate Data and Operations

Gary Hayslip

A secure and well-structured offboarding process is essential for protecting corporate data, maintaining operational integrity, and preserving the company's reputation.

Relationships with third-party vendors are integral to modern business operations, offering various services from software solutions to logistics support. However, when such partnerships end, ensuring a smooth and secure offboarding process is critical. Offboarding procedures are essential to protect sensitive corporate data, maintain uninterrupted business operations, and safeguard access to corporate assets. Below are strategic steps and considerations for effectively offboarding vendors while prioritizing your company's security and operational integrity.

1. Initiate the Offboarding Process with a Formal Notice

The offboarding process begins with a formal notification to the vendor about the decision to terminate the partnership. Your notification to the vendor should follow the terms in the initial contract, including any notice period requirements. The notification should be clear, professional, and concise, outlining the expectations and timeline for the offboarding process. It is essential that you follow the process in your contract. I have seen 30, 60, or 90-day notification requirements. I have witnessed notification requirements directing the business to provide cancellation notice by email or written letter on corporate letterhead. What is essential is to know the notification requirements, and if you have any questions, speak with your legal team.

2. Review Contractual Obligations and Documentation

Carefully review the contract for any clauses related to offboarding, data handling, and confidentiality that must be adhered to during the process. These clauses will include obligations for both sides of the agreement, such as the return or destruction of data and the timeframe for these operations. There will also be a settlement of accounts and the final delivery of services or products. It would be best to speak with your legal and procurement teams to answer any questions. All legal and compliance requirements must be understood and followed.

3. Secure and Retrieve Corporate Data

Data security is paramount during the offboarding process. Identify all the data shared with the vendor, including confidential and proprietary information, customer data, and operational data. Ensure the vendor securely returns all data or confirms its destruction according to the agreed-upon terms. This process might involve overseeing the deletion of data from the vendor's systems and obtaining certificates of destruction with applicable before and after screenshots to validate completion. I would pay special attention to the timeframe they have to return or destroy data. I have seen response windows for vendors to return data of up to six months, which may impact your onboarding of a replacement vendor. Another point about returning data to the business is understanding the format in which it will be returned. I once had to pay for professional services to change a returned data archive into a format my company could use; the effort took over three months. This unfortunate situation happened because of a contract I inherited as a new CISO, so I highly recommend you read the small print in your contracts if you didn't negotiate them. One final lesson learned here, not all data is equal in the protections assigned to it and the methods used for secure destruction. Internal corporate information, also known as material non-public information (MNPI) and intellectual property (IP) will require special protections to demonstrate the business is meeting its requirements of implementing due care. If the data you are retiring is one of these sensitive types, it's imperative you select methods that meet this extra level of scrutiny.

4. Revoke Access to Corporate Systems and Assets

The clock is ticking once you have notified the vendor that you are cancelling the relationship. When feasible, it's essential to immediately begin revoking the vendor's access to your corporate systems, networks, and physical assets. This process should include disabling login credentials and VPN access and removing permissions from corporate applications and databases. Ensure that any physical assets or devices provided to the vendor are also returned. The IT team should conduct a thorough audit to confirm that no unauthorized access points remain for the vendor and their personnel. I would also recommend the CISO review current processes such as incident response or business continuity if the departing vendor was a critical partner to understand the impact of changing this support vendor for a necessary business process.

5. Conduct an Exit Interview

This step is often overlooked as no one wants to talk to someone who has been a partner and now you're terminating the relationship. However, conducting an exit interview with the vendor can provide valuable insights into the partnership's performance, potential security risks, and areas for improvement in your vendor management processes. It also allows for a formal conclusion to the collaboration between the vendor and your team and ensures that both parties are clear on any outstanding obligations or concerns. I keep this as positive as possible when talking to an outgoing vendor. I look at this process as my organization matures and our needs change, and it's essential as the primary security executive for the business to ensure I have the correct tools and services we need for current services and future initiatives.

6. Update Documentation and Inform Stakeholders

Now that you have offboarded your vendor, it's time to update internal documentation and records to reflect the termination of the partnership. This process should include removing the vendor from your list of active suppliers, updating access logs, and revising both internal and external contacts lists. Besides updating lists and paperwork, you must inform relevant organizational stakeholders about the change, ensuring everyone knows about the offboarding and its implications for their operations.

7. Review and Adjust Business Operations as Necessary

Assess the impact of the vendor's offboarding on your business operations. This assessment may involve identifying interim solutions or quickly onboarding a new vendor to fill the gap. To ensure minimal disruption to current operations, I recommend completing an assessment before the cancellation notification is provided to the outgoing vendor so there are no surprises. I would also ask other business units that the offboarding might impact to review your assessment findings so all stakeholders understand why the vendor is being offboarded and can provide input for a replacement.

8. Learn and Improve Your Vendor Management Process

Finally, the experience of offboarding the vendor can be used to mature current vendor management and offboarding processes. I would recommend if this vendor was a critical stakeholder providing services required by your team that you formally document a vendor lessons learned process. Use this process and the report you develop to identify what worked well and where there were challenges and apply these lessons to future vendor engagements to enhance efficiency, security, and compliance.

Conclusion

Offboarding vendors is a critical process that, if not handled properly, can pose significant risks to your company's data security, business operations, and access to corporate assets. By following a structured and secure offboarding process companies can mitigate these risks, ensuring a smooth transition and maintaining the integrity of their operations and data. Remember, the goal is to end the relationship on a professional and secure note, paving the way for future partnerships and maintaining a positive reputation in the market.

Engagements End: The Critical Role of Proactive Offboarding Planning

Matt Stamper

Organizations ideally enter vendor or supplier relationships with the goal of long-term success; the reality is that engagements will sometimes end—sometimes abruptly!

No one enters a vendor or supplier relationship with the hope that it will end with conflict and litigation. In my view, organizations that do not invest the time and diligence during the onboarding process and cycle through vendors and suppliers on a routine basis add undue stress to their operations and risk to their business. Vendor and supplier relationships are complicated in the best of scenarios; frequent turnover among material providers should be avoided, and where there is high turnover, it's an opportunity to take pause and look at internal practices to see if they foment this continuous change. Under ideal circumstances, vendor offboarding should not come as a surprise to either party. As we've discussed throughout this book, there's value in transparency—establishing clear, unambiguous expectations regarding quality, service levels, lead times, etc. This transparency requires us to understand key elements of the vendor's or supplier's operating environment. Asking for 100% uptime or 100% on-time delivery is easy. What requires work is validating the vendor's or supplier's actual capacity to meet these objectives. Objectives should be strenuous but achievable. As discussed in Chapter 4, there's value in getting the onboarding due diligence right and establishing positive versus zero-sum engagements with vendors and suppliers.

Even when the onboarding process is managed well, there will be times when suppliers and vendors must be offboarded and alternative options evaluated. Our TPRM programs should plan for these scenarios proactively. If an engagement "goes south," it should not come as a surprise for either party, and the reasons for offboarding a vendor or supplier should not be a surprise. To avoid surprises and reduce the risk of service interruptions and potential litigation, ongoing stewardship and collaboration between the parties is required (Chapter 5 provides an approach to address these dynamics).

While it is recommended, from my perspective, to enter engagements with the best intentions, it's important to understand that vendor and supplier engagements that end abruptly are costly for both parties. Knowing that relationships can and will end should be integral to your TPRM program and should be planned for accordingly. In this chapter, we'll hit upon some of the important considerations to keep in mind should a termination be required.

Your TPRM team should develop a basic exit checklist contextualized to the products and services at hand that can be quickly used to validate how a termination should proceed. The primary goal of any termination is to minimize impacts on your organization. With respect to suppliers, this means having new suppliers identified that can produce the quantities and quality required for your organization. This is one of the primary reasons why ISO 9001:2015 (Quality management systems – Requirements) requires multiple bids from distinct providers to be incorporated into standard procurement procedures.[6] For service providers, this also means finding a provider that can provide similar services with similar capabilities and quality and at a price point largely consistent with the previous provider's services. It's important to note, however, that there are times when the discharged provider's quality did not meet expectations because the finances of the engagement required the provider to cut corners. Effectively, if you "starved" a provider and expected world-class service, it's unlikely you'll get world-class service if you intend to "starve" the next provider. Again, my perspective is that mutually beneficial relationships are more

[6] If you are interested in learning more about quality management standards, consider looking at the guidance from the ISO - https://www.iso.org/standards/popular/iso-9000-family.

enduring, introduce less long-term risk, and provide a level of predictability and resilience to support business operations compared to frequent changes predicated primarily on financial concerns versus quality and operational concerns.

Let's delve into the dynamics and considerations of offboarding a vendor or supplier. As I noted above, the best way to mitigate risks with third parties is to ensure that due diligence and stewardship activities reflect the intrinsic importance of the relationship. Turnover is costly, both financially, given the costs of new due diligence activities and onboarding and integration costs, as well as operationally, given the potential for service or supply disruption.

Your offboarding checklist should be sufficiently detailed to capture the key risk considerations associated with the soon-to-be ex-vendor or ex-supplier. Ideally, during the due diligence phase of your TPRM program, your organization evaluated and assessed several alternative options that may not have been the right fit at that time. It's now time to revisit these analyses and see if any previously vetted firms may offer an option for the displaced provider. With the pace of technological change and the ever-present geopolitical concerns, revisit your requirements to see if additional factors need to be evaluated. Effectively, there should be tight integration between the onboarding and offboarding processes, notably as it relates to requirements gathering and risk tolerances for the organization.

The list below contains considerations that should be validated in the context of your offboarding checklist and associated activities. Your TPRM team should make it a practice to revisit this list and the associated workflows at least annually to determine if changes are required.

Termination Clauses – The personnel focusing on offboarding vendors and suppliers should evaluate the impacts of any termination or auto-renew clauses with time thresholds that may have been part of the supplier's contract with your organization. Many managed services, for example, have auto-renewal clauses that require proactive notification within a given period of time (typically 30 to 60 days) to cancel the service. Your TPRM program should maintain a master schedule of service and product expiry dates to ensure that ample time is provided to evaluate options and that when changes do occur, they are not disruptive to the business. Also, some factors can override termination clauses, notably those related to quality and service delivery. As part of the onboarding process, termination for cause considerations in service agreements should be reviewed and understood by the TPRM team and the lines of business that use the given product or service.

Records of Service Issues and Associated Correspondence – Your TPRM team, in collaboration with organizational stakeholders, should maintain records of service- and product-impacting issues. These considerations don't help much if they have not been conveyed to the supplier to allow them to remediate and address the issue. Again, it's important to highlight the value of transparency and stewardship. If the provider cannot effect these improvements, the cancellation of service or purchases should not come as a surprise. These records are also invaluable should litigation be required. If your organization can show a clear fact pattern of issues impacting quality and that these issues were clearly communicated to the provider, the court would look more favorably on your position should any litigation occur.

Keeping these records is invaluable. Similar to the point above regarding auto-renewal or evergreen clauses, the onboarding process should have evaluated SLAs and whether the burden is on the client to notify the supplier of the issue or if the SLA process is proactive (e.g., auto-instantiated tickets when services are outside of agreed-to parameters and direct notification to the consuming entity's appropriate points of contact on their Authorized Personnel and Emergency Contact (APEC) list).

Data Deletion and Destruction – Our economy at the macro level and our organizations at the micro level run on data. Data processing is integral to many third-party relationships, and how the data should be governed and secured is a foundational element to any engagement with a third party used to process data. So, too, are the procedures and validations that occur when that engagement ends. While many service agreements have legal provisions to either delete or destroy data at the end of the contract, these provisions, from my perspective, bring only partial assurance. It's critical, and I don't use that term lightly, to ensure the data is deleted or destroyed consistent with your organization's requirements. There are real challenges in obtaining these validations. For example, data conveyed to the third party may be overly shared within the service provider's operating environment and potentially with that provider's third parties and suppliers. Unstructured data, including sensitive data conveyed in emails or attachments, tends to propagate expansively across a provider's network and rarely reflects the need-to-know or least-privilege provisions that may have been incorporated into the service agreement. Adding insult to injury, one client's data may be co-mingled with other client data in the service provider's system, making the disaggregation of this data technically challenging.

Ensuring that data is deleted or destroyed requires technical oversight and diligence. Your TPRM team may want to proactively engage the CIO or CISO teams to help address the particular nuance of how this should be accomplished. Beyond the aforementioned service agreements, it's good practice to ask for a formal attestation from the service provider that they did indeed delete or destroy information consistent with the agreement. Ask for verifications such as pre-and-post details showing the data before being deleted, deleted in its system, and with validation that caches, trash bins, etc., have been cleared and emptied. For many service providers, these requests may be disruptive to their day-to-day activities. Anticipate pushback from the provider. Ideally, data destruction and verification mechanisms should be negotiated prior to entering into the engagement.

Even for organizations that don't process personal data, let alone from residents of the European Union, there's value in reviewing how standard contractual clauses (SCCs) are used between data controllers and data processors. These contracts unambiguously address key topics such as data residency, onward transfer, purpose limitation, and other important privacy (data) controls. In that same vein, the GDPR's Article 28 can be referenced to provide excellent context on how third-party relationships should be governed to mitigate risks that data shared with third parties is used for nonauthorized derivate works, overly shared, and not used consistent with your organization's requirements and expectations.

Attestations, Verifications, and Validations – Offboarding a vendor relationship should be formalized, and, like all effective communication, there should be validations of understandings. If an organization notifies a vendor or supplier that they are terminating the engagement, it's important to ensure that the provider or supplier acknowledges this termination request in writing. Too frequently, requests to end services are sent by the contracting entity to the email address of a sales representative or other personnel who may no longer be with the provider. Effectively, the termination notice is lost in the provider's operating environment, and the cancellation is not recognized in a timely manner. This is one of the reasons why verifying administrative and billing points of contact with the APEC form is so important. Ensure that your cancellation notices are provided to the right department or individual. Ask that department or individual to acknowledge the receipt of the cancellation notice to your organization in writing. Store this acknowledgement in your vendor master file or a similar system where these details are maintained.

Your offboarding process should also request a final statement from the provider indicating that all invoices have been paid in full. No one likes to be surprised by an unexpected invoice. Your TPRM team should collaborate with your organization's primary users of the service or the goods supplied to see if there are other variables that the provider will need to validate and attest to. If your service agreement had non-disparagement clauses, these too should be validated and attested to, especially if the engagement is ending under contentious circumstances. It's also advisable to validate confidentiality clauses and how long these are enforced by the agreement.

Regulators – Depending upon the operating context of your organization, there may also be requirements to notify regulators regarding the change in vendors or suppliers. This may be something as perfunctory as tracking business associates in the context of HIPAA, where notification is not explicitly required, to more explicit requirements found in regulations such as the Defense Federal Acquisition Regulation Supplement (DFARS), the Federal Acquisition Regulation (FAR), and the International Traffic in Arms Regulation (ITAR). Specifically, DFARS 252.244-7001 requires notification of changes to material providers.[7] FAR 52.243-7 requires notification to the Administrative Contracting Officer of any changes that could impact the contract terms and conditions.[8] ITAR § 122.4(a) - Material Changes requires covered entities to notify the Directorate of Defense Trade Controls (DDTC) within five days of material changes.[9] Your TPRM should validate with your organization's counsel if any specific regulatory notifications may be required when one vendor or supplier is removed and replaced by another.

Internal Communications – No one likes to be caught off guard by developments that could have been reasonably communicated to organizational stakeholders in a timely manner. If a provider's services are widely used within your organization, you should notify applicable stakeholders of the change. Granted, the timing of notifications may be a sensitive issue until the change is formally approved and effected. As part of your offboarding checklist, the TPRM should validate the appropriate communication protocols to internal (and potentially external) stakeholders.

Post-Engagement Security Assessment – Your TPRM team will need to collaborate with the security team to ensure that a post-engagement security assessment is conducted. Specifically, the security team, likely in collaboration with the service desk and Infrastructure & Operations (I&O), should formally terminate any network connections or services between the contracting entity and the supplier. Similarly, there may have been service accounts and credentials for the provider's staff added to the contracting entity's domain or identity stores. Make sure that provider credentials that

7 Please reference – https://www.acquisition.gov/dfars/252.244-7001-contractor-purchasing-system-administration.

8 Please reference – https://www.acquisition.gov/far/52.243-7.

9 Please reference - https://www.ecfr.gov/current/title-22/chapter-I/subchapter-M/part-122/section-122.4.

may have been added to third-party applications and SaaS services are similarly validated and reviewed. These credentials and accounts should be disabled or deleted in a manner consistent with your organization's policy. Ensure that your security operations center (SOC) or security monitoring services look for any anomalous activity related to the provider, its services, and its personnel following the cancellation of the engagement. The security and I&O teams should also validate the status of any applications, scripts, third-party services, tools, or devices that were used by the provider and its personnel or by internal personnel. Once this assessment has been completed, its status and findings should be conveyed to appropriate personnel (e.g., legal counsel, CISO, CIO, etc.) for final review and approval.

Offboarding Risk Assessment – Conducting a post-engagement risk assessment is highly recommended for material and high-impact engagements. The assessment should determine why terminating the engagement was necessary and the factors that led to that decision. The assessment should determine if there were gaps in the onboarding due diligence or failures that may have occurred with ongoing stewardship not addressing issues that ultimately required the engagement to be terminated. These assessments should be focused on learning from previous concerns and challenges and not an excuse to blame individuals or departments for not managing the engagement correctly. There may be scenarios where the engagement ends for mutually agreeable reasons. These, too, should be documented and captured as part of the assessment. The time invested to analyze why engagements conclude will help inform and improve the onboarding process.

Ensure the assessment also looks at potential enterprise risk factors for the now-terminated engagement. The risk factors that should be validated include the following:

- Legal and Contractual Risks
- Reputational Risks
- Operational Disruptions
- Coordination Risks

- Data and Asset Retrieval
- Compliance Risks
- Implementation Risks with a New Vendor

To assess these factors, have the TPRM team collaborate with business units and line of business functions that were directly involved in the consumption of the vendor's products or services. Ask open-ended questions and validate understandings with these stakeholders.

The relationship between your onboarding and offboarding processes should be closed-loop. When your organization offboards vendors and suppliers, there is an inherent risk to your organization. These risks should be proactively assessed and inform your TPRM program. Under ideal circumstances, the lessons learned from a "failed" engagement will be critical to enhancing your onboarding processes and those actions for overseeing current and future engagements. The goal is to foment continuous learning and assessment capabilities for your TPRM program.

Insights and Actions

Chapter 7 discusses the final stage of the vendor management lifecycle: termination and offboarding. It emphasizes that effective offboarding is essential for minimizing disruption, protecting sensitive data, and ensuring smooth business operations. The process should be proactive, transparent, and well-documented, reflecting lessons learned from the entire vendor relationship. Here are the highlights that you should consider implementing in your third-party offboarding process.

Key Governance Concerns and Steps in Vendor Offboarding

- Performance Evaluation: Conduct comprehensive reviews of the vendor's performance throughout the contract, assessing whether SLAs and performance metrics were met or exceeded.
- Strategic Alignment: Evaluate whether the vendor's services, financial health, and key personnel still align with the organization's strategic objectives and future needs.
- Cost-Benefit Analysis: Assess the financial value delivered by the vendor, including total cost of ownership (TCO) and return on investment (ROI).
- Risk Assessment: Reassess risks associated with continuing, adjusting, or terminating the vendor relationship, including operational continuity, data security, compliance, and transition costs.
- Market Analysis and Vendor Comparison: Analyze market trends and compare alternative vendors to ensure the current vendor remains competitive in pricing, technology, and service quality.
- Stakeholder Feedback: Gather and analyze feedback from key stakeholders and end-users regarding their satisfaction with the vendor's services and relationship management.

- Contract Terms Review: Review existing contract terms for areas requiring renegotiation, such as pricing, service scope, or updated SLAs.
- Negotiation Strategy: Develop a strategy for contract renewal discussions, balancing organizational leverage with the need to maintain positive relationships.

Transition and Offboarding Best Practices

- Transition and Exit Planning: Plan for knowledge transfer, data migration, and minimal disruption to business operations when switching vendors or insourcing services.
- Legal and Compliance Implications: Understand penalties for early termination, data retention requirements, and regulatory obligations.
- Documentation and Record-Keeping: Ensure thorough documentation of the renewal or termination process, including rationale, negotiation records, and transition plans.
- Communication Plan: Develop a plan to inform internal stakeholders, employees, and possibly customers of the decision, ensuring clarity and vetting communications with legal counsel.

Practical Steps for Secure and Effective Offboarding

- Formal Notice: Initiate offboarding with a formal notification to the vendor, following contractual requirements.
- Contractual Obligations: Carefully review contract clauses related to offboarding, data handling, and confidentiality.
- Secure and Retrieve Corporate Data: Identify all data shared with the vendor, ensure its secure return or destruction, and obtain certificates of destruction if required.

- Revoke Access: Immediately revoke the vendor's access to corporate systems, networks, and physical assets.
- Exit Interview: Conduct an exit interview with the vendor to gather feedback and formally conclude the relationship.
- Update Documentation: Remove the vendor from active supplier lists, update access permissions, and inform relevant stakeholders.
- Review and Adjust Business Operations: Assess the impact of offboarding on business operations and identify interim solutions or new vendors as needed.
- Learn and Improve: Use the offboarding experience to mature vendor management processes and improve future engagements.

Additional Considerations for TPRM Teams

- Termination Clauses: Evaluate auto-renewal and termination clauses to avoid service disruptions.
- Records of Service Issues: Maintain records of service-impacting issues and communications with the vendor.
- Data Deletion and Destruction: Ensure data is deleted or destroyed according to organizational requirements, with technical oversight and formal attestations from the vendor.
- Attestations and Validations: Obtain written acknowledgments of termination notices and final statements from the vendor confirming all invoices are paid.
- Regulatory Notification: Notify regulators as required.
- Internal Communications: Inform internal stakeholders of the change in a timely manner.

- Post-Engagement Security Assessment: Conduct a security assessment to ensure all vendor access and credentials are revoked and monitor for anomalous activity.
- Offboarding Risk Assessment: Conduct a post-engagement risk assessment to identify gaps in onboarding or ongoing stewardship and inform future improvements.

Section 3

Managing and Optimizing

Resilience is accepting your new reality, even if it's less good than the one you had before.

~ Elizabeth Edwards, American Attorney and Author

Introduction

In Section 3, we begin to examine the external factors that impact the supply chain and provide a methodology for optimization. Dr. Andrea Little Limbago contributes two critical essays. In Chapter 8, "The Great Reset: Supply Chain Risk Management in the New Normal," she provides a comprehensive analysis of how global supply chains have transformed in response to recent disruptions and geopolitical shifts. She makes the point that no single event is entirely responsible for the "new normal," but rather, these changes have been building for some time and are unlikely to subside.

In Chapter 9, "Optimizing the Supply Chain Risk Management Program: Reasonable Rationalization," Chris Forbes provides a comprehensive framework for optimizing supply chain risk management (SCRM) programs, emphasizing the need for practical, agile, and financially sound approaches that align with business objectives and resilience goals. In our current environment where disruptions, seemingly out of our control, can have such profound impacts, his methodology for optimizing the supply chain and maintaining supply chain resilience is invaluable. Immediately following Chris' essay is a list of publications he references throughout.

Then in Chapter 10, "Managing and Monitoring Your Vendors," Andrea builds on one of the disruptions she describes in Chapter 8 and examines the growing and intertwined risks of sustainability, climate change, and third-party (vendor) management. Andrea examines the growing impact of a changing climate, highlighting its increasing influence on global supply chains and corporate risk management strategies. Whether or not companies take a stance on combating climate change is irrelevant to the impact that these changes will have on them, their suppliers, and their customers.

Chapter 8

The Great Reset: Supply Chain Risk Management in the New Normal

Dr. Andrea Little Limbago

Whether it's diversification, redundancy, or taking the first step toward visibility into geographic concentration risk, companies that gain transparency across their supply chain ecosystem and prioritize adaptation and resilience will gain the competitive advantage in the new normal.

2020 was a global inflection point. The COVID-19 pandemic exposed the fragility of global supply chains while also accelerating many technological and geopolitical shifts. Those who expected a simple return to the "Before Times" are increasingly bumping into the reality of the new normal, with global physical and digital supply chains transforming along geopolitical fault lines. These massive movements in global competition are having an equally massive impact on supply chain risk.

It wasn't long ago that geopolitics was an afterthought in supply chain risk management. Since joining the World Trade Organization in 2001, China's percentage of global trade jumped from 4% to 13%.[10] China surpassed the United States as the world's leading destination for foreign direct investment in 2020.[11] A few years later, the tone is quickly changing. Inbound foreign direct investment

10 https://asia.nikkei.com/Economy/China-s-trade-with-world-surges-ninefold-after-20-years-in-WTO.

11 https://www.wsj.com/articles/china-overtakes-u-s-as-worlds-leading-destination-for-foreign-direct-investment-11611511200.

(FDI) into China has collapsed, down 94% in the second quarter of 2023 from the same period in 2021.[12] Trade among geopolitical blocs increased by roughly 5% since Russia's invasion of Ukraine.[13] Fears over the expansion of this and other global conflicts, the expansion of Western export controls, China's updated data privacy and cybersecurity laws, and concerns about detention are among the many factors driving this change.[14]

Welcome to the new normal. Globalization is undergoing a significant transformation driven by geopolitics, including the U.S.-China trade rivalry, Russia's invasion of Ukraine, as well as massive decoupling of authoritarian and democratic regimes. Take these gigantic shifts and couple them with the economic uncertainty due to U.S. tariff policy fluctuations and global trade wars, and geopolitics are now front and center.[15] Geopolitical tensions already existed prior to the onset of COVID-19, but the pandemic surfaced and accelerated many of the ongoing transformations that are defining the new normal.

As if the geopolitical tensions—and the subsequent reglobalization of trade flows, technological bifurcation, and shifting regulatory environments—weren't enough, climate change adds yet another layer of risks to the new normal. How can organizations build resilience during these unprecedented global transformations? A new mindset is required, one that internalizes these global shifts and prioritizes collective resilience. Innovations in collaboration on par with global transformations are required.

12 https://www.economist.com/business/2023/09/26/ties-between-foreign-businesses-and-china-go-from-bad-to-worse.

13 https://www.wto.org/english/blogs_e/ce_ralph_ossa_e/blog_ro_12sep23_e.htm.

14 https://www.reuters.com/breakingviews/nomura-is-merely-first-line-new-china-risk-2023-09-25/.

15 https://www.bbc.com/news/articles/cx2epx15pj2o.

Supply Chain Security Risks in a Shifting Geopolitical Landscape

As the Russian invasion of Ukraine demonstrated, in addition to the horrific human toll geopolitical events can cause widespread disruption across a range of industries. From agriculture to energy to key metals, the Russian invasion caused significant global supply chain disruptions.[16] Unfortunately, conflict and instability are not limited to Russia's invasion. Conflict in Sudan shocked gold markets, protests in Canada and India disrupted the automotive and agricultural supply chains, and the Tigray War devastated manufacturing and crops.[17]

For decades, geopolitics was little more than an afterthought for supply chain risk management. Just-in-time strategies focused on hyper-efficiencies that fueled economic interdependence, with minimal consideration of national boundaries. Times have changed. In 2017, only 13% of executives had taken active steps to offset their geopolitical risk.[18] In contrast, a 2023 survey found that 97% of CEOs are adjusting their investment strategies due to geopolitical risks.[19]

The growing impact of geopolitics on global supply chains is perhaps most evident when discussing Taiwan and the semiconductor industry. Taiwan's dominance over the global semiconductor industry cannot be overstated. Producing 90% of advanced semiconductors, this "Silicon Shield" was long thought to protect Taiwan and deter military invasion.[20] Taiwan is also a core hub for the petrochemical, electronics, and financial industries.[21] The strength of the Silicon Shield is now in question as a record number

[16] https://news.ufl.edu/2023/02/russia-ukraine-global-supply-chain/.
[17] https://www.bloomberg.com/news/articles/2023-05-17/conflict-brings-sudan-s-lucrative-official-gold-trade-to-a-halt.
[18] https://dobetter.esade.edu/en/political-and-geopolitical-risk.
[19] https://fortune.com/2023/02/07/ey-ceos-changed-investment-strategy-geopolitical-challenges-international-politics-economy/.
[20] https://www.economist.com/special-report/2023/03/06/taiwans-dominance-of-the-chip-industry-makes-it-more-important.
[21] https://www.internsinasia.com/blog/taiwans-top-5-industries.

of Chinese warplanes and warships were spotted near the island throughout 2023, leaving many wondering whether the saber-rattling will turn into conflict.[22] More recently, China conducted a large-scale naval exercise in December 2024 in both the air and sea space around Taiwan.[23]

While significantly impacting supply chains, geopolitical risk strategies must extend beyond China and focus on broader global transformations and conflict hot spots. With the worst conflict in decades in the Middle East and Ukraine, as well as a series of coups in commodity-rich African states, geopolitical conflict will continue to cause massive human suffering and upend the global economy. As tensions continue to rise, geopolitical uncertainties will continue to send shocks across the interdependent global economy, deepening the biggest economic transformations in generations.

Shifting Supply Chains

Many organizations are altering their global supply chain footprint in response to these geopolitical risks. For instance, due to new cybersecurity laws and tightening ties to China, many corporations are fleeing Hong Kong, especially in the financial and technology industries.[24] Simon Cartledge has written on this topic and noted that investing or residing in Hong Kong used to be "a fairly risk-free matter" for corporations and notes that is no longer the case. A similar trend is occurring in oil and gas, where oil giants are moving investments into the Western Hemisphere due to concerns over expanding regional conflict in Ukraine and the Middle East.[25] This diversification aims to manage these geopolitical risks.

[22] https://abcnews.go.com/International/wireStory/taiwan-spotted-22-chinese-warplanes-20-warships-island-103109443.

[23] https://globaltaiwan.org/2025/01/the-prc-sends-a-message-to-the-international-community/.

[24] https://www.wsj.com/world/asia/hong-kong-china-corporate-headquarters-retreat-10454a9a?mod=hp_lead_pos7.

[25] https://www.wsj.com/business/energy-oil/exxon-chevron-look-to-the-west-in-an-increasingly-uncertain-world-6bc2ea38?mod=djem10point.

While many point to Russia's invasion as the turning point for global trade, the transformation of globalization has been ongoing for years. The U.S.-China trade war escalated between 2017 and 2020 when the U.S. negative balance of trade decreased from $375 billion to $310 billion.[26] A movement toward decoupling with China is not limited to the U.S. and only grew in relevance during the onset of the COVID-19 pandemic, as both the private and public sectors felt firsthand their single-source dependencies on China.

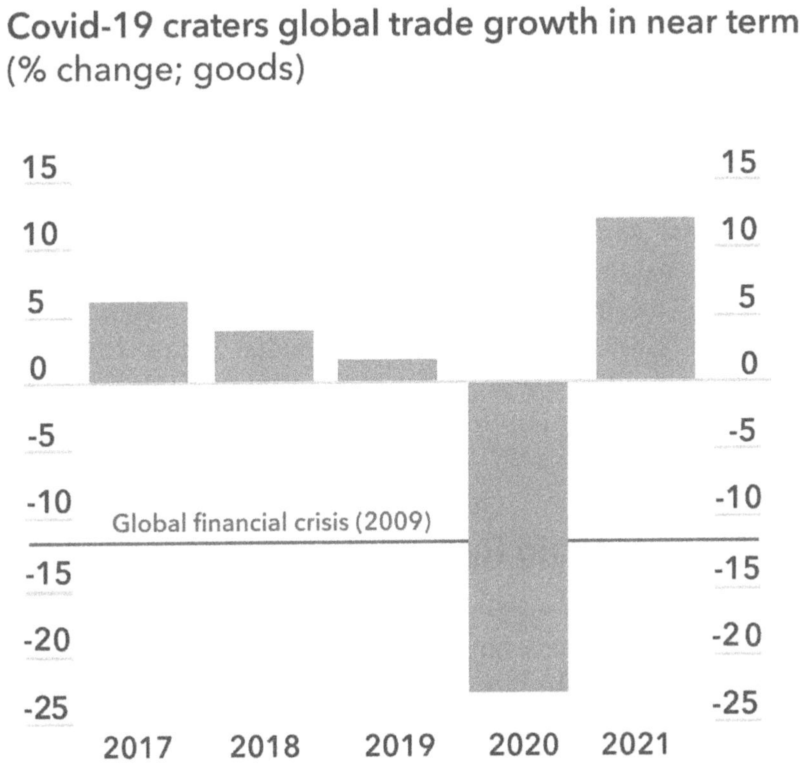

Figure 8.1 - Global Trade Growth Under Covid-19 [27]

The pandemic's impact on global trade was unprecedented. Geopolitical considerations notwithstanding, the global shock forced companies to reevaluate their global footprint and concentration risks. Since 2021, there has been record-breaking reshoring by U.S.

---

[26] https://warsawinstitute.org/u-s-china-trade-war-origins-timeline-consequences/.

[27] Source: The Economist Intelligence Unit.

companies, wherein companies return offshore operations to their domestic headquarters.[28]

However, following decades of globalization and hyper-specialized supply chains, home countries do not necessarily meet all necessary criteria for onshoring. And this is where geopolitics has additional influence. Allyshoring—or friendshoring—is a growing part of supply chain de-risking and diversification. Former U.S. Treasury Secretary Janet Yellin noted, "Working with allies and partners through friend-shoring is an important element of strengthening economic resilience while sustaining the dynamism and productivity growth that comes with economic integration."[29]

Labor uncertainty, economic fluctuations, concentration risks, and reglobalization of the global economy along geopolitical lines is already well underway. However, we are just in the early stages of corporations and governments derisking their supply chains in response to geopolitical shifts. As Taiwan Semiconductor Manufacturing Company (TSMC) founder Morris Chang has summarized, "There is no globalization anymore. There is no free trade anymore, the priority is national security only. I see global competition going on."[30]

Restrictions and Regulatory Landscape

Geopolitics are not only pushing organizations to reassess their global supply chain footprints, but they are also sparking some of the largest regulatory shifts in decades. Driven by security risks as well as human rights violations, governments across North America, Europe, and Asia are sanctioning Chinese and Russian companies in the thousands. Since 2016, the U.S. Department of Commerce has added over 1,300 Russian and Chinese companies to its Entity List. This is just one of many U.S. restrictions lists, with the UK, EU, and

[28] https://reshorenow.org/content/pdf/2022_Data_Report.pdf.

[29] https://www.cnbc.com/2022/07/19/us-treasury-secretary-on-supply-chain-resilience-use-friend-shoring.html.

[30] https://asia.nikkei.com/Business/Tech/Semiconductors/TSMC-s-Morris-Chang-says-tougher-competition-in-store-for-chipmaker.

Australia among the many other governments sanctioning Chinese and Russian companies.

In turn, China has issued its own Unreliable Entities list, adding aerospace and defense companies that are prohibited from import, export, and investment activities in China.[31] Following the corporate exodus from Russia in early 2022, Russia has imposed an exit tax on companies attempting to leave the country. Western companies still operating in Russia also face the real risk that the government could seize them.[32]

These tit-for-tat global sanctions contribute to the reglobalization of supply chains, as well as a growing technological bifurcation. Geopolitical strategic competition is especially targeting emerging technologies, with U.S. legislation, such as the CHIPS and Science Act, driving domestic production and export controls, including those on advanced AI chips to China and 21 other countries with which the U.S. has an arms embargo.[33] Additional bans by the U.S., Australia, Canada, the UK, and the EU targeting Chinese technology companies such as Huawei, ZTE, Hikvision, and Dahua, as well as investment restrictions in China, further entrench the technological bifurcation.[34]

Just as technologies are bifurcating, so too are data privacy and security risks. Digital authoritarianism—the use of digital information technology to surveil, repress, and manipulate domestic and foreign populations—introduces yet another layer of risk for global supply chains. Foxconn, a Fortune 500 supplier known for making Apple iPhones, is among the corporations impacted by China's regulatory landscape, as multiple Chinese locations were

[31] https://sanctionsnews.bakermckenzie.com/china-added-two-us-companies-to-the-unreliable-entities-list/.

[32] https://www.npr.org/2023/04/19/1170919522/many-american-companies-that-waited-to-exit-russia-are-now-struggling-to-leave.

[33] https://www.cnbc.com/2023/10/17/us-bans-export-of-more-ai-chips-including-nvidia-h800-to-china.html.

[34] https://www.reuters.com/world/white-house-detail-plans-restricting-some-us-investments-china-source-2023-08-09/.

searched under the auspices of tax evasion investigations.[35] Increasingly, authoritarian (and some non-authoritarian) governments are leveraging their domestic regulations to force access to sensitive data of corporations residing within their sovereign borders. For instance, Russia has probed the source code of some U.S. technology companies as a requisite for accessing the Russian market.[36]

This shifting regulatory environment introduces supply chain risks on multiple levels. These include security risks introduced by adversarial technologies in the corporate tech stack, regulatory compliance requirements of eliminating any of the thousands of restricted companies from your supply chain, and intellectual property and sensitive data access via foreign regulatory environments. The technological bifurcation that is underway introduces a new range of risks but also opportunities, as we'll discuss in the final section. But first, there is one additional feature of the new normal that knows no sovereign boundaries: climate change.

Climate Change

Climate change, no longer a distant possibility, is already dramatically increasing the frequency and severity of natural hazard events, causing a steady drumbeat of record-breaking forest fires, hurricanes, typhoons, droughts, heat waves, floods, and winter storms. The last decade broke numerous records in natural disaster-imposed devastation, with the last eight years being the hottest on record, and more records will regrettably be broken in the decade ahead.[37] From China's historic floods to Texas' ice storms and Australia's wildfires, natural hazards have upended supply chains across the globe.[38] The Texas ice storms alone cost supply chains $10 billion in disruptions, while China's flooding disrupted a diverse

[35] https://apnews.com/article/china-tax-inspections-foxconn-taiwan-business-cba0a0eb5154d6067c00a38575d907b0.

[36] https://www.reuters.com/article/us-usa-cyber-russia/tech-firms-let-russia-probe-software-widely-used-by-u-s-government-idUSKBN1FE1DT.

[37] https://www.nytimes.com/interactive/2023/climate/earth-hottest-years.html.

[38] https://www.strategicsourceror.com/2020/02/australian-wildfires-have-sizable.html.

range of supply chains, from pigs to coal, and led to the closure of a Nissan plant.[39] Water scarcity in the world's most populous cities is not a distant reality but effectively is already underway. The growing water stress increases the risks of conflict and humanitarian crises.[40]

Supply chain disruptions caused by catastrophic events, such as natural disasters and diseases, are among the most deadly and costly. Natural disasters have inflicted billions of dollars in damages and are already reshaping supply chains.[41] According to one study, adverse weather variation impacts profitability in at least 70% of businesses.[42] An October 2023 U.S. Senate hearing cited estimates that climate change could cost companies $120 billion by 2026, noting that the adverse impact of climate change on supply chains "has already begun."[43] Despite these growing risks and warnings from the United Nations, businesses are slow to heed these warnings.[44] Supply chains are at risk from physical disruptions due to climate change, and they are particularly vulnerable when there are high concentrations of suppliers exposed to climatic risks and low geographic diversification of supply sites.

Many of the most critical global supply chain hubs are also located in areas vulnerable to natural disasters. Taiwan not only sits along geopolitical fault lines, but also geological fault lines, and has a high risk of tectonic activity. Shanghai and Rotterdam are at heightened flood risk, while Los Angeles faces tectonic, tsunami, and wildfire risks. A severe natural disaster to these or other major global ports would ripple across supply chains. Following the record-breaking natural hazards in July 2023, University of Exeter research impact fellow David Armstrong McKay noted, "What used to be a rare event

39 https://www.weatheroptics.co/post/supply-chain-delays-likely-exceeded-10-billion-during-deep-south-winter-storm.

40 https://www.cbsnews.com/news/major-cities-are-running-out-of-water-a-new-report-for-world-water-day-says/.

41 https://www.ncei.noaa.gov/access/billions/.

42 https://www.sciencedirect.com/science/article/abs/pii/S014829631730334X.

43 https://www.supplychaindive.com/news/Senate-hearing-spotlights-climate-disruption-on-supply-chains/697936/.

44 https://www.reuters.com/business/sustainable-business/despite-mounting-climate-disasters-companies-slow-heed-un-call-fund-adaptation-2023-04-26/.

is becoming more common, and what used to be impossible in an unchanged climate is now becoming a real possibility."[45]

The Great Reset

Global supply chains must become resilient to these kinds of disruptions and focus on adaptation and diversification rather than simply optimizing. Companies that find their own unique balance of efficiency and resilience will thrive in the new normal, while those who fail to adapt will be left in a perpetual reactionary mode. Unfortunately, many still view these risks as futuristic and too often, the tyranny of the now supersedes longer-term planning.

But the future is now. These global transformations are already well underway, with significant implications for compliance, security, and continuity of operations. Instead of rejecting the new normal, companies must embrace it and, in fact, can leverage these shifts to produce positive change. Improved security, sustainability, and collaboration can also become defining features of organizations that thrive in this new normal. In fact, a new mindset focused on building collaborative resilience across entire supply chain ecosystems must become an integral component of de-risking supply chains.

Collective resilience captures this notion of leveraging collaboration to pursue strength in unity, sharing information to identify vulnerabilities and risks and evaluating the most insecure links within highly interdependent systems.[46] Concentration risks, such as those in Taiwan, can only be mitigated through collective action. At a strategic level, there has been a decisive movement toward collective resilience following Russia's invasion of Ukraine, with new alliances and cooperative agreements, such as the Quad's Cyber Challenge and the Chip Pact, introduced to achieve greater supply chain resilience.[47] The private sector must similarly follow suit and pursue innovations

45 https://www.washingtonpost.com/climate-environment/2023/07/31/july-hottest-month-extreme-weather-future/.

46 https://www.darkreading.com/vulnerabilities-threats/strength-in-unity-why-it-s-especially-important-to-strengthen-your-supply-chain-now.

47 https://thescif.org/combating-digital-authoritarianism-through-collective-resilience-insights-from-russias-invasion-c35955c1290d.

in collaboration to help strengthen resilience across their entire supply chain, while also addressing geographic or technological concentration risks. Most businesses rely heavily on a handful of cloud providers and cloud-based business services, introducing significant risks for single points of failure or access. Introducing new processes for information sharing or assisting in cybersecurity defenses could go a long way toward gaining greater supply chain visibility and proactively addressing vulnerabilities as well as concentration dependencies.

This great reset is necessary regardless of whether organizations prioritize it or not. At a symposium in the heart of Silicon Valley, Ken McCallum, Director General of MI5, warned, "If you're working today at the cutting edge of technology then geopolitics is interested in you, even if you're not interested in geopolitics."[48] This is not only true for emerging technologies; virtually no industry will be immune from the generational shifts that are underway. Companies need to integrate this new normal into their due diligence and continuous monitoring of supply chains. Whether it's diversification, redundancy, or taking the first step toward visibility into geographic concentration risk, companies that gain transparency across their supply chain ecosystem and prioritize adaptation and resilience will gain the competitive advantage in the new normal.

[48] https://www.bbc.com/news/uk-67142161.

Insights and Actions

Supply chain risk management must evolve to address the new realities of geopolitics, regulatory complexity, technological bifurcation, and climate change. The future belongs to organizations that prioritize resilience, transparency, and collaborative adaptation in their supply chain strategies.

Global physical and digital supply chains are transforming along geopolitical fault lines. Globalization is undergoing a significant transformation driven by geopolitics, including the U.S.-China trade rivalry, Russia's invasion of Ukraine, as well as massive decoupling of authoritarian and democratic regimes.

Those who expect a simple return to the "Before Times" are increasingly bumping into the reality of the new normal, encountering more and more frequent disruptions, surprises, and vulnerabilities within their supply chain. Whether from export controls or conflict or due to climate risks, a reglobalization of supply chains is underway, spearheaded by organizations seeking greater resilience and diversification.

Resilience in the new normal requires collective resilience. Collective security focuses on innovations in collaboration to pursue strength in unity, sharing information to identify vulnerabilities and risks, and elevating the most insecure links within highly interdependent systems.

Chapter 9

Optimizing the Supply Chain Risk Management Program: Reasonable Rationalization

Chris Forbes

Optimizing SCRM requires structured, data-driven methodologies to balance risk reduction, operational efficiency, and financial performance. Successful programs explicitly define unacceptable risks, justify investments, and continuously adapt to evolving threats—ensuring resilience and sustainable growth.

1.0 The Tangible Costs of Risk

Supply chain risk management (SCRM) is now essential across industries as innovation drives supply chains to operate faster and with greater unpredictability. Organizations must adopt practical, agile approaches to manage risk while supporting profitability. Effective SCRM requires alignment with business objectives, proactive hazard management, and a focus on resilience. Organizations must also ensure that risk-management investments deliver measurable returns by thoroughly understanding:

- True/Total Value at Risk (TVaR)
- Intangible and Psychological Costs
- Unacceptable Risks
- Effective Risk Responses
- Risk Optimization Strategies

Companies must carefully balance thoroughness with agility. Excessive analysis can delay critical action ("analysis paralysis"), while superficial assessments risk regulatory and shareholder scrutiny. This chapter offers a framework to navigate these competing demands.

Understanding True Value at Risk (TVaR)

Traditional financial measures offer partial views:

- Value at Risk (VaR) estimates maximum loss within normal conditions but may miss catastrophic events.
- Tail Risk highlights rare but severe losses that VaR may overlook.
- Conditional Value at Risk (CVaR) improves on VaR by calculating average losses during worst-case scenarios.

True Value at Risk (TVaR) builds further by using stress testing and scenario analysis to include operational, financial, strategic, and reputational risks, providing a more realistic and actionable picture.

Quantifying Financial Impacts: GAAP and IFRS

Under U.S. Generally Accepted Accounting Principles (GAAP), losses must be recognized when both probable and reasonably estimable, divided into:

- Probable: Recognize and record.
- Reasonably Possible: Disclose without recording.
- Remote: No action required.

International Financial Reporting Standards (IFRS) (IAS 37) similarly classify potential losses as Provisions, Contingent Liabilities, or Contingent Assets. Accountants must record insurance recoveries separately once they become probable. For example, the accountant must reflect disaster-related losses (such as floods or fires) or asset impairments if they meet the recognition standards.

The Hidden Costs of Risk

Risk underestimation occurs due to:

- Uninsured Losses: Focusing only on insured damages misses broader impacts.
- Risk Misperception: Underestimating the frequency and severity of extreme events.
- Long-Term Economic Impacts: Ignoring supply-chain disruptions and reduced earnings following events.
- Rising Disaster Frequency: Climate change amplifies the risk landscape, requiring updated modeling.

Organizations must model beyond insurance payouts and recognize the hidden risks affecting resilience and sustainability.

TVaR: A Pragmatic Approach

Accurately estimating the full financial impact of disruptions ensures adequate preparation. TVaR incorporates additional costs, such as overtime labor and external contractors, that arise from events beyond normal operations. Routine activities performed by internal staff do not require separate estimates. By applying TVaR, companies obtain a realistic, complete view of risk, allowing them to make smarter investment decisions and improve operational resilience.

1.1 Revenue: Current Losses

Current revenue losses occur immediately during a supply chain disruption and include:

- Lost Sales: Unfulfilled orders leading to direct revenue loss and potential customer migration to competitors.
- Discounts and price reductions to retain dissatisfied customers will result in revenue losses.

- Contractual penalties, fines, and extra fees may result from failing to meet service-level agreements.

Accurately capturing these figures is essential for understanding the actual financial consequences of disruptions.

1.2 Revenue: Future Losses

Future revenue losses are more challenging to quantify but can significantly impact financial health:

- Loss of Customer Trust: Ongoing decline in sales due to damaged loyalty.
- Lost Business Opportunities: Missed contracts and partnerships.
- Brand Reputation Damage: Reduced brand attractiveness, hurting market share.
- Competitive Disadvantages: Competitors gain market share by outperforming during a disruption.
- Increased Acquisition Costs: Additional marketing and sales efforts are needed to rebuild trust.

Organizations must carefully model potential future losses, factoring in both duration and severity.

1.3 Expenses: Asset Repair/Restoration

Costs related to asset restoration include:

- Direct Repairs: Labor, materials, and third-party services.
- Replacement Costs: Procurement and installation of irreparable assets.
- Salvage and Disposal: Managing damaged assets appropriately.

- Temporary Rentals: Leasing essential equipment to maintain operations during repairs.

1.4 Expenses: Additional Labor

Disruptions often necessitate increased labor, including:

- Overtime Wages: May be authorized to recover lost productivity.
- Temporary and Contract Labor: Additional expenses driven by disruptions when required to fill urgent staffing needs.
- Specialized Labor: The organization need to hire experts for complex repairs.
- Maintenance and Logistics Labor: Additional personnel will be needed to manage supply chain backlogs.

Proper labor cost forecasting is vital for recovery planning.

1.5 Expenses: Legal Services

Engaging external experts incurs costs such as:

- Legal Fees: Defense in lawsuits, contract disputes, or regulatory matters.
- Consulting Fees: Strategic advisors for recovery planning.
- Compliance Support: Ensuring adherence to evolving regulations.
- Litigation Support: Experts, forensic analysis, and evidence collection.
- Dispute Resolution: Mediation or arbitration costs.

1.6 Expenses: Indirect Expenses

Broader financial strain includes:

- Workers' Compensation Claims: Arising from disruption-related injuries.
- Insurance Premium Increases: May result from elevated risk exposure.
- Increased Borrowing Costs: May result from higher interest rates or stricter credit terms.
- Rent or Lease Increases: May be incurred from facility expansion to handle the overflow.
- Higher Administrative Costs: May be incurred during and after events, resulting in increased overhead.

1.7 Assets: Diminished Valuation and Useful Life

Supply chain disruptions often lead to:

- Lower Resale Value: Decreased market value for damaged goods.
- Lower Salvage Value: Reduced asset recoverability.
- Shortened Useful Life: Accelerated depreciation of assets.
- Impairment Losses: Permanent reductions in asset book value.

Organizations must adjust asset management strategies post-disruption.

1.8 Assets: Intangible Damage

Non-physical asset depreciation includes:

- Intellectual Property Devaluation: Reduced commercial value of intellectual property.
- Brand Reputation Loss: Weakened brand strength following service failures.
- Customer Goodwill Erosion: Lower customer retention rates.
- Loss of Strategic Contracts: Reduced business opportunities.

- Franchise and Licensing Devaluation: Weakened licensing revenue potential.

Intangible losses require strategic recovery efforts beyond immediate repairs.

1.9 Liabilities: Lawsuits

Disruptions can trigger legal and regulatory exposure:

- Legal Defense Costs: Defense against claims related to service failures.
- Settlements and Judgments: Financial penalties from adverse rulings.
- Reputational Damage Management: Costs related to public relations and customer compensation.

Organizations must accurately track contingent liabilities in their financial disclosures.

1.10 Liabilities: Regulatory Fines

Non-compliance during disruptions may result in:

- Fines and Penalties: Monetary sanctions.
- Sanction Costs: Operational and financial restrictions.
- Compliance Remediation Costs: Measures required to restore compliance status.
- Legal and Consulting Fees: Support navigating regulatory investigations.

Early identification and mitigation of regulatory risks preserve organizational credibility and financial strength.

2.0 The Intangible Cost of Risk

Supply chain disruptions often generate intangible costs that are difficult to quantify yet critical to organizational value and competitive strength. Unlike tangible losses such as shipment delays or asset repairs, intangible impacts include damaged brand reputation, diminished customer trust, and reduced employee morale.

For example, tangible costs include procurement penalties and alternative sourcing if a fire damages a supplier's facility. Intangible costs, however, stem from media coverage harming brand perception, customer attrition, and workforce uncertainty. Organizations should use scenario analysis, stakeholder surveys, and reputation modeling techniques to estimate these impacts. Integrating intangible costs into risk assessments strengthens resilience and strategic decision-making.

2.1 Strategic Setbacks

Disruptions can derail strategic initiatives, delay product launches, and weaken competitive positioning. A key supplier failure, for example, can stall market entry, enabling competitors to capture share.

These setbacks erode employee momentum, reducing productivity and amplifying uncertainty about corporate direction. Investor and partner confidence can also suffer, impacting funding opportunities and future strategic endeavors.

2.2 Fear and Uncertainty

Disruptions foster fear among employees, resulting in risk-averse behavior that hinders innovation; staff may hesitate to propose new ideas or pursue creative solutions.

2.3 Ignorance of Risks

Ignoring visible risks fosters organizational complacency and magnifies vulnerabilities. Overlooking supplier instability, for example, can cause sudden operational failures, prolonged recovery times, regulatory scrutiny, and reputational harm. Neglect also jeopardizes employee safety, product quality, and environmental responsibility, threatening long-term sustainability. Vigilant risk recognition and proactive mitigation are essential for avoiding these consequences.

2.4 Accepting Risks

A laissez-faire approach toward known risks destabilizes organizations. Dependence on a single supplier creates a single point of failure, endangering supply continuity and market position. Risk acceptance without proper contingency planning increases exposure to legal, regulatory, and reputational liabilities. It may also encourage unethical practices, eroding transparency and trust.

2.5 Over-Analyzing Risks

While thorough analysis is vital, excessive risk evaluation can cause "analysis paralysis," delaying decision-making and stalling strategic initiatives. Missed opportunities allow competitors to capitalize on inaction. Extensive indecision frustrates employees, undermines morale, and weakens leadership credibility internally. Externally, partners and investors lose confidence, impairing future collaboration and growth potential. Successful risk management requires balancing diligence with decisiveness. Research from the World Economic Forum underscores that overly complex risk management structures degrade responsiveness and operational efficiency.

2.6 Excessively Controlling Risks

Over-investment in risk controls can introduce operational inefficiencies. Excessive layers of control slow decision-making, inhibit innovation, and divert resources from core functions. This bureaucratic burden stifles organizational agility, particularly in fast-evolving markets. Moreover, excessive oversight diminishes employee autonomy, leading to disengagement and reduced morale. Bain & Company research shows that disproportionate investments in risk management often yield minimal additional benefit relative to the costs incurred.

2.7 Overconfidence

Overconfidence in risk management capabilities creates blind spots and strategic vulnerabilities. Organizations relying on past successes may dismiss emerging threats, leaving critical gaps unaddressed. Overconfidence suppresses open dialogue and feedback internally, weakening the organization's ability to adapt. Externally, stakeholders may perceive overconfident companies as reckless or complacent. McKinsey research indicates that organizations demonstrating unchecked overconfidence experience slower market adaptation and declines.

2.8 Psychological Stress from Risk

Persistent exposure to risk environments imposes heavy psychological burdens on employees. Chronic stress reduces motivation, impairs decision-making, and increases turnover, undermining operational stability. Forward-thinking organizations invest in employee well-being initiatives, fostering open conversations about stress management and providing resources to mitigate burnout. Cultivating a resilient, supported workforce is vital for maintaining operational performance during prolonged risk events.

2.9 Cost of Complexity

Risk management processes that become excessively complex can cripple operational efficiency. Layers of checks, approvals, and redundant procedures drain resources, lengthen response times, and reduce innovation potential.

Organizations must ensure that risk control structures remain proportionate, targeted, and adaptable. Research by Bain & Company and MIT reveals that excessive complexity frequently increases operational costs without corresponding improvements in risk mitigation outcomes.

2.10 The Cost of Capital

Elevated risk perceptions increase a company's cost of capital. Investors and lenders demand higher returns to compensate for perceived vulnerabilities, resulting in:

- Higher interest rates
- Tighter borrowing conditions
- Reduced investment interest

This financial strain limits an organization's agility, constrains innovation investment, and can negatively impact stock valuation. Maintaining a realistic, transparent risk management posture helps control financing costs and sustain long-term growth opportunities.

3.0 Cost-Benefit of Risk to Individuals

Understanding the psychological costs and benefits of dealing with risk is crucial in supply chain management, though these intangible factors can vary significantly among individuals based on personality and experience. Sections 3.1 and 3.2 explore how risk exposure positively and negatively impacts individuals, while Sections 3.3 through 3.10 highlight intangible benefits for organizational culture and workforce management.

3.1 Accelerating Achievements (The Good Side of Risk)

Engaging with risk can significantly enhance personal and professional development. Confronting uncertainty forces individuals out of their comfort zones, promoting growth, decision-making skills, and resilience. Taking calculated risks can lead to discovering hidden talents, developing critical thinking, and building confidence to manage future challenges effectively. Successful navigation of risks provides psychological rewards, including increased self-esteem, personal satisfaction, and a reinforced sense of accomplishment, driving continuous growth. For example, entrepreneurs launching new ventures develop critical skills and confidence by navigating initial uncertainties, creating lasting personal and professional growth.

3.2 Burdens and Burnout (The Bad Side of Risk)

However, sustained exposure to risk carries substantial psychological costs. Chronic uncertainty can lead to prolonged stress, anxiety, and decision fatigue, especially in high-stakes roles such as financial instrument trading or healthcare. Over time, this can result in burnout, characterized by emotional exhaustion, reduced productivity, and detachment from work. In extreme situations, such as military or emergency response roles, continuous exposure to high levels of risk may cause severe psychological conditions like Post-Traumatic Stress Disorder (PTSD). Additionally, negative risk experiences may lead individuals to become overly risk-averse, hindering innovation, or conversely, excessively risk-seeking, increasing potential exposure.

3.3 Confidence and Certainty (Outcomes of Optimization)

Systematic risk assessment and response planning significantly enhance confidence and reduce uncertainty within organizations. Methodical risk analysis clarifies potential outcomes and prepares teams for managing challenges effectively, providing a tangible sense of control and security. Organizations that proactively analyze and respond to risks foster a culture of preparedness and resilience, leading to confident decision-making and strategic clarity.

3.4 Deliberating Defenses (Preparing for Scrutiny)

Documented and structured risk management processes empower organizations to confidently defend decisions to auditors, regulators, and shareholders and in legal disputes. Consistent risk assessments and structured decision-making demonstrate transparency and evidence-based rationale, significantly improving defensibility. Clear risk documentation promotes dialogue with regulators, facilitates understanding of regulatory expectations, and ensures alignment with strategic business objectives, enhancing overall organizational resilience and regulatory standing.

3.5 Enhancing Efficiency (The Toil and the Toll)

Methodical risk management streamlines organizational efficiency, allowing precise resource allocation, reducing wasted efforts, and accelerating decision-making processes. Clear risk identification enables organizations to prioritize critical issues, improving responsiveness to opportunities and threats. This structured approach supports strategic alignment, maximizing outcomes while minimizing ongoing effort and creating sustainable efficiency and long-term value.

3.6 Finding Funds (Inviting Investments)

Practical risk analysis significantly boosts an organization's attractiveness to investors and lenders by demonstrating responsible risk management and strategic foresight. Organizations displaying thorough risk awareness and proactive mitigation strategies receive favorable lending terms, higher creditworthiness ratings, and greater investor confidence. Similarly, detailed risk assessments support asset-backed securitization efforts and strengthen pitches to venture capitalists, enhancing access to critical funding and growth capital.

3.7 Grounded Guidance (Method to the Madness)

A structured approach to risk analysis establishes clear standards for consistently evaluating and addressing risks across an organization. Such frameworks eliminate subjective biases, ensure reliable decision-making aligned with strategic goals, and foster adaptability to changing circumstances. A methodical approach encourages continuous improvement and cultivates a culture of accountability, significantly enhancing organizational resilience and credibility with external stakeholders.

3.8 Harnessing Harmony (United and Unified)

Standardized risk management processes and comprehensive team training ensure clarity, consistency, and effective communication across geographically distributed teams. This alignment supports leadership effectiveness, streamlines decision-making, and empowers teams to independently manage risks proactively. Clear documentation enables efficient communication with internal and external stakeholders, fostering a culture of proactive risk management, accountability, and organizational cohesion.

3.9 Identifying Inconsistencies (Uniform Understanding)

A consistent risk management framework across departments addresses risk perception and handling inconsistencies, enhancing organizational uniformity and decision quality. Standardized methodologies enable accurate risk comparisons, better strategic decision-making, and improved resource allocation. Such consistency builds stakeholder trust and reinforces a proactive organizational culture, promoting continuous improvement and robust risk management practices.

3.10 Joint Journey (Maturing Capabilities)

A clearly defined and documented risk management framework greatly supports capability maturity and organizational learning, especially in large, diverse organizations. Standardized training accelerates workforce onboarding, increases situational awareness, and ensures consistent application of risk principles. Employees gain a deeper understanding, improving judgment and decision-making skills. This ultimately fosters organizational wisdom and resilience, equipping the organization to thrive amidst evolving risks.

4.0 Unacceptable Risks and Mandatory Investments

Explicitly identifying and proactively managing unacceptable risks is crucial for ethical and sustainable supply chain management. Unacceptable risks involve potential severe harm, irreversible impacts, or fundamental ethical violations that potential gains cannot justify. Companies should clearly define these risks, establishing strong policies that guide ethical decision-making and ensure that profit never compromises the well-being of individuals, communities, or the environment.

Organizations should emphasize zero tolerance for activities endangering employees, customers, or communities. Ethical standards must extend throughout the supply chain, explicitly rejecting human rights abuses, environmental damage, or exploitation. Companies should also consider reputational risks seriously, recognizing that perceived unethical behaviors, like conflicts of interest or misinformation, can significantly damage public trust and company credibility.

4.1 Unacceptable Risks and National Security

Protecting national security is paramount, and companies should explicitly ensure that their operations never compromise critical infrastructure, sensitive data, or national defense capabilities. Policies should commit to safeguarding national interests, emphasizing rigorous due diligence to prevent security breaches. Organizations should proactively assess potential vulnerabilities, collaborating openly with government agencies when necessary to protect national security and contribute positively to broader societal stability.

4.2 Unacceptable Risks and Loss of Life

Organizations must never take risks that could result in loss of life or serious harm to human health. Organizational policies should prioritize human safety over financial or operational considerations. They should proactively address both immediate and long-term threats, such as chronic health conditions resulting from exposure to dangerous substances or unsafe conditions. Companies should incorporate robust safety standards and conduct regular assessments to identify and mitigate potential risks to employees, customers, and the surrounding communities. An ethical approach to risk management also considers indirect health impacts and potential harm spanning generations.

4.3 Unacceptable Risks and Public Health and Safety

Ensuring public health and safety goes beyond compliance, requiring companies to proactively evaluate the potential impacts of their operations, products, and supply chains. Rigorous due diligence should be undertaken when handling hazardous materials, manufacturing products, or managing high-risk supply chain activities. Organizations should also consider addressing secondary risks, such as environmental contamination, unsafe product use, and broader public safety concerns. Consistent monitoring, thorough risk assessments, and proactive mitigation efforts are essential in preserving public safety, maintaining consumer trust, and reinforcing the company's ethical reputation.

4.4 Unacceptable Risks and Legal Compliance

Companies should demonstrate an unwavering commitment to adhering to domestic and international legal frameworks and industry standards. They should implement regular training programs, perform consistent internal audits, and cooperate transparently with regulatory authorities. Additionally, companies should thoroughly vet their supply chain partners for compliance-related risks and swiftly take corrective action when violations occur. Such proactive measures will preserve organizational integrity, protect public trust, and ensure long-term operational stability.

4.5 Unacceptable Risks and Contractual Requirements

Meeting contractual obligations is essential for maintaining trust and reliability in business relationships. Companies should proactively manage contractual risks, ensuring clear communication of expectations internally and externally. Policies should reinforce adherence to contract terms, explicitly prohibiting actions or negligence that could result in contractual breaches. Regular contract reviews and proactive communication with partners help mitigate misunderstandings and potential disputes, ensuring operational stability and maintaining strong, trustworthy relationships throughout the supply chain.

4.6 Unacceptable Risks and Insurance Requirements

Companies should carefully maintain insurance coverage to manage potential losses effectively. Policies should emphasize maintaining sufficient coverage, adhering to policy conditions, and promptly addressing insurance claims. Regular insurance coverage assessments and thorough vetting of partner coverage minimize financial vulnerability and enhance resilience.

Organizations should establish clear protocols to avoid actions that could invalidate coverage or claims. They should also maintain transparent communication with insurers and continuously review policies to align with evolving business risks.

4.7 Unacceptable Risks and Environmental Damage

Environmental responsibility is a core component of organizational ethics. Policies should explicitly require compliance with environmental regulations, proactive assessment of ecological risks, and mitigation of environmental impacts throughout the supply chain. Companies should hold their suppliers and partners accountable for maintaining sustainable practices. Continuous monitoring and proactive action to minimize environmental damage demonstrate corporate accountability, enhance reputation, and ensure alignment with global sustainability standards.

4.8 Unacceptable Risks and Economic Damage

Proactively preventing economic harm is crucial for organizational and community stability. Companies should recognize their broader economic responsibility and avoid actions that could significantly disrupt local economies or the financial health of suppliers and partners. Thorough financial and operational assessments should be conducted regularly to identify vulnerabilities and implement safeguards. By fostering sustainable economic practices and prioritizing shared value, companies enhance their resilience, contribute positively to local economic stability, and protect themselves from reputational and financial risks.

4.9 Unacceptable Risks and Shareholder Harm

Consistent and proactive risk management enhances investor confidence and long-term organizational sustainability, ensuring that business practices align with shareholder interests and expectations.

4.10 Unacceptable Risks of Going Out of Business

The ultimate risk any company faces is business failure. Companies should explicitly recognize existential threats and proactively prepare for scenarios that could disrupt operations or threaten organizational viability. Comprehensive risk management practices, including scenario planning, stress testing, and contingency planning, help safeguard against unexpected catastrophic events.

Organizations should routinely assess supplier reliability, geopolitical risks, internal governance, and operational resilience. Maintaining robust governance structures, ethical operations, and precise strategic planning mitigates existential threats, protecting the organization's continuity and stakeholder confidence.

5.0 Risk Investment Options

Effective resource allocation for risk mitigation and treatment requires thoughtful analysis and a structured methodology. It is a strategic priority within supply chain risk management.

Companies should promote cooperation between multiple departments to create this methodology, including supply chain, finance, risk management, and legal teams. Varied input encourages a comprehensive risk assessment and shared responsibility and creates a proactive company culture around risk management.

Clear evaluation criteria are essential for risk investment analysis. These include likelihood, impact, cost-effectiveness, unintended consequences, and alignment with overall business objectives. Consistent criteria ensure transparent and strategic decisions about risk mitigation investments.

The following sections explore specific investment options, detailing their advantages and disadvantages and outlining the scenarios for which they are most suitable. This information equips organizations to allocate resources strategically, enhancing supply chain resilience while balancing cost efficiency and operational effectiveness.

Organizations should also carefully balance their investment levels. Excessive risk mitigation can negatively impact profit margins and operational efficiency. An optimized risk response strategy balances mitigation benefits, associated costs, administrative burdens, and potential operational delays.

5.1 Investing in Resilience, Resistance, Prevention, and Mitigation

Supply chain resilience involves the capacity to withstand disruptions while maintaining operational and financial stability. Investments in resilience aim to build adaptive strength and flexibility, recognizing that some risks, especially uncontrollable ones, are inherent in global supply chains.

Common resilience strategies include diversifying suppliers to reduce dependency, developing contingency and response plans, and enhancing supply chain visibility through technology. Advanced systems like real-time tracking and predictive analytics enable early risk identification and effective responses. These investments help mitigate impacts from unavoidable disruptions, such as natural disasters or geopolitical instability.

5.2 Investing in Avoidance

Risk avoidance prioritizes long-term sustainability over short-term gains by strategically deciding not to engage in activities with unacceptable risk levels or misalignment with organizational goals.

Practical risk avoidance measures include refraining from entering unstable markets, avoiding complex or high-risk transactions, and maintaining strict ethical standards. Organizations employing strategic risk avoidance benefit from enhanced financial performance and greater resilience against disruptive events.

5.3 Investing in Redundancy

Investing in redundancy involves maintaining duplicate assets or processes as backups in case of primary system failures. While redundancy is costly, it provides additional protection, ensuring critical supply chain operations during disruptions.

Redundancy can include maintaining multiple suppliers, establishing parallel facilities, and diversifying transportation methods. These proactive investments significantly reduce potential disruptions' financial and operational impacts, enhancing organizational stability.

5.4 Investing in Recovery

Organizations investing in recovery capabilities acknowledge that disruptions may still occur despite proactive prevention measures. Effective recovery investments involve developing comprehensive disaster recovery and business continuity plans, establishing rapid response teams, and training personnel in crisis management. While potentially costly, investing in recovery capabilities substantially mitigates downtime, financial losses, and reputational damage, leading companies to outperform competitors in post-disruption recovery periods.

5.5 Investing in Inspection

Inspection investments focus on early identification and mitigation of risks within the supply chain through audits and assessments. Organizations can proactively identify weaknesses and implement timely solutions by utilizing recognized industry standards (e.g., ISO certifications, SOC reports). Effective inspection programs enhance supply chain transparency and risk management efficiency, significantly reducing the likelihood of costly disruptions.

5.6 Investing in Isolation and Insulation

Isolation and insulation investments aim to shield critical operations from identified threats. These strategies may involve outsourcing risky activities to specialized third parties or establishing physical and virtual barriers to reduce exposure. Although these investments carry costs, they minimize potential disruptions and reduce vulnerability, safeguarding core business functions and overall supply chain integrity.

5.7 Investing in Legal and Legislative Indemnity

Organizations may engage proactively with policymakers and industry associations to advocate for legislative protections or indemnities against certain risks. By shaping legal and regulatory frameworks, organizations can mitigate liability exposure and promote operational stability. Active involvement in legislative processes supports industry-wide risk management, providing a predictable operational environment that encourages innovation and strategic investment.

5.8 Investing in Insurance

Insurance investments transfer financial risk to insurers, protecting against unpredictable yet potentially catastrophic losses, such as natural disasters, cyberattacks, or supply chain disruptions. Types of coverage include property, business interruption, and liability insurance. The strategic use of insurance provides critical financial security, reducing the burden of unforeseen events and supporting rapid operational recovery. Organizations increasingly recognize the importance of comprehensive insurance coverage as a key element of risk management.

5.9 Investing in Reserves (Self-Insurance)

Financial reserves, including cash and lines of credit, represent proactive internal risk management strategies, especially when external insurance is unavailable or prohibitively expensive. Reserves ensure liquidity during disruptions, enabling continued operations and rapid recovery. Organizations maintaining robust reserves demonstrate enhanced financial resilience, which is particularly valuable in volatile economic conditions or during significant operational disruptions.

5.10 Investing in Detection and Responsiveness

Investments in detection and responsiveness prioritize rapid identification and agile responses to emerging risks. These investments involve real-time monitoring technologies, flexible operational processes, and strong partnerships that enable swift adaptation to disruptions. Companies investing in detection and responsiveness significantly reduce disruption impacts, maintaining operational continuity, minimizing losses, and preserving stakeholder confidence. Enhanced agility and adaptability emerge as significant competitive advantages, positioning organizations to manage future uncertainties effectively.

6.0 SCRM Program Optimization and Rationalization

Implementing a structured Risk Investment Optimization (RIO) methodology has become a key competitive advantage in supply chain risk management. Clear policies for measuring the costs and benefits of risk investments are essential to ensure resources are allocated effectively, and risk mitigation efforts yield measurable returns. A systematic RIO approach enables companies to optimize risk management decisions, strengthen operational resilience, and protect financial performance. Collaboration across supply chain management, finance, risk, and operations ensures that analyses are comprehensive, accurate, and aligned with strategic objectives. A formal RIO process provides significant advantages to companies by offering a structured and objective framework to evaluate the financial viability of risk mitigation strategies.

Second, RIO enhances transparency and accountability. When companies document assumptions, calculations, and rationales behind decisions, they create a clear audit trail and demonstrate due diligence to stakeholders such as investors, regulators, and customers who demand visibility into risk practices.

Third, a standardized RIO process facilitates effective prioritization. By ranking initiatives based on costs and expected returns, companies can allocate resources to the highest-value opportunities, aligning investments with overall risk appetite and strategic goals while avoiding overinvestment in low-priority areas.

Research underscores the benefits of RIO. Aon Foto fully evaluates mature risk management programs, which experience 30% lower earnings volatility. Deloitte reported that 70% of companies using structured RIO frameworks improved their risk identification and mitigation capabilities. These findings highlight that systematic risk investment optimization strengthens both financial outcomes and overall risk posture.

6.1 Cost-Benefit Analysis (CBA)

Cost-benefit analysis (CBA) is a foundational methodology used in economics, public policy, and business to evaluate whether a project, policy, or investment's benefits outweigh its costs. CBA provides a structured, quantifiable approach to decision-making, ensuring that choices maximize overall value. Central to this method is the identification and meaningful quantification of both costs and benefits.

Formally, CBA involves systematically comparing a project's total expected costs and benefits, typically expressed in monetary terms. It accounts for the time value of money by discounting future cash flows to present value, allowing decision-makers to understand how future impacts relate to current investments.

Key Steps in Cost-Benefit Analysis

Defining the Scope: The process begins with clearly defining the project's objectives, stakeholders, and time horizon. Establishing whether a project is short- or long-term helps frame the evaluation appropriately.

Identifying Costs and Benefits: Costs include direct expenses like labor and materials and indirect costs such as opportunity costs or environmental impacts. Benefits include increased revenue, savings, or improved quality. Tangible and intangible factors must be considered, even if intangibles like reputation or public health are more challenging to quantify.

Quantifying Costs and Benefits: Once identified, all costs and benefits must be expressed in monetary terms. Surveys, studies, or willingness-to-pay models may be needed to estimate the value of intangibles. The goal is to allow meaningful comparisons across all elements.

Discounting for Time: Future costs and benefits must be discounted to present value using a discount rate that reflects either the opportunity cost of capital or social preferences. The present value formula is:

$$PV = \frac{FV}{(1+r)^t}$$

Where:

- PV represents the present value,

- FV is the future value of the cost or benefit.
- r is the discount rate, and
- t is the number of years into the future.

Decision Metrics

Net Present Value (NPV): Calculated by subtracting the present value of costs from the present value of benefits:

$$NPV = \sum_{t=1}^{n} \frac{R_t}{(1+r)^t} - C_0$$

Where:

- R_t is the net cash inflow (or benefit) during the period t,
- r is the discount rate,
- t is the time (in years),
- n is the total number of periods, and
- C0 is the initial investment or cost.

A positive NPV indicates that benefits exceed costs, making the project economically viable.

Benefit-Cost Ratio (BCR): The ratio of present value benefits to present value costs:

$$BCR = \frac{\sum \text{Present Value of Benefits}}{\sum \text{Present Value of Costs}}$$

A BCR greater than 1.0 signals a favorable investment, while a BCR below 1.0 suggests that costs outweigh benefits.

Managing Uncertainty

No CBA is complete without addressing uncertainty. Sensitivity analysis tests how changes in assumptions impact results, while risk analysis evaluates the probability of different outcomes. These techniques enhance the robustness of recommendations.

Making Recommendations

Final recommendations should consider NPV, BCR, and sensitivity analyses. Projects with a high NPV or BCR significantly greater than one are typically favored. However, ethical considerations, public opinion, and alignment with strategic goals should also influence final decisions. CBA is a powerful but not singular tool in comprehensive decision-making.

6.2 Return on Investment (ROI)

Return on Investment (ROI) is a fundamental metric for evaluating the efficiency and profitability of investments across business functions, including supply chain risk management (SCRM). ROI helps organizations assess the financial gains or losses generated relative to the cost of a project, making it an essential decision-making tool for initiatives aimed at improving operations, mitigating risks, or boosting profitability.

Formally, ROI quantifies profitability by comparing net benefits gained from an investment to its total cost, expressed as a percentage:

$$ROI = \frac{\text{Net Return on Investment}}{\text{Cost of Investment}} \times 100$$

A positive ROI indicates a profitable investment, while a negative ROI signals a loss. High ROI values suggest more financially efficient initiatives.

Methodology for Calculating ROI

A formalized ROI methodology enables companies to evaluate and prioritize risk mitigation strategies systematically. Developing such a methodology requires collaboration across the supply chain, finance, operations, and risk management functions, ensuring that financial and operational aspects are considered. Key steps in ROI calculation include:

1. Define the Investment Scope

Clearly outline the project's goals, timeline, and key performance indicators (KPIs). For example, investments might involve implementing warehouse management systems, upgrading logistics infrastructure, or adopting new risk mitigation technologies.

2. Identify All Costs

Accurately capture:

- Capital Expenditures (CapEx): Include initial outlays for technology, infrastructure, or consulting.
- Operational Expenditures (OpEx): Include ongoing maintenance, labor, and training costs.
- Indirect Costs: Include potential downtime, productivity loss, or delayed projects.

Comprehensive cost accounting is crucial to avoid overestimating ROI.

3. Quantify Net Benefits

Benefits in a supply chain context include:

- Cost Savings: Reduced transportation, labor, or inventory costs.
- Increased Revenue: Higher customer satisfaction and market access.
- Risk Mitigation Savings: Avoided disruption costs.
- Process Improvements: Gains from faster cycle times or optimized resource use.

Net benefits equal total realized gains minus any ongoing operational costs.

4. Calculate ROI

With quantified costs and benefits, apply the ROI formula. For instance, a $500,000 technology investment generating $750,000 in benefits yields:

$$ROI = \frac{\text{Net Benefits} - \text{Costs}}{\text{Costs}} \times 100$$

Thus, the company gains $0.50 in profit or savings for every dollar spent.

$$ROI = \frac{750,000 - 500,000}{500,000} \times 100 = 50\%$$

5. Consider Time-Related Factors

To ensure accurate financial comparisons over multi-year horizons, one should use a suitable discount rate to discount future benefits to present value for long-term investments.

6. Conduct Sensitivity Analysis

Since future costs and benefits can vary, sensitivity analysis will test how different assumptions impact ROI, which is critical in supply chain projects as market, supplier, or geopolitical factors can introduce uncertainty.

7. Compare ROI Against Alternatives

Comparing the ROI of multiple investment opportunities ensures that capital is allocated to initiatives with the highest relative returns, maximizing overall value.

Strategic Value of ROI in SCRM

Companies that systematically apply ROI to risk management decisions achieve more substantial financial outcomes. Research by Aberdeen Group shows that firms with mature ROI frameworks experience a 25% increase in Return on Invested Capital (ROIC). Similarly, Deloitte reports that 75% of companies using ROI in risk investment decisions improved financial performance and cost savings. By integrating ROI into decision-making, companies enhance risk mitigation while ensuring that resilience investments contribute directly to economic success.

6.3 Benefit-Cost Ratio (BCR)

The **Benefit-Cost Ratio (BCR)** is a straightforward metric used to evaluate whether a project or decision's benefits outweigh its costs. The specific application varies by context, but the calculation follows a consistent structure.

Identification of Costs and Benefits: First, identify all direct and indirect costs and tangible and intangible benefits. Costs may include labor, materials, and equipment, while benefits could involve revenue increases, cost savings, or quality improvements.

Quantification: Assign monetary values to all identified costs and benefits. Direct values are typically easy to quantify; intangibles like customer satisfaction or environmental improvements may require proxy measures or estimation techniques.

Time Value of Money: Future costs and benefits must be discounted to present value terms using a discount rate that reflects the opportunity cost of capital.

With discounted values established:

- Net Present Value (NPV) is the difference between total benefits and costs.
- BCR is calculated as:

$$BCR = \frac{\sum \text{Present Value of Benefits}}{\sum \text{Present Value of Costs}}$$

Interpretation: A BCR greater than 1.0 signals a favorable investment, while a BCR below 1.0 suggests that costs outweigh benefits.

Widely used in public policy, infrastructure, and business investment decisions, BCR provides a simple numerical snapshot of a project's value. However, it should be considered alongside broader financial and strategic analyses for a complete evaluation of feasibility and desirability.

6.4 Risk-Adjusted Return on Capital (RAROC)

Risk-Adjusted Return on Capital (RAROC) is a vital performance metric that measures profitability while factoring in risk exposure. It helps organizations balance risk and return, ensuring optimal capital allocation across complex supply chains.

RAROC is calculated as:

$$\text{RAROC} = \frac{\text{Net Income} - \text{Expected Losses}}{\text{Economic Capital}}$$

Calculating RAROC consistently for ongoing operations and new investments enables decision-makers to quantify the risks of current supply chains, such as vendor reliability or market volatility, and assess whether operations remain optimized for risk-adjusted returns.

RAROC helps evaluate risks like demand uncertainty and geopolitical instability for proposed expansions. Clear RAROC policies guide capital deployment, prioritizing investments that maximize returns relative to risk.

Organizations with robust RAROC frameworks have integrated risk prevention, protection, and response into broader supply chain management processes. According to a 2022 McKinsey study, companies with defined RAROC methodologies achieved 15% higher returns on supply chain investments by focusing capital on high-impact risk mitigation strategies.

RAROC provides critical benefits:

- **Prioritization**: It identifies which risk reduction initiatives deliver the highest value relative to capital invested, preventing overinvestment in low-yield areas.

- **Strategic Planning**: Quantifying risk-adjusted returns enables long-term growth planning while maintaining agility and risk control.

Embedding RAROC into decision-making ensures companies remain resilient, agile, and financially optimized amid evolving threats.

6.5 Risk-Benefit Analysis (RBA)

Risk-benefit analysis (RBA), which has roots in 19th- and early 20th-century economic theories, is a process used to assess a specific decision's potential risks and benefits. It is frequently employed in healthcare, environmental policy, and engineering to aid decision-making.

Standard RBA methodologies include:

- **Quantitative Risk Assessment** (QRA): Quantifies risk probability and severity. It is often used in the chemical, nuclear, and aviation sectors.
- **Cost-Benefit Analysis** (CBA): Evaluates economic costs and benefits, factoring in risk and uncertainty.
- **Decision Tree Analysis:** Maps decision pathways with associated probabilities and impacts.
- **Monte Carlo Simulation**: Uses random sampling to model probable outcomes under uncertainty.
- **Fault Tree Analysis** (FTA): Identifies causes of system failures from a top-down perspective.
- **Failure Mode and Effects Analysis** (FMEA): Systematically identifies potential failures in processes or designs.
- **Health Risk Assessment** (HRA): Evaluates health hazards in public and environmental domains.

- **Benefit-Cost Ratio (BCR):** Compares financial benefits to costs, considering risk factors.

The choice of methodology depends on the decision context, risk nature, and data availability. Multiple techniques are often combined to provide a comprehensive assessment.

6.6 Opportunity Costs Between Investment Returns and Risk Reductions

Companies must carefully allocate financial resources between growth initiatives and risk reduction. Opportunity cost, the value of the foregone alternative, guides these choices and ensures that capital supports revenue growth and resilience.

Balancing investments between risk reduction and income generation is critical. Investments in resilience, such as supply chain redundancy or cybersecurity, safeguard business continuity but can limit immediate profitability. Conversely, focusing solely on growth without mitigating risks can expose the organization to significant disruptions, undermining gains.

In volatile industries, prioritizing resilience delivers more significant long-term benefits. However, over-investing in risk mitigation may constrain growth and innovation. Leading companies adopt structured methodologies to compare investment options using Cost-Benefit Analysis (CBA), Risk-Adjusted Return on Capital (RAROC), and scenario planning frameworks.

A 2023 World Economic Forum report found that companies with formal methodologies for comparing risk reduction and growth investments achieved a 12% higher Return on Invested Capital (ROIC) than peers without such structures. These methodologies help align capital allocation with both current risks and future opportunities.

A well-defined comparative framework typically includes:

- **RAROC Assessment**: Quantifies the return from mitigating risks.

- **CBA for Growth Initiatives**: Measures the speed and size of returns on income-generating investments.
- **Cost Savings Analysis**: Identifies operational efficiencies that free capital for future resilience or expansion.

Companies that formalize their capital allocation policies, such as designating specific percentages for growth, risk mitigation, and cost-saving initiatives, achieve greater financial agility. A 2021 Deloitte study found that companies with defined capital allocation frameworks were 20% more likely to recover quickly from supply chain disruptions, demonstrating the importance of proactively accounting for opportunity costs in investment planning.

6.7 Measuring Risk's Impact on Supply Chain Efficiency

Efficiency measures the relationship between outputs and inputs, aiming to maximize production with minimal resource use. Although the basic concept is simple—output divided by input—the efficiency calculation, especially in supply chains, can be highly complex.

Supply chains typically assess efficiency across two primary domains: financial and operational. Organizations use hundreds of metrics, including raw material utilization, Inventory Turnover Ratio, Overall Equipment Effectiveness (OEE), Perfect Order Fulfillment (POF), and Cash-to-Cash Cycle Time.

In the context of supply chain risk management (SCRM), it is crucial to recognize that risk mitigation strategies can introduce friction, potentially impacting operational efficiency. Evaluating multiple risk investment options requires understanding not just their direct costs but also their effects on the organization's primary objective: maintaining optimal efficiency.

For example, a low-cost risk control (Option A) might cause substantial efficiency reductions, whereas a higher-cost option (Option B) might maintain higher operational performance. Costs alone are insufficient to determine the better investment; impacts on efficiency must also be factored in.

To address this complexity, companies should develop a **Risk Investment Scoring Methodology** based on ten critical dimensions:

- Financial Costs (minimizing expenses)
- Risk Reduction (mitigating adverse outcomes)
- Operational Minimalism (streamlining steps)
- Speed to Market (accelerating delivery)
- Necessary Diligence (ensuring thoroughness)
- Compliance (avoiding legal penalties)
- Conduciveness to Resilience (enhancing durability)
- Response Acceleration (quick reaction to events)
- Restoration and Resumption (rapid recovery)
- Insurance Optimization (managing shared risks)

Weights can be assigned to each dimension based on company-specific priorities, allowing for customized, data-driven investment decisions.

6.8 Decision Framework

Multi-Criteria Decision Analysis (MCDA) is widely applied across industries to address complex decisions involving multiple, often conflicting, objectives. MCDA provides a structured process to balance quantitative and qualitative factors, enabling more transparent and justifiable choices.

Several popular MCDA frameworks include:

- **Analytic Hierarchy Process (AHP): P**rovides a structured decision hierarchy using pairwise comparisons.

- **Analytic Network Process (ANP)**: Similar to AHP but accounts for interdependencies between factors.

- **ELECTRE**: Uses outranking methods to compare alternatives in pairs.

- **PROMETHEE**: Ranks alternatives based on preference functions.

The general MCDA process includes:

1. **Define the Decision Problem and Objectives**: Clarify goals, stakeholders, and success measures.
2. **Identify Decision Criteria**: List all critical quantitative and qualitative factors.
3. **Select Alternatives**: Identify the strategies or solutions under consideration.
4. **Evaluate Alternatives**: Measure performance against each criterion.
5. **Weight the Criteria**: Assign relative importance to each criterion.
6. **Score the Alternatives**: Aggregate weighted scores.
7. **Rank the Alternatives**: Order options from most to least preferred.
8. **Perform Sensitivity Analysis**: Test how changes in criteria or assumptions impact the ranking.
9. **Make a Decision**: Select the best alternative, incorporating stakeholder input where necessary.
10. **Implement and Monitor**: Execute the decision and track its outcomes to ensure objectives are met.

MCDA strengthens decision-making by allowing structured comparisons even when trade-offs between conflicting priorities are inevitable.

6.9 Justifying Supply Chain Friction

Although essential for resilience, implementing Supply Chain Risk Management (SCRM) strategies often introduces operational friction. If not managed carefully, these challenges can offset the benefits of risk mitigation.

Common sources of friction include:

- **Cost Increases:** Include direct expenses (insurance, redundancies) and indirect costs (training, longer lead times).
- **Process Complexity**: Enhanced tracking, documentation, and compliance requirements that slow operations.
- **Reduced Flexibility:** Stricter operating protocols limit adaptability to market shifts.
- **Longer Lead Times**: Supplier diversification and quality checks can delay material flow.
- **Resource Diversion**: Personnel and capital diverted from growth initiatives to risk activities.
- **Lower Efficiency**: Additional checks and redundancies may slow processes and add bureaucracy.
- **Innovation Constraints**: Overemphasizing risk avoidance can stifle new initiatives and technology adoption.
- **Supplier Relations**: Burdensome risk requirements may strain vendor partnerships.
- **Regulatory Burdens**: Compliance efforts require ongoing resources and specialized expertise.
- **Slower Market Responsiveness**: Layered decision-making can delay reactions to trends and customer demands.

Successfully balancing these frictions with the benefits of risk management is vital for maintaining operational effectiveness and long-term organizational resilience.

6.10 SCRM Program Optimization Methodology

Optimizing a Supply Chain Risk Management (SCRM) program involves balancing operational improvements, cost control, risk reduction, and compliance requirements. Effective programs align tightly with the organization's mission, strategic goals, values, and culture.

Key steps in the optimization framework include:

1. **Define Scope and Structure**: Clarify the program's objectives, roles, responsibilities, processes, tools, and metrics.
2. **Understand Stakeholder Expectations**: Identify and address the needs, preferences, and concerns of internal and external stakeholders.
3. **Assess Current State**: Evaluate strengths, weaknesses, opportunities, and threats to determine the maturity and effectiveness of the existing program.
4. **Benchmark Against Standards**: Compare current practices to best practices, industry standards, regulatory mandates, and peer organizations.
5. **Prioritize Gaps and Improvements**: Identify improvement opportunities based on impact, urgency, feasibility, and cost-benefit considerations.
6. **Develop a Roadmap**: Establish clear action plans, timelines, milestones, resource needs, risks, and contingencies.
7. **Execute with Agility**: Implement flexible initiatives, open communication, and continuous feedback loops.
8. **Monitor and Measure Performance**: Track outcomes against baseline metrics and program goals.
9. **Evaluate and Learn**: Conduct evaluations to extract lessons learned and identify best practices.
10. **Drive Continuous Improvement**: Adapt the program over time to address evolving risks, expectations, and operational environments.

Conclusion

This chapter explored the challenges of and strategies for optimizing SCRM programs, emphasizing the need for structured methodologies to guide decision-making and resource allocation. Effective risk management requires balancing resilience investments with operational efficiency, applying financial analysis tools such as Cost-Benefit Analysis (CBA), Return on Investment (ROI), and Risk-Adjusted Return on Capital (RAROC). Ultimately, successful SCRM optimization enables organizations to address unacceptable risks, justify operational friction, and achieve sustainable resilience and growth.

REFERENCES

- Accenture. Study on Supply Chain Disruptions and Resilience. Accenture Research, 2021.
- vecnarobotics.com
- Allianz Global Corporate & Specialty (AGCS). Global Supply Chain Insurance Market Outlook (2021–2028). Allianz SE, 2021.
- Bain & Company. Supply Chain Risk Management Investment Analysis. Bain white paper, c.2019.
- Center for Responsive Politics (OpenSecrets). "Lobbying spending reached a record high of $3.7 billion in 2021, with significant focus on health, tech, and finance issues"
- sciencedirect.com
- Deloitte. Global Survey of Supply Chain Executives (Risk Preparedness). Deloitte Consulting, n.d.
- Deloitte. Annual Supply Chain Risk Management Survey. Deloitte Consulting, n.d.
- Federal Emergency Management Agency (FEMA). NFIP Agent Marketing and Outreach Research Report. FEMA Federal Insurance Directorate, 2023
- agents.floodsmart.gov
- Gartner. Risk Management Programs Benchmark (ROI Analysis). Gartner Research, 2022.

- Gartner. Supply Chain Technology Investment Survey. Gartner Research, 2021.
- Global Business Coalition for Education. "Business Action on Education" Survey Findings. GBC-E Report, 2021.
- Institute for Supply Management (ISM). Supply Chain Disruption Survey Report. ISM, 2020
- fastercapital.com
- McKinsey & Company (2021). Supply Chain Resilience Survey – Redundancy vs. Efficiency. McKinsey Global Institute, 2021.
- McKinsey & Company (2022). Resilience for Sustainable, Inclusive Growth. McKinsey Research, 2022
- mckinsey.com
- MIT Center for Transportation & Logistics (CTL). Global SCALE Risk Initiative. Massachusetts Institute of Technology, https://ctl.mit.edu/research/current-projects/global-scale-risk-initiative
- World Economic Forum (2020). Systems Leadership: Managing Complexities and Realizing Opportunities. Cologny/Geneva: WEF White Paper, 2020
- https://www.weforum.org/whitepapers/systems-leadership-managing-complexities-and-realizing-opportunities
- World Economic Forum (2023). "Emerging research shows firms that invest in resilience outperform their peers in terms of value and longevity."
- weforum.org

Insights and Actions

Organizations must quantify True Value at Risk (TVaR) beyond traditional financial metrics to understand complete risk exposure. Traditional risk measures, such as Value at Risk (VaR), only capture losses under normal conditions and overlook catastrophic tail risks that can devastate organizations. True Value at Risk encompasses ten critical cost categories, including current and future revenue losses, asset repair and restoration expenses, additional labor costs, legal services, indirect expenses, diminished asset valuations, intangible damage to intellectual property and brand reputation, lawsuit liabilities, and regulatory fines. Additionally, organizations must account for significant intangible costs, such as strategic setbacks, employee fear and uncertainty, psychological stress, complexity burdens, and increased cost of capital, which can compound financial impacts and undermine long-term competitive positioning.

Systematic risk investment optimization using financial analysis tools is essential for balancing resilience with operational efficiency. Organizations must implement structured methodologies, including Cost-Benefit Analysis (CBA), Return on Investment (ROI), Benefit-Cost Ratio (BCR), and Risk-Adjusted Return on Capital (RAROC), to objectively evaluate risk mitigation investments. Research indicates that companies with mature risk management programs experience 30% lower earnings volatility. Those utilizing structured frameworks, meanwhile, improve their risk identification capabilities by 70% and achieve 15% higher returns on supply chain investments. The ten primary risk investment options—resilience/prevention, avoidance, redundancy, recovery, inspection, isolation, legal indemnity, insurance, reserves, and detection/responsiveness—each require careful evaluation against opportunity costs to ensure optimal capital allocation between growth initiatives and risk reduction.

Supply chain friction from risk management must be strategically justified through multi-criteria decision analysis and continuous program optimization. While SCRM strategies necessarily introduce operational friction through increased costs, process complexity, reduced flexibility, longer lead times, and resource diversion, organizations must systematically justify these trade-offs using Multi-Criteria Decision Analysis frameworks that balance ten critical dimensions: financial costs, risk reduction, operational minimalism, speed to market, necessary diligence, compliance, resilience enhancement, response acceleration, restoration capability, and insurance optimization. Successful SCRM optimization requires a ten-step methodology that encompasses scope definition, stakeholder alignment, current state assessment, benchmarking, gap prioritization, roadmap development, agile execution, performance monitoring, evaluation and learning, and continuous improvement. This approach enables organizations to address unacceptable risks while maintaining competitive operational effectiveness.

Identify the Tangible and Intangible Costs of Risk

SCRM is essential for modern, fast-moving supply chains. Organizations must balance thorough risk analysis with agility—avoiding both "analysis paralysis" and superficial assessments.

The chapter introduces the concept of True/Total Value at Risk (TVaR), which goes beyond traditional financial measures to include operational, strategic, and reputational risks using stress testing and scenario analysis.

Costs from disruptions are categorized as:

- Immediate revenue losses: Lost sales, discounts, penalties.
- Future revenue losses: Loss of customer trust, missed business opportunities, brand reputation damage.
- Direct expenses: Asset repair, additional labor, legal services.
- Indirect expenses: Insurance, borrowing costs.
- Asset impacts: Diminished value, accelerated depreciation, impairment losses, intangible damage (brand reputation loss, customer goodwill erosion).
- Liabilities: Lawsuits, regulatory fines.

Quantify Intangible Costs and Organizational Impact

- Disruptions also cause intangible costs that are more difficult to quantify: strategic setbacks, fear and uncertainty, ignorance or inappropriate acceptance of risks, over-analysis, over-control, overconfidence, psychological stress, and increased complexity.
- These factors can erode morale, slow innovation, and increase the cost of capital.

Recognize the Human Element

- Engaging with risk can accelerate personal and professional growth, but sustained exposure to risk and uncertainty can lead to stress and burnout.
- Systematic and documented risk management enhances confidence, efficiency, investment attractiveness, and organizational learning.

Define and Manage Unacceptable Risks

- Organizations must explicitly identify and manage unacceptable risks—those that could cause severe harm, violate ethics, or threaten survival (e.g., national security, public health, environmental damage, legal compliance).
- Policies should enforce zero tolerance for risks that could result in loss of life, legal violations, or existential threats.

Choose Your Risk Investment Options

- Resilience and mitigation: Diversifying suppliers, contingency planning, technology for visibility.
- Avoidance: Not engaging in high-risk activities.
- Redundancy and recovery: Maintaining backups, disaster recovery plans.

- Inspection and insurance: Audits, comprehensive insurance, reserves.
- Detection and responsiveness: Real-time monitoring, agile processes.

Balancing investment levels is crucial; over-investment can reduce profitability and efficiency.

Consider a Structured Risk Investment Optimization (RIO) Methodology for Measuring and Prioritizing Risk Investments

- Financial analysis tools such as Cost-Benefit Analysis (CBA), Return on Investment (ROI), Benefit-Cost Ratio (BCR), and Risk-Adjusted Return on Capital (RAROC) are explained, with guidance on their application and interpretation.
- Multi-Criteria Decision Analysis (MCDA) frameworks help balance conflicting objectives and support transparent, justifiable choices.

Manage Supply Chain Friction

Risk management introduces operational friction (costs, complexity, slower responsiveness), which must be justified and balanced against the benefits of resilience.

Continuous Improvement Is Essential

Optimization involves defining scope, understanding stakeholder expectations, assessing current state, benchmarking, prioritizing improvements, developing a roadmap, executing with agility, monitoring, and continuous learning.

Chapter 10

Managing and Monitoring Your Vendors

Dr. Andrea Little Limbago

Sustainability and climate risks are converging with third-party risk management. Companies that proactively address both ESG and climate adaptation—through compliance, transparency, and resilience—will be better positioned to manage regulatory, reputational, and operational risks in a rapidly changing environment.

Companies often view sustainability and climate change as future risks, which are often deprioritized in favor of near-term objectives and quarterly earnings. However, the impact of climate risk on companies and their supply chains is, unfortunately, a current reality that will cost companies over a trillion dollars in the upcoming years.[49] The various kinds of climate-related risks are often bundled together under a single umbrella despite the distinct requirements and strategies required to address them.[50] This makes it difficult for companies to address these risks and contributes to the deprioritization of sustainability, especially among supply chains.

Part of the problem rests in many of the regulations themselves, which remain nascent but are gaining momentum. The proposed climate risk regulations from the U.S. Securities and Exchange Commission (SEC) are a case in point.[51] The SEC's Climate-Related

[49] https://www.forbes.com/sites/rosecelestin/2021/03/05/climate-change-will-cost-companies-13-trillion-by-2026/?sh=2223a76a6cdc.

[50] https://www.npr.org/2023/10/12/1205068747/climate-change-emissions-companies-disclosure-sec-california.

[51] https://www.sec.gov/files/33-11042-fact-sheet.pdf.

Disclosures would have required companies to assess and release their natural hazards risks, such as hurricanes and flooding, the potential impact of these natural hazards on business operations, as well as Scope 1, 2, and 3 emissions and climate-related targets and goals. While these are certainly pertain to the environment, the first focuses on how companies respond to extreme natural hazard events, while the latter focuses on what companies are doing to mitigate their contributions to climate change. Distinct strategies are required to address supply chain risks related to climate adaptation and resilience compared to those focused on a company's impact on the environment.

On the one hand, ensuring climate resilience and continuity of operations requires assessing the potential risks of climate change on a company's global footprint and operations. Do they have core suppliers in earthquake-prone regions? Are data centers in areas with increasing drought concerns? These are physical risks that impact the continuity of operations and have a heightened potential for contagion across third-party ecosystems if a disruption ripples upstream or downstream in a partner ecosystem.

In contrast, a company's impact on the environment is better captured by the evolving environment, social, and governance (ESG) regulations. What is a company's carbon footprint? Do they have environmental targets and policies? At a strategic level, the difference comes down to compliance and reputational risks found within ESG compared to the physical (even existential) and continuity of operations risks due to extreme natural hazard risks, with financial risks associated with each. Each of these provides two distinct but interconnected risks associated with climate change that require different strategies and preparation for companies. This chapter unpacks the intertwined risks associated with climate change and sustainability and provides a useful heuristic for companies when thinking about their own third-party risk strategies within a shifting regulatory environment and the acceleration of extreme weather events.

Sustainability: ESG Risk

ESG is a hotly debated and evolving corporate and third-party risk that is gaining momentum due to the steady drumbeat of regulations across Europe and the United States. Due to its relative nascency compared to other regulatory issues, ESG lacks a common standard, and at times there is significant variation of factors and requirements, making compliance difficult. There are also dramatically different approaches to ESG from country to country, with the United States shifting focus away from ESG on the regulatory front while Europe continues to expand its focus. This section highlights some of the most prominent emerging ESG regulations and what to expect in this growing space when it comes to third-party risk.

E: Environmental Risk

As mentioned earlier regarding the SEC's proposed regulations, companies may need to prepare for climate impact disclosure in the coming years, largely centered on emissions. Importantly, the regulations do not focus solely on direct emissions from a specific corporate building or headquarters but increasingly include indirect emissions as well as those within a company's supply chain. These are referred to as Scope 1, 2, and 3 emissions. Scope 1 emissions are emissions directly controlled by a company, Scope 2 are the indirect emissions stemming from energy purchased and used by a company, such as through electricity, and Scope 3 are emissions by a company's suppliers across the supply chain.

On January 1, 2024, the EU's Corporate Sustainability Reporting Directive (CSRD) came into effect, requiring companies to disclose information pertaining to environmental and social issues.[52] Mandatory energy usage and costs, emissions metrics and targets, and other sustainability reporting vetted by a third party are among the new compliance requirements. A similar directive, the EU's Corporate Sustainability Due Diligence Directive (CS3D), focuses on companies taking responsibility for the impact of their activities

[52] https://eur-lex.europa.eu/legal-content/EN/TXT/?uri=CELEX:32022L2464.

and also includes social impact. The CS3D isn't phased in until 2030 and is addressed in more detail in the next section.

The CSRD includes some of the most rigorous requirements to date, focusing not only on a company's own business but also those of its suppliers, as well as on data supported by independent assessors to avoid greenwashing. However, although it came into effect, each member state had flexibility on how to integrate it into its own national legal system. France was the first member state to implement the law and introduced severe penalties for non-compliance, including up to €75,000 euros or the possibility of up to five years' imprisonment.[53]

The U.S. Chamber of Commerce has issued an impact assessment of European legislation on companies inside and outside the EU and notes concerns over the burden it will place on companies and the potential for excessive legal risks.[54] However, just as the CCPA followed the GDPR for cyber disclosures, California is similarly on the heels of EU legislation and has introduced a Scope 3 climate disclosure law. The Climate Corporate Data Accountability Act (SB 253), signed into law in the fall of 2023, requires companies to report their carbon footprint, which includes that of their suppliers. While the disclosure requirements do not come into effect until 2026, given the general lack of preparedness and the resources required for compliance, market forces are moving sustainability away from an ethical corporate decision to a financial and regulatory one in many parts of the globe.

S: Social Risk

While substantively distinct from environmental sustainability, social sustainability is garnering increased regulatory attention and is frequently grouped with environmental due diligence. The CS3D, commonly referred to as the EU Supply Chain Act, is a case in point

[53] https://www.forbes.com/sites/maryfoley/2023/12/21/france-introduces-possible-jail-time-as-penalty-for-non-compliance-with-sustainability-disclosure/?sh=1a28bb8e34db.

[54] https://www.uschamber.com/international/u-s-chamber-of-commerce-position-on-the-eu-corporate-sustainability-due-diligence-directive.

as it is focused on both human rights and environmental impact. The EU Supply Chain Act is making the largest strides in this area, as is Germany's Supply Chain Due Diligence Act. The German regulation took effect in January 2023 and includes disclosure of both human rights and environmental impacts across corporate supply chains. The first complaints have already been filed against several global corporations for failures to ensure worker safety in Bangladesh.[55]

The EU Supply Chain Act focuses on due diligence and requires companies to disclose both upstream and downstream adverse impacts and their actions to identify, assess, mitigate, and prevent them. The adverse impacts cover a range of areas, including child labor, slavery, and labor exploitation, as well as environmental impacts, including pollution, deforestation, and water consumption.

Distinct from environmental sustainability, the social sustainability regulatory requirement to eliminate unethical labor risks from supply chains is gaining momentum. The U.S. Uyghur Forced Labor Prevention Act (UFLPA) and the California Transparency in Supply Chains Act both introduce new regulatory and reputational risks aimed at eliminating forced labor from supply chains by requiring disclosures and greater auditing of partners and third parties.[56] Canada, the UK, and Australia have all passed similar legislation with legally binding requirements for transparency and disclosure across supply chains.[57] The United States-Mexico-Canada Agreement (USMCA), the replacement for NAFTA, includes provisions against forced labor and the import of any goods produced in part or whole with forced labor.[58]

55 https://www.complianceweek.com/regulatory-policy/large-companies-in-crosshairs-early-under-german-supply-chain-act/33495.article.

56 https://www.dhs.gov/uflpa-entity-list, https://oag.ca.gov/SB657.

57 https://www.afslaw.com/perspectives/alerts/canada-passes-legislation-forced-labor-and-supply-chain-due-diligence,
https://www.legislation.gov.uk/ukpga/2015/30/contents/enacted,
https://www.legislation.gov.au/C2018A00153/latest/text.

58 https://crsreports.congress.gov/product/pdf/IF/IF11308.

Voluntary guidelines are also proliferating. Japan has released guidelines for corporate due diligence on third-party human rights violations that mirror those found in the UN Guiding Principles on Business and Human Rights, as well as the Organization for Economic Cooperation and Development's guidelines.[59] The G7 issued a Joint Statement focused on removing forced labor from supply chains while also targeting corruption, which is often inextricably linked to both unethical labor and environmental degradation and is a core component of governance discussed next.[60]

Before moving to governance, it is important to note that diversity and inclusion is generally considered under the "S" umbrella of ESG, but it too is facing a dynamic regulatory landscape in the United States. From executive orders to shifting corporate reports, diversity, equity, and inclusion (DEI) policies are at an inflection point.[61] Nevertheless, prior to these latest shifts, for the most part DEI lacked the regulatory teeth to tackle unethical labor and environmental sustainability. This will likely remain a dynamic situation. Nasdaq now requires companies listed on the exchange to have women and minority directors on their boards, a ruling upheld by a U.S. appeals court in October 2023; a similar California law was struck down in 2022.[62] In contrast, in 2022, the EU passed the Women on Boards Directive, requiring stock exchange-listed boards to contain at least 40% women by 2026.[63] DEI remains a moving target for regulatory risks, although reputational and financial risks may have a negative impact.[64]

59 https://www.shrm.org/topics-tools/news/japan-publishes-guidelines-corporate-human-rights-due-diligence.

60 https://www.whitehouse.gov/briefing-room/statements-releases/2021/06/13/fact-sheet-g7-to-announce-joint-actions-on-forced-labor-in-global-supply-chains-anticorruption-and-ransomware/.

61 https://www.whitehouse.gov/presidential-actions/2025/01/ending-illegal-discrimination-and-restoring-merit-based-opportunity/.

62 https://www.reuters.com/legal/legalindustry/californias-board-diversity-law-struck-down-what-now-2022-04-05/.

63 https://www.forbes.com/sites/paologaudiano/2022/11/30/eu-law-set-to-increase-gender-diversity-on-company-boards/?sh=45b9b03c33ea.

64 https://www.forbes.com/sites/marcuscollins/2023/07/16/the-material-cost-of-canceling-diversity/?sh=68606dc140cb.

G: Governance

As the World Economic Forum notes, "G" is at the heart of sustainable businesses. Behind every social or environmental malfeasance lies poor governance. From corruption and accountability to transparency and business ethics, governance is foundational to sustainability.[65] Unlike "E" and "S," most governance regulatory frameworks have been in existence for decades, including anti-bribery, anti-money laundering, board oversight and reporting, and conflict-of-interest regulations and frameworks.

However, government intervention in corporate business—especially by foreign governments—is garnering renewed attention as geopolitical tensions rise. In the U.S., the Foreign Corrupt Practices Act was enacted in 1977 and prohibits U.S. citizens or companies from bribing foreign officials in exchange for business.[66] That kind of behavior falls under corruption and is not new.

What is new is the growing concern of government intervention in corporate business, for instance by state-owned enterprises (SOEs). For example, in late 2023, the Kremlin warned that it would confiscate U.S. and European assets if the G7 decided to confiscate frozen Russian central bank reserves.[67] The story is similar in China, where the Chinese regulatory landscape and risk of government involvement in corporate business are driving many to leave China. In the U.S., foreign ownership, control, or influence (FOCI) risk is impacting everything from utilities to elections to metro trains.[68] SOEs and various levels of government intervention are increasingly a governance concern as geopolitical tensions rise. The "Build America, Buy American Act" is a case in point; it requires all iron,

65 https://www3.weforum.org/docs/WEF_Defining_the_G_in_ESG_2022.pdf.

66 https://www.trade.gov/us-foreign-corrupt-practices-act.

67 https://www.reuters.com/world/kremlin-says-it-has-list-western-assets-be-seized-if-russian-assets-are-2023-12-29/.

68 https://www.wsj.com/finance/investing/the-big-risk-causing-investors-to-shun-china-c0710fdd?mod=djem10point.

steel, and manufactured products used in infrastructure to be produced in the U.S.[69]

In sum, governance, as well as environmental and social risks, comprise sustainable business behavior. ESG focuses specifically on the business and its behavior as it impacts the environment and society and the governance over both. The business risks are regulatory, reputational, and financial and, for the most part, are within the company's ability to control and shape. Each of these, in turn, introduces third-party risks, both financially and reputationally. We turn to this in the next section. In contrast, how companies approach the risks posed by climate change is completely different. Climate adaptation and resilience require companies to view the existing and future risks posed by climate change, which they cannot alone control and which shape rather than require corporate adaptation.

Sustainability: Climate Resilience and Adaptability

California has distinct bills addressing ESG (the aforementioned SB 253) but also introduced SB 261, which requires the disclosure of climate-related financial risks focused on assessments of financial impacts due to extreme natural hazard events related to climate change.[70] This reflects the distinct requirements and steps needed for compliance with ESG versus climate resilience. In contrast, as previously mentioned, the SEC integrates both ESG and climate adaptation into a singular proposal, requiring climate-related disclosures in corporate periodic reports. Specifically, it would mandate companies to disclose:

> "the impact of climate-related events (severe weather events and other natural conditions) and transition activities on the line items of a registrant's consolidated

[69] https://www.whitehouse.gov/omb/management/made-in-america/build-america-buy-america-act-federal-financial-assistance/.

[70] https://leginfo.legislature.ca.gov/faces/billTextClient.xhtml?bill_id=202320240SB261.

> financial statements, as well as on the financial estimates and assumptions used in the financial statements."[71]

These requirements, which have since been withdrawn, are related but distinct from various ESG disclosures, such as Scope 1 to 3 emissions, and inherently involve different risks and mitigation strategies.[72] In this context, climate-related risks pertain more to climate resilience, or the ability to mitigate, respond to, or recover from climate-related shocks, such as hurricanes and floods.[73] Climate adaptation is a core component of this strategy and reflects the processes of adjusting to both current and future anticipated impacts of climate change.[74]

Despite the whiplash on the regulatory front, climate adaptation continues to pose a real risk across supply chains. Natural hazard-focused climate risks involve physical risks, material and transition costs, as well as potential liability risks from insurance or emerging regulatory risks from shifting legal frameworks. Contagion is also a much greater risk, especially given the skewed concentration of some industries or suppliers in specific regions of the world. Although regulations are a moving target, these climate-related risks should be a top concern now, not something to be addressed in the distant future. Unfortunately, many executives still view the impact of climate change as a future concern. Most executives equate climate risks to financial risks; however, less than a quarter view climate change as a serious risk, with fewer than a quarter preparing for climate-related disruptions in the next 12 to 18 months, according to one study.[75] As the next section details, these disruptions are already having a significant financial and operational impact, especially across third-party organizations and supply chains.

[71] https://www.sec.gov/news/press-release/2022-46.

[72] https://www.sidley.com/en/insights/newsupdates/2025/04/sec-ends-defense-of-climate-related-disclosure-rules.

[73] https://toolkit.climate.gov/steps-to-resilience/steps-resilience-overview.

[74] https://www.un.org/en/climatechange/climate-adaptation.

[75] https://www.marketplace.org/2023/08/23/just-half-of-ceos-see-climate-change-as-a-risk-to-their-business/.

Climate Adaptation and Resilience and Third-Party Risk

Operational disruptions induced by natural hazards have significant effects on supply chains, inflicting billions of dollars in damages and reshaping supply chains.[76] Extreme weather events led to estimated global economic losses of $313 billion dollars in 2022.[77] The global cost of natural disasters is only expected to continue to increase going forward, with 2023 assessed to be the hottest year on record and accompanied by sea level rise and extreme weather events that once were viewed as black swans becoming more frequent. In fact, the last decade broke numerous records in natural disaster-imposed devastation, with the last eight years the hottest on record.[78]

A steady drumbeat of record-breaking forest fires, hurricanes, typhoons, droughts, heat waves, floods, and winter storms across the globe is costing businesses billions of dollars. Supply chains are at risk from physical disruptions due to climate change, and they are particularly vulnerable when there are high concentrations of suppliers exposed to climatic risks and low geographic diversification of supply sites. As Sanjay Patnaik of the Brookings Institution notes, the range of risks spans all aspects of operational resilience, "From supply chains to the location of plants, to even things like, 'Do I have enough water in my vicinity in the future the next couple of years that I need for my manufacturing?'"[79] Climate-related disruptions are already introducing a new range of financial burdens and, as trends continue, will do so going forward.

For example, the 2011 Tohoku earthquake and subsequent tsunami in Japan upended automotive supply chains across the globe, with car part facilities temporarily shutting down in the United States, Thailand, the Philippines, and Indonesia. In September 2017, Hurricane Maria battered the Caribbean Island of Puerto Rico,

---

76 https://www.ncei.noaa.gov/access/billions/, https://cepr.org/voxeu/columns/how-natural-disasters-reshape-supply-chains-lessons-covid-19-crisis.

77 https://www.aon.com/weather-climate-catastrophe/index.aspx.

78 https://www.nytimes.com/interactive/2023/climate/earth-hottest-years.html.

79 https://www.marketplace.org/2023/08/23/just-half-of-ceos-see-climate-change-as-a-risk-to-their-business/.

knocking out the main production facility of Baxter International, which supplies 41% of the saline solution used in the United States, leading to widespread shortages in hospitals across the country. In March 2021, a widely publicized maritime accident in the Suez Canal caused the canal to close for six days, costing the global economy an estimated $6 billion and generating knock-on disruptions across third-party ecosystems that lasted for months.

Understanding the growing impact of these natural hazards—and building the resilience and adaptation needed to withstand them—will be critical to maintaining global supply chains and should be a top priority when assessing third-party risk. Deutsche Bank executive Markus Müller summarizes well the danger of underpricing and deprioritizing climate risk. In a client note, he contends, "The temptation is to assume that the effects...of global heating...will accumulate only gradually... However, this isn't guaranteed."[80] He describes the "fat-tail" risks associated with climate change, which seem unlikely but could be catastrophic, and the outcomes of which are dangerously underexplored.

Looking Ahead: Mitigation, Adaptation, and Resilience

Over 15 years ago the Harvard Business Review claimed, "Companies that manage and mitigate their exposure to climate-change risks while seeking new opportunities for profit will generate a competitive advantage over rivals in a carbon-constrained future."[81] That was true then and it will be even more accurate over the next 15 years.

Third-party risk and sustainability will be even more interconnected as the impacts of climate change and climate-related regulations accelerate. However, they should be viewed as related but distinct risks for companies, given the different approaches required for mitigation, adaptation, and resilience. ESG focuses on how a

[80] https://www.investmentnews.com/esg/news/deutsche-bank-exec-warns-of-growing-climate-risk-245042.

[81] https://hbr.org/2007/03/competitive-advantage-on-a-warming-planet.

company is contributing to climate change and the steps it is taking to help minimize that impact, while climate adaptation and resilience focuses on what companies are doing to derisk from the physical and operational impacts of climate disruptions in light of increasing extreme weather and natural hazard events.

ESG-focused sustainability risk strategies require introspection and a transparent evaluation of a company's—including its partners'—impact on the environment and society. While this used to be viewed as a nice-to-have and pertaining solely to reputational risks, the regulatory environment from Europe is quickly making ESG a mandatory consideration for organizations, with potential financial, legal, and reputational impacts. This entails a broad assessment of third-party businesses and their sustainability footprint, including contributions to environmental degradation as well as social and governance risks.

In contrast, climate-related disclosures focused on climate adaptation require different third-party derisking strategies. Climate adaptation and resilience must assess a company's global footprint—and that of their third-party relationships—overlaid with the wide range of growing natural hazard risks as well as continuous monitoring of natural hazards. Diversification away from key areas at heightened natural hazard risk, continuity of operations plans, and greater visibility of shifting third-party dependencies are all essential components of this derisking strategy.

Visibility across all partner ecosystems is essential to both kinds of climate-related disclosures and disruptions. Businesses must look holistically at what actions they can take to limit future warming and risks (ESG), adhere to growing regulations (ESG and climate adaptation), as well as mitigate the physical and contagion effects of natural hazard extreme events (climate adaptation). However, as long as climate-related risks continue to take a back seat to other corporate priorities, businesses may continue to be caught off guard in a regulatory environment that remains a moving target and as extreme natural hazard events disrupt companies in a hyper-connected global economy.

Insights and Actions

Companies must elevate climate and sustainability risks from future concerns to immediate priorities and integrate them into third-party risk management and supply chain strategies to ensure business continuity and regulatory compliance in the face of accelerating climate events and evolving global standards.

Companies often view sustainability and climate change as a future risk which is deprioritized in favor of near-term objectives and quarterly earnings. However, the impact of climate risk on companies and their supply chains is unfortunately a current reality, costing companies over a trillion dollars in the upcoming years. This includes climate adaptation as well as climate impact assessments across your supply chain.

Global regulations are emerging that focus on the societal and environmental impact of supply chains. Generally, under the umbrella of environmental, social, and governance (ESG) frameworks, these nascent regulations are in flux, often due to government transitions and private sector feedback addressing the scope and compliance requirements.

Although the business cost due to natural hazards continues to grow, there are fewer regulations addressing climate resilience. Organizations must gain visibility into supplier concentration risks in areas prone to natural disasters and seek strategies to diversify, derisk, and adapt to climate extremes.

Section 4

Legal and Regulatory

It is difficult to make our material condition better by the best law, but it is easy enough to ruin it by bad laws.

~ Theodore Roosevelt, 26th President of the United States

Preamble

The famous race car driver, Mario Andretti, is quoted as saying "It is amazing how many drivers, even at the Formula One level, think that the brakes are for slowing the car down." Of course, he meant that with good brakes that one could rely on, you could push the car faster. If you had no way of slowing down, how fast could you approach an intersection or a turn? And speaking of intersections, what if, as you approached the intersection, you noticed there were no stop signs, no traffic lights, heck, no lane markings? There are police, but they seem to be pulling drivers over for seemingly no discernable consistent reason. You'd find it impossible, or at the least nerve-wracking, to try to make it through to the other side. You might limit the number of times you ventured down that road and wish you were driving a tank when you did.

The point of this analogy is not that all laws and regulations are equal in perceived value to traffic laws that keep you safe, fairly. And it is certainly true that laws, regulations, and most definitely, courts, can add much to the cost of doing business. But we can all agree that laws and regulations are necessary to support trust between the transacting parties, whether consumers, corporations or governments. A statement widely attributed to Nobel laureate economist Paul Romer says, "The most important difference between the United States and Somalia is not income, but the extent of trust. In the United States, you can write a check to a stranger and be confident it will be honored. In Somalia, you can't."

In Section 4, Matt Stamper, Dr. Andrea Little Limbago, and Chris Forbes present a moderate dose of why we have the hodge-podge of corporate laws and regulations we're subjected to and a large dose of how to navigate these laws and regulations safely and fairly.

Chapter 11

Legal Implications

Introduction

In Chapter 11, we turn our attention to the legal and regulatory front. We begin with Matt's essay, "Legal Implications of TPRM," which examines the critical legal aspects of Third-Party Risk Management (TPRM), emphasizing the importance of thorough, well-crafted contracts and the necessity of close collaboration among legal, security, and operational teams. Matt stresses that successful TPRM depends on contracts that are clear, unambiguous, and aligned with both legal and operational realities. He makes the powerful point that proactive, cross-functional collaboration is essential to manage asymmetries, clarify responsibilities, and ensure that legal agreements effectively mitigate third-party risks throughout the vendor relationship lifecycle. Matt goes on to address the concept of legally defensible "reasonable security" as a mitigation strategy for both regulatory enforcement and product liability tort.

In her essay, "Third-Party Regulatory Shifts," Andrea addresses the impact of the regulatory landscape. She notes that third-party risk is more dynamic and challenging than ever, which requires organizations to adopt comprehensive, continuous risk management strategies. The shifting multi-national regulatory landscape creates new perils for executives and companies as they navigate personal and corporate liability, making collaboration across the executive team and with suppliers essential for navigating this evolving environment and mitigating both regulatory and reputational risks.

Legal Implications of TPRM

Matt Stamper

Ambiguity in contracts—especially regarding roles and responsibilities—creates risk. Use detailed roles and responsibilities (R&R) matrices that clearly delineate which party is responsible for each service component, reducing uncertainty and aligning operational reality with legal agreements.

Contracting third-party services extends far beyond traditional pricing and delivery terms. The contracts we use and the terms they contemplate can have critical implications for successful third-party risk management. Effective TPRM programs require the proactive input of the organization's legal team to ensure that legal agreements, notably master services agreements, mitigate legal and reasonably anticipated operational risks. Throughout my career, I've always benefited from close collaboration with both general and external counsel. Their insights complemented my security and operational perspectives, and collectively, we reached a consensus on specific terms that minimized the risks to the organization.

Asymmetries and Ambiguity – Both Are Bad

Before delving into some of the contract provisions I look for and review in service agreements, I want to address two critical topics. The first is that of the potential asymmetries that may exist between the procuring and supplying entities. Large companies have clear advantages when they procure from smaller entities. They can require aggressive—some might say egregious—terms and conditions of their providers. While this is understandable from the perspective of the larger entity, be wary of T&Cs that can undermine the viability of the much smaller provider. Smaller providers, to grow market share and meet investor commitments, may agree to these T&Cs without the ability to deliver some of the more strenuous requirements. Larger organizations also typically have full-time internal counsel. While these attorneys may be overworked, they are not an hourly expense for the organization. For many smaller organizations, negotiating terms and conditions is a direct expense. These expenses may ultimately change the underlying financial status of an engagement.

Asymmetries can surface in multiple places throughout the relationship. For example, large cloud service providers may have master service agreements that are effectively one-sided, and their "legal" assurances for data security and other requirements may not be sufficient from the procuring entity's perspective. A smaller CSP, however, may be willing to agree to requirements that the larger cloud provider would never entertain. Effectively, the smaller CSP may appear less risky "legally" when compared to the T&Cs provided by the much larger provider. However, operationally, there may be orders of magnitude less risk with the larger CSP than a smaller organization willing to enter into an agreement that it may not be able to fulfill operationally. This nuance requires collaboration between stakeholders to make an informed risk decision. Legal counsel may favor agreements written in their organization's favor, while operational stakeholders would accept this legal risk knowing that the larger provider is more stable operationally. Delve into this dynamic.

This leads to the second topic that needs to be addressed regarding the legal implications of the TPRM program—ambiguity. As I noted in the *CISO Desk Reference Guide*, "declare war on ambiguity." Ambiguity serves no one. Ambiguity surfaces its ugly head everywhere in TPRM. My career began in IT managed services. For those familiar with the Open Systems Interconnection or OSI model, I drafted a variation that effectively looked at roles and responsibilities by the service layer.[82] In this case, I wanted to ensure that our clients understood what our firm did and, most importantly,

[82] If you want to explore the OSI model, here's a good reference: https://www.iso.org/ics/35.100/x/.

didn't do for each technology layer. In this case, I drafted a services stack that included the following service components:

- Applications
- Databases
- Operating Systems
- Hypervisors
- Networks
    - IP
    - Backup/Administrative
- Storage
- Data Center

I wanted to eliminate ambiguity with our clients regarding which services we provided and where our services effectively started and stopped. Unlike many traditional roles and responsibilities matrices, we showed client and provider responsibilities on the same line for each service or function.

The following table is an illustrative roles and responsibilities (R&R) matrix for application administration with a third party. The level of detail will be predicated on the criticality of the services to be provided and the inherent risk of the relationship. Critical relationships require a more detailed understanding of service demarcation points and the associated roles and responsibilities.

Function/Activity	Client Responsibility	Provider Responsibility
Service Layer: Application Services		
Licensing	The client will provide the required software licenses and obtain applicable maintenance agreements with the manufacturer.	The provider will validate that the software is licensed correctly and that the maintenance agreements name the provider as an authorized support contact.
User Administration	The client will determine which users should have access to the application and their associated entitlements.	The provider will monitor application activity, including access and authentication based on the user profiles established by the client. The provider will enforce the authentication mechanisms required by the client.
API Inventory, Throttling, and Monitoring	The client will maintain an inventory of publicly accessible endpoints and any throttling thresholds related to the same.	The provider will provide API gateway security services, configured per client specifications, and monitor API endpoint usage consistent with throttling and rate-limiting requirements.
Code & Repository Administration	The client will maintain all code bases for the application.	The provider will oversee the security of the CI/CD pipeline as directed by the client.
Application Performance Management	The client will determine the performance standards and thresholds associated with the application.	The provider will provide infrastructure services engineered to meet the performance standards required of the application, including network, compute, memory, and storage services.
System Logging	The client will identify which logs will be centralized and forwarded to the provider's SIEM for monitoring and performance management.	The provider will validate log sources, event per second metrics, and desired responses based on event IDs to provide infrastructure services to the application.

Figure 11.1 – R&R for Application Management with a Third Party

Service Demarcation

Showing a particular function with the client's and the provider's requirements noted side-by-side in this way helped to reduce uncertainty. Spend time with your team to determine where these service demarcation points exist and identify deliverables, timeframes, and other relevant details. In short, declare war on ambiguity to ensure that key goods or services are supplied or provided as envisioned.

The time spent reviewing the nuances of asymmetries between the parties and areas where ambiguity may surface is time well spent. Codify and document these understandings. The value of detailed roles and responsibilities matrices cannot be overstated.

Contracts and legal obligations associated with TPRM efforts are areas where these asymmetries and ambiguity can surface. Ideally, contracts should be unambiguous and aligned with the actual relationship between the entities. Too frequently, the contracts do not reflect the actual business relationship and the contemplated operations between the two organizations. This gap between the operational reality and the legal agreement introduces unnecessary risks. Cases in point include contracting services that may have unrecognized regulatory or contractual obligations at one extreme of the spectrum, to delaying the provisioning and onboarding of services pending a thorough legal review and contract negotiation when the risk factors that necessitated the review are not part of the service. We frequently see this when data elements such as PII or PHI are mistakenly considered part of the service or engagement. This is where the collaboration between counsel and the TPRM team meets reality. Modifying legal terms and conditions does not come cheap. Whether internal or external, legal services are never inexpensive. For this reason, it's important to work proactively to understand which clauses and legal protections are absolute versus negotiable. If every agreement is negotiated, TPRM legal validation will never scale financially. As a case in point, if the contemplated services have a total contract value of $100,000, spending $15,000 on legal fees to negotiate T&Cs fundamentally changes the economics of the relationship. Ensure that your firm knows which conditions are readily negotiated versus non-starters.

Key Contract Provisions

Certain provisions from master services agreements warrant evaluation by your TPRM team. What is acceptable will vary from one organization to another based on their specific operating environment and their risk tolerances. Spend time validating your organization's expectations for the following risk factors.

Product and Service Definitions and Descriptions – A clear definition of the scope and purpose of the relationship between the two entities is critical. In the context of privacy, purpose limitation is a foundational principle. Personal data should only be used for its specified purpose. Ensure that the purpose and scope of your agreements are clear and reflective of the engagement or service at hand. Use the roles and responsibilities matrices and service demarcation guidelines to clarify these understandings.

Audit Rights – Audit rights have become a standard term with many service provider agreements. Where appropriate, ensure that your agreements include the ability to audit a service provider's operations and engagement/service documentation. These clauses typically put the onus on the auditing entity to pay for the audit. There are also third-party audits, including SOC 2 Type 2 audits, that can complement direct audits of a provider's operations. The degree of specificity in this clause should reflect the underlying value of the relationship. Critical providers warrant audit clauses that specify fees, the availability of resources and documentation, and how much advance notice is required to perform an audit.

Privacy Rights – Data subject rights and data protection addendums may be required for services and engagements where personal data in its various forms is in scope.[83] The European Union's General Data Protection Regulation (GDPR), specifically *Chapter III – Rights of the Data Subject*, offers comprehensive examples of data subject rights that should be contemplated, including the following factors:

- Access
- Rectification
- Purpose limitation and limits on profiling
- Deletion
- Portability

[83] In *Data Privacy Program Guide: How to Build a Privacy Program that Inspires Trust*, Justine Phillips, David Goodman, and I discuss the myriad privacy dynamics that organizations confront, including the specific rights afforded to data subjects resulting from global privacy regulations.

For organizations operating in the U.S. and servicing California residents, the California Consumer Privacy Act (CCPA), as amended, also offers some important additions to these privacy rights, including the right to know the sources of personal data collected, how such data is used, whether it is shared or sold to any third parties, and the various rights afforded to the consumer (the Data Subject in EU terms) to control how their data should be used. Spend time with your privacy officer and legal counsel to determine the nature and extent of specific privacy clauses required based on the contemplated relationship. Counsel should validate expectations related to purpose limitation and on-ward transfer clauses. Moving data across jurisdictional boundaries has important implications and may result in penalties and fines if standard contractual clauses (or similar) are absent.

Governing Law and Venue – Jurisdictional considerations may extend beyond obligations associated with cross-border data transfers of personal data. Litigation is expensive. As we discuss in Chapter 7 regarding the offboarding of vendors, if the engagement ends litigiously, lawyering up in non-local venues can be expensive. Work with your legal team to validate if there are requirements related to governing law and its venue. This factor is obviously more critical for companies that operate internationally or in multiple states here in the U.S. In *Data Privacy Program Guide: How to Build a Privacy Program that Inspires Trust*, I described how I assisted a firm that did employment and income verification services. Based on client demand, the company's CEO wanted to validate if these services could be delivered compliantly internationally in markets including Mexico, South Korea, Japan, Taiwan, Germany, Ireland, and the UK. To facilitate the international expansion of the application and its service, we sought in-country counsel and reviewed residency requirements, country-specific privacy regulations, and licensing requirements. We thoroughly vetted governing law considerations given the sensitive data that the application processed. Ensure that your TPRM team validates the considerations associated with governing law and venue for the product or service at hand.

Data Security – As with privacy clauses, working with the CISO and CIO is a good idea to evaluate the nature of required security controls and service availability requirements. Similar to privacy addendums, security provisions are increasingly found in service agreements. Validate which security protections may be needed. Examples could include the use of multi-factor authentication to gain access to in-scope systems, cryptographic services for data at rest and in motion, administrative controls such as the requirement to have the provider's security program certified (e.g., ISO 27001), audited (e.g., SOC 2 Type 2 audit reports), or to follow a given security framework or standard (e.g., the NIST Cybersecurity Framework or the Center for Internet Security's Critical Security Controls). The TPRM team must ensure it has the requisite security knowledge, or access to staff who do, to determine requirements and evaluate prospective provider responses. Granted, I'm biased, but CISOs are especially skilled at finding sources of risk that could occur with a third party's operations.

Security measures and requirements are too important not to be addressed in most service agreements. If these requirements are not specifically called out in a data protection addendum, your organization should codify its expectations concerning security practices that it either expects or will deliver in the contemplated engagement between the parties. Here, the concept of reasonable security practices should be used to guide the level of detail that this addendum or section captures. Reasonable security has become a hot topic given its reference in the CCPA/CPRA (see 1789.81.5), which requires the following:

> "A business that owns, licenses, or maintains personal information about a California resident shall implement and maintain reasonable security procedures and practices appropriate to the nature of the information, to protect the personal information from unauthorized access, destruction, use, modification, or disclosure."

What precisely is reasonable is subject to some debate. Here, too, spending time with the CISO would be valuable. Given the litigious nature of the U.S. business climate, I strongly recommend asking a simple question to help determine if reasonable security practices exist. "Would it be reasonable not to have a given security function, practice, or tool in place?" I've given presentations on this topic and used my variant of the OSI model to ask this question for each technology layer. As an example, for application security, would it be reasonable not to have the following capabilities:

- Penetration testing
- Code reviews
  - Static
  - Dynamic
  - Runtime
  - Software Composition Analysis
- Input validation
- API Security
- Web Application Firewalls

The level of detail noted in a security addendum will be predicated on the materiality of the relationship between the entities. For defense contractors subject to the Defense Federal Acquisition Regulation Supplement (DFARS), the level of specificity for required security controls is notable. Indeed, the requirements for controlled unclassified information (CUI) and federal contract information (FCI) can number in the low 100s (as conveyed in NIST 800-171), with an even larger number of determination statements (the validations required for each control).[84]

Incident Response – Where sensitive data is in scope, service agreements should address incident response procedures and breach notification timeframes. While it may be obvious, if your firm has obligations to notify its clients of a data breach within 48 hours, your vendors' terms cannot exceed that threshold. I've worked with several firms that have created a master schedule of breach notification

[84] To learn more about DFARS requirements and the specific control objectives of NIST SP 800-171 and NIST SP 800-171a, there's no better source than the actual Special Publication. These can be found here: https://csrc.nist.gov/pubs/sp/800/171/r3/final. It's critical to also validate the requirements noted in the assessment guidance: https://csrc.nist.gov/pubs/sp/800/171/a/r3/final.

obligations that they use to validate if their service providers have obligations that allow them to meet their internal requirements. Whether addressed in the agreement or elsewhere, validate incident response protocols with the service provider. Topics to review include the availability of staff and personnel to support investigations, procedures to support privileged communication and maintain the confidentiality of sensitive information during an incident, and how forensic data would be shared among the respective entities. The incident response procedure may also require the support of law enforcement and regulatory authorities. Work with your legal counsel to document how these scenarios should be addressed. Create playbooks for scenarios that require the development of muscle memory. Incident response is never easy. It's worse when it involves a third party over whom you have no operational control. For critical vendors and suppliers, spend the time necessary to understand how the organizations would work together during an incident involving their services but impacting your firm's data and operations. We discuss incident response requirements in Chapter 6.

But Wait, There's More!

Third Parties' Third Parties – Our vendors also have their service providers and their respective suppliers. For certain industries, including healthcare with HIPAA and the defense sector with DFARS and ITAR, your contracts may need to be structured so that sub-processing relationships are documented and agreed to before contracting. These agreements may need to specify specific jurisdictions, the nationality of personnel, and the provenance of software and components. Where regulatory requirements are front and center, pause to ensure these requirements are identified, resources allocated, and the requisite validations are occurring. As we'll discuss in Chapter 12, privacy and cybersecurity regulations are bringing the effectiveness of TPRM programs front and center. In that chapter, we discuss strategies to ensure that organizations have TPRM capabilities that align with regulations (and contractual obligations) and reduce overall operational risk.

Where subservices are integral to the engagement, confirm that flow-down clauses are established to ensure, at least legally, that the provider's providers are subject to consistent security, privacy, and governance obligations. The same level of diligence is warranted for the provider's contractors and their use of staff augmentation services. Be sure to validate their practices related to the same, notably how they address background checks for their employees and contractors. Few companies deliver services independently, so your provider's providers should be a topic that requires appropriate diligence.

Limitations of Liability – The topic of limitations of liability warrants proactive collaboration between the TPRM team and legal counsel. Similar to earlier comments where contracts may be disconnected from the actual services contemplated, limitations of liability clauses frequently create challenges between the procuring entity and the service provider. For the procuring entity, the goal is to have the provider face unlimited liability. From the service provider's perspective, they want to limit liability to the least amount tenable (typically something lower than the contract value). These disparate incentives almost ensure that the parties will be on opposite sides of the table. Conflicts over limitations of liability can quickly undermine what would have been an otherwise productive and mutually beneficial engagement.

I have found that the risk factors that go into the calculus are generally poorly understood, creating challenges with the negotiations. As a case in point, when I worked in the colocation industry, we'd rent out locking cabinets in our data centers for around $1,000 per month. The fees included the cabinet, a redundant 20-AMP power circuit, remote support services, and access controls to the facility. One client requested a $1 million liability limit for their cabinet. Our standard liability limit was three months of the service fees. There's a clear disconnect here. Their logical rationale was that they had seven figures of expensive servers and storage arrays in the cabinet. However, our firm had zero operational control over this hardware. We simply gave them a cabinet and the redundant power circuits. The client was responsible for ensuring that their hardware was configured and managed correctly and that their hardware used the allocated redundant power circuits correctly. From our perspective, if our firm accepted the liability target of our client, that $1,000 per month cabinet would likely need to be 10 times more expensive to address our exposure. This was a price point well above market levels. Differing perspectives of liability and the operational context of the environment challenged a relationship that the IT teams of the two companies had already agreed to.

Risk factors vary based on the perspective of each entity. For the client, they had expensive IT hardware that they wanted to protect. From our perspective, an annual contract worth $12,000 in revenue was insufficient to warrant the potential seven-figure financial exposure. It took multiple discussions with multiple stakeholders to help change how these risk factors were viewed and how they should be addressed. I noted that this is where business interruption insurance and other insurance products come into play. This example is a microcosm of the challenges that limitations of liability have with TPRM programs. There are valid disagreements as to what level of liability is acceptable. These perspectives are more challenging when service demarcation points are vague and roles and responsibilities for the engagement are unclear. Too many projects or engagements have been either delayed or canceled because the parties couldn't reach a clear fact pattern related to risk, risk ownership, risk treatment options, and how these should be addressed with limitations of liability.

Limitations of liability are even more challenging with software and services provided by SaaS providers and software manufacturers. Enterprise and end-user licensing agreements typically disclaim all warranties (expressed or implied) and limit liability to the purchase price of the software or a limited number of months for the subscription fees. Effectively, the software industry has limited exposure to the damages caused by insecure or faulty software. It will be interesting to see whether the case between Delta Airlines and CrowdStrike changes this dynamic.[85]

Another dynamic that we'll likely see is that software companies may be more exposed, regardless of their attempts otherwise, to financial liability as more software is used to control physical operations and critical infrastructure. The case of Boeing should be front and center as we can see how poor-quality software can lead to the loss of life.[86]

These material risks have not been lost on policymakers. The White House's National Cybersecurity Strategy, released in March 2023, noted the Biden Administration's intent to change the relationship between software companies and their clients.

> "The Administration will work with Congress and the private sector to develop legislation establishing liability for software products and services. Any such legislation should prevent manufacturers and software publishers with market power from fully disclaiming liability by contract, and establish higher standards of care for software in specific high-risk scenarios." (National Cybersecurity Strategy, March 2023, page 21)

Market power is a clever euphemism for the asymmetries referenced earlier. Anticipate these disconnects and distinct risk perspectives as an ongoing dynamic of TPRM programs. Ideally, work with counsel proactively to assuage their concerns and determine what's required to reach an acceptable middle ground between the parties when it comes to "limiting liability."

Data Retention and Data Destruction – In Chapter 7, we delve into the dynamics of ending relationships with service providers where the final status of data becomes a critical consideration. This topic requires the input of the organization's legal counsel to ensure that

85 The news media is replete with perspectives on this topic, but this article from CNBC is worth a skim: https://www.cnbc.com/2024/12/17/crowdstrike-moves-to-dismiss-delta-suit-citing-contract-terms.html.

86 This article details the linkages between safety and software code, notably in the case of Boeings 737 Max: https://spectrum.ieee.org/how-the-boeing-737-max-disaster-looks-to-a-software-developer.

mandated regulatory requirements or contractual obligations associated with the data shared with that provider are handled as required. If your organization requires data to be destroyed at the end of an engagement, it's imperative that your contract stipulates how this destruction would be verified and evidenced. Don't leave these expectations up to the whims of the provider. Provide detailed expectations of what your firm will need if data is to be destroyed or deleted at the end of the engagement and the type and level of evidence you'd require to corroborate the same. Retention requirements should also be reviewed. It's not enough to have these codified in the agreement. If the data is particularly sensitive, subject to regulatory requirements, or valuable for other reasons, speak with operational stakeholders of the firm to verify how they retain and/or destroy data. Too frequently, contractual requirements never reach the operational stakeholders who are expected to fulfill these expectations. We discuss this and other dynamics of onboarding providers in Chapter 4.

Service Level Agreements (SLAs) – SLAs also warrant attention. SLAs have two components: the provider's purported uptime commitment and the consequences if those uptime commitments are not met. Like many factors related to TPRM, careful analysis of the nuance and details is required. It's important to understand how availability commitments are measured and whether factors such as maintenance windows are part of the calculation. In the managed services and data center industries, as examples, maintenance windows may be excluded from downtime calculations. Providers may declare maintenance windows for various reasons, including emergency maintenance, a euphemism for unplanned downtime, or a service outage. Providers can use these exclusions to avoid paying penalties associated with missing uptime targets. Indeed, the opportunities for shenanigans with SLAs are notable. Not only can providers use maintenance windows to change the actual financial calculus of not meeting commitments, but they can also change the reporting obligations and place the burden on the customer to notify the provider if they detect an outage. Determining which entity is obligated to notify the other of service-impacting issues is a factor that should not be overlooked.

Another trick that can be used to game SLAs is to offer SLA targets that far exceed the provider's actual uptime capabilities. Companies can offer 100% uptime guarantees, knowing that their financial exposure is limited by making SLA credits nominal. From a marketing perspective, the provider benefits from boasting a 100% uptime guarantee. The consuming entity may be shocked when an outage occurs and discover that the credits likely wouldn't buy a cup of coffee at Starbucks.

Availability targets should be backed with rigorous engineering and fault-tolerant architecture. As an example, when I started my career at AT&T (this was pre-breakup and before the acquisition by SBC), AT&T's long-distance network had "five nines" of availability. To achieve this required fault tolerance and redundancy throughout the network, the figure below shows that the difference between the "nines" is notable.

SLA Metrics	Downtime in Minutes	Downtime in Hours	Downtime in Days
99.999%	5.26	0.09	0.00
99.990%	52.56	0.88	0.04
99.900%	525.60	8.76	0.36
99.700%	1,576.80	26.28	1.09
99.500%	2,628.00	43.80	1.83
99.000%	5,256.00	87.60	3.65

Figure 11.2 – SLA Objectives and Downtime

Based on the criticality of the service or application, make sure that your TPRM team reviews not only the contract language of the SLA but, equally importantly, the underlying environment. It's important to determine if the provider has single points of failure or high-risk dependencies that could bring down the application or service.

Given how litigious certain business environments can be, spending collaborative time to work through the myriad legal implications of your TPRM is advisable. While it's easy to think that contracts are only legal counsel's purview, this can be a risky assumption. Operational, security, privacy, and other business functions are needed to ensure the service agreements are drafted correctly and accurately reflect the engagement. The insights garnered through this collaboration will result in more effective TPRM programs and, ultimately, less risk for the organization.

Third-Party Regulatory Shifts

Dr. Andrea Little Limbago

The regulatory environment for third-party risk is rapidly evolving, with new and complex requirements emerging globally. These changes significantly impact cybersecurity executives, corporate leadership, and organizations as a whole, introducing heightened personal liability and compliance risks.

In October 2022, Uber CISO Joseph Sullivan was convicted for his handling of a 2016 data breach. This sent shock waves through the security community, with personal liability now a growing concern among cybersecurity executives. Over 60% of cybersecurity executives are concerned about their own liability following cyber-attacks.[87] There is plenty of advice for CISOs on how to avoid liability, but with the shifting regulatory landscape, CISOs—and corporate executives writ large—increasingly have a full plate of compliance risks.[88]

From timely Securities and Exchange Commission (SEC) disclosures to ethical labor violations to deforestation to banned technologies, today's third-party regulatory environment is challenging for even the most vigilant companies. Despite increased investments in third-party risk, in the past two years over 45% of organizations have experienced some form of business disruption due to third parties.[89]

This chapter covers a wide range of regulatory shifts that should be top of mind when considering third-party regulatory risk. The global

87 https://www.infosecurity-magazine.com/news/cisos-worried-personal-liability/.

88 https://www.darkreading.com/cybersecurity-operations/a-cisos-guide-to-avoiding-jail-after-a-breach.

89 https://www.darkreading.com/cyber-risk/it-s-time-to-rethink-third-party-risk-assessment-.

regulatory environment is extremely dynamic, attempting to keep up with geopolitical shifts, a growing threat landscape, and a technology revolution. This chapter is divided into those regulatory risks that first are technology focused, followed by an emphasis on human and environmental regulations in the final portions of the chapter.

Specifically, the first regulatory risk covered is executive liability and accountability following a cyber-attack. This is followed by a focus on export controls, and the hardware and software that is increasingly targeted by sanctions and other forms of financial or commercial restrictions. Next, we'll turn to AI-powered technologies, which are subject both to export controls as well as data privacy challenges as the European Union and others introduce regulations that create guardrails around the technology. Finally, we wrap up with those non-cyber regulations that are increasingly posing regulatory risks: unethical labor and climate risks.

In short, third-party regulatory shifts are causing unprecedented levels of complexity as well as uncertainty. Gaining visibility across this range of risks requires collaboration across the executive team, and across suppliers because they are simply too expansive and cross-cutting for one individual to manage alone. Each organization must optimize tight resources against this growing regulatory landscape, but first things first. To better prepare for these ongoing changes, it is first essential to understand them. The following is a brief overview of the wide range of third-party regulatory risks that are altering the compliance—and the third-party risk—landscape.

Cyber and the C-Suite

As mentioned, personal liability is a top concern for today's cybersecurity executives. While Sullivan was sentenced to a three-year probation, the October 2023 SEC charges against SolarWinds' CISO renewed concerns over personal liability.[90] In 2023, the SEC also adopted new cybersecurity disclosure rules to inform risk

[90] https://www.techtarget.com/searchsecurity/feature/CISOs-on-alert-following-SEC-charges-against-SolarWinds.

management.[91] The rules aim at consistent disclosures, similar to financial events, and require the disclosure of any cybersecurity incident deemed material in Current Reports on Form 8-K as well as in Annual Reports on Form 10-K. What is deemed material remains a key challenge, as the CrowdStrike global IT outage stemming from a faulty update proved. Two C-suite executives were named in a class-action suit against the company, while other customers are similarly blaming the company for the outage's impact.[92]

The U.S. is not alone in regulating breach liability. The EU's NIS2 directive similarly includes provisions referencing CISO liability.[93] Given this growing emphasis on CISO liability, between 2024 and 2025 fully 93% of organizations made policy changes to address this risk.[94] Nevertheless, almost half remain uncertain on accountability for a breach.

The SEC disclosure rules also encourage Board accountability over cyber governance and resilience.[95] These rules require companies to disclose a cyber incident within four business days of its discovery, with the intent to gain information not just on the attack but on the materiality and impact of it. However, most disclosures so far fail to describe the kind of breach or its material impact.[96] Given that each U.S. state, Washington, DC, Puerto Rico, Guam and the Virgin Islands all have distinct breach disclosure laws, the disclosure timeline is also inconsistent with many of the U.S. state-level data breach disclosure time frames.

In addition to the regulations, there is a growing list of standards used for third-party procurement guidelines. There are a series of standards targeting the public and private sectors, including ISO 27001, the NIST Cybersecurity Framework, CMMC, FedRamp,

91 https://www.sec.gov/newsroom/press-releases/2023-139.

92 https://www.cybersecuritydive.com/news/crowdstrike-class-action-suit-investors/723053/.

93 https://digital-strategy.ec.europa.eu/en/policies/nis2-directive.

94 https://www.helpnetsecurity.com/2025/03/19/ciso-liability-policy/.

95 https://news.mit.edu/2024/now-corporate-boards-have-responsibility-cybersecurity-too-0429.

96 https://www.forbes.com/sites/bobzukis/2024/03/04/companies-are-already-not-complying-with-the-new-sec-cybersecurity-incident-disclosure-rules/.

and SOC2. The Digital Operational Resilience Act (DORA) and the Network and Information Systems (NIS2) are two EU-based initiatives focused on the financial and critical infrastructure systems, respectively.[97] Both include reporting requirements and processes to have in place not only for a company's own defensive posture, but also for those processes and controls across their supply chain ecosystem. As this cyber regulatory landscape expands, the unique requirements, controls, and/or certification procedures can be financially costly or resource intensive and therefore require integration into strategic planning. These guidelines often enhance defensive postures, but as these guidelines become integrated into procurement processes, they may introduce new financial burdens or approaches to third-party partnerships.

Export Controls

In February 2024, a U.S. House of Representatives report titled "The CCP's Investors" identified numerous linkages between U.S. investment flows and the Chinese military and human rights abuses.[98] Since that time, numerous reports and investigations have linked U.S. private sector investment dollars to Chinese companies on existing U.S. banned lists.[99] Several pieces of bipartisan legislation have also been proposed to limit U.S. dollars from potentially funding Chinese surveillance and military capabilities as well as human rights abuses.[100]

While the investment flows have dominated the headlines, export controls aimed at curbing Chinese technological and military capabilities and human rights abuses have been on the rise for quite some time. These banned lists take many forms in the U.S., ranging from various Treasury OFAC lists, such as the Non-SDN

97 https://www.infosecurity-magazine.com/opinions/cyber-resilience-nis2-dora/

98 https://selectcommitteeontheccp.house.gov/sites/evo-subsites/selectcommitteeontheccp.house.gov/files/evo-media-document/2024-02-08 FINAL VC Report.pdf.

99 https://www.reuters.com/business/finance/wall-street-steered-billions-blacklisted-chinese-companies-probe-wsj-reports-2024-04-18/.

100 https://www.pionline.com/legislation/china-investments-targeted-4-bipartisan-house-bills.

Communist Chinese Military Companies List, to Homeland Security's Uyghur Forced Labor Prevention Act (UFLPA), which just recently updated its compliance guidance strategy.[101] These restrictions lists target a range of national security, human rights, economic, and technological risks to U.S. national interests. Increasingly, they are also coordinated with U.S. allies and are part of a foreign policy strategy among like-minded countries to counter the risks posed by authoritarian governments across the globe.

The U.S. Department of Commerce's Entity List is among the more prominent banned lists, focused on curbing activities contrary to U.S. national security and foreign policy interests. Since 2016, approximately 650 Chinese companies have been added to the Entity List. China is not the biggest target for these lists; since 2016, over 700 Russian companies have been added to the Entity List. In each case, there has been a sharp rise since 2019, a trend that likely will not abate any time soon as geopolitical tensions persist.

The AI Supply Chain

With hundreds of billions of dollars devoted to artificial Intelligence (AI) investments, coupled with budgetary cuts to enable greater corporate investments in AI, the mad dash toward AI continues virtually unabated. As is often the case with new technologies, security often remains an afterthought. But unlike other major technological leaps, the regulatory landscape is trying to keep up. This is largely due to the highly impactful (and risky) areas seeking to leverage AI, as well as the rising awareness of AI hallucinations, coupled with a high-stakes geopolitical race to be the first to achieve augmented general intelligence (AGI). The graph below illustrates these concepts with respect to semiconductor investments.

[101] https://www.dhs.gov/uflpa-strategy.

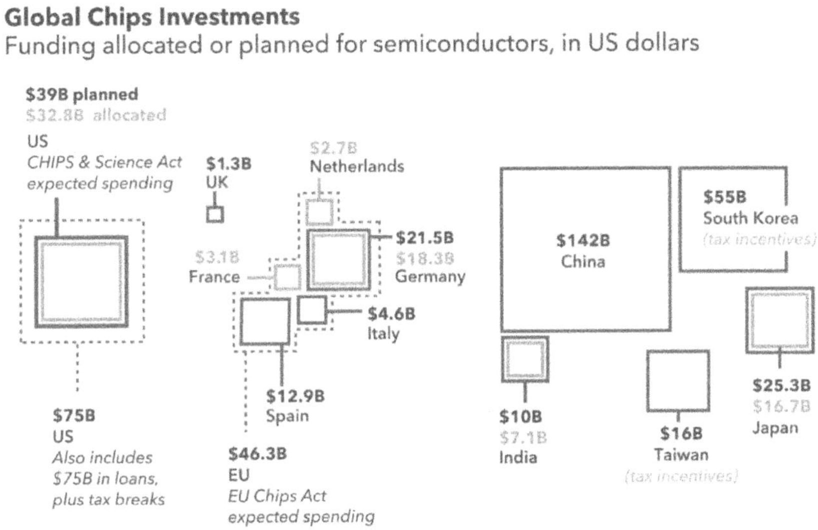

Figure 11.3 – Global Chips Investments[102]

In August 2024, the EU Artificial Intelligence Act (EU AI Act) came into force as the world's first significant piece of AI legislation.[103] The legislation takes a risk-based approach to the use of AI, establishing a taxonomy of risk levels to guide the level of scrutiny and transparency. For instance, AI-weapons systems require very different oversight than those that may inform recipe or book recommendations. The EU AI Act categorizes different kinds of data based on the risk they represent and universally stresses the need to minimize bias and defines areas of unacceptable risk, such as social scoring systems.

Because the EU AI Act applies to any business operating in Europe, the global ramifications are similar to those for the GDPR; the law applies even if a company is not EU-based. Outside of Europe, the AI regulatory landscape is shifting as well. In the United States, at least 40 states introduced some form of AI legislation during the

102 Sources for this composite graphic are Bloomberg reporting and research and the Semiconductor Industry Association.

103 https://artificialintelligenceact.eu/.

2023-24 legislative session.[104] The UK is in early stages of drafting AI legislation, as are Argentina, Singapore, China and many, many others.[105] [106] The Hiroshima AI Process Friends Group was launched in May 2023 and includes 49 countries aiming to enforce safe, secure, and trustworthy AI.[107]

With the vast potential of AI, the security and regulatory considerations are generally overlooked as a third-party risk. As discussed in Chapter 9, forward-leaning organizations would benefit from elevating these AI-related risks into their broader risk management framework. Whether selecting the NIST AI Risk Management Framework, the EU AI Act, or any of the growing range of frameworks and policies, just as AI increasingly integrates into every aspect of business, so too must it become a core element of third-party risk management.

Human Rights and Unethical Labor

While the previous sections of this essay focused largely on technology domains, the next three regulatory shifts highlight the social and environmental regulations shaping third-party risk. Unethical labor is one of the most prominent areas for emerging regulations, introducing significant financial and reputational risks, not to mention the human toll. Industries as diverse as fast-fashion and automotive are receiving fines and reaching settlements for unethical labor.[108] [109] A May 2024 Department of Labor settlement imposed almost $5 million in fines against poultry processors and distributors in California.[110]

104 https://www.ncsl.org/technology-and-communication/artificial-intelligence-2024-legislation.

105 https://www.bloomberg.com/news/articles/2024-04-15/uk-starts-drafting-ai-regulations-for-most-powerful-models?embedded-checkout=true.

106 https://iapp.org/media/pdf/resource_center/global_ai_law_policy_tracker.pdf.

107 https://www.soumu.go.jp/hiroshimaaiprocess/en/index.html.

108 https://abcnews.go.com/Business/wireStory/shein-discloses-found-2-cases-child-labor-supply-113110749.

109 https://www.washingtonpost.com/business/2024/05/30/hyundai-child-labor-alabama/.

110 https://www.dol.gov/newsroom/releases/whd/whd20240502.

The Uyghur Forced Labor Protection (UFLPA) Act is arguably the most prominent regulatory advance in the United States, introducing entity lists of companies deemed to produce, mine, or manufacture goods with forced labor.[111] The Act also places the burden of proof on buyers from the Xinjiang region that purchased goods were not made with forced labor. Companies were fined almost a billion dollars in its first year, a number likely to grow as the entities list expands.[112]

The EU Supply Chain Act similarly focuses on eliminating human rights violations and unethical labor from corporate supply chains.[113] Companies have four years before it comes into effect in 2029, but reputational repercussions exist today. The German Supply Chain Act (aka the Lieferkettensorgfaltspflichtengesetz) similarly aims to reduce human rights violations within supply chains. Given the lack of third-party visibility and due diligence required, this has proven to be a bureaucratic burden to such an extent that delaying it for two years is under review.[114]

As this regulatory environment shifts and more laws are enacted, it is not surprising that fines and penalties are also on the rise. In the United States alone during 2022-2023, child labor violations exceeded $8 million and represented an almost 90% increase from 2019.[115] These fines don't take into account the reputational damage, which can take years or even decades to recover.[116]

111 https://www.cbp.gov/trade/forced-labor/UFLPA.

112 https://www.cnbc.com/2023/04/17/feds-seize-goods-tied-to-forced-labor.html.

113 https://www.weforum.org/agenda/2024/03/eu-human-rights-environment-due-diligence-supply-chains/#:~:text=What%20is%20the%20CSDDD%3F,protection%20across%20their%20supply%20chains.

114 https://www.reuters.com/world/europe/german-government-considers-pausing-supply-chain-law-two-years-says-minister-2024-06-07/.

115 https://www.washingtonpost.com/business/2023/10/19/child-labor-violations-2023/.

116 https://www.thefashionlaw.com/visibility-is-central-to-a-successful-supply-chain-heres-what-brands-need-to-know/.

Environmental Impact

By 2025, companies doing business in the EU will need to comply with the EU Regulation on Deforestation-free Products.[117] The law is intended to stop the expansion of agricultural land in the following areas: cattle, wood, cocoa, soy, palm oil, coffee, rubber, and some derived products. Exporters of those products to EU countries must prove that they did not contribute to or originate from deforested land.

This regulation reflects a growing third-party risk trend wherein buyers are at regulatory risk due to the environmental impact of their suppliers. The EU and German laws mentioned in the previous section not only have a human rights component but also an environmental component. While the final version of the EU law is less strict than earlier versions, many companies will still be impacted.[118] EU due diligence rules address pollution and biodiversity impact and apply to companies with over 500 employees and net global turnover of €150 million.[119] To comply, companies need to integrate supply chain assessments in these areas for adverse impacts and remedy any adverse impacts discovered. Non-compliance may result in sanctions.

The German law initially targeted larger companies and incrementally applies to smaller companies each year, and it is under pressure to both loosen standards as well as conform to the EU law. For instance, only large companies with over 3,000 employees were initially accountable in 2023, which then expanded to companies with over 1,000 employees in 2024. As originally implemented, the environmental component of the German law focuses on environmental standards such as chemical pollutants or waste management.[120] With the adoption of the EU's Corporate

[117] https://environment.ec.europa.eu/topics/forests/deforestation/regulation-deforestation-free-products_en.

[118] https://www.theguardian.com/world/2024/mar/15/eu-approves-watered-down-human-rights-and-supply-chain-law.

[119] https://ec.europa.eu/commission/presscorner/detail/en/ip_23_6599.

[120] https://www.bmz.de/resource/blob/154774/lieferkettengesetz-faktenpapier-partnerlaender-eng-bf.pdf.

Sustainability Due Diligence Directive (CS3D), even tighter restrictions apply in very similar areas to the German law.[121] Under the CS3D, companies with an annual revenue beyond 400 million euros can be fined up to 5% of their annual revenue.

The U.S. lacks federal legislation that is equivalent to the legislation in Europe. The Inflation Reduction Act incentivizes progress toward greener supply chains but does not include regulatory requirements.[122] The SEC Climate Risk Disclosures rules passed in March 2024 immediately encountered legal challenges.[123]

Under the SEC's rule, companies were required to disclose Scope 1 and 2 emissions, with Scope 3 emissions requirements removed prior to the final version. Each of these scopes pertain to different sources of emissions, with Scope 1 focused on a company's direct emissions, Scope 2 those indirect emissions created through electricity, heat, etc. purchased from external sources, while Scope 3 refers to suppliers' emissions from upstream and downstream in the supply chain.

In March 2025, the SEC voted to end their defense of the climate-related disclosures.[124] However, Scope 1 through 3 emissions remain a key concern in other regulations from Europe and at the state level.

Climate Resilience

The SEC's Climate Risk Disclosures rules not only focused on a company's impact on the environment, but also addressed those risks associated with climate change. Because both sustainability and climate resilience are often grouped together within a single regulation, compliance can be confusing since they require different strategies.

[121] https://www.sdcexec.com/safety-security/regulations/article/22934137/baker-donelson-eu-corporate-sustainability-due-diligence-directive-and-german-supply-chain-act-what-to-expect-in-2025.

[122] https://www.forbes.com/sites/jonmcgowan/2024/06/30/sec-climate-disclosure-rule-is-in-peril-with-new-supreme-court-opinion/.

[123] https://www.sec.gov/newsroom/press-releases/2024-31.

[124] https://www.sec.gov/newsroom/press-releases/2025-58.

Climate resilience refers to the ability to adapt or mitigate the impact of climate change, such as extreme temperatures or increased flooding in some areas. The SEC rule specifically required companies to disclose "climate-related risks that have had or are reasonably likely to have a material impact on the registrant's business strategy, results of operations, or financial condition." These include the actual and potential material impacts of these risks and their impact on the business outlook as well as the financial expenses of mitigation. In addition, the Bipartisan Infrastructure Law (BIL) is one of many infrastructure laws that require new investments and projects to integrate climate resilience.[125]

The SEC Climate Disclosure rules were paused in April 2024 due to lawsuits, and then withdrawn in March 2025, and several related efforts have met similar fates.[126] Executive Order 14008 on Tackling the Climate Crisis at Home and Abroad ordered federal agencies to integrate climate resilience into their strategies, elevating it as a national security priority, including at international forums.[127] This executive order, and several others, were rescinded in January 2025.[128]

For the majority of organizations, these rules and regulations were not directly impactful. The EU still offers guidance but lacks the regulatory teeth of the environmental impact laws. Europe is warming faster than any other continent, with 2024 its hottest year on record.[129] [130] Natural disasters caused more than $417 billion in economic losses in 2024 and are expected to cause $145 billion in

125 https://www.phmsa.dot.gov/legislative-mandates/bipartisan-infrastructure-law-bil-infrastructure-investment-and-jobs-act-iija.

126 https://www.wsj.com/articles/sec-accepts-pause-on-its-climate-rule-b2afe8d9.

127 https://www.whitehouse.gov/briefing-room/presidential-actions/2021/01/27/executive-order-on-tackling-the-climate-crisis-at-home-and-abroad/.

128 https://www.whitehouse.gov/presidential-actions/2025/01/initial-rescissions-of-harmful-executive-orders-and-actions/.

129 https://www.worldbank.org/en/news/press-release/2024/05/15/europe-urgently-needs-to-increase-its-disaster-and-climate-resilience

130 https://commission.europa.eu/news/2024-warmest-year-record-europe-finds-european-state-climate-report-2025-04-15_en.

damages in 2025.[131] [132] Despite the lack of climate resilience regulations, climate change nevertheless imposes a significant risk across third-party networks.

Conclusion

The regulatory landscape of third-party risk continues to evolve, introducing a range of challenges and opportunities for organizations. Gaining visibility across your extended supply chain is especially crucial given that many regulatory violations may occur upstream in the value chain. This is especially true in the sub-tiers, as the deeper and more complex the inter-relationships, the greater the likelihood of violations.

Companies should not view third-party risk assessments as a one and done checkbox, but rather an ongoing process. From classifying vendors based on the kind of risk or potential exposure to ongoing vigilance and monitoring, organizations must gain visibility into their third-party relationships and formulate a standardized process for continuously monitoring both the third parties and the regulatory environment.

The following chapters provide a deep dive into specific regulations and how they impact third-party risk. Chapter 14 details those risks at various phases of the AI supply chain, while Chapter 12 provides additional nuance on the shifting regulatory landscape focused on sustainability, and then looks globally and provides an overview of China's regulatory environment and unique considerations for data and supply chain security. The only certainty in this uncertain regulatory environment is that it continues to change and evolve in unprecedented ways, introducing opportunities and risks for companies as they manage third-party risk.

131 https://riskandinsurance.com/natural-disasters-cost-global-economy-417-billion-in-2024-gallagher-re/.

132 https://www.weforum.org/stories/2025/05/costs-climate-disasters-145-billion-nature-climate-news/.

Insights and Actions

When your organization contracts third-party services from material vendors, ensure that service demarcation points are clearly defined and unambiguous. Too often, what the contracting entity thinks it's procuring differs from what it actually procures. Use roles and responsibilities matrices to clarify understandings and ensure that the statement of work has the appropriate level of detail based on the criticality of the contemplated service. Validate, as well, that key provisions in service agreements are consistent with your organization's requirements, notably breach notification, data retention, and minimum data and privacy requirements.

Governments around the world are introducing regulations that target global supply chains to enhance security, transparency, accountability, and environmental and social impact. Geopolitical shifts are the impetus for many of these, as are concerns over cybersecurity, the technologies powering the global economy, and shifting perspectives on corporate governance.

The breadth of third-party risks continues to grow, ranging from C-suite accountability for breaches to climate resilience, export controls, and the AI supply chain. While each is distinct, there are interdependencies among them, and they are often viewed more as a check-the-box process rather than a coherent strategy within organizations.

Organizations must evolve across people, processes, and technology to effectively address the shifting regulatory environment. Gaining visibility across this range of risks requires collaboration across the executive team and with suppliers, as they are too expansive and crosscutting for one individual to manage alone. Collective resilience and innovations in collaboration are critical to meet these challenges.

Key Contract Provisions to Evaluate

- Product and Service Definitions: Clearly define the scope and purpose of the relationship, especially regarding data use and privacy.

- Audit Rights: Include the right to audit the provider's operations, with specifics on fees, documentation, and notice periods.
- Privacy Rights: Address data subject rights (access, deletion, portability, etc.) and ensure compliance with regulations like GDPR and CCPA.
- Governing Law and Venue: Specify jurisdiction for dispute resolution, particularly in cross-border or multi-state relationships.
- Data Security: Codify security requirements, referencing standards (e.g., ISO 27001, NIST CSF) and practices (e.g., multi-factor authentication, penetration testing). Define "reasonable security" in line with legal requirements.
- Incident Response: Set clear breach notification timelines and cooperation protocols for investigations and regulatory responses.
- Third Parties' Third Parties: Address sub-processors and flow-down clauses to ensure consistent security and privacy obligations throughout the supply chain.
- Limitations of Liability: Carefully negotiate liability caps, balancing the interests of both parties and aligning with the actual risk exposure.
- Data Retention and Destruction: Specify requirements for data handling at contract termination, including verification of destruction.
- Service Level Agreements (SLAs): Scrutinize uptime commitments, maintenance windows, notification obligations, and the real value of SLA credits.

Personal Liability and Accountability

- High-profile cases (e.g., Uber CISO conviction, SEC charges against SolarWinds' CISO) have made personal liability a top concern for cybersecurity executives.
- Over 60% of cybersecurity leaders are worried about their own liability following cyber incidents.
- The SEC now requires prompt disclosure of material cybersecurity incidents, with board accountability for cyber governance and resilience.
- The EU's NIS2 directive also includes CISO liability provisions, and 93% of organizations made policy changes in response to these risks.

Technology-Focused Regulations

- Export Controls: Increasing restrictions on technology exports, especially to China and Russia, with lists like the Entity List and the Uyghur Forced Labor Prevention Act (UFLPA).
- AI Regulation: The EU AI Act (effective August 2024) introduces a risk-based approach to artificial intelligence, requiring transparency and minimizing bias. Similar regulatory activity is underway in the U.S. and globally.
- Standards and Frameworks: Organizations must comply with standards like ISO 27001, NIST Cybersecurity Framework, CMMC, FedRAMP, SOC2, DORA, and NIS2, all of which impose new controls and reporting requirements.

Human Rights and Unethical Labor

- Regulations such as the UFLPA and the EU Supply Chain Act target forced labor and human rights abuses in supply chains.

- Companies face significant fines and reputational damage for non-compliance. For example, child labor violations in the U.S. increased by almost 90% from 2019 to 2023.
- The burden of proof is increasingly on buyers to ensure products are not made with forced labor.

Environmental and Climate Regulations

- The EU Regulation on Deforestation-free Products requires proof that certain goods do not originate from deforested land.
- The EU and German laws mandate environmental due diligence and climate risk disclosure, with potential fines up to 5% of annual revenue for non-compliance.
- The SEC's climate risk disclosure rules (now withdrawn in the U.S.) required companies to report on climate-related risks and emissions.
- Despite regulatory uncertainty in some regions, climate change and natural disasters continue to pose significant risks to supply chains.

Consider This Additional Practical Guidance

- Avoid contracts that are disconnected from operational reality, as this creates unnecessary risk.
- Not all contract terms are equally negotiable; organizations should know which are absolute requirements and which are flexible, to avoid excessive legal costs.
- Collaboration across legal, privacy, security, and business teams ensures contracts accurately reflect the intended engagement and reduce operational risk.
- The regulatory and market landscape is evolving. The software industry's liability limitations are being scrutinized,

especially as software increasingly controls critical infrastructure. Organizations should stay up to date with changes in regulations as policymakers are considering legislation to increase software vendors' liability for damages caused by insecure or faulty products.

Chapter 12

Regulatory Impacts

Introduction

In Chapter 12, we move on to regulation. Matt begins with his essay, "Regulatory Context of TPRM," by outlining the significant regulatory actions that every business must comply with and then describes the functions and tools that companies should put in place to address the resulting myriad requirements. He then presents a slimmed-down version that would be suitable for an SMB to address its regulatory obligations, recognizing that they have neither the same level of exposure nor the same resources with which to tackle the regulatory burden.

Then, in her essay, "China's Regulatory Environment—and the Ripple Effects," Andrea examines the growing impact of China's evolving regulatory environment on global third-party risk management, especially for organizations with direct or indirect supply chain ties to China. While exploring the real-world impacts of these changes, Andrea examines the knock-on effects, including exposure to forced labor, corruption, governance risks, and geopolitical and economic tensions.

To round out this chapter and complete Section 4, Chris provides a soup-to-nuts treatise on regulatory process and structure. The context he offers for the history, purpose, and structure, along with the required outcomes for regulation we must comply with, is essential reading and sets one up perfectly for the systemic program Chris provides for integrating regulatory compliance into your supply chain operations and governance.

Immediately following Chris' essay is a list of publications he references throughout.

Regulatory Context of TPRM

Matt Stamper

Successful regulatory compliance is not just about following rules, but embedding a proactive, informed, and collaborative approach into the fabric of the organization, enabling it to adapt to the ever-changing regulatory environment while maintaining trust and operational resilience.

Organizations confront overlapping and frequently conflicting regulations requiring some form of vendor or supply chain risk management. Similar to the dynamics of complying with myriad privacy regulations, addressing this muddled regulatory landscape requires resources and a well-defined strategy. While larger organizations may have teams dedicated to TPRM, in small to medium-sized businesses (SMBs) compliance may fall to a single individual with numerous other day-to-day responsibilities. Managing regulatory compliance is only prioritized when audits and regulatory inquiries are pressing. Being in a reactive state when confronting regulations is never advisable.

In this chapter, I distill some of the guidance outlined in Section 1 of this book as an effective approach to addressing the challenges with regulatory compliance. Chapter 11 also brings in the legal implications of TPRM. These earlier chapters provide valuable context to your organization as you address regulatory requirements for your program.

Even with large, dedicated teams, regulatory compliance is not for the faint of heart. With many regulations numbering in the hundreds of pages and with nuanced requirements, complying with the "chapter and verse" of specific regulatory requirements can be daunting. Here in the U.S., for example, many regulations require appropriate oversight and risk management over third-party services. Cases in point include, but are not limited to, the following:

- The Health Insurance Portability and Accountability Act (HIPAA) from the U.S. Department of Health and Human Services
- The Gramm-Leach-Bliley Act (GLBA) from the Federal Trade Commission
- The Defense Federal Acquisition Regulation Supplement (DFARS) from the U.S. Department of Defense
- The Interagency Guidance on Third-Party Relationships: Risk Management from the Board of Governors from the Federal Reserve Board
- The Federal Information Security Management Act, overseen by the Office of Management and Budget
- The Foreign Corrupt Practices Act, overseen by the Securities and Exchange Commission and the Department of Justice

Federal regulations may also intersect with state and international regulations, including privacy regulations like the California Privacy Rights Act (CPRA). International privacy regulations also call out specific requirements related to the oversight of third parties (data processors), as is the case with the European Union's General Data Protection Regulation (see Article 28 for a detailed list of requirements), India's Personal Data Protection Bill (PDPB), and Japan's Act on the Protection of Personal Information (APPI), among many others. New York State's Department of Financial Services Cybersecurity Regulation (also known as 23 NYCRR Part 500) also spells out specific requirements for evaluating the risks and governance considerations of using third-party service providers and associated services. In short, there is no shortage of regulations spanning most industries that call on organizations to assess and manage third-party risk. With so many regulations and distinct provisions related to TPRM, complying with the letter of the law for each may be intractable for all but the largest organizations. A principled-based approach to TPRM may be the only viable solution to "comply." There are successful analogs that suggest a principle-based approach may be in order.

As illustrated by the juxtaposition between U.S. Generally Accepted Accounting Principles (GAAP) and International Financial Reporting Standards (IFRS), how to comply with multitudinous regulations varies based on organizational context and, frankly, the risk tolerances of the organization's leadership team, who will need to determine what level or degree of compliance is warranted. Despite the term "Principles" in GAAP, GAAP is fundamentally a rules-based approach to accounting. Conversely, IFRS is principle-based. Whether your organization should take a principle-based approach or strictly comply with a regulation or standard will be predicated on your organization's risk tolerances and approach to compliance. There have been movements toward more "top-down" principled approaches akin to the refinements that the Public Company Accounting Oversight Board (PCAOB) made when it deprecated Audit Standard 2 (noted for being prescriptive and detailed) to Audit Standard 5, which is principle-based, risk-focused, and emphasizes the role of management, notably with evidencing managerial reviews and approvals over accounting functions and treatment decisions.

So, how would a principle-based approach to TPRM look for most organizations? Would a principle-based approach be legally defensible if regulators were to come knocking at the door? As I've noted in various talks on the topic of reasonable security, for better or worse (it's worse), the U.S. has a litigious business culture, and regulators have historically used consent orders, fines, penalties, and threats of debarment to help enforce regulations. Essentially, TPRM leaders should posit whether it would be reasonable *not* to incorporate certain functions and capabilities into their TPRM programs. By asking the question, "Is it reasonable not to have this capability or function?" the organization's leadership team and members of the TPRM program can reach a consensus on what level of capability is required to mitigate regulatory and compliance risk for the organization.

Recommended TPRM Governance and Administrative Functions

Here is a list of TPRM governance and administrative functions that I believe are necessary to have a principle-based and defensible TPRM program when confronting a sea of regulations.[133] Spend some time with your team and evaluate the current state of the items below within your organization. Your organization's designated TPRM leader should undertake this review. I would strongly recommend that counsel be fully engaged in the process to ensure that regulatory requirements and contractual obligations are given the appropriate analysis.

Tone at the Top – First and foremost, the tone at the top must be clear. A senior executive needs to oversee and coordinate the TPRM program. This executive should be accountable for the TPRM program and report on its status at a cadence acceptable to the board of directors and executive leadership team. There's a notable red flag if the tone at the top is ambivalent. If TPRM functions are ambiguous with respect to roles and responsibilities, ownership, and risk treatment tolerances and decisions, it's clear that the executive leadership team has not devoted sufficient time and attention to making TPRM an organizational priority. There are ways to codify the tone at the top organizationally, including establishing a standing committee (or agenda item) and charter to formalize understandings and expectations.

TPRM Committee – Depending on the organization's existing committee structure and committee practices, the topic of TPRM may be handled as a standing agenda item with a pre-existing risk committee or similarly risk-oriented committee (See Section 1 of this

[133] In a litigious business culture, determining "legally defensible" TPRM actions can be challenging. Plaintiff's attorneys can and will have different perspectives regarding the reasonableness and adequacy of actions taken by the organization.

book for additional details on the role of committees in supporting the TPRM program). If the inherent risk factors associated with third-party services and suppliers are sufficiently critical for the organization, consider a stand-alone TPRM committee that meets quarterly. Ensure that the committee's standing agenda captures the considerations outlined in the TPRM charter, including the role of key stakeholders in evaluating vendor and supply chain risks. The committee should oversee key assessments of vendors and suppliers, as well as a list of defined key risk indicators (KRIs) for the TPRM program. The committee's meeting minutes are important evidence of the organization's commitment to oversee and manage third-party risk factors germane to the organization's operating environment. Attendance is also essential to evidence executive engagement and oversight of TPRM functions. When key executives cannot attend committee meetings, they should have a clearly identified and authorized delegate to support decision-making on TPRM actions.

TPRM Program Charter – A senior executive, ideally the organization's CEO, CFO, or General Counsel, should approve a TPRM charter. The charter should outline who is accountable for overseeing and administering the TPRM program, the role of various organizational stakeholders (e.g., finance and accounting, IT, privacy, security, legal, and lines of business), how conflicting perspectives on third-party risk should be adjudicated within the organization, and every manager's role in bringing third-party risk considerations to an appropriate committee for its evaluation and assessment. Beyond spelling out the need for a TPRM committee (or standing agenda item in a similarly focused committee), the charter should require that the TPRM program maintain a risk register of identified risk factors that require executive attention.

TPRM Policy – Your TPRM program should have a policy that outlines expectations for the program and defines key terms, including which vendors or suppliers are classified as material. The TPRM policy should have standard disciplinary language (such as "Failure to comply with the policy may lead to disciplinary action up to and including termination.") that is reviewed by counsel and should document the organization's requirements for vendor and supplier audits, assessments, and reviews. The policy should also outline other expectations for the program, including reviews of the vendor master file, maintaining an inventory of applicable regulations, expectations for stewardship over key partners, and other functional activities. Like the charter, the policy should be executed by a senior executive and acknowledged by department leaders from various lines of business as well as functional areas, including privacy, legal, IT, and security.

Risk Register – The TPRM program should maintain a high-level risk register that identifies material risks and key considerations related to the program. Items that appear on the risk register cannot be addressed directly by the TPRM team, absent input from the committee or the executive leadership team. As noted below, the status of KRIs tied to the TPRM program provides data-driven insights to inform resourcing and prioritization decisions for the committee and the executive leadership team.

Key Risk Indicators (KRIs) – The TPRM program should be data-driven. To help foment a more empirical approach to TPRM, KRIs should be established and tracked to ensure that organizational stakeholders are kept current regarding the program's coverage, capabilities, and status. Some basic KRIs to consider including in your inventory of KRIs would be the following:

- Percent of material vendors or suppliers assessed within the last six months
- Percent of material vendors with external audits or certifications with negative audit findings
- Percent of material vendors with risk factors that warrant compensating or mitigating controls
- Percent of material vendors with contract expiry terms of less than 60 days
- Percent of material vendors without breach notification clauses in their contracts and service agreements

Spend time with your team to ensure that your portfolio of KRIs accurately reflects the organizational context and risk priorities. The process of identifying and fine-tuning KRIs can be quite instructive for the TPRM team. As part of this effort, identify the data source for the information required to report on the KRI.

TPRM Calendar – Calendars are powerful tools for noting the cadence and time required for different corporate functions. Build a TPRM calendar that captures the dates of reviews, assessments, audits, and stewardship activities with material providers. For example, if an assessment takes two weeks to complete, capture that time commitment in the calendar. Good calendar management practices ensure that TPRM stakeholders are not unaware of upcoming requirements for audits and assessments. Ensure that key activities have appropriate reminders to notify stakeholders within the TPRM team of the forthcoming activity. When used well, calendars, along with KRIs, can help clarify resourcing requirements and time allocations for TPRM functions. Ensure distribution lists and notification settings are reviewed with the TPRM team for accuracy and completeness.

RACI Matrices Tied to High-Priority/High-Impact TPRM Functions – RACI matrices are powerful tools for governance and oversight. Draft and maintain RACI matrices for key TPRM functions, including onboarding, assessments and audits, offboarding, and other critical activities across your TPRM program, such as detailed security and privacy assessments. Make sure that assignments noted in RACIs are kept current. Ensure stakeholders noted in the "Consulted" and "Informed" columns know their roles in the process. Depending on the breadth and depth of the individuals and their experience within your TPRM team, internal members may be able to provide the subject matter expertise typically provided by the "Consulted" role. Other resources should be proactively identified when the team is small or certain expertise may not be readily available. Clearly, if the team is small, or there is not enough diversity in experience to inform TPRM decisions, this is a factor that should be captured in the risk register and should be addressed by the committee or executive leadership team for adjudication.

Vendor Master File – Ensure that the TPRM team has an opportunity to evaluate how the vendor master file is managed and maintained, recognizing that there may ultimately be several overlapping vendor inventories for the organization. These separate inventories should be documented, indicating their specific role or function. Many excellent applications beyond the organization's ERP can provide useful details regarding a vendor or a supplier's relationship with the organization. Ideally, the system used to track vendor details can be customized to meet the needs of the TPRM program. The TPRM team should note the expiry dates on contracts, the dollar value of the engagement, key risk factors assessed (e.g., operational, privacy, or security risks), and specific contract provisions (e.g., SLAs and breach notification clauses). Where specific details are not captured, the TPRM should collaborate with the accounting team to see if modifications and refinements can be added to the application. These discussions and any changes made should be documented as evidence of the organization's review of its vendor inventories.

Vendor and Supplier Categorization and Priority Ranking – The aforementioned vendor master file (or a similar inventory tool) should categorize vendors based on defined criteria. This classification can be as basic as "material" or "non-material" vendors, where materiality is defined in the TPRM policy. Other approaches include separating and classifying vendors based on function or the data elements they process. The goal is to provide evidence of the organization's review of its universe of suppliers and vendors and to prioritize these relationships based on their value and risk to the organization. If the criteria are pre-established and agreed to, again via the TPRM policy or charter, the classification and prioritization should be straightforward but will take time to complete. I strongly recommend that the organization's most critical relationships have a designated executive or line of business sponsor with the organization. Effectively, as part of the categorization and prioritization process, ensure that the most material and critical relationships are clearly noted and that these relationships are proactively managed according to defined criteria.

Inventory of In-Scope Regulations – It's critical that the TPRM team maintains currency and awareness of the various regulations applicable to the company's operating environment. One approach is to maintain a master schedule of these regulations and ensure that the appropriate committee receives an annual update on those deemed most material to the organization and the organization's current status for complying with the identified in-scope regulations. Many law firms provide regulatory summaries that can be incorporated into these reviews. I strongly recommend that the TPRM team take a disciplined approach to this regulatory landscape review and force-rank those regulations that have the most impact on or present the most risk to the organization. As an overly simplified example, for a defense contractor, DFARS may take precedence over other regulations. Companies in healthcare should likely focus on HIPAA. With the support of counsel, it's important that the TPRM team lists in-scope regulations in the order of their precedence.

Risk and Control Matrices for Critical Regulations – While I'm advocating a principle-based approach to complying with in-scope regulations, there are times when documenting the specific requirements of a given regulation is in order. For example, DFARS requires defense contractors to comply with defined controls to secure controlled, unclassified information (CUI) and federal contract information (FCI) as outlined in NIST SP 800-171 and its accompanying audit guide, NIST SP 800-171a. These documents provide explicit control requirements and the associated determination statements to validate the controls over CUI and FCI.

There's value in mapping the requirements of a material regulation to a structured risk control matrix (RCM). Like the risk register noted above, risk control matrices are typically in the form of a spreadsheet unless they are embedded into an application that provides similar functionality. The RCM should minimally have the following structured elements (think columns in the context of a spreadsheet):

- **Risk Statement** – A statement indicating what risks are being mitigated and controlled by the organization's TPRM program.

- **Control Objective** – A statement defining the control activities' end state (e.g., material third-party vendors are assessed for risk). Where an RCM is tied to a specific regulation, the control objectives should be verbatim and with the regulation's specific reference.
- **Control Activities** – A brief description of the specific activities and functions employed to meet the control objective and minimize the likelihood and impact of the risk materializing.
- **Control Type** – Controls can be categorized by their type. The three most common types are manual, hybrid, or automated. Like "preventative" controls noted below, automated controls are preferred over hybrid and manual controls.
- **Control Classification** – Controls can be classified as "preventative," "detective," or "corrective." Generally, preventative controls are deemed more effective than detective controls and clearly more effective than corrective controls.
- **Control Owner** – The control owner is analogous to the "accountable" party noted in a RACI matrix. This should be the department head who is ultimately accountable for the design, implementation, and ongoing governance of a given control or suite of controls.
- **Control Frequency** – The cadence of a control and the impact of a control failure should inform how frequently it is evaluated and assessed.

Collectively, the tools and functions noted above will help provide a principle-based approach to meeting regulatory requirements. By using a committee, defining program goals with the charter, and codifying understandings in the TPRM policy, the organization's core expectations will be broadly understood by stakeholders. Using a risk register and KRIs to track the coverage and efficacy of program functions and capabilities will help executive stakeholders make informed decisions regarding compliance risks and resourcing. Where warranted, distilling regulations into their mandated controls and mapping these into risk control matrices will help prevent specific regulatory requirements from being overlooked. Calendars and RACI matrices further this principled approach by ensuring that roles and responsibilities are documented and understood and that key governance and third-party risk management functions are calendared and resourced accordingly. Maintaining documentation on risk treatment decisions (e.g., transfer, mitigate, accept) is also foundational to a principle-based approach. It's important to evidence management's oversight of the TPRM program, including its capabilities, resourcing, and functions. In the aggregate, these strategies will put your organization's TPRM program on a solid foundation. Where detailed and resourced regulatory compliance is required, these expectations will not surprise the organization or its leadership team.

A Special Callout to Small and Medium-sized Enterprises (SMBs)

Throughout this book, we've discussed critical elements of designing and operating a comprehensive TPRM program. Under-resourced, smaller organizations confront unique challenges in designing and operating programs that mitigate third-party risks absent dedicated teams and sophisticated tooling. Here are five easy-to-implement techniques that can be used to ensure that your program is reasonably prepared to address third-party risks.

1. **Compile and maintain a list of your most material vendors and suppliers.** This list does not need to be comprehensive, but it should minimally capture those relationships that underpin your organization's operations. Try to keep the initial list to less than 25 providers for manageability.

2. **Assign an accountable party to each identified material relationship** and validate key services and risks associated with each vendor. If risks that require additional treatment

and attention are identified, add that risk to a simple risk register to ensure that the risk factor is captured and tracked. Draft a simple vendor summary to ensure that the variables most germane to your organization are tracked consistently.

3. In the absence of a designated, accountable party for the TPRM program, **establish a committee of key organizational stakeholders** and review the status of material vendors and any identified risk factors that warrant the committee's attention. Have the committee meet each quarter to provide an update on key factors for those "most" material providers.

4. **Determine the appropriate response to identified risks.** Options could include alternative or additional suppliers and vendors, updated contract terms, and insurance, among other approaches. Review the desired approach with committee members and document and agree to the desired course of action.

5. **Update your vendor master file to capture the variables that are most germane to your baseline program.** Minimally, ensure mechanisms to categorize and sort provided services, notably for those services where sensitive data may be shared or where the provider's services are integral to the organization's operations. If your vendor master file allows for the tracking of expiry dates for services, create a basic calendar reminder to review material vendor services several months prior to the expiry to ensure adequate time to renegotiate terms and/or request modifications to services aligned with your organization's priorities and risk tolerances.

While the five points noted above are certainly not comprehensive, they offer a low-cost, easy-to-implement starting point for a TPRM program. I cannot stress enough the value of collaborative effort and the insights that ensue with well-governed committees. Consider drafting a basic charter to outline expectations for the committee. See that the committee meets at least quarterly to ensure that TPRM factors are reviewed in a timely manner. Every organization can find an hour or two per quarter to address TPRM considerations. These basic steps will ensure that the organization is not caught flat-footed by third-party risks that should have been reasonably anticipated.

China's Regulatory Environment—and the Ripple Effects

Dr. Andrea Little Limbago

While most data compliance conversations focus on the EU's GDPR, China's data and cybersecurity regulations have become a significant but underappreciated governance risk. With a large share of critical goods (pharmaceuticals, electronics, apparel, etc.) sourced from China, many organizations are exposed to these risks—often unknowingly.

When discussing data protection regulations and compliance, the European Union's General Data Protection Regulation (GDPR) or many of its progeny usually come to mind. In contrast, China's series of cyber and data regulations over the last few years are rarely discussed in those data compliance and risk conversations, despite the fact that so many third-party relationships lead back to China.

In the U.S., roughly 90% of active pharmaceutical ingredients, 40% of apparel, and 48% of electronics are sourced from China, not to mention the numerous other raw materials, machinery, and textile dependencies, among many others.[134] As proprietary and/or financial data frequently moves across suppliers, companies are likely at risk of China's regulatory environment but may not know it. Just as many were caught off guard over their dependency on China during the COVID-19 pandemic, the same may soon be true over their data exposure as these regulations start to have an impact. Regulations that enable data access and storage requirements may go against the interests of those organizations. In short, China's regulatory environment is a significant governance risk, and yet it garners

134 https://fortune.com/2023/05/30/corporations-china-decoupling-usa-trade-globalization-economy-politics-sonnenfeld-bass-tian/.

minimal attention in data governance and third-party risk conversations.

Background

Following China's 2023 Counter Espionage Law, the U.S. Chamber of Commerce released a statement citing growing risks to businesses due to legal uncertainties and risks of doing business there.[135] Their statement notes the "wide range of documents, data, or materials" at risk due to the new law. A similar statement released by the National Counterintelligence and Security Center explains, "These laws provide the PRC government with expanded legal grounds for accessing and controlling data held by U.S. firms in China."[136]

The Counter Espionage Law broadens an existing law by expanding the definition of espionage beyond state secrets to any documents, data, or materials related to national security without specifying the parameters of what that entails.[137] This law is only the latest in a series of laws aimed at increasing national security and data protection that, in reality, introduce significant risks for U.S. companies—and their partners—operating in China.

The 2021 Personal Information Protection Law (PIPL) and Data Security Law (DSL), along with the 2017 Cybersecurity Law, together comprise the main data governance architecture in China. On the surface, the PIPL shares features with the GDPR, including a focus on personal information rights, a data controller equivalent, and an extraterritorial scope for data protections.[138] The PIPL deviates from the GDPR with national security exemptions, a common theme that enables the PRC government with unfettered data access. On the day the PIPL was introduced, Yahoo shut down

[135] https://www.uschamber.com/international/u-s-chamber-statement-on-concerns-over-prc-investment-climate.

[136] https://www.dni.gov/files/NCSC/documents/SafeguardingOurFuture/FINAL_NCSC_SOF_Bulletin_PRC_Laws.pdf.

[137] https://www.reuters.com/world/asia-pacific/china-passes-revised-counter-espionage-law-state-media-2023-04-26/.

[138] https://iapp.org/news/a/analyzing-chinas-pipl-and-how-it-compares-to-the-eus-gdpr/.

its remaining services in China, noting an "increasingly challenging legal and business environment."[139]

The DSL and Cybersecurity Law similarly introduce new data governance challenges, ranging from the extraterritorial reach of data laws inside and outside of China to cross-border data flow restrictions and data localization requirements. An additional law, the Cyber Vulnerability Reporting Law, requires companies to report vulnerabilities directly to a government authority prior to public disclosure.[140] In fact, this extends beyond corporations. Participants in major hacking competitions in China are required to disclose vulnerabilities directly to the government.[141] This gives the Chinese government a jump on remediation or potentially exploiting these vulnerabilities.

These new laws have already had an impact across a range of areas. For instance, the 2021 laws created a 90% loss of global shipping location data from China, which was instrumental in identifying port congestion and other shipping disruptions.[142] International research, especially in the areas of health and academic data, has also taken a hit.[143] Some have coined China a "data black hole" due to the growing data restrictions and lack of data transparency, as well as the difficulty in assessing corporate databases and economic databases.[144] There is also the issue of "vanishing data" where the government limits access to the foundational economic data needed to make informed investments and other corporate decisions.[145]

139 https://www.wired.com/story/china-personal-data-law-pipl/

140 https://www.wired.com/story/china-vulnerability-disclosure-law/.

141 https://www.bloomberg.com/news/articles/2025-04-30/chinese-hacking-competitions-fuel-the-country-s-broad-cyber-ambitions?embedded-checkout=true.

142 https://www.reuters.com/world/china/off-grid-chinese-data-law-adds-global-shipping-disruption-2021-11-17/.

143 https://www.nature.com/articles/d41586-023-01638-1.

144 https://www.bloomberg.com/news/articles/2023-10-18/china-is-becoming-a-data-black-hole-short-seller-aandahl-says.

145 https://www.wsj.com/world/china/china-economy-data-missing-096cac9a?st=5xkUS1&reflink=article_copyURL_share.

But Wait, There's More!

The shifting data regulations are not the only growing data risks for companies doing business in China. Police raids on several U.S. companies have sparked growing concern on both personal security and data security. Due diligence firms have been targeted, as have consulting companies, including the imprisonment of a senior researcher on espionage charges related to work for a consulting company.[146] Bain & Company, Mintz Group, and Capvision are among those raided by Chinese law enforcement.[147] China has also opened an investigation into Micro Technology on national security grounds, suspended Deloitte's operations in Beijing for several months, launched an investigation into Foxconn, and issued several bans preventing U.S. defense contractors from selling in China.[148]

Although Mintz employees were released in March 2025, this risk remains.[149] In early January 2024, the Chinese Ministry of State Security detained the head of a consulting agency, claiming they worked as a spy for the British government.[150] Chinese police also arrested three employees of one of the world's largest advertising companies, WPP Plc.[151] A Japanese trading firm employee has also been detained, as has a former employee of Safe Ports, a U.S. logistics company.[152] In response, Safe Ports CEO Lucy Duncan expressed

[146] https://www.aljazeera.com/economy/2023/5/10/chinas-foreign-companies-on-edge-after-national-security-raids.

https://www.reuters.com/world/china/chinese-police-query-bains-shanghai-office-staff-company-spokesperson-2023-04-26/, https://www.cnn.com/2023/08/22/economy/china-mintz-consulting-fine-intl-hnk/index.html.

[148] https://www.ft.com/content/454ef0c7-cd2c-4cbc-a581-aed2bf8b186f, https://www.axios.com/2023/10/25/china-investigation-foxconn-warning-us-taiwan.

[149] https://www.npr.org/2025/03/25/g-s1-55655/china-releases-staff-of-an-american-due-diligence-firm-in-move-to-woo-investors.

[150] https://www.nytimes.com/2024/01/08/world/asia/china-spying-britain.html.

[151] https://www.bnnbloomberg.ca/wpp-employees-arrested-and-offices-raided-by-chinese-police-1.1987509.

[152] https://www.reuters.com/world/china/china-formally-arrests-astellas-employee-suspected-spying-japan-urges-release-2023-10-19/.

her disbelief at the accusations and proclaimed, "It is impossible to do business in China."[153]

Other Western companies are finding themselves on China's Unreliable Entity List, often a tit-for-tat retaliation stemming from U.S. and Western sanctions targeting Chinese companies. For instance, in 2024 and 2025, China places numerous U.S. defense companies on the unreliable list. This follows a series of additions to the list since its introduction in 2020.[154] As part of the ongoing escalation/de-escalation of the trade war, in May 2025 many companies were removed from the list.[155] Nevertheless, U.S./China trade relations are so uncertain that it is likely this tool of economic statecraft will be used again in the future.

President Xi Jinping is also revitalizing corporate-based militias, a move reminiscent of the era of Mao Zedong.[156] Over the last few years, dozens of Chinese companies have announced the creation of People's Armed Forces Departments. Some maintain this is more indicative of concerns about internal stability; for companies doing business in China, it reflects the tight control of the Chinese government over domestic companies, as well as potential internal instability risks.

Finally, forced labor, corruption, and governance introduce additional regulatory risks. For example, the U.S. Uyghur Forced Labor Prevention Act (UFLPA), enacted in December 2021, prohibits the importation of goods made from forced labor, specifically targeting the Xinjiang Uyghur Autonomous Region of China.[157] The government's crackdown on corruption introduces benefits, such as cleaning up a system notorious for bribery and graft, as well as significant disruptions. Over the past ten years, nearly five

[153] https://www.theguardian.com/world/2024/feb/15/china-holds-citizen-on-spying-charges-after-she-did-admin-work-for-us-company.

[154] https://www.cnbc.com/2020/09/21/china-releases-details-on-unreliable-entity-list-raising-uncertainty-for-foreign-businesses.html

[155] https://www.newsweek.com/china-suspends-sanctions-export-restrictions-us-companies-trump-trade-talks-2072559.

[156] https://www.ft.com/content/d6b2e4d6-2f84-4ef9-bf99-10d76d92d045.

[157] https://www.dhs.gov/uflpa-entity-list.

million individuals have been disciplined for their corrupt behavior.[158] These were largely party officials, but the crackdown has also decreased lending and put foreign firms on guard for probes, such as those targeting Bain & Company, Mintz Group, and Capvision.

What Does This Have to Do with Third-Party Risk?

Regardless of which industry you are in, there's a good chance China has developed a near monopoly of items critical to your business. From COVID lockdowns to widespread floods to protests at factories, with the majority of supply chains leading back to China—whether directly or indirectly—the hyper-connectivity that created great efficiencies also introduces significant data risks as well as operational risks.[159]

Given this shifting regulatory regime and growing movement toward data sovereignty, the UK government issued recommendations for those concerned about their data within China.[160] These include getting specialist legal advice before establishing projects in China and understanding the nuances of cross-border data transfers, as not all sectors must comply. For those pressured to transfer source code or other IP, they recommend seeking Embassy support.

A 2022 study of U.S. companies highlighted the core challenges of data localization, regulatory ambiguity, and inconsistent enforcement as top data, privacy, and cybersecurity concerns.[161] While responses varied by industry, a common theme emerged around the necessity to map and gain visibility of their data flows. In the longer term, some are considering separate product offerings and

[158] https://www.reuters.com/breakingviews/chinas-war-corruption-turns-into-high-wire-act-2024-01-18/.

[159] https://asia.nikkei.com/Business/Business-trends/Factory-strikes-flare-up-in-China-as-economic-woes-deepen.

[160] https://www.gov.uk/government/publications/overseas-business-risk-china/overseas-business-risk-china.

[161] https://www.uschina.org/reports/how-american-companies-are-approaching-china%E2%80%99s-data-privacy-and-cybersecurity-regimes.

disconnecting any footprint in China from their broader global operations.

The regulatory uncertainty and inconsistent enforcement have already led to the termination of major deals, and a record-low level of optimism about doing business in China.[162] The number of German firms exiting or considering existing China has doubled over the last few years, as European companies writ large are shifting investment and trade strategies away from China.[163] As European Chamber president Jens Eskelund explains, business confidence in China is "pretty much the lowest we have on record."[164]

Despite the decreasing confidence and growing security concerns, breaking up is hard to do. In 2022, the U.S.-China goods trade hit a record high.[165] Nevertheless, there are signs of significant shifts in global trading patterns. In 2023, for the first time in decades, the United States bought more goods from Mexico than from China.[166] Rather than full decoupling, many are pursuing a derisking strategy, including supply chain stress tests and audits, as well as seeking alternative suppliers.[167]

Conclusion

The regulatory concerns associated with China's anti-espionage law, data and cybersecurity policies, including data localization, government access to data, inspections, and personnel risks and detentions, have introduced unique third-party risks. Even for those

[162] https://www.reuters.com/technology/intel-walk-away-54-bln-acquisition-tower-semiconductor-sources-2023-08-16/, https://www.reuters.com/technology/intel-walk-away-54-bln-acquisition-tower-semiconductor-sources-2023-08-16/.

[163] https://www.reuters.com/world/china/more-german-firms-leave-china-or-consider-exit-survey-2024-01-24/.

[164] https://apnews.com/article/china-foreign-companies-investment-trade-a47887e2c89050d291ebd169b0989cc4.

[165] https://www.bloomberg.com/news/articles/2023-02-07/us-china-trade-climbs-to-record-in-2022-despite-efforts-to-split?embedded-checkout=true.

[166] https://www.nytimes.com/2024/02/07/business/economy/united-states-china-mexico-trade.html.

[167] https://www.economist.com/the-economist-explains/2023/05/31/what-does-de-risking-trade-with-china-mean.

not doing business directly in China, the extraterritorial nature of their regulations, coupled with the hyper-dependence of global supply chains on China, likely means these risks impact your organization even if you don't think they do.

The heightened geopolitical tensions further exacerbate these risks. U.S. Executive Orders are making investment in certain Chinese industries more difficult, while another aims at blocking transfers of personal data to "countries of concern," including China.[168] Concerns over national security risks associated with data collection by Chinese companies—ranging from automobiles to TikTok—highlight the data risks and concerns over China's data policies and governmental access.[169] Heightened rhetoric and military exercises around Taiwan are yet another concern for global stability, as is the ongoing trade conflict between the U.S. and China.

Nevertheless, due to decades of hyper-connectivity and interdependence, it's nearly impossible to avoid China.[170] As most companies do not have full visibility into their extended supply chains or data flows, it would be advantageous to integrate China's uncertain digital regulatory environment into any third-party risk assessment. Fortunately, many of the recommendations coincide with strong cyber hygiene, but nevertheless, the data localization, access, and inspections introduce an additional layer of risk. As long as China continues to expand data sovereignty policies and tensions exist between the U.S. and China, China's regulatory environment must be integrated into any comprehensive third-party risk strategy.

[168] https://asia.nikkei.com/Politics/International-relations/US-China-tensions/Eyeing-China-Biden-limits-personal-data-transfers-to-U.S.-rivals.

[169] https://www.cnbc.com/2024/02/29/us-says-to-investigate-national-security-data-risks-from-chinese-vehicles.html.

[170] https://www.wsj.com/world/china/u-s-companies-are-finding-it-hard-to-avoid-china-213997b7.

Regulatory Compliance Challenges and Strategies

Chris Forbes

Regulatory compliance is a dynamic and challenging process, requiring organizations to be agile, well-informed, and proactive.

Essay Overview

"The law is reason, free from passion." *Aristotle*

Our founding fathers rooted regulations and administrative law in the U.S. Constitution. The delegation of legislative power begins in Article I, Section 1 of the Constitution, which vests all legislative powers in Congress. Article I, Section 8 of the Constitution empowers Congress to "regulate Commerce with foreign Nations, and among the States."

In one of the earliest instances of American administrative law, the Tariff Act of 1789 granted the president of the United States the authority to impose and suspend tariffs and established a customs duty on imported goods. This act empowered the president to adjust tariff rates within certain bounds and address fluctuations in the value of foreign currencies. The Tariff Act of 1816 granted the president the authority to suspend tariffs altogether in times of emergency or national interest to alleviate the economic burden on American consumers and businesses during the War of 1812. Subsequent tariff acts conferred even more discretion upon the president, allowing for the imposition of retaliatory tariffs against countries that engaged in unfair trade practices. The use of tariffs sparked intense political debates, with proponents arguing for the benefits of protectionism and critics denouncing the potential for abuse and corruption.

Congress delegates authority to agencies to create and enforce regulations. The U.S. Supreme Court has held that Congress cannot wholly delegate its legislative power. However, it can delegate authority to agencies if it provides an "intelligible principle" to guide its actions (nondelegation doctrine). Modern courts have generally held that when Congress delegates authority to a federal officer or agency, subdelegation to subordinate officials is presumptively permissible unless expressly prohibited. The Supreme Court has emphasized that decisions of "magnitude and consequence" should rest with Congress or be explicitly delegated to an agency. I will cover more recent court rulings, such as the Chevron doctrine, later in this chapter.

In its first 100 years, the federal government established numerous regulatory offices. Mainly designed to promote and develop the young nation and its industries, these agencies included the Army Corps of Engineers (1824), the Patent and Trademark Office (1836), the Comptroller of the Currency (1863), the Copyright Office of the Library of Congress (1870), and the Bureau of Fisheries (1871). Two other agencies, the Internal Revenue Service (1862) and the Civil Service Commission (1883) were established to facilitate government administration.

In 1887, Congress authorized the first independent regulatory agency, the Interstate Commerce Commission (ICC), to regulate economic activity. The ICC explicitly oversees the railroad industry to ensure fair rates, eliminate rate discrimination, and regulate other aspects of common carriers.

In 1946, Congress passed the Administrative Procedure Act (APA), which standardized agency rulemaking and adjudication processes. The APA established procedures for these processes, including requirements for public notice and comment periods, which help ensure accountability in exercising delegated authority.

In 1951, Executive Order 10250, issued under the authority granted by 3 U.S.C. § 301, formalized the presidential delegation of functions to department heads and other officials.

Legal experts have struggled to establish a universal definition for regulation and to produce a comprehensive list of regulatory programs and regulated activities because of the remarkable diversity of forms and functions. Kenneth Meier, a scholar on regulation, defined regulation as "any attempt by the government to control the behavior of citizens, corporations, or subgovernments." This definition encompasses programs and activities in which regulation is either the primary goal or secondary effect.

The regulatory process typically has six identifiable stages: legislation, rulemaking, implementation, enforcement, judicial review, and dispute resolution. But the sequence of these stages is neither neat nor predictable. For example, any stage can lead directly to dispute resolution. When creating new rules, agencies follow specific procedures, including public notice and comment periods. Administrative agencies can also act quasi-judicially, conducting hearings and issuing decisions. We can see concrete examples of these practices in the Department of Defense (DoD) Defense Federal Acquisition Regulation Supplement (DFARS) Cybersecurity Maturity Model Certification (CMMC) process that has unfolded and evolved over the past six-plus years.

Regulation addresses market imperfections and failures in a free market system. It aims to correct market failures such as natural monopolies, destructive competition, and externalities.

- **Natural Monopolies:** Natural monopolies occur when a single supplier can provide a good or service more efficiently than multiple suppliers. Unregulated natural monopolies can restrict output, elevate prices, and reduce consumer welfare. Regulation of natural monopolies, such as public utilities, involves controlling prices, output quality, and profit margins to protect consumers from exploitation.

- **Destructive Competition:** Regulation helps maintain stability in industries characterized by destructive competition. Overly vigorous competition can lead to product quality deterioration, bankruptcies, and the emergence of monopolies. For example, competing firms may engage in price wars without regulation, leading to unsustainably low prices and financial distress. Regulation can help prevent such destructive competition, ensuring the survival of multiple businesses and preserving consumer choice.

- **Externalities:** Externalities are costs or benefits that result from a transaction but are not reflected in the market price. Negative externalities, such as air pollution and water contamination, impose costs on third parties not directly involved in the transaction. Regulations aim to address these inefficiencies and inequities by establishing standards and limits on activities that generate negative externalities. For example, environmental regulations may require businesses to install pollution control equipment or restrict their emissions.

Corporations and civic groups have long argued against regulations, which they see as inefficient and bureaucratic, slower and more expensive than private sector solutions, easily abused by government overreach and intrusion, and often filled with unintended consequences.

- **Inefficiency and Bureaucracy:** Critics argue that command and control regulation, with its uniform rules and monitoring mechanisms, can be cumbersome, ineffective, and inefficient. They contend that the rigidity of such rules may stifle innovation and hinder economic growth. Moreover, the bureaucratic processes associated with regulation can be time-consuming and costly for small businesses.

- **Private Sector Solutions:** Proponents of free markets assert that the private sector can address pollution control and safety more effectively than government regulation. Businesses are motivated to develop innovative and cost-efficient solutions to these challenges to gain a competitive advantage. Critics of regulation argue that government intervention frequently stifles innovation and experimentation within the private sector.

- **Government Overreach and Intrusion:** Some critics argue that excessive regulation stifles economic growth, innovation, and individual freedoms. They contend that government regulations often go beyond what is necessary to protect public health, safety, and the environment and impose unnecessary burdens on businesses and consumers. Overly intrusive regulations can discourage investment, entrepreneurship, and job creation.
- **Unintended Consequences:** Regulation can sometimes have unintended consequences, leading to unintended market distortions or negative impacts on other industries. For example, regulations aimed at protecting consumers from harmful products may inadvertently create barriers to entry for new businesses or stifle innovation in specific sectors. Additionally, too stringent or poorly designed rules may lead to unintended environmental or economic consequences.

Today, U.S. regulations and administrative laws are vast, complex, and constantly in flux. There are over 430 federal agencies and upwards of 5,000 entities nationwide when you count state agencies and self-regulating organizations. Estimates for the current volume of laws and regulations are over 1 million pages. In 2022, federal regulations were estimated to cost the U.S. economy approximately $3.079 trillion, equivalent to 12% of the nation's Gross Domestic Product (GDP). Firms allocate between 1.3% and 3.3% of their total wage bill to regulatory compliance activities.

This expenditure increased at an annual rate of about 1% from 2002 to 2014. The average U.S. firm incurs annual regulatory compliance costs of about $277,000, with manufacturers paying approximately

$29,100 per employee and small manufacturers with fewer than 50 employees paying an average of $50,100 per employee.

Regardless of the intended goals and unintended consequences, regulations have forced companies to change their mindsets and behaviors in significant ways:

1. Continuous monitoring and analysis of applicable laws and regulations
2. Robust documentation of executive decision-making
3. Stronger audit trails for company compliance
4. More rigorous risk management and analysis beyond mandatory laws and regulation
5. Sharing information with regulators or law enforcement
6. Greater transparency and mandatory notifications to impacted customers and communities
7. Incentivizing socially responsible behaviors by penalizing harm to customers, communities, shareholders, and the environment
8. Reducing gambling with other people's money and safety by reducing reckless practices
9. Countering complacency and motivating companies to take appropriate actions
10. Serving as an effective deterrent to criminal activities

1.0 Proliferation of Regulators

"Justice may be blind, but she has very sophisticated listening devices."—*Edgar Argo*

Regulatory entities and bodies are crucial in overseeing, standardizing, and enforcing rules within various industries and sectors. Regulators are categorized based on their nature, scope, and degree of government involvement. Below is a comprehensive summary of the different types and categories of regulatory entities and bodies.

1.1 Governmental Regulatory Agencies

Governments create agencies through statutory laws to regulate specific industries, safeguard public interests, and uphold the law. These agencies operate with government funding and employ government personnel. A prime example is the Office of the Comptroller of the Currency (OCC), which regulates and supervises national banks and federal savings associations as part of the U.S. Department of the Treasury. Another key player is the Securities and Exchange Commission (SEC), an independent federal agency tasked with overseeing securities markets and protecting investors. A third example is the Environmental Protection Agency (EPA), which regulates environmental laws to protect human health and the environment. A fourth example is the Food and Drug Administration (FDA), which ensures the safety and efficacy of food, drugs, and medical devices.

1.2 Independent Government Regulatory Bodies

These agencies possess the in-depth knowledge to operate and regulate specific industries to ensure compliance with laws and protect public interests. The federal government funds these agencies, and their employees are federal workers, but they function independently from executive control to prevent political interference in their regulatory decisions. Examples include the Federal Communications Commission (FCC), which regulates interstate and international communications, and the Federal Aviation Administration (FAA), which oversees all aspects of civil aviation in the U.S. A third example is the Nuclear Regulatory Commission (NRC), which oversees nuclear reactor safety and nuclear material usage.

1.3 State Regulatory Agencies

Operating at the state level, these agencies regulate within their jurisdiction, complementing or supplementing federal regulations. Their authority stems from state laws, and they address state-specific regulatory needs, often collaborating with federal agencies. Examples include State Insurance Commissions, which regulate insurance companies and practices within the state, and State Departments of Financial Institutions, overseeing state-chartered financial institutions.

1.4 Quasi-Governmental Organizations

While affiliated with the government, these entities operate independently, exhibiting public and private sector characteristics. They may receive government funding but are not entirely under government control, and their employees may not be classified as government employees. Examples include the Federal Reserve Banks, the 12 regional banks within the Federal Reserve System, and the U.S. central bank. Another example is the Federal Deposit Insurance Corporation (FDIC), an independent agency that insures deposits and supervises financial institutions for safety and soundness. A third example is Fannie Mae and Freddie Mac, government-sponsored enterprises overseeing and supporting the housing finance market.

1.5 Self-Regulatory Organizations (SROs)

SROs are industry groups that establish and enforce industry regulations and standards, subject to a degree of government oversight. They are funded and operated by industry participants, with legislation or government agencies granting them authority. Their primary aim is to maintain industry integrity and protect consumers. Key examples include the Financial Industry Regulatory Authority (FINRA), which regulates brokerage firms and exchange markets in the U.S., and the Payment Card Industry Security Standards Council (PCI SSC), which is responsible for developing security standards for payment card processing. A third example is the National Association of Realtors (NAR), which sets ethical standards for real estate professionals.

1.6 International Regulatory Bodies

These organizations oversee regulations that transcend national borders, promoting international cooperation and standardization.

Their membership comprises multiple countries or international entities, and they develop guidelines and standards that are adopted globally. While not directly enforceable, they rely on member compliance. Notable examples include the Basel Committee on Banking Supervision, which provides recommendations on banking regulations concerning capital, market, and operational risks. Additionally, the International Organization of Securities Commissions (IOSCO) develops standards for securities regulation. A third example is the World Trade Organization (WTO), which regulates international trade between nations.

1.7 Professional Associations and Regulatory Coordinating Bodies

These membership-based organizations set professional standards, conduct certifications, and may enforce ethical guidelines within specific professions. They develop codes of conduct and professional standards and can impose sanctions on members for violations. Prominent examples include the American Bar Association (ABA), which sets academic and ethical standards for legal professionals, and the American Medical Association (AMA), which influences medical practice standards and policies. Regulatory Coordination Bodies facilitate coordination among various regulatory agencies, encourage information-sharing among their members and multiple agencies, promote unified regulatory approaches and policy harmonization, and work to address regulatory gaps and overlaps. Examples include:

- Financial Stability Oversight Council (FSOC), which identifies risks to U.S. financial stability and promotes market discipline.
- Joint Forum, which works on issues common to the banking, securities, and insurance sectors.
- American Institute of Certified Public Accountants (AICPA), which represents Certified Public Accountants (CPAs) in the United States and provides guidance, standards, training, and advocacy to CPAs and the accounting profession.

- The American Bar Association (ABA) is a professional organization for attorneys and legal professionals in the United States. It oversees professional licensing and ethical standards for lawyers, judges, law students, and related legal professionals.

1.8 Non-Governmental Organizations with Regulatory Influence

While not official regulators, these organizations significantly influence industry practices through standard-setting. They operate independently of government control, developing voluntary standards widely adopted by industries and influencing policy and best practices. Key examples include the National Institute of Standards and Technology (NIST), a U.S. Department of Commerce non-regulatory agency that promotes innovation, security, and industrial competitiveness. NIST's primary mission is to advance measurement science, standards, and technology to enhance economic security, improve quality of life, facilitate trade, and enhance productivity. Another example is the International Organization for Standardization (ISO), which develops and publishes international standards across various sectors. A third example is the Institute of Electrical and Electronics Engineers (IEEE), which sets electrical and electronics engineering industry standards.

1.9 Non-Statutory Bodies

The origin and authority of the regulatory body distinguish statutory and non-statutory bodies. Legislative bodies create statutory bodies through statutes, granting them direct legal authority to enforce regulations such as the Occupational Safety and Health Administration (OSHA). In contrast, executive decisions or industry agreements establish non-statutory bodies. These organizations lack direct legal enforcement power unless their standards are incorporated into law. Examples of non-statutory bodies include the Financial Action Task Force (FATF), which develops policies to combat money laundering; the International Organization of

Securities Commissions (IOSCO); the Egmont Group of Financial Intelligence Units, the International Association of Insurance Supervisors (IAIS), the World Customs Organization (WCO), the Internet Corporation for Assigned Names and Numbers (ICANN), and the World Wide Web Consortium (W3C), which develops protocols and guidelines for the web.

1.10 Central Banks and Monetary Authorities

These institutions are critical in managing a nation's currency, money supply, and interest rates. They are responsible for implementing monetary policy and regulating member banks and financial institutions. Examples include the Federal Reserve System (the Fed) in the United States, the European Central Bank (ECB), which manages the Euro and implements EU monetary policy, and the Bank of England, the Central Bank of the United Kingdom, overseeing monetary policy and financial stability. Monetary authorities include international financial institutions that provide financial support and economic development advice to promote global financial stability. Examples include the International Monetary Fund (IMF), which stabilizes international exchange rates and financial systems, and the World Bank, which provides loans and grants for development projects.

2.0 Purpose of Regulations

"The law isn't justice. It's a very imperfect mechanism. If you press exactly the right buttons and are also lucky, justice may show up in the answer."—*Raymond Chandler*

There are many theories of regulation that try to explain why governments intervene in the free-market economy to regulate businesses and individuals. The **public interest theory** suggests that regulation is enacted to address market failures, such as externalities, asymmetric information, and monopoly power. These market failures impede the efficient functioning of the market, and regulations aim to correct them. However, the public interest theory does not fully explain all forms of regulation.

The **regulatory capture theory** offers an alternative perspective. It suggests that special interest groups can influence politicians and regulators to shape regulations that benefit their narrow interests rather than the broader public good. This phenomenon is known as regulatory capture.

The **economic theory** and **public choice theory** of regulation provide complementary explanations for the existence of regulation. These theories emphasize the role of self-interest and rent-seeking behavior in shaping regulatory outcomes. Rent-seeking refers to efforts by individuals or groups to obtain economic benefits through political means rather than through productive activities. According to these theories, regulation can be viewed as wealth redistribution, where interest groups compete for favorable regulations that transfer wealth from one group to another.

The "bootleggers and Baptists" phenomenon illustrates a special case where seemingly unrelated groups can align to influence regulation. In this scenario, special interest groups (bootleggers) who seek to profit from a particular activity join forces with public interest groups (Baptists) who genuinely believe in the social benefits of that activity. This alliance can result in regulations that may not be in the best interests of the broader public.

I would offer another option: **regulations should be designed for the good of the nation and its citizens** and must strike a balance across as many competing priorities as possible while minimizing potential harm.

2.1 Protection of National Sovereignty, National Security and Defense

Regulations and administrative laws are critical in upholding national sovereignty by reinforcing national security and defense mechanisms. They provide the legal foundation for border control, cybersecurity, defense procurement, and counterterrorism measures, ensuring that national interests are protected from foreign threats and domestic vulnerabilities. Regulatory bodies, such as the Department of Homeland Security and the Department of Defense, implement rules that govern the activities of private contractors, manage the flow of sensitive information, and protect critical infrastructure from external threats. The government is equipped to respond efficiently to emerging and persistent security risks through these frameworks, safeguarding the nation's sovereignty and public safety.

2.2 Preserve the Rule of Law and Justice

Preserving the rule of law and pursuing justice are cornerstones of democratic governance, supported by regulations that ensure fairness, accountability, and adherence to the law. Judicial and law enforcement regulations, such as sentencing guidelines and due process protocols, guarantee that justice is consistently applied and accessible. They provide for an independent judiciary and maintain checks on the executive branch, creating a balance of power that upholds democratic principles. By defining the legal framework within which all citizens and entities operate, regulations prevent abuses of power and protect individual rights, fostering public trust in the justice system.

2.3 Economic Stability, Fair Competition, Social Equity

Regulations are vital in promoting economic stability, fair competition, and social equity, ensuring that markets operate transparently and equitably. Financial regulations, like those implemented by the Securities and Exchange Commission (SEC) and the Federal Reserve, protect the economy from speculative risks and market manipulation, preserving stability. Antitrust laws prevent monopolistic practices, ensuring smaller businesses have a fair competition opportunity fostering innovation and consumer choice. Social regulations, such as minimum wage and anti-discrimination policies, enhance social equity by safeguarding worker rights and promoting inclusive economic growth. These regulatory frameworks create an economic environment that balances the pursuit of profit with the welfare of the broader population.

2.4 Promote International Trade and Commerce

Regulations that promote international trade and commerce are designed to attract investments, encourage foreign exchange, and position the country as a critical player in the global economy. Trade regulations, such as tariffs, quotas, and free trade agreements, provide structure and predictability, making cross-border transactions more transparent and reliable. Agencies like the U.S. Trade Representative work to establish trade standards that benefit domestic businesses while adhering to international obligations. Such regulatory frameworks foster economic growth and facilitate diplomatic ties, fostering an environment where international trade thrives, investments are encouraged, and mutual economic benefits are realized.

2.5 Protect the Safety and Soundness of the Financial System

Financial regulations are essential in maintaining the stability and resilience of the financial system by reducing systemic risks that could lead to financial crises. Agencies such as the Federal Deposit Insurance Corporation (FDIC) and the Consumer Financial Protection Bureau (CFPB) oversee the banking and financial services industries, ensuring institutions operate within safe and sound practices. Regulations that mandate adequate capital reserves, transparent reporting, and risk management practices help mitigate the risk of financial instability, thus protecting both consumers and the broader economy. These measures also enhance confidence in the financial system, reassuring citizens and businesses that their assets are safeguarded.

2.6 Infrastructure Development and Maintenance

Regulations supporting infrastructure development and maintenance provide guidelines and standards for building and maintaining the physical framework of society, such as roads, bridges, utilities, and public transportation. Agencies like the Department of Transportation and the Federal Highway Administration establish construction, safety, and sustainability standards, ensuring that infrastructure projects meet public safety and environmental requirements. These regulatory standards contribute to economic productivity by enhancing connectivity and reliability, enabling people and goods to move efficiently across regions. Effective infrastructure regulation fosters long-term economic growth and resilience by ensuring that infrastructure assets are safe, durable, and environmentally responsible.

2.7 Public Welfare and Social Services

Public welfare and social services regulations underscore the government's commitment to supporting the greater good and ensuring all citizens have access to essential resources. Social Security, Medicare, and unemployment benefits are regulated to provide safety nets for vulnerable populations, promoting social stability and economic inclusivity. Regulatory oversight ensures these programs operate transparently and ethically, fostering public confidence that the government is acting in its best interests. Through these regulations, society reaffirms its commitment to equality and compassion, supporting the well-being of individuals and communities.

2.8 Protect Health and Safety

Health and safety regulations safeguard public well-being, ensuring workplaces, products, and public spaces are free from harmful hazards. Agencies like the Occupational Safety and Health Administration (OSHA) and the Food and Drug Administration (FDA) create occupational health, food safety, and consumer goods standards to reduce risks that could lead to injuries, illnesses, or fatalities. These regulations protect workers and consumers, fostering environments where people can work, shop, and live without exposure to preventable risks. Therefore, effective health and safety regulations are fundamental to maintaining a high quality of life and public trust.

2.9 Environmental Conservation

Environmental regulations are critical in preserving natural resources and preventing environmental degradation, ensuring sustainability for future generations. Laws such as the Clean Air Act and the Clean Water Act, enforced by the Environmental Protection Agency (EPA), set pollution control and resource management standards, encouraging businesses and individuals to minimize their ecological footprint. These regulations protect biodiversity and address climate change by regulating emissions and promoting renewable energy. Through these laws, the government demonstrates a commitment to balancing economic growth with environmental responsibility.

2.10 Government Accountability and Transparency

Regulations promoting government accountability and transparency are essential in maintaining public trust and ensuring fiscal responsibility. Laws like the Freedom of Information Act (FOIA) and the Government Performance and Results Act (GPRA) require government agencies to operate openly, provide accessible information, and report on their performance. Fiscal responsibility regulations ensure that public funds are used effectively and ethically, preventing misuse and enhancing government efficiency. By creating mechanisms for oversight and public engagement, these regulations empower citizens to hold their government accountable, reinforcing democratic principles and ethical governance.

3.0 Powers and Authorities

"Laws are spider webs through which the big flies pass, and the little ones get caught."—*Honoré de Balzac*

Regulators wield a range of powers and authorities that enable them to enforce compliance across industries, ensuring that businesses adhere to standards designed to protect the public interest. These powers encompass administrative control through established laws, regulations, and guidelines; they grant regulators the authority to request information, conduct audits, issue or revoke licenses, and enforce corrective actions. Together, these regulatory tools create a framework within which companies are held accountable for their practices, particularly in critical areas like supply chain management, which has implications for everything from consumer safety to national security.

3.1 Administrative Control through Laws, Regulations, and Guidelines

One of the most fundamental powers of regulators is their authority to establish laws, regulations, and guidelines that set the standards companies must follow. These rules create a structured environment where companies operate, shaping how they manage everything from ethical sourcing to data protection. By establishing clear expectations, regulators ensure businesses adhere to practices promoting safety, transparency, and accountability in their supply chains. For example, companies might be required to demonstrate that their suppliers comply with specific labor standards or environmental laws, creating a baseline of responsibility across the entire production chain.

3.2 Mandatory Information Sharing and Notifications

Regulators also have the authority to mandate information sharing and notifications, which are essential for identifying and mitigating risks within the supply chain. Companies may be required to report certain activities, potential violations, or emerging risks to regulatory bodies or law enforcement. This obligation enables regulators to monitor high-risk sectors and respond quickly to issues threatening public safety or market stability. Such transparency obligations are critical in managing supply chain risks, particularly when violations in one segment can lead to broader reputational or operational risks.

3.3 Audit and Examination Authority

Regulatory agencies can conduct audits and examinations of companies and their critical third parties to assess compliance with regulatory standards and evaluate operational risks. By examining a company's books, records, and processes, regulators can identify areas of vulnerability, assess the robustness of risk management practices, and verify adherence to legal obligations. This authority is essential in complex supply chains where multiple entities contribute to a final product, and regulatory oversight helps mitigate risks such as fraud, safety violations, or substandard practices.

3.4 License Issuance, Suspension, and Revocation

The power to issue, suspend, or revoke licenses is a critical regulatory tool enabling regulators to control which companies can operate in specific sectors. This authority ensures that only those companies that meet compliance and quality standards can conduct business within regulated industries. If a company fails to meet these standards or poses a risk to public safety, its license may be suspended or revoked, effectively barring it from operations. This measure is a preventative and corrective tool, as companies are incentivized to uphold high standards to maintain operating licenses. Companies can check with the state bar associations and state courts for published disciplinary actions against attorneys.

3.5 Imposing Financial Penalties and Fines

Financial penalties are a crucial enforcement tool, allowing regulators to impose fines for non-compliance as a deterrent against unsafe or unethical practices. By imposing monetary penalties, regulators create financial incentives for companies to maintain compliance and discourage risky behaviors that could compromise the integrity of supply chains. These fines are a tangible reminder of the costs associated with regulatory violations, emphasizing the importance of proactive compliance management.

3.6 Enforcing Corrective Actions (Cease and Desist Orders and Consent Orders)

When companies engage in unlawful activities, regulators can issue cease-and-desist or consent orders, requiring immediate corrective action. Cease-and-desist orders demand an end to specific activities, while consent orders involve agreements in which the company consents to implement corrective measures. These orders are potent tools for regulators to swiftly address violations and rectify harmful practices, particularly within supply chains where one entity's actions can impact numerous downstream participants.

3.7 Mandatory Staffing and Governance Changes

When regulatory violations are linked to inadequacies in leadership or governance, regulators can mandate staffing and governance changes. This form of penalty requires companies to appoint qualified individuals to crucial roles or to restructure board oversight to improve compliance. Such measures ensure that those responsible for managing supply chain practices are sufficiently qualified and compliant, enhancing oversight and risk management.

3.8 Third-Party Approvals, Restrictions, and Audits

To ensure comprehensive compliance, regulators may restrict third-party vendors with substandard practices from participating in regulated industries. By setting standards for third-party approvals, regulators help companies vet suppliers and other critical partners, enhancing the reliability and accountability of their supply chains. Additionally, regulators may require audits of third parties to verify that they meet the same standards applied to primary companies, thus reinforcing compliance throughout the supply chain.

3.9 Recommendations, Matters Requiring Attention (MRA), and Matters Requiring Immediate Attention (MRIA)

Regulators may issue formal recommendations, including Matters Requiring Attention (MRA) and Matters Requiring Immediate Attention (MRIA), to guide companies in improving their risk management practices. MRAs and MRIAs serve as early warnings, alerting companies to compliance issues that could escalate into more significant violations if unaddressed. By responding to these recommendations, companies can enhance their operational practices, better manage risks, and prevent regulatory infractions before they occur.

3.10 Risk-Based Monitoring and Audits

Regulatory agencies often implement risk-based monitoring and auditing, tailoring their oversight based on the specific risks posed by different companies or sectors. This approach ensures that regulatory resources are allocated efficiently, with greater scrutiny applied to high-risk activities or entities. Risk-based monitoring allows regulators to stay agile, responding to emerging threats within supply chains and adapting oversight to reflect evolving risks. This method enhances the effectiveness of regulatory efforts and provides companies with guidance on areas where they should prioritize their compliance initiatives.

4.0 Process for Regulatory Evolution

"Laws are like sausages; it is better not to see them being made."— *Otto von Bismarck*

The process of regulatory evolution ensures that regulations adapt to changes in technology, industry practices, and societal needs. This process is often iterative, involving ongoing review, public input, and revisions. Regulatory bodies assess the effectiveness of existing laws, identify emerging risks, and update regulations to meet new challenges. Regular reviews and amendments are part of this process, allowing regulators to refine guidelines, close loopholes, and address unforeseen issues. This evolution maintains the relevance of regulations and supports their role in protecting the public and promoting fair market practices.

4.1 Authority Needed to Succeed

Regulatory agencies are established with specific authorities and organizational structures that empower them to fulfill their missions. These agencies, such as the Environmental Protection Agency (EPA) or the Securities and Exchange Commission (SEC), derive authority from congressional acts and operate within clearly defined mandates. Organizationally, they are structured to allow specialized divisions to focus on different aspects of compliance, enforcement, and education. This structure enables regulators to address complex issues within their jurisdictions effectively. It ensures that each agency has the expertise to uphold environmental conservation, financial stability, and consumer protection standards.

4.2 Analysis of the Mission and the Challenges

The regulatory process involves a detailed analysis at each stage, focusing on the mission and specific problems regulations aim to address. This analytical approach begins with legislative assessment, as congressional staffers examine the potential impact of proposed regulations. Legal staff, including federal clerks, may analyze conflicting perspectives during litigation, but the most comprehensive analyses occur within regulatory agencies. These analyses, carried out by agency staff and their surrogates, guide the rulemaking process and help ensure adequate and relevant regulations.

Legal Analysis: Legal analysis is the foundation of any regulatory process, beginning with an assessment of legislative or judicial mandates defining new regulations' scope and authority. Agencies must determine what the law requires or allows them to accomplish, including deadlines, study requirements, or public participation mandates. Typically, agency rule writers work closely with their general counsel's office to clarify statutory expectations before drafting regulations, setting the groundwork for all subsequent steps in rulemaking.

Policy Analysis: Policy analysis aligns regulatory actions with the broader priorities and values of the current administration and agency leadership. Presidential directives, agency leadership preferences, and political factors shape regulators' approach to developing rules. For example, regulatory priorities have varied across administrations, from aggressive regulatory action at the FDA under David Kessler to a free-market approach at the Federal Energy

Regulatory Commission (FERC) that avoided price controls during the California energy crisis. By integrating these policy considerations, agencies can create regulations that reflect the administration's broader objectives and avoid potential issues when the rules are later reviewed.

Scientific and Technical Analysis: Scientific and technical analysis is essential for public safety, environmental protection, or industry standards and regulations. Agencies like OSHA and the FAA rely on scientific expertise to respond to safety incidents and to integrate state-of-the-art technologies into regulatory frameworks. For certain agencies, such as the EPA, scientific analysis is crucial to identifying and implementing the "best available technology" to limit pollution. However, technical analysis becomes challenging when regulations address complex, understudied issues, such as environmental or worker health risks, due to limited data, high costs, and potential resistance from the regulated industries.

Risk Analysis: Risk analysis is central to health, safety, and environmental protection regulations. By assessing the potential risks posed by substances or activities, agencies determine whether rules should aim to eliminate, reduce, or mitigate those risks. Disputes often arise over acceptable risk levels, leading to extended debates within scientific communities. The absence of uniform standards for risk assessment across agencies further complicates the process, as risk tolerance may differ across regulations. Despite these challenges, risk analysis remains a powerful tool for designing effective regulatory programs.

Cost-Benefit Analysis: Cost-benefit analysis, particularly emphasized since the Reagan administration, is designed to ensure that regulatory benefits outweigh their costs. This approach was solidified by Executive Order 12044 under President Carter and remains a core component of the regulatory process. Agencies assess economic costs and benefits, exploring alternative regulatory approaches and evaluating the most efficient options. Although beneficial for setting priorities and controlling regulatory burden, cost-benefit analysis can be complex, especially when benefits are difficult to quantify.

Other Required Analyses: Many regulations also require additional analyses, such as the Regulatory Flexibility Act (RFA) assessment for small business impact or an Environmental Impact Statement (EIS) under the National Environmental Policy Act (NEPA). Each analysis follows guidelines that may include public review and comment, adding another layer of scrutiny to ensure that regulations consider diverse impacts and align with the public interest.

4.3 Jurisdictions and Organization Structures

Jurisdictional and legal structures define the scope and reach of regulatory agencies across federal, state, and local levels in the U.S. Federal agencies operate under mandates that allow them to regulate matters affecting interstate commerce or national interest. In contrast, state and local agencies handle issues within their specific geographic areas. This layered approach ensures comprehensive coverage and that regulations are tailored to the needs and nuances of each jurisdiction. Legal structures such as the Administrative Procedure Act guide the regulatory process, providing transparency, procedural fairness, and mechanisms for public engagement at all levels.

4.4 The Seven-Stage Regulatory Lifecycle

The seven stages of administrative law rulemaking typically follow a structured process to ensure transparency, public participation, and thorough evaluation. Here's a breakdown of each stage:

1. **Identifying the Need for Regulation:** Agencies determine whether a new rule or modification to an existing rule is necessary. This stage involves analyzing the problem that needs to be addressed, whether it stems from a legislative mandate, public need, or emerging risk.

2. **Drafting the Rule:** Agency staff, often with input from experts, draft a preliminary version of the rule. During this phase, agencies assess legal, policy, technical, and economic factors to ensure the rule effectively addresses the identified issues.

3. **Notice of Proposed Rulemaking (NPRM):** The agency publishes a Notice of Proposed Rulemaking in the Federal Register. This notice informs the public of the proposed rule, its rationale, and the legal authority for its enactment and initiates the public comment period.

4. **Public Comment Period:** The public is invited to submit feedback, comments, and concerns about the proposed rule. Typically lasting between 30 and 90 days, this period allows stakeholders, businesses, and individuals to participate in the regulatory process and influence the final rule.

5. **Review and Analysis of Comments:** The agency considers all public comments. Based on substantive feedback, agencies may revise the proposed rule, refining or altering provisions to address public concerns, technical issues, or emerging insights.

6. **Finalizing the Rule:** After analyzing public comments and making any necessary adjustments, the agency issues a final rule that is published in the Federal Register. This final rule explains how public input was considered and any changes made in response to feedback.

7. **Implementation and Enforcement:** Once the final rule is published, it becomes effective immediately or after a set period. The agency then oversees compliance and enforces the rule, which may include monitoring, audits, inspections, or guidance to ensure the rule's goals are achieved.

4.5 The 12 Principles of Regulations

Good regulation is guided by principles designed to ensure fairness, efficiency, and responsiveness. The 12 principles in the Principles of Regulation section of Executive Order 12866, issued by President Bill Clinton in 1993, provide a framework for federal agencies to follow in developing and implementing regulations. Here is a summary of the 12 principles:

1. **The Necessity of Regulation:** Agencies should only regulate when a substantial problem or market failure exists and when regulation will benefit society.
2. **Cost-Benefit Analysis:** Regulations should be based on an analysis showing that the benefits justify the costs.
3. **Public Involvement:** Agencies should encourage meaningful participation from the public, especially from stakeholders directly affected by the regulations.
4. **Risk Assessment:** Regulations should address real risks, and agencies should use scientific data to ensure regulation is proportional to the problem.
5. **Performance-Based Regulation:** Regulations should be designed to achieve specific objectives, focusing on outcomes rather than prescribing particular methods or procedures.
6. **Market-Oriented Approaches:** Where appropriate, agencies should consider market-based approaches and incentives, like taxes or subsidies, instead of command-and-control methods.
7. **Coordination Across Agencies:** Agencies should coordinate to reduce redundancies and conflicting rules and ensure consistency.
8. **Transparency and Accountability:** Agencies must clearly explain the regulatory action's purpose, basis, and rationale to the public.
9. **Review and Update Regulations:** Agencies should regularly review regulations to ensure they are up-to-date, necessary, and effective.
10. **Minimization of Burdens:** Regulations should impose the least burden on society, especially for small businesses and lower-income sectors, while achieving their objectives.

11. **International Compatibility:** Regulations should promote U.S. competitiveness and, where feasible, be consistent with international standards.

12. **Regulatory Flexibility:** Regulations should allow flexibility, permitting alternatives or variances to achieve regulatory goals effectively.

4.6 Participation in Industry Forums

Regulatory agencies often participate in industry forums to remain informed about sector developments, emerging risks, and technological advancements. Industry forums provide a collaborative space where regulators, companies, and other stakeholders can exchange information, discuss challenges, and explore best practices. These forums foster mutual understanding, allowing regulators to gain insights into industry operations while companies gain clarity on regulatory expectations. Participation in such forums supports proactive regulatory approaches and enhances trust and cooperation between industry and regulators.

4.7 Regulatory Oversight, Inspections, and Examination

Regulatory oversight, inspections, and examinations are essential for verifying compliance and maintaining regulatory standards. Regulatory bodies assess adherence to the law through routine and risk-based inspections to detect potential violations early. These inspections may involve examining records, conducting on-site visits, or auditing specific processes. Oversight ensures that companies adhere to standards consistently and allows regulators to enforce corrective actions when needed. It also reinforces public confidence by holding companies accountable for safe and ethical practices.

4.8 Responding to and Remediating Issues and Findings

Companies are expected to respond promptly to regulatory findings, often through remediation plans that address identified issues. Responses include policy changes, operational control improvements, or increased staff training. Remediation demonstrates a company's commitment to compliance and is often viewed favorably by regulators. For ongoing compliance, companies may establish dedicated teams to monitor regulatory changes, implement internal audits, and respond swiftly to emerging risks. Effective remediation aligns companies with regulatory standards, protects their reputation, and mitigates potential penalties.

4.9 Dispute Resolution

When companies believe regulators have erred, dispute resolution mechanisms allow them to seek redress. Companies can file complaints, file appeals, or request reviews by oversight committees, agency panels, or inspectors general. These procedures check regulatory actions, ensuring that decisions are fair and based on sound evidence. If unresolved, companies may pursue judicial reviews, where courts assess the legality of regulatory actions. These pathways protect companies from arbitrary decisions and reinforce the principles of due process and accountability in regulatory enforcement.

After promulgating a rule, an affected party may challenge its validity in court. A court may overturn a rule on several grounds, including constitutional violations, such as violations of due process or equal protection, and procedural violations, such as a failure to comply with the required rulemaking procedures.

Courts also review the substance of rules to determine whether they are supported by substantial evidence. Substantial evidence is relevant, reliable, and sufficient to support a conclusion. In rulemaking, considerable evidence means enough evidence in the record to support the agency's determination that the rule is necessary and appropriate.

In addition to challenging a rule on constitutional or procedural violations or lack of substantial evidence, an affected party may also challenge a rule on the grounds that the agency abused its discretion. Abuse of discretion occurs when an agency makes a decision that is arbitrary, capricious, or otherwise not in accordance with the law.

For example, an agency may abuse its discretion if it decides without considering all of the relevant evidence, relies on irrelevant or unreliable evidence, or makes a decision that is not supported by the facts.

Courts review formal rulemaking for substantial evidence, while informal rulemaking is reviewed for arbitrariness, capriciousness, or abuse of discretion. Formal rulemaking is a more rigorous process that includes public notice and comment, while informal rulemaking is a less formal process that does not require public notice and comment. The different standards of review reflect the different degrees of formality and public participation involved in the two types of rulemaking.

4.10 Congressional Oversight, Inquiries, and Reviews

Congressional oversight plays a crucial role in reviewing regulatory agencies' actions to ensure that they operate within their mandates and effectively serve the public. Through hearings, inquiries, and reports, Congress assesses regulatory actions, evaluates agency performance, and may recommend reforms. Congressional committees also hold agencies accountable for their spending, efficiency, and adherence to legislative intent. This oversight ensures that regulatory bodies remain responsive to democratic principles and that their actions reflect public policy objectives, providing an additional layer of accountability and transparency in government operations.

5.0 Problems with the Current Regulatory System

"We must not confuse law with justice. Law is a mechanism; justice is a goal."—*Bertolt Brecht*

The U.S. regulatory system is essential in setting standards and ensuring compliance across various sectors. However, it faces several significant challenges that complicate its effectiveness, efficiency, and fairness. Key issues include overlapping jurisdictions, inconsistencies between federal and state regulators, the overwhelming volume of laws and precedents, and an imbalance of influence that favors corporations and lobbyists. Additionally, accountability, enforceability, and the inherent complexity of compliance further undermine the system's objectives. These factors collectively impact regulatory processes' clarity, reliability, and equity across the U.S.

5.1 Multiple Agencies with Overlapping Responsibilities

One major problem is the overlapping authority among federal regulatory agencies. For example, in the financial sector, the Federal Reserve (FRB), Office of the Comptroller of the Currency (OCC), and Federal Deposit Insurance Corporation (FDIC) all oversee different aspects of banking and finance, yet their responsibilities often overlap. This duplication can lead to conflicting guidelines and create unnecessary complexities for regulated entities. Companies may struggle to meet differing requirements, adding compliance burdens without necessarily enhancing oversight or risk management.

5.2 Federal vs. State Regulators (Who Is In Charge)

Another challenge arises from the division of authority between federal and state regulators. In many sectors, such as environmental protection and financial services, state laws may impose additional requirements beyond federal regulations, creating a dual compliance burden. Jurisdictional conflicts can arise over which level of government has the final say, leading to inconsistent enforcement and complicating companies' efforts to stay compliant across state lines. Another example is the Health Insurance Portability and Accountability Act (HIPAA), which is a U.S. federal law that provides baseline privacy and security standards to protect individuals' protected health information (PHI). If a state law provides greater privacy protections or rights to individuals, the state law takes precedence over federal HIPAA. Examples include stricter requirements for patient consent, additional safeguards for specific health conditions (e.g., HIV/AIDS, mental health, substance abuse), or more stringent reporting and notification rules following a data breach. Compliance with state laws does not negate the requirement to comply with federal HIPAA, and both must be followed, with the stricter rule prevailing in case of conflict.

5.3 Impossible to Reconcile Millions of Pages of Laws and Regulation

The sheer volume of U.S. regulatory content presents a massive challenge. With over 100,000 laws, rules, and regulations, thousands of court cases setting precedents, and more than a million pages of text, the regulatory landscape is both dense and complex. Companies must devote significant resources to navigating these requirements, and any oversight or misinterpretation can lead to costly penalties or legal challenges. The system's complexity can stifle smaller businesses lacking the resources for comprehensive legal compliance and defense.

5.4 Regulatory Overreach and Reading Between the Lines

Regulatory overreach occurs when agencies extend their authority beyond the letter of the law, often by interpreting statutes too broadly. Agencies may attempt to impose rules not explicitly authorized by legislation, which can lead to accusations of "reading between the lines" and regulatory overreach. This tendency creates uncertainty for businesses, as they may face regulatory demands beyond statutory requirements, leading to legal challenges and a lack of trust in regulatory bodies.

5.5 Tipping the Scales of Justice

The influence of corporations and lobbyists on the regulatory process is a persistent problem. Large companies and industry groups can "tip the scales of justice" by swaying legislation, regulatory priorities, and enforcement decisions in their favor through lobbying efforts. This influence may result in less stringent or less consistently enforced rules, undermining public trust and creating an uneven playing field that disadvantages smaller competitors.

5.6 Rules Without Enforcement Are Meaningless

Regulations without effective enforcement lack impact and fail to meet their intended objectives. In some cases, responsibility for compliance verification has been delegated to private accounting firms, which may need more authority or resources to enforce regulations strictly. Without a robust and consistent enforcement mechanism, regulations become realities, diminishing their protective effects on consumers, employees, and the public.

5.7 Every Company Must Independently Analyze and Develop Compliance Systems

The regulatory system requires each company to develop, implement, and manage its compliance framework, which can be costly and inefficient, particularly for small and mid-sized businesses. This decentralized approach leads to significant duplication of effort as companies individually analyze the same regulations and create unique compliance systems rather than benefiting from standardized tools or shared resources.

5.8 Gaming the System

The regulatory environment in the U.S. often permits "gaming the system," where companies adopt a mindset of "full speed ahead until the law stops us." Instead of proactively managing compliance, some companies prioritize investments in legal maneuvers to exploit regulatory loopholes or delay enforcement. Companies may also decide that paying the penalties and fines associated with non-compliance is an acceptable cost of doing business. This attitude can result in unethical practices and harm to stakeholders and ultimately require more stringent oversight to mitigate emerging risks.

5.9 Regulators Are Not Accountable or Measured on Results

Accountability is a critical issue for regulatory agencies, which are not always evaluated on their effectiveness or the costs of their regulations. Agencies may operate with limited transparency regarding their performance or the outcomes of their regulatory actions, leading to a lack of accountability. Without concrete metrics to assess impact and cost-effectiveness, regulators have little incentive to refine their practices or seek more efficient enforcement methods.

5.10 Courts and the Chevron Doctrine

The judicial system's role in the regulatory process often focuses on overseeing punishment rather than actively dispensing justice or reducing risks. Challenging regulatory decisions in court is slow, costly, and uncertain. The Chevron doctrine, which grants agencies deference in interpreting ambiguous statutes, has further raised questions about the scope of regulatory powers, and recent rulings have scrutinized this deference in cases of regulatory overreach. High-profile cases, like SolarWinds regarding financial control breaches, highlight the tension between judicial oversight and regulatory authority. Additionally, class-action lawsuits and jurisdictional challenges create significant costs, which larger companies may use strategically to stifle competition or delay compliance, further complicating the regulatory landscape.

6.0 Program for Regulatory Compliance

"The good lawyer knows the law; the great lawyer knows the judge."—*Author Unknown*

Establishing an effective regulatory compliance and legal management strategy is essential for navigating complex regulatory environments. This practice involves creating a structured program that systematically parses legal requirements into individual components to ensure compliance. By grounding the program in the law and breaking down each requirement, companies can design compliance mechanisms that align with regulatory demands and ensure thorough adherence to both the spirit and the letter of the law.

6.1 Grounded in the Law and Colored by Examination

Regulatory examination handbooks provide critical guidance on what regulators will look for during audits and reviews. By integrating these handbooks into the compliance program, companies can anticipate regulatory expectations and prepare documentation and evidence that aligns with regulatory standards. This proactive approach helps ensure the company is well-prepared for examinations and can demonstrate compliance with clear, organized documentation.

6.2 Consider Recent Regulatory and Court Case Precedents

Incorporating recent regulatory and court case precedents into the compliance strategy provides valuable insight into how regulations are interpreted and enforced. Understanding recent cases highlights trends in legal interpretation and enforcement priorities, helping companies align their practices with current regulatory expectations. Monitoring legal outcomes ensures compliance practices remain relevant and responsive to evolving interpretations.

6.3 Monitor and Respond to Regulatory Changes and Case Outcomes

Maintaining an ongoing process to monitor and respond to regulatory changes and case outcomes is crucial for staying up-to-date in a dynamic regulatory landscape. Regularly reviewing regulatory updates, court decisions, and enforcement actions allows companies to adjust their compliance efforts and proactively address emerging risks before they become issues during an examination or audit.

6.4 Bring in Outside Counsel with Expertise

Engaging outside counsel with expertise in the specific regulatory area strengthens a company's compliance program. Specialized legal experts provide insights into complex regulations and can advise on best practices, risk management, and potential loopholes. Their guidance is precious when navigating novel or ambiguous regulatory requirements, ensuring the company is fully informed and well-prepared.

6.5 Size the Impacts of Non-Compliance

Analyzing the potential impact of non-compliance and considering penalties, legal costs, and the burden of prolonged court involvement is essential for prioritizing compliance efforts. This risk-based approach allows companies to allocate resources effectively and implement more robust controls in areas where non-compliance could result in significant legal or financial repercussions. Understanding these impacts helps justify the importance of compliance initiatives at all levels of the organization.

6.6 Going Beyond Governance, Risk, and Compliance (GRC)

Regulatory compliance involves more than traditional Governance, Risk, and Compliance (GRC) frameworks. Companies should be "exam-ready," which requires maintaining solid evidence and a thorough analysis of each identified risk and its mitigative solution. Documentation should be comprehensive, detailing the measures in place and the rationale for those measures, demonstrating that the organization is prepared to meet regulatory expectations with transparent and well-documented compliance practices.

6.7 Cultivating a Culture of Compliance

Creating a culture of compliance starts with tone at the top. Leadership must visibly commit to regulatory adherence and model this commitment through actions and policies. Promoting radical transparency and consistent internal enforcement strengthens the compliance culture by reinforcing that regulations should be respected and actively supported across all levels. A culture that prioritizes compliance and breaks down organizational barriers is more likely to achieve sustainable regulatory success.

6.8 Root Out Bureaucratic Inefficiencies

Identifying and eliminating bureaucratic inefficiencies within the compliance program can improve response times, streamline processes, and reduce costs. Simplifying compliance workflows, reducing redundant tasks, and creating efficient reporting mechanisms allow the compliance team to operate effectively and keep pace with regulatory demands. This focus on efficiency supports a more agile and responsive compliance function. Many organizations have successfully adopted Lean or Six Sigma principles to streamline compliance processes. For instance, JPMorgan Chase implemented lean techniques to simplify internal compliance procedures, cutting redundant reporting tasks, improving compliance responsiveness, and significantly reducing associated overhead costs (PricewaterhouseCoopers 2020). Another example is GE's enterprise-wide initiative to streamline regulatory compliance through workflow automation and centralized compliance management tools, which resulted in a 30% decrease in compliance operating costs and faster internal response to regulatory changes and demands (Harvard Business Review 2019).

6.9 Influence Future Regulatory Improvements

Companies can contribute to shaping future regulatory improvements by participating in public comment periods, engaging with industry associations, and providing constructive feedback to regulators. By actively contributing to the regulatory process, companies can advocate for practical solutions that meet regulatory goals while addressing industry concerns. Engaging in this way can build constructive relationships with regulators and encourage a more collaborative approach to regulatory challenges.

6.10 Building Positive Relationships with Examiners

Dealing with examiners as individuals and fostering respectful, professional relationships can significantly improve the regulatory experience. Companies can facilitate open communication and constructive feedback by treating examiners as partners rather than adversaries. This approach ensures that regulatory examinations are conducted efficiently and potential issues are addressed collaboratively, ultimately fostering a more positive and effective compliance environment.

Conclusion

Companies face regulatory challenges due to overlapping jurisdictions, dense and ever-changing rules, and high compliance costs. Effective compliance requires organizations to integrate regulatory expectations directly into their governance structures, prioritize monitoring regulatory changes and relevant case precedents, and actively engage specialized external legal expertise to clarify ambiguities. Additionally, executives must foster a culture of compliance, embedding transparent decision-making, accountability, and rigorous documentation into daily operations.

Executives should also build constructive relationships with regulators, seeing them as strategic partners rather than adversaries. Organizations can influence regulatory improvements through active participation in industry forums and public comment processes, which helps shape practical regulations and positions companies as compliance leaders. Businesses can mitigate risks, reduce costs, and ensure long-term operational resilience by prioritizing proactive compliance strategies, streamlining processes, regularly auditing for bureaucratic inefficiencies, and investing in robust internal controls. Ultimately, the lessons learned underscore that successful regulatory management is less about reacting to rules and more about embedding compliance strategically within organizational culture and governance.

REFERENCES

- Meier, Kenneth J. *Regulation: Politics, Bureaucracy, and Economics.* New York: St. Martin's Press, 1985.
- Administrative Procedure Act of 1946, 5 U.S.C. §§ 551–559.

- Executive Order 10250. "Providing for the Performance of Certain Functions of the President by the Secretary of the Interior and Other Officers of the Executive Branch," June 5, 1951, 3 U.S.C. § 301.
- "Tariff Act of 1789," 1 Stat. 24 (1789).
- "Tariff Act of 1816," 3 Stat. 310 (1816).
- Administrative Procedure Act, Pub. L. No. 79-404, 60 Stat. 237 (1946).
- Clinton, William J. "Executive Order 12866," Federal Register 58, no. 190 (October 4, 1993): 51735-51744.
- Freedom of Information Act (FOIA), 5 U.S.C. § 552 (1966).
- Government Performance and Results Act (GPRA), Pub. L. No. 103-62, 107 Stat. 285 (1993).
- "Chevron U.S.A., Inc. v. Natural Resources Defense Council, Inc.," 467 U.S. 837 (1984).
- U.S. Small Business Administration, Office of Advocacy. "The Impact of Regulatory Costs on Small Firms." Washington, DC, 2014.
- Dudley, Susan, and Melinda Warren. "Ten Thousand Commandments: An Annual Snapshot of the Federal Regulatory State." Competitive Enterprise Institute, 2022.
- Executive Order 12866, 58 FR 51735, 3 CFR, 1993 Comp., 638–649.
- PricewaterhouseCoopers, "Leveraging Lean Principles to Enhance Compliance Efficiency," PwC Financial Services White Paper, 2020.
- Harvard Business Review, "Simplifying the Complexities of Corporate Compliance," HBR Case Study, 2019.

Insights and Actions

The U.S. regulatory landscape is vast, complex, and costly, requiring strategic navigation rather than reactive compliance. With over 430 federal agencies, 5,000 regulatory entities nationwide, and more than one million pages of laws and regulations, the U.S. regulatory system costs approximately $3.079 trillion annually (12% of GDP), with firms allocating 1.3 to 3.3% of their wage bill to compliance activities. The system suffers from overlapping jurisdictions among agencies, such as the Federal Reserve, OCC, and FDIC, conflicts between federal and state authorities, regulatory overreach through broad statutory interpretation, and inconsistent enforcement, which allows for "gaming the system." Organizations must develop sophisticated compliance frameworks that go beyond traditional GRC approaches to systematically parse legal requirements, monitor regulatory changes, and maintain exam-ready documentation.

Your program's target operating model should clearly identify regulatory requirements that mandate specific and defined capabilities. As you and your team review the regulatory context of your TPRM program, validate the disclosure obligations and timescales associated with it. Your program should maintain an inventory of both contractual obligations and regulatory requirements. Your TPRM program committee should review the compliance status of in-scope regulations at least annually. Where gaps and challenges are identified, these should be noted on the program's risk register for prioritization and resourcing.

Core TPRM Governance and Administrative Functions

- Tone at the Top: Senior executive oversight and clear accountability are crucial.
- TPRM Committee: A cross-functional committee should oversee key vendor assessments and risk indicators.
- TPRM Charter and Policy: Formal documentation of roles, responsibilities, and expectations, signed by senior leaders.

- Risk Register and Key Risk Indicators (KRIs): Maintain a risk register and track KRIs to inform decisions and resource allocation.
- TPRM Calendar: Schedule and track assessments, audits, and reviews.
- RACI Matrices: Clearly define roles and responsibilities for critical TPRM functions.
- Vendor Master File: Maintain a detailed, up-to-date inventory of vendors, contracts, and risk factors.
- Vendor Categorization: Classify and prioritize vendors based on risk and materiality.
- Inventory of In-Scope Regulations: Track and prioritize applicable regulations, updating the committee annually.
- Risk and Control Matrices: For key regulations, map requirements to specific controls, owners, and assessment frequencies.

Regulators wield comprehensive powers, including administrative control through laws and guidelines, mandatory information sharing and notifications, audit and examination authority, license issuance/suspension/revocation, financial penalties and fines, corrective action enforcement, mandatory staffing and governance changes, third-party approvals and restrictions, formal recommendations (MRA/MRIA), and risk-based monitoring. These authorities enable regulators to enforce compliance across supply chains, encompassing ethical sourcing, labor standards, cybersecurity, and environmental protection, making regulatory alignment essential for operational continuity and market access in critical sectors.

Success demands moving beyond reactive compliance to building a culture grounded in law and examination expectations, incorporating recent regulatory and court precedents, continuously monitoring regulatory changes, engaging specialized outside counsel, accurately assessing the impacts of non-compliance, and maintaining comprehensive documentation. Organizations must cultivate radical transparency with tone-setting leadership, eliminate bureaucratic inefficiencies through lean processes, influence future regulatory improvements through active participation in public comment periods and industry forums, and build positive relationships with examiners as strategic partners. This proactive approach enables companies to mitigate risks, reduce costs, ensure long-term operational resilience, and position themselves as leaders in compliance rather than followers.

Due to its unique role in the global economy and its status as a supplier to the world, as well as its business exposure and data risk, China's regulatory environment requires significantly greater attention to third-party risk strategies. China's domestic data laws and business environment are increasingly impactful to foreign companies. China's cybersecurity laws introduce limitations, such as localized data storage and government access upon request. Police raids on corporations, bans on foreign companies, unethical labor practices, and arrests or detentions of foreign personnel further exacerbate the risks of doing business.

Strategies for Effective Compliance

- Proactive Monitoring: Continuous tracking of regulatory changes and court precedents is essential.
- Risk Assessment: Companies should regularly assess their compliance risks and prioritize areas of highest exposure.
- Expert Guidance: Engaging outside counsel and compliance experts helps navigate complex requirements.
- Culture of Compliance: Leadership must foster a culture where compliance is valued and integrated into daily operations.

- Efficiency and Automation: Streamlining compliance processes and leveraging technology can reduce costs and improve responsiveness.
- Positive Relationships with Regulators: Building constructive relationships with examiners and participating in industry forums can facilitate smoother compliance experiences.

Given the significant probability of an extended supply chain dependency on China, China's uncertain digital regulatory environment must be factored into any third-party risk assessment. Strong cyber hygiene, including data segmentation and security, is paramount, given the data localization and access laws. As long as China continues to expand data sovereignty policies and tensions exist between the U.S. and China, China's regulatory environment must be integrated into any comprehensive third-party risk strategy.

Expanding Regulatory Reach

China's legal framework—including the 2023 Counter Espionage Law, the Personal Information Protection Law (PIPL), Data Security Law (DSL), and Cybersecurity Law—grants the government broad authority over data and operations:

- The Counter Espionage Law expands the definition of espionage, allowing the government to access a wide array of documents and data, creating legal uncertainty for foreign firms.
- The PIPL, while similar to GDPR in some respects, includes national security exemptions that allow unfettered government access to data.
- Laws require data localization, restrict cross-border data flows, and mandate vulnerability disclosures to the government before public release.

Third-Party and Supply Chain Exposure

Most global supply chains are deeply intertwined with China, making it nearly impossible to avoid exposure to these regulatory and operational risks. Regulatory ambiguity, inconsistent enforcement, and data localization requirements are top concerns for U.S. and European firms, leading some to consider "derisking" or shifting investments elsewhere.

Geopolitical and Economic Tensions

- U.S.-China trade relations remain volatile, with ongoing use of "Unreliable Entity Lists" and retaliatory sanctions.
- U.S. Executive Orders are making certain investments and data transfers to China more difficult.
- Military tensions around Taiwan and the broader U.S.-China rivalry add further instability.

Section 5

Supply Chain Risks

Some risks that are thought to be unknown, are not unknown. With some foresight and critical thought, some risks that at first glance may seem unforeseen, can in fact be foreseen. Armed with the right set of tools, procedures, knowledge and insight, light can be shed on variables that lead to risk, allowing us to manage them.

~ Daniel Wagner, CEO of Country Risk Solutions

Introduction

In Section 5, we offer two essays that address supply chain risk. In Chapter 13, Chris Forbes provides a comprehensive overview of the complexity, unpredictability, and critical importance of robust risk management for organizations dependent on global supply chains and third-party providers. In his essay, "Supply Chain Risk Management: What Could Possibly Go Wrong and How Bad It Could Be," he unpacks a holistic, adaptive approach that blends rigorous methodologies, advanced technology, cross-functional collaboration, and continuous improvement to anticipate, mitigate, and respond to the full spectrum of supply chain risks. In addition to the analytical approach, Chris also extolls the value of building a strong risk culture, fostering communication, and integrating risk management with business strategy. Taken together, the analytical and the cultural are vital for resilience and long-term stability in an increasingly fragile global supply chain environment. Immediately following Chris' essay is a list of publications he references throughout.

Then, in Chapter 14, Dr. Andrea Little Limbago explores the rapidly evolving landscape of artificial intelligence (AI) and its profound impact on third-party risk management in her essay, "AI and Third-Party Risk." As organizations rush to adopt generative AI (GenAI) tools like ChatGPT and Google Gemini, security concerns are often sidelined, introducing new and complex supply chain risks. She examines the risks to supply chains from AI tools across several vectors, including data quality and security, model output and prompt injection, and the regulatory environment. She concludes by exploring security and governance best practices, as well as financial and environmental considerations.

Chapter 13

Supply Chain Risk Management: What Could Possibly Go Wrong and How Bad It Could Be

Chris Forbes

Building a strong risk culture, fostering communication, and integrating risk management with business strategy are vital for resilience and long-term stability in an increasingly fragile global supply chain environment.

1.0 Essay Overview

Supply Chain Risk Management (SCRM) has become essential for organizations of all sizes, particularly those dependent on third-party providers for products, services, or logistics. Global supply chains introduce complexity, geopolitical risk, and regulatory inconsistency. Disruptions such as natural disasters, supplier insolvency, cyberattacks, or trade restrictions can significantly impact operations and financial stability.

While forecasting risks offers a competitive advantage, overconfidence in prediction remains dangerous. Bertrand Russell noted, "The demand for certainty... is an intellectual vice." Aristotle and Confucius similarly cautioned that wisdom lies in acknowledging uncertainty. Risk management must accept that some events are unpredictable and prepare accordingly.

Although research has improved our ability to forecast large-scale trends, short-term and low-frequency disruptions, such as supply chain failures, remain challenging to predict consistently. As Robert G. Wilmers observed, "You can reduce risk, but you cannot create certainty."

This chapter outlines the SCRM lifecycle and examines the challenges that hinder its effectiveness. It highlights gaps in data, inconsistent methodologies, and the difficulty of balancing control rigor with operational flexibility. It also reviews the broader tools, standards, and governance framework ecosystem. Ultimately, it offers ideas for refining SCRM strategies to improve resilience, reduce exposure, and support more adaptive and efficient decision-making.

2.0 Supply Chain Risk Management Lifecycle

Modern risk management draws from various disciplines, including statistics, finance, and actuarial science. Foundational contributions include **Probability Theory** (e.g., Pascal and Fermat), **Actuarial Science** (e.g., Halley and Dodson), **Modern Portfolio Theory** (e.g., Markowitz), and **Corporate Finance** (e.g., Black-Scholes).

Risk, broadly defined, is the potential for loss or harm due to uncertainty. In Supply Chain Risk Management (SCRM), risk is the probability that an adverse event will create a financial or operational impact. The Society for Risk Analysis (SRA) emphasizes that risk involves both outcomes and uncertainty. It is not simply the result but the **combination of consequence and unpredictability**.

Risk metrics, such as probability distributions, expected loss values, and variance, are tools for evaluating exposure. Effective risk management requires identifying, prioritizing, and mitigating threats, including measurable risks and unquantifiable uncertainties like natural disasters or geopolitical shocks.

Many companies build SCRM on the foundation of an **Enterprise Risk Management (ERM)** program. ERM provides lifecycle methodologies, including risk appetite definitions, quantification methods, and impact modeling. A mature SCRM lifecycle includes ten key elements:

1. **Asset Inventory**: Identify and assess assets, partners, suppliers, and distribution channels for criticality and exposure.
2. **Vulnerability Assessment**: Detect weaknesses across assets and processes based on value and susceptibility.
3. **Hazard and Threat Cataloging**: Document threat events and estimate their probability of reaching exposed assets.
4. **Threat Modeling**: Analyze cross-dependencies, impacts, and cascading failure risks.
5. **Business Impact Assessment (BIA)**: Estimate losses under threat scenarios.
6. **Inherent Risk Estimation**: Evaluate raw, unmitigated exposure based on likelihood and impact.
7. **Control Design and Deployment**: Apply safeguards to lower threat probability and severity.
8. **Testing and Audits**: Assess control performance and identify gaps.
9. **Residual Risk Estimation**: Recalculate risk levels post-mitigation.
10. **Financial Risk Analysis**: Determine risk acceptance thresholds using capital planning, insurance coverage, and strategic objectives.

An end-to-end lifecycle is the foundation of a robust SCRM program, enabling organizations to anticipate threats, allocate resources, and sustain resilient operations.

2.1 Supply Chain Assets Inventory

Supply chains are complex, interconnected systems that rely on multiple internal and external parties. As such, they are inherently vulnerable to a wide range of risks. Effective risk mitigation starts with understanding what is at stake, which means identifying and documenting the assets that support supply chain operations.

The saying "you can't protect what you can't see" is particularly relevant here. As Vince Lombardi famously said, "Hope is not a strategy." Without a clear asset inventory, organizations can only hope that disruptions will not occur.

Most Supply Chain Management programs agree on the value of asset inventories. However, there is less consensus on what qualifies as a "supply chain asset." Traditional views limit assets to what the company owns and controls. In contrast, leading SCRM programs advocate for a broader definition, including any asset that can materially affect operations, finance, compliance, customer satisfaction, or stakeholder trust.

Common SCRM asset categories include:

- **Physical assets** – Facilities, warehouses, and transportation infrastructure
- **Human assets** – Employees, contractors, partners, and emergency responders
- **Information assets** – IT systems, operational data, and intellectual property
- **Financial assets** – Cash flow, reserves, credit lines, and access to capital
- **Reputational assets** – Brand equity, public trust, and media presence
- **Supplier/partner assets** – External facilities, resources, and logistics services

Beyond listing assets, companies must document physical characteristics (e.g., location, construction materials), digital attributes (e.g., lifecycle, value), and inherent susceptibilities. No asset is immune, and each has conditions that make it vulnerable to specific threats.

It is also essential to evaluate how assets relate to one another. Clusters and dependencies can amplify risk, leading to cascading failures, collateral damage, and overexposure. Comprehensive asset inventories form the foundation for meaningful risk assessments.

2.2 Supply Chain Vulnerabilities and Weaknesses

After identifying supply chain assets and their susceptibilities, the next step is to assess those assets for vulnerabilities and weaknesses in their operational context. In risk management, three terms—**susceptibility**, **vulnerability**, and **weakness**—have distinct meanings:

- **Susceptibility** refers to an asset's inherent predisposition to harm under specific conditions. It is generally a permanent characteristic.
- **Vulnerability** is a specific flaw that a threat can exploit to cause harm. It is a gap in defense.
- **Weakness** describes systemic limitations, such as poor training, resource shortages, or weak governance. These often expose the organization to multiple threats.

These conditions evolve, so regular reassessment is necessary. To illustrate, consider a manufacturing facility:

- The building, made of wood, is **susceptible** to wildfires—a permanent trait.
- If the protective fire barrier is overgrown, it creates a **vulnerability** by nullifying the intended protection.
- A sprinkler system with limited capacity reflects a **weakness**, as it cannot handle large-scale fires.

Remediation requires targeted action:

- Replace wood siding with fire-resistant material to reduce **susceptibility**.
- Maintain the fire barrier to eliminate the **vulnerability**.
- Upgrade the sprinkler system to address the **weakness**.

These concepts tie directly to **resistive strength** and **resilience**:

- **Resistive strength** is an asset's ability to withstand threats through inherent qualities.
- **Resilience** is the ability of an asset to recover quickly after disruption, involving processes, systems, and adaptive strategies.

Organizations should build processes to identify and reassess vulnerabilities and weaknesses continuously. Doing so improves resistance to threats and the ability to recover, as well as critical components of supply chain reliability and risk readiness.

2.3 Supply Chain Hazard Catalog and Threat Events

Effective Supply Chain Risk Management (SCRM) begins with identifying potential hazards, understanding their operational impacts, and deploying proactive mitigation strategies. While not all disruptions are preventable, many can be anticipated, enabling organizations to act early and strengthen resilience. Hazards generally fall into five major categories:

1. Natural and Environmental Hazards

- **Weather Events:** Hurricanes, floods, and extreme temperatures disrupt logistics.
- **Geological Events:** Earthquakes or volcanic activity may turn off key infrastructure.

- **Climate Shifts:** Long-term environmental changes affect agriculture and resource availability.
- **Toxins/Pollution:** Hazardous conditions endanger human safety and operations.

2. **Technological and Cybersecurity Hazards**

- **Hardware/Software Failures:** Equipment breakdowns and software defects cause downtime.
- **Cyber Threats:** Ransomware, data breaches, and privilege abuse exploit vulnerabilities.
- **Counterfeit Components:** Non-compliant parts may create hidden risks.

3. **Infrastructure and Supply Hazards**

- **Infrastructure Failures:** Power, water, or telecom outages halt operations.
- **Transport Delays:** Interruptions in shipping or rail disrupt delivery schedules.
- **Supply Disruptions:** Supplier insolvency or material shortages impact production.

4. **Human Error and Workforce Hazards**

- **Insider Threats:** Malicious or accidental actions compromise systems.
- **Labor Disruptions:** Strikes or regulatory changes threaten continuity.
- **Workplace Incidents:** Safety events and pandemics affect workforce availability.

5. **Industry, Economic, and Geopolitical Hazards**

- **Geopolitical Unrest:** Conflict, sanctions, or regulatory changes disrupt global trade.
- **Exchange Rate:** Swings in exchange rates and inflation cause economic instability.

Many organizations use **all-hazard catalogs** to manage these risks systematically. The **NFPA 1600 Standard**, endorsed by the U.S. Department of Homeland Security, provides a structured framework for threat identification, emergency planning, and business continuity.

These catalogs incorporate inputs from FEMA, geological studies, historical data, local authorities, and global institutions (e.g., WHO, UNDRR). Leveraging these resources enables organizations to model threats, improve scenario planning, and boost resilience across complex supply chain networks.

2.4 Supply Chain Threat Models and Likelihood of Occurrence

A threat model is a structured approach to identifying, assessing, and prioritizing risks that could disrupt a supply chain. It illustrates how hazards or adversaries may exploit vulnerabilities or exceed the resistive strength of assets, leading to operational or financial impact. These models support decision-making by enabling organizations to visualize threat scenarios, plan defenses, and define necessary controls. Threat modeling can be **threat-oriented**, **asset/impact-oriented**, or **vulnerability-oriented**. Combining these approaches helps reduce bias and improve accuracy. Common methodologies include:

- **HAZOP (Hazard and Operability Study)**: Identifies operational deviations in the chemical, energy, and pharmaceutical sectors.

- **FMEA (Failure Modes and Effects Analysis)**: Evaluates failure points in manufacturing and aerospace.
- **Fault Tree Analysis (FTA), Event Tree Analysis (ETA),**
- **Attack Trees** and **STRIDE** for cybersecurity threats.

These models inform scenario planning by identifying how threats unfold, what assets are impacted, and how controls influence outcomes. Cross-functional teams, engineers, operations leaders, and cybersecurity experts are essential in building accurate, context-specific threat models.

After scenario creation, organizations must estimate the **likelihood of occurrence**, the probability that a specific threat will affect a supply chain asset, which includes:

- Historical incident data
- Industry reports and audits
- Expert judgment and surveys
- Simulations (e.g., FAIR, Monte Carlo)
- Market behavior and peer benchmarks

For high-value assets, quantitative precision is preferred; for others, a **qualitative scale** is sufficient:

Rating	Label	Probability Example
1	Rare	<1% – e.g., once in a decade
2	Unlikely	1–10% – e.g., once in several years
3	Possible	10–50% – occasionally
4	Likely	50–90% – annually
5	Almost Certain	>90% – multiple times per year

Modeling should continue until the **Point of Diminishing Returns**, where added data no longer improves confidence. Consider intent, targeting, training, and environmental factors for human threats. A threat with no asset exposure (e.g., volcano risk in a safe region) can be assigned a zero likelihood. Well-designed threat models and probability analysis empower organizations to manage critical supply chain risks proactively.

2.5 Business Impact Assessments and Magnitude of Potential Losses

A fundamental aspect of Supply Chain Risk Management (SCRM) involves evaluating the possible consequences of disruptions when threats affect vital supply chain elements. A well-organized **Business Impact Assessment (BIA)** serves this purpose by assisting organizations in determining recovery priorities and distributing resources effectively. Organizations commonly utilize numerous industry-recognized BIA frameworks.

- **ISO 22317** – Guidelines for business continuity analysis
- **NIST SP 800-34** – Contingency planning for federal systems
- **DRII** – Business continuity professional practices

- **BCI Good Practice Guidelines (GPG)** – Holistic continuity planning approaches

Most frameworks follow similar steps, including identifying essential business functions, assessing their dependencies, estimating the impact of disruption, and defining recovery priorities.

Common impact categories include:

- **Operational Impact:** Includes lost production, delays, restarts, and inefficiencies due to raw material or logistics failures.
- **Financial Impact:** Includes direct costs (e.g., expedited shipping) and indirect losses (e.g., reduced profit margins, missed revenue).
- **Market and Customer Impact:** Order fulfillment issues can erode customer satisfaction and loyalty, opening the door to competitors.
- **Reputational Impact**: Failure to deliver products or services can harm brand image and stakeholder confidence.
- **Legal and Compliance Impact**: Regulatory fines and contract breaches may arise from delays or failures.
- **Supplier and Partner Impact**: Disruptions can cascade downstream, causing financial or operational strain on partners.
- **Strategic Impact**: Prolonged disruptions may shift suppliers, markets, or long-term direction.
- **Employee Morale and Productivity**: Increased workload or crisis response duties may affect employee well-being and retention.
- **Innovation and Growth Impact**: Crisis management often diverts attention from strategic initiatives and R&D.

- **Inventory Management Impact**: Disruptions may cause stock imbalances, overstock, or critical shortages.
- **Capacity Utilization Impact**: Inefficient use of assets due to idle production or logistical bottlenecks.
- **Health and Safety Impact**: Reduced resources or pressure to maintain output can lead to safety risks.

To support consistent analysis, companies often define qualitative impact scales like the following:

Rating	Label	Definition
1	Insignificant	Minimal or no disruption or cost. No lasting effect.
2	Minor	Slight financial loss (<5%), minor delays, little impact on goals.
3	Moderate	Noticeable delays or costs (5–10%), moderate disruption or rework.
4	Major	Severe cost implications (10–25%), project delays, reputational damage.
5	Catastrophic	A catastrophic risk event is a critical failure resulting in significant financial loss (greater than 25%) and potential long-term harm to brand or economic stability.

These categories help risk managers communicate potential consequences clearly to executives and boards, enabling timely and informed decision-making.

2.6 Inherent Risk: Probability and Frequency of Impacts and Losses Over Time

In Supply Chain Risk Management (SCRM), **inherent risk** refers to the level of exposure to threats in the absence of any controls or mitigation. It represents the baseline risk under natural operating conditions and is a starting point for prioritizing resource allocation and control strategies.

Qualitative Inherent Risk Assessment

Organizations often use scales to categorize inherent risk. A standard five-point qualitative model includes:

Rating	Label	Definition
1	Very Low	Minimal impact and likelihood; no significant threats
2	Low	Low probability; minor consequences
3	Moderate	Moderate chance; noticeable but manageable impact
4	High	High likelihood and significant disruption
5	Very High	Near-certain occurrence with severe consequences

Scales help rank risks and support executive decisions on where to focus mitigation efforts.

Quantitative Inherent Risk Assessment

In quantitative models, risk is often expressed as:

Risk = Probability × Impact

For instance, a 50% chance of a $1 million loss yields an expected risk of $500,000. Tools like **Monte Carlo simulations** help visualize possible outcomes, including best-, worst-, and median-case losses.

Example: If malware costs $1,000 per incident and is expected 100 times annually, the **Annualized Loss Expectancy (ALE)** is $100,000.

Organizations often favor median values to avoid distortion from outliers (e.g., one $1 million loss among frequent $1,000 losses).

Risk Scenarios and Narratives

Frameworks like **NIST RMF**, **ISACA Risk IT**, and **COSO ERM** recommend crafting risk scenarios to contextualize risk. A scenario should include:

- Asset at risk
- Threat actor and motive
- Vulnerability exploited
- Frequency and conditions of the event
- Financial and operational consequences

Examples:

- "Cybercriminals lock manufacturing systems for three days, resulting in $4 million in downtime and recovery costs."
- "Insider breach leaks customer data, damaging the brand and requiring a legal response."

Concise formats include:

- **ISACA**: "[Event] caused by [cause] resulting in [consequence]."
- **OpenFAIR**: "[Actor] impacts [asset] via [method]."

Inherent Risk in Decision-Making

High-risk scenarios (rated High or Very High) often trigger:

- Additional modeling
- Budget adjustments
- Escalation to executive oversight

Organizations should set risk thresholds for action and calculate supporting metrics such as detection time, recovery costs, and potential increases in insurance premiums. Understanding inherent risk provides a foundation for control design, residual risk analysis, and strategic planning.

2.7 Supply Chain Risk Mitigations, Control Strength, and Control Effectiveness

Mitigating supply chain risks requires a layered approach that combines proactive planning, operational flexibility, and effective control implementation. Organizations should routinely assess vulnerabilities and deploy strategies such as supplier diversification, contingency planning, real-time visibility tools, and resilient design. A core component of this effort is maintaining a documented **Inventory of Risk Controls**, including each control's name, scope, owner, and purpose. Controls fall into two primary categories:

- **System Controls**: Apply to specific systems, assets, or processes
- **Enterprise/Common Controls**: Apply broadly across the organization or supply chain

Controls must be evaluated for **Effectiveness**, which is the degree to which they reduce the **likelihood** or **impact** of a threat. Effectiveness is typically rated using this scale:

Rating	Label	Definition
1	Not Effective	Frequent issues; no meaningful mitigation
2	Partially Effective	Inconsistent results; no improvement plan
3	Most Effective	Some problems; improvement plan in progress
4	Effective	Reliable with minimal issues
5	Very Effective	Proven control with no known failures

Control Strength refers to how well a control mitigates the targeted risk. **Control Accuracy** measures how consistently and precisely the control performs without false positives or negatives.

Rating	Label	Definition
1	Very Low Accuracy	High error rate or unreliability
5	Very High Accuracy	Near-perfect, consistent performance

To calculate **Residual Risk**, subtract (Control Effectiveness – 1) from the initial probability or impact score.

> Example: If Probability = 5 and Control Effectiveness = 5 → Residual Risk = 1

While no control reduces risk to zero, strong, accurate, and well-maintained controls significantly lower exposure, supporting more resilient supply chain operations.

2.8 Control Coverage Issues, Gaps, Certainty, and Competence

Organizations must perform periodic **control testing** to ensure risk controls function as intended and validate whether controls meet objectives and respond effectively under operational conditions. There are three key testing types:

- **Test of Design**: Evaluates whether the control structure is appropriate to mitigate the identified risk.
- **Test of One**: Confirms control functionality through a single execution—often used during rollout or after updates.
- **Test of Effectiveness**: Simulates threat scenarios to verify real-world control performance.

Risk assessors rely on control test results, audit findings, and incident reports to rate control effectiveness. When no evidence is available, a default rating of "1 – Not Effective" is applied to ensure conservative analysis.

Frequent testing and **continuous monitoring are recommended in high-risk environments,** using Operational Technology (OT), third-party audits, and independent assessments.

Human oversight remains critical. To strengthen **SCRM competence**, organizations must define required skill sets and invest in formal training, certifications, and ongoing education. While cost-effective, training-based controls can be inconsistent and must be reinforced through supervision and repeatable processes.

Documented test results support **audit readiness**, legal defense, and **root cause analysis** (RCA) while contributing to long-term control improvements and organizational transparency.

2.9 Residual Risk: Cumulative Reduction of Inherent Risk

Residual risk is the remaining exposure after controls are applied. It reflects the net threat level that must be actively managed. There should be a clear, logical linkage between **Inherent Risk, Control Effectiveness**, and **Residual Risk.**

If controls are ineffective or absent, residual risk mirrors inherent risk. Adequate controls reduce risk accordingly and can be communicated in several formats:

- **Qualitative:** Labels such as Low, Moderate, High
- **Quantitative:** Probability (%) × Estimated Loss ($)
- **Descriptive:** Narrative statements summarizing the threat and impact

Example: "There is a 10% chance that flooding will impact the distribution center, causing $1 million in damage and delays."

These formats allow leadership to understand and prioritize exposure, allocate resources, and determine mitigation urgency.

2.10 Risk Registers, Reserves, Appetite, and Governance

A **risk register** consolidates key risk scenarios, mitigation strategies, residual ratings, and assigned owners. It is a central tool for risk governance and should align across business functions. Key governance mechanisms include:

- **Risk Acceptance:** Formal approval to tolerate residual risk within defined thresholds.
- **Risk Appetite:** Strategic definition of acceptable risk exposure.
- **Risk Budgets and Authority:** Defined limits and decision-making roles for approving risk-based actions.
- **Risk Accountability:** Linking executive decisions to compensation with clawback clauses in negligence cases.

Effective governance ensures risks are visible, managed, and strategically aligned, promoting a culture where risk oversight strengthens enterprise resilience.

3.0 Risk Management Is Getting It Wrong

Despite its critical role, risk management has not yet evolved into a fully mature, standardized discipline. Risk management remains inconsistent and fragmented across industries, unlike statistics, which is built on shared terminology, reproducible methods, and mathematical rigor.

Statistics offers a structured foundation: data collection, analysis, interpretation, and evidence-based decision-making. Risk management, by contrast, swings between **subjective qualitative approaches** and **emerging quantitative models**. This inconsistency complicates benchmarking, weakens cross-industry collaboration, and erodes executive confidence.

Qualitative techniques such as **interviews, expert panels, and scenario analysis** provide valuable insights but are inherently subjective and difficult to replicate. Prioritizing risks as "low," "moderate," or "high" lacks mathematical precision and often fails to inform decisions under uncertainty.

Quantitative methods offer more substantial forecasting potential, including **probability analysis, Monte Carlo simulations**, and **sensitivity analysis.** However, these tools lack a consistent framework or common vocabulary, limiting their comparability and credibility. While risk management is gaining academic attention, it still lacks the foundational maturity seen in more established disciplines.

3.1 Incomplete Supply Chain Inventories Create Blind Spots

Accurate, real-time asset inventories are essential for effective SCRM. Yet many companies operate with **dangerous visibility gaps**, lacking clear insight into what assets they rely on, where those assets reside, and who owns them.

A 2019 study in the *International Journal of Production Economics* noted key challenges: **non-standard data practices, aging technologies**, and the **global complexity of supplier networks.** These limitations make asset traceability difficult and blind spots inevitable. Only a few regulations mandate transparency:

- **FSMA** – food supply traceability
- **DSCSA** – pharmaceutical tracking
- **Dodd-Frank 1502** – conflict mineral disclosures
- **FAR/DFARS** – defense supply documentation

Most sectors still rely on voluntary disclosures, leaving critical gaps in visibility.

3.2 No Standards for SCRM Hazards, Threats, and Probability Data

A standardized All-Hazards Catalog or central threat repository is significantly lacking for SCRM. Organizations struggle to compare, share, or benchmark risk information due to the absence of consistent definitions or centralized data, hindering collaboration and policy development and weakening regulatory alignment. Advanced methods such as chaos theory, Markov chains, and extreme value modeling show promise but lack widespread adoption because of insufficient data. Regulatory reporting requirements like those for SEC Forms 8-K and 10-K improve investor awareness, yet supply chain-specific threat disclosures remain rare. The insurance sector can accelerate progress if brokers share aggregated claims data, allowing organizations to benchmark exposure, understand threat frequency, and improve resilience through informed risk strategies.

3.3 SCRM Is Incapable of Assessing Supply Chain Vulnerabilities

Modern supply chains are deeply interconnected, globally distributed, and often lack transparency, making it difficult for SCRM teams to assess vulnerabilities across multiple tiers. Companies depend on complex networks of suppliers and logistics partners operating in diverse regulatory environments, creating widespread blind spots.

Most third-party risk and procurement functions were designed for compliance and documentation, not active risk analysis. Consequently, many organizations lack the tools, talent, and data integration necessary to map supply chain assets, evaluate threat exposure, or identify critical dependencies.

Geopolitical shifts, cyber threats, and regulatory changes rapidly evolve supply chain risks. Accurate vulnerability assessment now requires real-time visibility, continuous monitoring, and cross-functional collaboration.

SCRM should look to the cybersecurity field, which uses standardized frameworks like CWE, CVSS, STIX, and TAXII to classify and share vulnerabilities. SCRM urgently needs similar protocols to ensure consistent identification, scoring, and communication of supply chain weaknesses.

3.4 Combinatorial Complexity Between Threats and Assets

A familiar SCRM axiom—"Hazard sources trigger threat events that reach exposed assets and overpower resistive strength"—provides a simplified view of risk. Risk is shaped by **combinatorial complexity**, where numerous interdependent factors intersect unpredictably.

Conditional probability helps estimate risk, but accurate modeling requires deep insight into dependencies across assets, suppliers, and geographies. For instance, while earthquakes can be regionally forecasted, predicting which supply chain assets will be impacted—and whether their resistive strength will hold—is far more complex. Resistive strength is not static; it evolves based on asset design, aging, maintenance, and control maturity. Effective modeling must factor in **secondary disruptions**, feedback loops, and cascading failures.

The **2017 COSO ERM Framework** emphasizes that rare, high-impact risks are difficult to quantify due to data gaps, model error, and statistical uncertainty. To improve, SCRM must adopt **Model Risk Management** (MRM) practices, using advanced simulation, scenario testing, and analytics to capture the full scope of risk interactions.

3.5 Incomplete and Inconsistent Business Impact Assessments

One of the core challenges in SCRM is producing accurate Business Impact Assessments (BIAs) when threats intersect with vulnerable assets. For example, a wildfire near a distribution center could affect logistics, infrastructure, utilities, and personnel simultaneously. While BIAs are commonly used in Business Continuity Planning (BCP), many remain incomplete, inconsistent, or biased.

Traditional BIAs depend on self-assessments by business units, which are frequently distorted by **cognitive biases**. These include the **Dunning-Kruger Effect**, where individuals overestimate their expertise, and **Optimism Bias**, which leads to underestimating adverse outcomes. Additional biases, such as **Loss Aversion**, **False Consensus**, **Confirmation Bias**, and **Status Quo Bias** further compromise results. BIAs often fail to consider **second-order effects** and cascading failures across business functions.

Moreover, many BIAs evaluate risk in isolation, assuming a single-event scenario. In reality, organizations often face **multiple related disruptions**. Companies should adopt the **Annual Loss Expectancy** (ALE) model: **ALE = SLE × ARO** (**SLE**: Single Loss Expectancy, **ARO**: Annual Rate of Occurrence).

ALE helps estimate **cumulative risk exposure**, guiding capital reserves, insurance planning, and resource prioritization. Evolving BIAs to reflect complex, real-world dynamics is essential to enhancing SCRM maturity.

3.6 Inherent Risk Is Overly Complex and Unwieldy

Inherent risk reflects an organization's baseline exposure before any controls are applied. Yet current practices often compress three key dimensions: the **probability of occurrence**, **impact magnitude**, and **loss range** into a single, oversimplified score. Each of these dimensions varies significantly:

- **Probability** is influenced by threat actors, location, and operational context
- **Impact** depends on which assets are affected and how
- **Loss range** includes financial, reputational, and regulatory consequences

Reducing these into a single "High" or "Medium" rating leads to misinterpretation. For example:

- **Scenario A**: 25% chance of a $1 million one-time loss
- **Scenario B**: 50% chance of a recurring $500,000 loss

A single risk score fails to differentiate that both have the same expected value ($250,000), yet Scenario B carries ongoing exposure. Organizations should **break down inherent risk** into components to improve clarity, include transparent assumptions, and use narrative-driven context to support informed decision-making.

3.7 SCRM Control Strategy Is Systemically Challenging

Designing effective control strategies is foundational to risk management, yet SCRM presents unique obstacles. Unlike IT or physical security, where companies control the protected assets, many supply chain assets lie beyond direct oversight, limiting the effectiveness of conventional "block-the-threat" tactics.

Risk treatment strategies generally fall into seven categories:

- **Risk Acceptance**: Tolerating known risks
- **Risk Avoidance**: Exiting or avoiding high-risk activities
- **Risk Alternatives**: Substituting with less risky options (e.g., financial hedging)
- **Risk Limits**: Thresholds that trigger interventions
- **Risk Contingencies**: Prearranged backup plans or partners
- **Risk Mitigation**: Reducing threat likelihood, impact, or duration
- **Risk Transfer**: Offloading risk via insurance or outsourcing

Controls also follow a seven-type framework:

- **Directive** (e.g., policies, training)
- **Deterrent** (e.g., warning signs, penalties)
- **Detective** (e.g., alerts, monitoring systems)
- **Compensating** (e.g., backups for weak controls)
- **Corrective** (e.g., damage recovery tools)
- **Preventive** (e.g., access controls, screening)
- **Recovery** (e.g., rapid restoration procedures)

Evaluating controls requires analyzing their cost, effectiveness, and overlap. No control is flawless, and **defense-in-depth** (multiple-layered safeguards) improves effectiveness but increases operational complexity and cost. SCRM control strategies must prioritize **resilience, redundancy, and partnership coordination** over rigid command structures, especially in globally distributed, decentralized environments.

3.8 Residual Risk Is Imprecise and Indefinite

Residual risk reflects the exposure that remains after implementing all controls. Ideally, it represents an acceptable threshold, but in practice, it is often based on **subjective inputs** and **assumptions** about control effectiveness, impact likelihood, and scenario modeling.

Even well-designed risk models can generate **false confidence**, leading to an underestimation of exposure. Residual risk should never be treated as resolved, and it must be **continuously reviewed**, especially as threats evolve and control performance degrades over time. Proactive reassessment is essential to avoid complacency and ensure residual risk aligns with the organization's risk appetite.

3.9 Risk Aggregation Disagrees with Risk Appetites

Managing risk would be far simpler if risks occurred one at a time. The challenge lies in aggregating hundreds of open risk scenarios and determining how they interact. Aggregation is crucial for understanding capital adequacy, insurance coverage, and systemic vulnerabilities.

First, SCRM needs to determine if multiple severe events, such as cascading failures and widespread regional issues, could occur at the same time or in rapid succession, which would require multi-layered contingency plans and increased capital reserves for resilience.

Second, risk aggregation must include **contingency dependencies** (e.g., reciprocal support agreements or shared backup providers) that may be unavailable during widespread crises.

Third, regulators increasingly demand scenario analysis involving **concentration risks** and cascading failures, especially for critical infrastructure.

Finally, as the number of accepted risks grows, the probability of an incident increases. A broader risk portfolio means a higher chance of simultaneous or compounded events, increasing exposure, and testing the organization's risk appetite.

3.10 Risk Prioritization and Capital Planning Are Disconnected

Many organizations overlook the critical link between **risk prioritization** and **capital planning**. Without alignment, even well-designed strategies may lack the funding to implement controls or recover from disruptions. Organizations must plan for the following:

- **Capital reserves** to absorb incident-related losses
- **Insurance** to transfer risk
- **Funding** for risk treatments, such as controls and system upgrades

However, risk is dynamic, while budgets are often static. As geopolitical, regulatory, and technological risks evolve, outdated budgets may underfund critical initiatives or misallocate resources to lower-priority threats. Additional challenges include:

- **Financial blind spots** – Risk costs are excluded from planning.
- **Reactive decision-making** – Crisis responses overshadow strategy.
- **Slow remediation** – Controls remain untested or incomplete.

Bridging this gap requires **defined risk thresholds**, **decision triggers**, and integrated planning between **risk, finance, and operations**. Capital must be treated as a **strategic buffer** for resilience, not just a performance enabler, to reduce exposure proactively before incidents occur.

4.0 SCRM Program Design Elements and Ideas for Improvement

Designing an effective SCRM program requires adaptability to rapidly evolving threats such as cyberattacks, climate risks, and geopolitical instability. Success depends on real-time analytics, continuous monitoring, and skilled professionals to interpret dynamic data. Fostering a risk-aware culture is equally vital. Employees and supply chain partners must be trained to identify threats, follow protocols, and collaborate during disruptions. Clear communication and trusted relationships enhance transparency and response. Finally, SCRM must align with the overall business strategy, balancing cost efficiency and operational resilience. Executive support and strategic integration are essential for sustained risk management success.

4.1 Improving SCRM Asset Management

SCRM leaders often face fragmented visibility due to the distributed ownership of supply chain assets. Even when SCRM operates through centralized services, data on assets is dispersed across business units.

Emerging strategies for improving asset oversight include:

- **Advanced Analytics:** Tools like digital twins and control towers enhance visibility across tiers.
- **IoT and AI Integration:** Real-time tracking and predictive alerts help identify risks early.
- **Blockchain:** Improves traceability through tamper-proof transaction records.
- **Low-Code Platforms:** Help speed up the deployment of customized supply chain applications.
- **Multi-Tier Supplier Collaboration:** AI tools reveal risks beyond Tier 1.
- **ESG and Scope 3 Compliance:** Sustainability regulations require more insight into supplier data.

These technologies improve transparency, support compliance, and strengthen risk response strategies.

4.2 Strengthening Vulnerability Sharing and Responsible Disclosures

Effective SCRM extends beyond organizational boundaries. Sharing intelligence through **Information Sharing and Analysis Centers (ISACs)**, commercial vendors, and **public-private partnerships** enables faster threat detection and collective defense. **Industry ISACs** such as Health-ISAC, FA-ISAC, and Transportation ISAC pool intelligence and coordinate responses. **Vendors** like SecurityScorecard, BitSight, SOCRadar, and BlackKite provide real-time insights and cyber risk ratings. **Government partnerships** with the FBI, DHS, and DoD facilitate early warnings and infrastructure protection. If willing to share anonymized claims data, insurance brokers could offer valuable insights into disruption trends. By embracing collaborative intelligence, organizations can reduce blind spots, improve threat visibility, and build more resilient supply chains.

4.3 SCRM Threat Intelligence

Modern supply chains increasingly rely on threat intelligence to anticipate and mitigate disruptions. Organizations are shifting toward frequent assessments, real-time monitoring, and independent validation of supplier ecosystems. Key developments include:

Advanced Analytics and AI: Predictive analytics uses historical and machine learning data to forecast disruptions. Prescriptive analytics recommends targeted mitigation strategies. AI detects real-time anomalies in supply chain behavior.

Real-Time Data Integration: IoT sensors continuously monitor operations. Data fusion provides a unified risk view. Cloud platforms support fast, collaborative decision-making.

Cybersecurity Integration: Threat intelligence sharing increases cyber threat visibility. Security ratings assess third-party cybersecurity posture. Incident response planning addresses potential disruptions proactively.

Third-Party Risk Management: Enhanced due diligence and continuous monitoring improve supplier oversight. Supply chain mapping identifies critical dependencies and vulnerabilities.

Risk Quantification and Prioritization: Assesses the financial impact and risk-ranks the potential impacts, allowing organizations to plan scenario preparations and resource allocation better.

These capabilities strengthen resilience, enabling proactive risk management and more substantial supply chain stability.

4.4 Supply Chain Threat Models and Digital Twins

Digital twins are real-time virtual models that simulate supply chain behavior under various conditions. They enable scenario testing and performance analysis, supporting vulnerability identification, resilience planning, and continuous improvement. Benefits include improved decision-making, cost savings, and enhanced customer satisfaction. Despite these advancements, SCRM lacks a standardized threat modeling framework, like MITRE ATT&CK in cybersecurity. A shared taxonomy aids the consistent assessment and communication of risks. A unified framework would improve threat visibility, support standard tools and practices, and foster collaboration, ultimately elevating SCRM maturity and strengthening global supply chain resilience.

4.5 Business Impact Assessments and Magnitude of Potential Losses

As supply chains grow more complex, organizations shift from static to **scenario-based BIAs** that simulate disruptions like pandemics or geopolitical events. These models evaluate cascading impacts across operations, enabling more strategic planning. **Dynamic BIAs** integrate real-time data and analytics, keeping impact assessments current as conditions evolve. **Third-party risk** is now routinely included, capturing vendor disruptions and performance issues. Modern BIAs combine **qualitative expertise** with **quantitative data** for accuracy. Dashboards and visualization tools improve communication, helping leaders prioritize response strategies and align recovery plans across business units.

4.6 Inherent Risk: Probability and Frequency of Impacts and Losses

Building resilience starts with **Secure by Design,** embedding risk controls, security, and fault tolerance into supply chain architecture from the outset, which ensures vulnerabilities are addressed early, not retrofitted. Designing for resiliency includes **supplier diversification**, **continuous monitoring**, and **redundant systems** to maintain operations during disruptions. **Fault-tolerant strategies**, such as backup vendors and real-time visibility tools, enable continuity when primary systems fail.

Organizations should also implement **feedback loops**, leveraging stakeholder input and analytics to refine operations and adjust to emerging risks. To prepare for **cyberattacks, climate events**, and **geopolitical disruptions**, companies must integrate these risk vectors into their **BIAs** and **inherent risk models**, improving foresight and safeguarding critical supply chain assets.

4.7 Supply Chain Risk Mitigations, Control Strength, and Control Effectiveness

Implementing supply chain controls is complex and costly. To improve scalability and efficiency, SCRM leaders are adopting **standardized control frameworks** tailored to specific industries (e.g., NIST CSF, HIPAA). Families of controls are organized into **reference architectures**, helping organizations visualize data flows and vulnerabilities and optimize protections. **Control Design Patterns** offer reusable templates for common risk scenarios, accelerating deployment. **Effectiveness Metrics** enable performance tracking, gap identification, and informed investment decisions. Continuous measurement supports ongoing refinement. **Collaboration and Knowledge Sharing** across industries enhance innovation and speed adoption. By contributing to shared frameworks, companies strengthen collective resilience. These practices help scale control environments, improve risk posture, and boost operational efficiency across global supply chains.

4.8 Control Coverage Issues, Gaps, Certainty, and Competence

SCRM professionals must regularly test and enhance controls to keep pace with evolving threats. Traditional frameworks often lack visibility into sub-tier suppliers and systemic dependencies. **Expanded Control Coverage** uses tools like blockchain and AI sensors to monitor logistics partners, utilities, and infrastructure in real-time. **Improved Control Accuracy** is achieved through machine learning, enabling faster, more precise detection of anomalies. **Control Certainty** grows through independent audits, automated validation, and red teaming. Standardized metrics and certifications help benchmark performance. **SCRM Competence** remains critical. Organizations are investing in training, cross-functional rotations, and certification programs to build teams capable of managing global supply chain risks. These enhancements create more adaptive, intelligent, and resilient control environments.

4.9 Residual Risk: Cumulative Reduction of Inherent Risk

Residual risk—the exposure remaining after controls are applied—must be actively monitored and refined. Organizations now use **advanced aggregation techniques** to capture complex risk interdependencies. **Correlation Analysis** identifies risk clusters and amplification patterns. **Scenario-based aggregation** models compound events to guide prioritization. **Monte Carlo Simulation** estimates outcomes across thousands of scenarios using probability distributions. Additional tools include:

- **Concentration Risk Analysis:** Detects overreliance on key suppliers or regions.
- **Cascading Failure Modeling:** Traces disruption upstream and downstream.
- **Collateral Damage Assessment:** Evaluates indirect and external shocks and impacts.
- **Unforeseen Scenarios:** Planning establishes response roles and recovery actions.

These methods improve residual risk visibility and support informed, forward-looking SCRM decisions.

4.10 Risk Registers, Reserves, Appetite, and Governance

The risk register is the foundation of effective SCRM governance, consolidating risk scenarios, mitigation plans, and decision points. To be effective, it must integrate into enterprise-wide governance frameworks with several key components:

- **Capital Reserve Reviews** ensure financial readiness for worst-case scenarios.
- **Risk Appetite Reviews** align tolerances with evolving strategy.
- **Cost-benefit Reviews** justify mitigation investments and support resource planning.
- **Risk Response Reviews** evaluate control performance and scalability.
- **Communication Platforms** centralize dashboards for executive visibility.
- **Decision Thresholds** trigger appropriate escalation.
- **Governance Structures** define roles, responsibilities, and accountability paths.

A unified approach promotes transparency, informed decisions, and enterprise-wide resilience.

5.0 SCRM Key Risk Indicators (KRIs)

As supply chains grow more complex and risk-prone, organizations are leaning on **Key Risk Indicators (KRIs)** to detect vulnerabilities before they escalate into significant disruptions. KRIs function as early warning signals—quantifiable metrics highlighting emerging risks and guiding mitigation efforts. By continuously monitoring these indicators, organizations can better protect their operations, reduce losses, and enhance resilience. SCRM professionals commonly group KRIs into **ten categories**, each tied to a critical supply chain function. The top three KRIs for each category are listed below, along with their calculation methods:

5.1 Raw Material Risks

- **Availability:** (%) = (Available Critical Inventory / Required Inventory) × 100
- **Price Volatility Index:** Standard deviation of price movements over time
- **Supplier Concentration:** (%) = (Suppliers providing >50% of input) / (Total Suppliers)

5.2 Supplier Risks

- **Financial Stability:** Credit rating or score from financial institutions
- **On-Time Delivery:** (%) = (On-Time Deliveries / Total Deliveries) × 100
- **Supplier Dependency:** (%) = (Top Supplier Purchase Value / Total Purchase Value)

5.3 Production and Warehousing Risks

- **Capacity Utilization:** (%) = (Actual Output / Max Output) × 100
- **Inventory Turnover:** = Cost of Goods Sold / Avg. Inventory
- **Warehouse Utilization:** (%) = (Used Space / Total Space) × 100

5.4 Manufacturing Quality Risks

- **Defect Rate:** (%) = (Defective Units / Total Units) × 100

- **First Pass Yield (FPY):** (%) = (Passed First Try / Total Tested) × 100
- **Rework and Scrap Rate:** (%) = (Reworked + Scrapped Units / Total Units Produced) × 100

5.5 Customer Demand Risks

- **Forecast Accuracy:** (%) = (1 - |Forecast - Actual| / Actual) × 100
- **Order Fulfillment:** (%) = (Orders Fulfilled On Time / Total Orders) × 100
- **Lead Time Variability:** Standard deviation of order fulfillment times

5.6 Delivery and Transportation Risks

- **On-Time Delivery Rate:** (%) = (Timely Deliveries / Total Deliveries) × 100
- **Transport Cost Variance:** (%) = (Actual - Budgeted) / Budgeted
- **Transit Time Variability:** Standard deviation of transit durations

5.7 Natural Disaster and Environmental Risks

- **Disaster Exposure Index:** Weighted sum of regional hazard risks
- **Environmental Compliance Rate:** (%) = (Incidents / Inspections) × 100
- **Climate Impact Metric:** Composite index based on environmental indicators

5.8 Geopolitical Risks

- **Country Risk Rating:** Aggregated score from geopolitical risk databases
- **Trade Restriction Alerts:** Count of relevant sanctions or trade actions
- **Political Exposure:** (%) = (Imports from High-Risk Countries / Total Imports) × 100

5.9 Regulatory Compliance Risks

- **Audit Score:** Average or cumulative score from regulatory audits
- **Regulatory Change Volume:** Number of material law or policy changes
- **Incident Response Time:** Average time from incident detection to closure

5.10 Financial and Currency Risks

- **Currency Variance:** (%) = (Current Rate - Baseline) / Baseline
- **Payment Delays:** (%) = (Late Payments / Total Payments) × 100
- **Credit Exposure:** Weighted average of credit risk scores from key partners

By regularly tracking these KRIs, companies can pinpoint weak areas in their supply chain and implement proactive strategies to manage risk and improve resilience.

Conclusion and Closing Thoughts

Supply Chain Risk Management (SCRM) must balance minimizing risk with enabling strategic growth. Risk is inherent to business, and

SCRM should support—not replace—executive judgment. Risk models offer insights, not certainty; leadership must determine when the need for action outweighs further analysis. Compliance ensures legal adherence, but only proactive risk management addresses real vulnerabilities. A strong risk culture fosters humility, communication, and readiness. Global supply chains are fragile and essential. Strengthening them requires more than good intentions—thoughtful design, collaborative accountability, and resilient frameworks. The future depends on deliberate, informed actions to ensure continuity, trust, and long-term stability.

REFERENCES

- Business Continuity Institute. Global Supply Chain Resilience Report. DHL, accessed March 18, 2025, https://www.dhl.com/global-en/home/insights-and-innovation/insights-and-innovation/resilience.html.
- Business Continuity Institute. The Global Supply Chain Report. BCI, accessed March 18, 2025, https://www.thebci.org.
- Deloitte. The Cost of Supply Chain Disruptions. Deloitte Insights, accessed March 18, 2025, https://www.deloitte.com/global-supply-chain-disruptions.
- Disaster Recovery Institute International. Professional Practices for Business Continuity Management. Disaster Recovery Institute International (DRII), accessed March 18, 2025, https://www.drii.org.
- Federal Emergency Management Agency (FEMA). "Emergency Management." Accessed March 18, 2025, https://www.fema.gov.
- International Organization for Standardization. ISO 22317: Security and Resilience—Business Continuity Management Systems—Guidelines for Business Impact Analysis. Geneva: International Organization for Standardization, accessed March 18, 2025, https://www.iso.org/standard/50054.html.

- International Journal of Production Economics. "Supply Chain Visibility." International Journal of Production Economics, 2019.
- MITRE. "MITRE ATT&CK Framework." MITRE Corporation, accessed March 18, 2025, https://attack.mitre.org.
- National Fire Protection Association. "NFPA 1600: Standard on Continuity, Emergency, and Crisis Management." National Fire Protection Association, accessed March 18, 2025, https://www.nfpa.org/codes-and-standards/1/6/0/nfpa-1600.
- National Institute of Standards and Technology (NIST). "SP 800-34: Contingency Planning Guide for Federal Information Systems." National Institute of Standards and Technology (NIST), accessed March 18, 2025, https://csrc.nist.gov/publications/detail/sp/800-34/rev-1/final.
- Society for Risk Analysis (SRA). "Risk Analysis Definitions." Society for Risk Analysis (SRA), accessed March 18, 2025, https://www.sra.org.
- U.S. Congress. "Dodd-Frank Wall Street Reform and Consumer Protection Act, Section 1502 (Conflict Minerals)." Public Law 111-203, 111th Cong., July 21, 2010.
- U.S. Congress. "Drug Supply Chain Security Act (DSCSA)." Public Law 113-54, 113th Cong., November 27, 2013.
- U.S. Congress. "Food Safety Modernization Act (FSMA)." Public Law 111-353, 111th Cong., January 4, 2011.
- U.S. Securities and Exchange Commission (SEC). "Form 10-K, Annual Report." Accessed March 18, 2025, https://www.sec.gov.
- U.S. Securities and Exchange Commission (SEC). "Form 8-K, Current Report." Accessed March 18, 2025, https://www.sec.gov.

Insights and Actions

The Nature of Supply Chain Risk

Effective SCRM requires a structured lifecycle that encompasses asset inventory, vulnerability assessment, hazard cataloging, threat modeling, business impact assessment, inherent risk estimation, control design and deployment, testing and audits, residual risk calculation, and financial risk analysis. However, current risk management practices are systematically flawed due to incomplete supply chain inventories creating dangerous blind spots, lack of standardized hazard and threat probability data preventing meaningful benchmarking, inability to assess multi-tier supplier vulnerabilities, combinatorial complexity between threats and assets that exceeds current modeling capabilities, and inconsistent business impact estimates distorted by cognitive biases—collectively undermining the reliability and effectiveness of risk management decisions.

Unlike the discipline of statistics, which relies on shared terminology, reproducible methods, and mathematical precision, risk management oscillates between subjective, qualitative approaches and emerging quantitative models without consistent frameworks or a common vocabulary. This immaturity manifests in oversimplified inherent risk assessments that compress probability, impact magnitude, and loss range into single scores, systemically challenging control strategies for assets beyond direct organizational control, imprecise residual risk calculations based on subjective assumptions, and disconnected risk prioritization and capital planning processes—creating false confidence and potentially dangerous underestimation of exposure across global supply chain networks.

Organizations must adopt emerging technologies, including digital twins for real-time virtual modeling, IoT and AI integration for predictive analytics and continuous monitoring, blockchain for tamper-proof traceability, and low-code platforms for rapid application deployment. Success also demands the sharing of collaborative intelligence through Industry Sharing and Analysis Centers (ISACs), commercial threat intelligence vendors, and public-private partnerships to reduce blind spots and enable collective defense. Additionally, companies must implement comprehensive Key Risk Indicators (KRIs) across ten critical categories—raw materials, suppliers, production/warehousing, manufacturing quality, customer demand, delivery/transportation, natural disasters, geopolitical factors, regulatory compliance, and financial/currency risks—providing early warning systems that enable proactive risk mitigation rather than reactive crisis management.

Challenges and Gaps in SCRM

- Incomplete Inventories: Many organizations lack real-time, comprehensive asset inventories, creating blind spots and undermining risk assessments.
- Lack of Standardization: There are no universal standards for hazard/threat data, making benchmarking and collaboration difficult.
- Difficulty in Assessing Vulnerabilities: Complex, opaque, multi-tiered supply chains hinder visibility and vulnerability assessment.
- Combinatorial Complexity: Interdependencies and cascading failures make risk modeling and aggregation challenging.
- Biased and Incomplete BIAs: Business impact assessments often suffer from cognitive biases and fail to capture second-order effects or concurrent disruptions.
- Overly Simplified Inherent Risk: Reducing risk to a single score can mask important differences in probability, impact, and loss frequency.
- Control Limitations: Many supply chain assets are outside direct control, making traditional risk mitigation strategies less effective.

- Imprecise Residual Risk: Residual risk calculations are often subjective and must be continuously reviewed as conditions change.
- Disconnected Risk Prioritization and Capital Planning: Budgets may not align with evolving risk landscapes, leaving organizations underprepared for major incidents.

Consider These Five Best Practices for Program Design and Improvement

- Technology and Analytics: Advanced tools (digital twins, IoT, AI, blockchain) can improve visibility, traceability, and risk response.
- Collaboration and Intelligence Sharing: Industry ISACs, vendor risk ratings, and public-private partnerships enhance threat detection and resilience.
- Continuous Monitoring: Real-time data integration, frequent assessments, and scenario-based BIAs are essential for modern SCRM.
- Control Frameworks: Standardized controls (e.g., NIST CSF) and reference architectures help scale and benchmark risk management.
- Governance: A robust risk register, clearly defined risk appetite, capital reserves, and defined decision thresholds are critical for effective oversight.

The Phases of the SCRM Lifecycle

A mature SCRM program follows a structured lifecycle, drawing from disciplines like statistics and finance. The ten key elements are:

- Asset Inventory: Identify all critical assets, including physical, human, informational, financial, reputational, and supplier/partner assets.

- Vulnerability Assessment: Detect weaknesses and susceptibilities in assets and processes.
- Hazard and Threat Cataloging: Document and estimate the likelihood of various threats (natural, technological, human, geopolitical, etc.).
- Threat Modeling: Analyze dependencies and potential cascading failures.
- Business Impact Assessment (BIA): Estimate losses under different scenarios, using frameworks like ISO 22317 and NIST SP 800-34.
- Inherent Risk Estimation: Assess raw exposure before controls are applied.
- Control Design and Deployment: Implement safeguards to reduce risk.
- Testing and Audits: Assess control effectiveness and identify gaps.
- Residual Risk Estimation: Recalculate risk after mitigation.
- Financial Risk Analysis: Set risk acceptance thresholds and plan capital reserves and insurance.

Chapter 14

AI and Third-Party Risk

Dr. Andrea Little Limbago

AI offers transformative opportunities but introduces significant third-party risks that must be managed holistically. Organizations should integrate AI-specific risks into their broader third-party risk management programs, prioritize data quality and security, and prepare for a fast-evolving global regulatory landscape.

The AI revolution is here, and with that comes enormous opportunities and risks. Due to the vast potential of AI and the enormous pressure to leverage it, organizations are rushing toward the latest open-source tools, especially those utilizing Generative AI (GenAI), such as ChatGPT, CLAUDE, Mistral, Google Gemini, and LLAMA.[171] As often happens with new technologies, market pressures are seemingly pushing security to the back burner in the C-suite.[172]

AI introduces a new form of third-party risk, with a supply chain consisting of the data inputs, outputs, and the model itself, each of which require security assessments and considerations. For instance, researchers discovered over 100 malicious AI models on the popular open-source AI platform, Hugging Face.[173] There are also privacy and intellectual property (IP) risks if sensitive data is disclosed

171 https://www.cnbc.com/advertorial/2023/09/21/pressure-to-adopt-ai-grows-for-leaders-across-industries-study-finds-.html.

172 https://www.darkreading.com/cyber-risk/ai-models-take-off-leaving-security-behind.

173 https://thehackernews.com/2024/03/over-100-malicious-aiml-models-found-on.html?utm_source=dlvr.it&utm_medium=linkedin&m=1.

through AI-assisted chat services, making it accessible to the company producing the technology or to hackers who have found side channels into the data.[174] These side-channel attacks exploit the indirect characteristics of the systems to extract information, such as energy usage or token length sequences, which can inadvertently leak information about the underlying text or behavior. Researchers have also demonstrated the ability to spread data-stealing prompt injection worms through large language model (LLM)-powered email assistants.[175]

Despite these risks, AI is foundational to the ongoing digital revolution, and organizations that fail to leverage AI securely will likely be left behind. The AI arms race is underway, and like most technologies, has dual-use applications. Malicious hackers from China, Russia, and Iran are leveraging AI to enhance their cyberattacks.[176] Businesses are also locked in an AI arms race, an extremely expensive one at that, due to the potential upsides.[177] However, to reap the full potential of AI, security must not be an afterthought. AI security must be elevated and integrated into broader third-party risk strategies and processes for organizations to truly reap the benefits and minimize the risks associated with this foundational technology which is driving the latest technological revolution.

What is Artificial Intelligence?

There is minimal agreement on the definition of artificial intelligence (AI). For many, AI has evoked images of futuristic robots with innate human intelligence. In reality, AI is increasingly viewed as an umbrella term that describes computational systems that leverage inputs (i.e., data) to autonomously produce outputs (e.g., recommendations, predictions, correlations, etc.). Astro Teller, the

174 https://arstechnica.com/security/2024/03/hackers-can-read-private-ai-assistant-chats-even-though-theyre-encrypted/.

175 https://www.schneier.com/blog/archives/2024/03/llm-prompt-injection-worm.html.

176 https://dialogo-americas.com/articles/hackers-from-china-russia-iran-use-ai-tools-microsoft-says/.

177 https://www.bbc.com/news/articles/cx7dx48ev91o.

co-founder and CEO of X (Alphabet's moonshot factory), summarizes AI as algebra on steroids.[178]

Given the lack of consensus on an AI definition, it is most practical to lean on the legal landscape. On the regulatory front, the EU's AI Act defines an AI system as "a machine-based system designed to operate with varying levels of autonomy, that may exhibit adaptiveness after deployment and that, for explicit and implicit objectives, infers, from the input it receives, how to generate outputs such as predictions, content, recommendations, or decisions that can influence physical or virtual environments."[179]

The EU AI Act goes on to define risk as well, specifying the probability of an occurrence of harm and its severity. Foundationally, the EU AI Act was introduced to minimize potential harm from AI systems, a topic that is growing in awareness in sync with the growing omnipresence of AI systems. It is just one example of the growing concern surrounding potential harm resulting from AI systems.

In the U.S., NIST similarly defines AI based on machine-driven automation.[180] The AI Risk Management Framework refers to an AI system as an engineered or machine-based system that can, for a given set of objectives, generate outputs such as predictions, recommendations, or decisions influencing real or virtual environments. Both the U.S. and EU definitions build upon the OECD's recommendations for AI systems, with a consistent focus on systems designed to operate with varying levels of autonomy.[181]

When looking at global standards, the ISO/IEC 22989:2022 views AI as "a technical and scientific field devoted to the engineered system that generates outputs such as content, forecasts, recommendations or decisions for a given set of human-defined objectives."[182] Within the open-source security community, the

178 https://foreignpolicy.com/podcasts/the-geopolitics-of-business/moonshots-ai-astro-teller/.

179 https://www.euaiact.com/article/3.

180 https://nvlpubs.nist.gov/nistpubs/ai/NIST.AI.100-1.pdf.

181 https://oecd.ai/en/.

182 https://www.iso.org/obp/ui/en/#iso:std:iso-iec:22989:ed-1:v1:en.

Open Worldwide Application Security Project (OWASP) is an authoritative source. It defines AI as "a broad term that encompasses all fields of computer science that enable machines to accomplish tasks that would normally require human intelligence."[183] Machine learning and generative AI are two subcategories of AI.

These all have in common a focus on machine-driven outputs but fail to elevate data as part of the definition. Of course, the importance of data is generally introduced throughout the various regulations and standards; however the lack of inclusion of data in core definitions highlights the broader narrative around AI, which often ignores data quality and security risks. This chapter aims to highlight the crucial role of data in AI systems when discussing AI third-party risks from a holistic perspective. For simplicity's sake, we can view these potential risk vectors based on the core components of the AI system: the input, model, and output.

A Holistic Approach to Third-Party Risk and AI

Manipulation of AI systems is not a new phenomenon, but it takes on broader implications thanks to corporate pressures to integrate GenAI and agentic AI. AI manipulation is often viewed under the umbrella of adversarial machine learning (ML), which refers to extracting information about the characteristics of an ML system and/or manipulating inputs into an ML system to obtain a preferred outcome.[184] Machine learning is one form of AI, but these concerns are relevant across the broad class of AI systems. In the context of LLMs, OWASP compiled a top ten list of risks for LLM applications, such as model theft, supply chain vulnerabilities, and data poisoning.[185] CSO Online largely agrees and specifies prompt injection, prompt extraction, poisoned models, and phishing as the

[183] https://genai.owasp.org/resource/llm-applications-cybersecurity-and-governance-checklist-english/

[184] https://www.nccoe.nist.gov/ai/adversarial-machine-learning.

[185] https://genai.owasp.org/resource/owasp-top-10-for-llm-applications-2025/.

top risks of LLMs.[186] For example, LLMs greatly assist targeted phishing campaigns, thereby improving the quality and quantity of phishing attacks.[187]

Data Inputs/Training Data

The old data science adage of "garbage in, garbage out" is extremely relevant when discussing the role of data in AI systems. As a *Harvard Business Review* article succinctly noted, "poor data quality is enemy number one to the widespread, profitable use of machine learning."[188] AI models are impacted twice by poor data quality: first during model training using historical data and then again when the new data is used for future decisions. If the inputs into the AI system are compromised, then any courses of action taken are equally compromised. Data poisoning—or the intentional manipulation of training data going into an AI system—is especially relevant for third-party risk when the data going into an AI system is from a third party and openly accessible.

The risk of data poisoning is especially concerning in the large language models (LLMs) powering many of the GenAI capabilities because they inherently include both the training data and the algorithms. Many researchers have already warned of data manipulation that could lead to misinformation or IP theft in open-sourced GenAI models.[189] A malicious payload could also be uploaded to a training set and triggered once deployed through a series of questions or prompts. In this manner, training data poisoning serves as a backdoor to introduce flaws, vulnerabilities, or other manipulations to the model.[190]

---

[186] https://www-csoonline-com.cdn.ampproject.org/c/s/www.csoonline.com/article/1294996/top-4-llm-threats-to-the-enterprise.html/amp/.

[187] https://hbr.org/2024/05/ai-will-increase-the-quantity-and-quality-of-phishing-scams.

[188] https://hbr.org/2018/04/if-your-data-is-bad-your-machine-learning-tools-are-useless.

[189] https://www.wsj.com/tech/ai/as-generative-ai-takes-off-researchers-warn-of-data-poisoning-d394385c.

[190] https://www.technologydecisions.com.au/content/security/article/how-attackers-are-weaponising-genai-through-data-poisoning-and-manipulation-1588457173.

For instance, there are numerous examples of Russian and Chinese campaigns that flood the data inputs via websites explicitly created to provide disinformation for scraping into LLM training models.[191] However, data poisoning is not just used by attackers; it is also a means by which some artists are attempting to defend intellectual property that they believe was used for training without their consent. A tool named Nightshade was specifically created for this purpose by the University of Chicago to protect digital artwork from AI replication or misuse.[192]

Model Corruption

Similarly, just as data corruption is a growing concern, so too is algorithm corruption. For instance, over 100 poisoned models were discovered on the Hugging Face AI platform alone.[193] Model corruption or poisoning reflects another potential AI supply chain risk that enables attackers to inject malicious code through openly available models.

The PyTorch compromise is another example. PyTorch is an open-source machine learning framework used to create deep neural networks and expedite development and deployment.[194] In 2022, one of PyTorch's libraries was compromised when a malicious package bearing the same name as a trusted package was uploaded to the code repository. Often referred to as dependency confusion, this occurs when a malicious package is registered with the same name as a trusted third-party software library. In this case, the seemingly trusted package collected system information, read files, and then exfiltrated the data.

In both of these attacks, machine learning model repositories provided the means by which attackers inserted malicious code. As

---

[191] https://www.washingtonpost.com/technology/2025/04/17/llm-poisoning-grooming-chatbots-russia/.

[192] https://www.technologyreview.com/2023/10/23/1082189/data-poisoning-artists-fight-generative-ai/.

[193] https://www.darkreading.com/application-security/hugging-face-ai-platform-100-malicious-code-execution-models.

[194] https://www.techrepublic.com/article/pytorch-ml-compromised/.

one security engineer summarized, "Machine learning pipelines are a brand-new supply chain attack vector, and companies need to look at what analysis and sandboxing they are doing to protect themselves. ML models are not pure functions. They are full-blown malware vectors ripe for exploit."[195]

Collaboration platforms such as Hugging Face and GitHub are essential for model implementation, but security tends to lag behind user adoption. In early 2024, two researchers successfully exploited GitHub's default settings by becoming a repository contributor and introducing backdoors and malicious code.[196] These kinds of CI/CD misconfigurations reflect an additional attack vector and supply chain attack where a fork in a public repository could potentially introduce malicious code onto self-hosted machines.[197]

Model Output

Finally, model output can also be corrupted, with prompt injection attacks a growing concern as LLMs become embedded in corporate and personal life. Prompt injection attacks reflect an additional form of AI supply chain compromise wherein finely targeted prompts manipulate the model output. The UK's National Cyber Security Centre (NCSC) issued a warning in August 2023 about prompt injection attacks, noting that while the LLM technology is exciting, our understanding is still "beta."[198] They recommend that users proceed with caution, given numerous examples of prompts being used to manipulate the output and reveal sensitive data, provide harmful guidance, and/or produce biased output. There are numerous legal cases underway, in fact, based on potential harm caused by LLMs, ranging from poor dietary advice to suicide.[199]

195 https://www.darkreading.com/cloud-security/ml-model-repositories-next-big-supply-chain-attack-target.

196 https://www.hackster.io/news/a-critical-supply-chain-attack-on-the-pytorch-infrastructure-raises-concerns-and-a-bug-bounty-e53bdf9524ca.

197 https://thehackernews.com/2024/01/tensorflow-cicd-flaw-exposed-supply.html

198 https://www.ncsc.gov.uk/blog-post/exercise-caution-building-off-llms.

199 https://www.reuters.com/sustainability/boards-policy-regulation/google-ai-firm-must-face-lawsuit-filed-by-mother-over-suicide-son-us-court-says-2025-05-21/.

Even with guardrails in place, prompts can circumvent them by tricking models into revealing information, such as email content, and have been used to demonstrate security flaws in the most widely used GenAI tools. For instance, researchers have been able to jailbreak OpenAI's ChatGPT and Google Gemini through a series of prompts that can subvert the guardrails that are in place to leak personally identifiable information and restrictions on content and language.[200]

Data leaks are an additional security risk associated with model outputs and can occur through numerous vectors. Researchers found several vulnerabilities in the open-source AI framework Ray that were undergoing active exploitation and fixed all but one.[201] The final vulnerability was disputed and never fixed, allowing attackers to manipulate the data and models so that they could control a company's computing power and leak sensitive data. Industries from education to healthcare to video analytics have been impacted.

Ray AI is not alone. Anthropic experienced a data leak when a contractor sent names and accounts receivable files to an unauthorized third party.[202] These kinds of leaks are not limited to AI systems but rather reflect general third-party risk when sharing sensitive data. Similarly, a GitHub repository used for AI models and image recognition was not secured, accidentally leaking 38TB of data.[203] This, again, is not limited to AI models but is more reflective of broader third-party data risks.

However, there are new data leak concerns that are unique to AI and LLMs. Because many GenAI tools save a user's chat history, if sensitive data or IP are disclosed in any of the prompts, those companies, in turn, can access that sensitive data.[204] For highly

200 https://www.cpomagazine.com/cyber-security/prompt-injection-vulnerability-in-google-gemini-allows-for-direct-content-manipulation/.

201 https://www.scmagazine.com/news/flaw-in-ray-ai-framework-potentially-leaks-sensitive-data-of-workloads.

202 https://www.techradar.com/pro/security/anthropic-confirms-it-suffered-a-data-leak-ai-wunderkid-says-human-error-behind-customer-info-breach.

203 https://www.pcmag.com/news/microsoft-ai-employee-accidentally-leaks-38tb-of-data.

204 https://www.forbes.com/sites/siladityaray/2023/05/02/samsung-bans-chatgpt-and-other-chatbots-for-employees-after-sensitive-code-leak/?sh=7c688d726078.

regulated industries like the financial industry, this introduces additional regulatory risks by exposing sensitive financial information. In fact, in a poll of UK CISOs, one in five CISOs believe their staff have leaked sensitive information via a GenAI tool.[205] Samsung banned ChatGPT after source code and meeting notes were leaked on the platform.[206]

Regulatory Environment and Risks

As referenced earlier, the European Union's Artificial Intelligence Act (EU AI Act) is the world's first comprehensive AI regulation.[207] It was approved in March 2024, introducing some of the most stringent guardrails around the use of AI. Following in the footsteps of the GDPR, even though it is a European regulation, the ban applies to any company that operates in or sells to European consumers. The EU AI Act creates a tiered system of use cases, with unacceptable risk scenarios subject to fines of up to 35 million Euros or 7% of the company's global turnover. Prohibited uses of AI include biometric classification for socio-economic inference and identification, social scoring systems, and influencing behavior in harmful ways.

The EU AI Act also includes provisions specifically for GenAI, requiring companies to provide summaries of the data used to train the models and comply with EU copyright law. For those that may cause "systemic risk," there will be extra vigilance, with OpenAI and Google Gemini included in that category.[208] They also must disclose how much energy their models use, reflecting increased attention to the links between computational energy consumption and climate concerns. The EU AI Act went into force in August 2024, with compliance phased in over the following years.

[205] https://www.infosecurity-magazine.com/news/fifth-cisos-staff-leaked-data-genai/.

[206] https://www.bloomberg.com/news/articles/2023-05-02/samsung-bans-chatgpt-and-other-generative-ai-use-by-staff-after-leak.

[207] https://artificialintelligenceact.eu/the-act/.

[208] https://apnews.com/article/ai-act-european-union-chatbots-155157e2be2e42d0f1acca33983d8c82.

In the U.S., the October 2023 executive order (EO) on AI was the first major federal policy push toward AI regulation.[209] The EO similarly took a risk-based approach, requiring the publication of red-teaming safety results for foundational models that may impact critical areas such as national security and public health. It also aimed to address disinformation risks by introducing watermarks to clearly identify any AI-generated content and directs additional research to focus on preventing bias and discrimination and protecting privacy. While it largely focuses on risks, the EO also offered guidelines for innovation, including the use of AI for cyber defenses, prioritizing privacy-preserving technologies, transforming education, and specifying actions aimed at creating the foundation for the U.S. to be a global leader in AI. A January 2025 Executive Order superseded it, removing many of the guardrails deemed to limit innovation.[210]

Those EOs reflect the shifting landscape of a U.S. federal approach and the ongoing policy fluctuations while AI barrels ahead. In the meantime, many states are introducing their own AI laws, creating a patchwork of challenges for corporate compliance.[211] The New York state bills (S7623 and A9315) are among the more prominent, augmenting the July 2023 law that requires companies to audit their AI systems for hiring.[212] The new proposals would take further steps toward transparency and require bias audits of AI systems. California lawmakers are aggressively pursuing AI legislation, with 20 AI laws signed in 2024 and additional proposals working their way through the legislature.[213] The National Telecommunications and

[209] https://www.whitehouse.gov/briefing-room/statements-releases/2023/10/30/fact-sheet-president-biden-issues-executive-order-on-safe-secure-and-trustworthy-artificial-intelligence/.

[210] https://www.whitehouse.gov/presidential-actions/2025/01/removing-barriers-to-american-leadership-in-artificial-intelligence/.

[211] https://apnews.com/article/artificial-intelligence-ai-explained-policy-technology-regulations-discrimination-d3226c9139d3d06af263e7ff467d0666.

[212] https://news.bloomberglaw.com/daily-labor-report/new-york-citys-ai-hiring-bias-law-creates-hurdles-for-companies.

[213] https://www.whitecase.com/insight-alert/raft-california-ai-legislation-adds-growing-patchwork-us-regulation.

Information Administration (NTIA) has also called for audits and transparency to push companies toward trustworthy AI systems.[214]

A similar picture is emerging globally. Brazil may well be the first political system wherein a regulation was written entirely by GenAI.[215] Since then, Brazil has introduced new legislation focused on AI and is one of at least eight countries in Latin America that have introduced AI laws.[216] Canada has also introduced the Artificial Intelligence and Data Act (2023), while China's Generative AI Services Law, South Korea's proposed AI Liability Act, and Indonesia's Governance of Artificial Intelligence and Regulations reflect the evolving regulatory landscape in Asia. Finally, in Africa, Nigeria is creating a national AI strategy while Kenya has proposed an AI bill, among the many ongoing shifts in that region.

International governmental organizations are introducing new voluntary standards, such as ISO 42001, aimed at the responsible development of AI, focusing on transparency and ethical considerations. Importantly, it takes a whole-of-organization approach, highlighting the necessity for leadership commitment toward responsible AI. This is essential given that the pressures to integrate AI often trump security considerations, which can in turn lead to detrimental organizational outcomes.[217] The United Nations is stepping into AI guidance by adopting a resolution focused on safe and secure systems while focusing on a sustainable development angle.[218]

214 https://www.ntia.gov/press-release/2024/ntia-calls-audits-and-investments-trustworthy-ai-systems.

215 https://apnews.com/article/brazil-artificial-intelligence-porto-alegre-5afd1240afe7b6ac202bb0bbc45e08d4.

216 https://www.context.news/ai/latin-america-joins-global-ai-regulations-race-as-threats-grow.

217 https://www-cnbc-com.cdn.ampproject.org/c/s/www.cnbc.com/amp/2024/05/03/ai-engineers-face-burnout-as-rat-race-to-stay-competitive-hits-tech.html.

218 https://press.un.org/en/2024/ga12588.doc.htm.

Toward Secure, Compliant, and Resilient AI Systems

With AI technologies and policy responses seemingly changing by the day, it is difficult to know not only how to prepare for today but be resilient against upcoming advances. Fortunately, there are several authoritative sources to help organizations optimize the gains and capabilities of AI while also minimizing both the policy and adversary risks.

For instance, the NIST AI Risk Management Framework (AI RMF 1.0) offers guidelines on how to achieve trustworthiness in your AI systems.[219] Consistent with the emerging global regulations, AI RMF 1.0 highlights: 1) identification of context to inform risk tolerance; 2) measure, track, and assess identified risks; and 3) prioritize and act on identified risks based on impact. All of these are part of building a culture of AI governance within an organization. NIST provides very detailed breakdowns across each of these areas and is highly recommended reading for organizations seeking secure and trustworthy AI and compliance with existing and forthcoming regulations.

AI RMF 1.0 builds upon existing frameworks, such as the OECD Framework for the Classification of AI Systems.[220] ISO 42005 offers organizations guidance on AI impact assessments.[221] The Biden White House also produced the Blueprint for an AI Bill of Rights, which focuses on safety and security, as well as mitigating biases, privacy concerns, and opt-out capabilities (when relevant), but has since been supplanted.[222] There also have been more industry-specific guidelines, such as the U.S. Department of Treasury's report *Managing Artificial Intelligence – Specific Cybersecurity Risks in the Financial Services Sector*. The report recommends that financial institutions should strengthen their risk management practices by

[219] https://nvlpubs.nist.gov/nistpubs/ai/NIST.AI.100-1.pdf.

[220] https://www.oecd.org/publications/oecd-framework-for-the-classification-of-ai-systems-cb6d9eca-en.htm.

[221] https://www.iso.org/standard/44545.html.

[222] https://www.whitehouse.gov/ostp/ai-bill-of-rights/.

integrating AI systems as part of their frameworks.[223] The report explains, “It is very likely that often overlooked third-party risk considerations such as data integrity and data provenance will emerge as significant concerns for third-party risk management.”

These frameworks are a good first step in creating an organization-wide culture of security when it comes to AI. They understandably focus on the processes but do not go deep into technology. Fortunately, the security industry again has guidelines on that front. The Open Worldwide Application Security Project (OWASP) created the LLM AI Cybersecurity & Governance Checklist based on their three pillars of reliable, resilient, and responsible systems.[224] Their guidelines include several areas familiar to those working in cybersecurity, such as red teaming, security and privacy training, asset inventory, and an AI RACI chart for governance. They also include Model Cards and Risk Cards that detail information about the model architecture, training data, performance metrics, and potential biases or limitations.

Researchers are also moving quickly to create new defenses against these threats.[225] Many focus on defending against prompt injection attacks, such as spotlighting to detect multiple sources of input, structured queries that separate prompts and data, and information hierarchies that define how the model should behave when given conflicting priorities.[226] AI systems are also benefiting from the evolution of MLSecOps and prioritizing security within the development pipeline.[227] This helps organizations safeguard against supply chain vulnerabilities introduced by AI systems. There also are relevant analogies from SBOMs and HBOMs with the emergence of

[223] https://home.treasury.gov/system/files/136/Managing-Artificial-Intelligence-Specific-Cybersecurity-Risks-In-The-Financial-Services-Sector.pdf.

[224] https://owasp.org/www-project-top-10-for-large-language-model-applications/llm-top-10-governance-doc/LLM_AI_Security_and_Governance_Checklist-v1.pdf.

[225] https://www.forbes.com/sites/lanceeliot/2024/04/04/prompt-engineering-and-the-newly-released-prompt-shields-and-spotlight-prompting-techniques-are-useful-for-protecting-your-generative-ai-from-baddies-and-even-yourself/?sh=7828a4371807.

[226] https://arxiv.org/pdf/2404.13208.pdf.

[227] https://www.techtarget.com/searchitoperations/tip/Secure-your-machine-learning-models-with-these-MLSecOps-tips.

MLBOMs (or AIBOMs). MLBOMs track names, locations, and versions, as well as information and meta-data, including ownership and requirements.[228]

Finally, there are two additional risk considerations when deploying AI systems at the enterprise level: the financial and environmental impacts. The cutting-edge chips required to deploy AI are in short supply, and GenAI models can cost billions to train and maintain.[229] While the costs may, for now, hinder some adoption of AI, the environmental impact of AI is also drawing attention, which could potentially introduce Environmental, Social, and Governance (ESG) risks as well.[230] In order to minimize energy costs and achieve greater data accuracy, organizations are exploring small language models for greater optimization and efficiency.[231]

Conclusion

The AI hype cycle persists, with companies that emphasize AI being rewarded with financial benefits.[232] The vast potential of AI to impact all aspects of society provides significant new opportunities for improvements across all aspects of society. However, like most technologies, there also are substantial risks associated with AI, which have largely been cast aside in the mad rush to implement AI-driven systems.

Fortunately, existing third-party risk processes are applicable to AI systems as well, especially when viewed through an AI supply chain lens. Despite corporate pressures, organizations must take a more nuanced approach to AI that integrates risk management as part of the broader AI strategy. This not only will help ensure more secure

228 https://www.darkreading.com/vulnerabilities-threats/mlboms-are-useful-for-securing-ai-ml-supply-chain.

229 https://www.nytimes.com/2024/04/29/technology/ai-startups-financial-reality.html.

230 https://www.theverge.com/2023/10/10/23911059/ai-climate-impact-google-openai-chatgpt-energy.

231 https://www.siliconrepublic.com/machines/ai-small-language-models-cost-energy-microsoft-google.

232 https://www.msn.com/en-us/money/other/ai-washing-how-companies-are-using-ai-hype-to-bump-up-their-share-prices/ar-BB1mmF7B.

and robust AI systems, but organizations who implement these policies now will be better prepared for the imminent regulatory changes emerging across the globe.

Insights and Actions

AI introduces a new form of third-party risk, with a supply chain consisting of the data inputs, outputs, and the model itself, each of which require security assessments and considerations. As organizations seek to optimize AI innovations, security must not be an afterthought but rather an integral part of the implementation.

Malicious actors are increasingly targeting the AI supply chain, manipulating training data, corrupting the outputs, and injecting payloads and malicious code to alter the algorithms.

The AI regulatory landscape continues to evolve, with the EU AI Act the first global regulation. Accidental data leaks, biases, and hallucinations are many of the challenges in addition to adversarial AI attacks that pose risk. There are existing AI risk frameworks—such as those from NIST and OWASP—that organizations should review and integrate into their strategic approach toward and internal policies on AI security.

Organizations must inform their usage of AI and prepare mitigation strategies across the following risk vectors.

AI as a Third-Party Risk Vector

- AI systems have their own supply chains: data inputs, models, and outputs—all of which require security assessment.
- Malicious actors have already exploited open-source AI platforms (e.g., Hugging Face), injecting poisoned models and leveraging prompt injection attacks.
- Sensitive data leaks, intellectual property exposure, and side-channel attacks are real risks, especially when AI chatbots are used without proper controls.

The Importance of Data Quality and Security

- "Garbage in, garbage out" is especially true for AI; poor or poisoned training data can compromise model integrity and outputs.
- Data poisoning attacks are increasingly used to manipulate AI models, sometimes even by artists seeking to protect their work.
- Model corruption and supply chain attacks (e.g., dependency confusion in open-source libraries) are growing threats.

Model Output and Prompt Injection

- Prompt injection attacks can manipulate AI outputs, bypass safety guardrails, and cause data leaks or harmful recommendations.
- Even with guardrails, attackers have demonstrated the ability to jailbreak leading GenAI tools, exposing sensitive data or bypassing content restrictions.

Regulatory Environment

- The EU AI Act (effective August 2024) introduces strict requirements and tiered risk categories for AI use, with heavy fines for non-compliance and special rules for GenAI.
- The U.S. regulatory approach is evolving, with executive orders and a patchwork of state laws focusing on transparency, bias audits, and risk-based controls.
- Other countries and international organizations are introducing their own AI regulations and standards, adding to compliance complexity.

Security and Governance Best Practices

- NIST's AI Risk Management Framework (AI RMF 1.0), ISO standards, and OWASP guidelines provide organizations with strategies for trustworthy, resilient, and responsible AI deployment.
- Recommendations include robust asset inventories, red teaming, security/privacy training, model and risk cards, and strong governance structures.
- Emerging practices like Model Bills of Materials (MLBOMs) help track AI components and dependencies.

Financial and Environmental Considerations

- The high cost and energy consumption of advanced AI models introduce additional risks, including potential ESG (Environmental, Social, Governance) concerns.
- Organizations are exploring smaller, more efficient models to balance performance, cost, and sustainability.

Conclusion

Throughout *Mastering Third-Party Risk: A Practical Handbook for Managing Vendor, Third-Party, and Supply Chain Threats in Every Organization*, we have shared our perspectives and expertise with you and hope that sharing our journeys helps you make more informed decisions as you build and improve your programs.

We've written this book with several goals in mind. First, to establish the foundational governance elements for a third-party risk management program, as our experience has shown that a solid structure and agreed-upon roles are essential for success. Second, we examined third parties, ranging from simple relationships with regional vendors to complex global supply chains. And finally, we turned our lens outward and to the future to address the growing challenges posed by international geopolitical pressures, climate change, and emerging technologies, such as artificial intelligence.

We want to leave you with a final thought. One of the foundational principles of CISO DRG Publishing is the strength of community in our business. Whether it's in the specific field of cybersecurity or the broader field of risk management, the desire—and, as importantly, the need—to share best practices works to our collective advantage. So be engaged; don't just attend conferences and collect freebies from sponsors; be a part of the information and experience sharing. Let others benefit from your experience as you grow your network and learn from others.

We welcome your feedback and invite you to visit our website: http://www.cisodrg.com or our LinkedIn company page: https://www.linkedin.com/company/ciso-desk-reference-guide.

Index

O

P

R

S

T

V

W

About the Authors

Bill Bonney is a security evangelist, author, and consultant. As co-author of the Cybersecurity Canon Hall of Fame books the *CISO Desk Reference Guide: A Practical Guide for CISOs Volumes 1 and 2*, Bill is dedicated to providing the practical advice needed to combat the ongoing scourge of cybercrime. Prior to co-founding CISO DRG Publishing, Bill was Vice President of Product Marketing and Chief Strategist at UBIQ, a maker of high-speed encryption software, Vice President of Product Marketing and Principal Consulting Analyst at TechVision Research, and Director of Information Security and Compliance at Intuit, maker of personal and small business financial products.

Bill holds multiple patents in data protection, access, and classification, and was a founding member of the board of directors for the San Diego CISO Round Table. Bill is a highly regarded speaker and panelist addressing technology and security concerns. In addition to co-authoring the two volumes of the *CISO Desk Reference Guide*, Bill has also co-authored the *CISO Desk Reference Guide Executive Primer: An Executive's Guide to Security Programs* and written *Protect Your Business: A Small Business Owner's Guide to Basic Network Security* and *Protect Your Practice: Basic Cybersecurity for Healthcare, Legal and Accounting Professionals* to help extremely small companies improve their security. He holds a Bachelor of Science degree in Computer Science and Applied Mathematics from the State University of New York at Albany.

LinkedIn Profile: https://www.linkedin.com/in/billbonney

Chris Forbes is president and CEO of Forbes Asset Management, Inc., an executive advisory firm focused on technology risk, information security, and privacy. Chris has over 40 years of global experience, including 3x Chief Information Security Officer (CISO), 2x Chief Privacy Officer (CPO), Chief Information Officer (CIO), Chief Technology Officer (CTO), and US Navy veteran.

Chris began his career in 1981, programming mainframe computers and early PCs. In 1982, Chris enlisted in the US Navy and spent six years as an Electronics Technician and Nuclear Reactor Operator on two ballistic missile submarines and qualified Engineering Watch Supervisor. After his tour of duty, Chris returned to computer programming as a DoD Contractor working at the Pentagon. In the early 90's, Chris started working for several large global financial services and banking companies. In 2001, Chris was the Chief Technology Officer for an international automotive company and was given his first Chief Information Security Officer (CISO) role.

Chris has advised CEOs and Boards of Directors on technology and security turnaround strategies, optimized business technology models, assisted with mergers and acquisitions (M&A), driven designs for new technology products, overhauled organizational and operational effectiveness, and delivered countless financial efficiency improvements. Prior firms include the Federal Reserve, JPMorgan Chase, BNY Mellon, BNP Paribas, AXA, Barclays, TD Ameritrade, DaimlerChrysler, Banc of California, Allianz, City National Bank, and Royal Bank of Canada.

Chris is working on several research projects, including Complete Information Security Strategy, Multiyear Transformational Roadmaps, Comprehensive Security Programs, Reference Enterprise Security Architecture, Predictable Threat Modelling, and Certifiable Security Levels.

Gary Hayslip is an experienced Global Security Executive with a proven track record of delivering innovative security programs that protect billion-dollar enterprises at every touchpoint. He is intensely focused on driving continuous improvement to maximize the efficiency of security programs while minimizing costs. As an insightful thought leader, he possesses strong business acumen and a commitment to organizational mission, values, and goals. He has demonstrated the ability to collaborate with all levels of an organization to champion new ideas, gain buy-in, and build consensus. Hayslip brings extensive experience in information technology, security leadership, physical security, and risk management to his role as the Chief Information Security Officer for SoftBank Investment Advisers – The Vision Fund and Vision Fund II, as well as SoftBank Group International – The LATAM Fund, The Opportunity Fund, and The Tech Fund. His previous executive positions include multiple roles as Chief Information Security Officer, Chief Information Officer, Deputy Director of IT, and Chief Privacy Officer for the U.S. Navy (Active Duty), the U.S. Navy (Federal Government employee), the City of San Diego, California, and Webroot Software.

Hayslip is a proven cybersecurity expert with excellent communication and public speaking skills. He is skilled at explaining complex security and risk concepts to audiences with different levels of knowledge. Hayslip has earned a reputation as a highly effective communicator, author, and keynote speaker. He co-authored the *CISO Desk Reference Guide: A Practical Guide for CISOs – Volumes 1 and 2*, The *CISO Desk Reference Guide Executive Primer: An Executive's Guide to Security Programs* and *Develop Your Cybersecurity Career Path: How to Break into Cybersecurity at Any Level.* He also recently authored *The Essential Guide to Cybersecurity for SMBs*, a guide aimed specifically at security practitioners protecting startups and small businesses. These books are among the top resources for helping CISOs improve their leadership and business skills. Hayslip currently serves as an independent director on several boards and advises various other security and technology firms. He is an active member of the cybersecurity community and belongs to professional organizations such as ISC2, NACD, ISACA, and InfraGard. Hayslip holds several professional certifications, including CISSP, CISA, and CRISC, and holds a Bachelor of Science degree in Information Systems Management from the University of Maryland, University College and an MBA from San Diego State University.

LinkedIn Profile: http://www.linkedin.com/in/ghayslip

Twitter: @ghayslip

Dr. Andrea Little Limbago is a cybersecurity and national security executive with two decades of experience building innovative products and leading operationally-focused research and external engagements. She is currently the Senior Vice President of Applied AI at Interos, architecting the company's global supply chain risk research and computational models, driving the data strategy, and providing extensive thought leadership in cybersecurity, geopolitics, and geo-economics.

Andrea is also a Senior Fellow at the National Security Institute's Cyber and Tech Center at George Mason, a regular contributor to the Cyberwire podcast, and a Cyber Guild Luminaire. Prior to Interos, Andrea was the Chief Social Scientist at Virtru, Endgame, and Berico Technologies. She also taught political economy and conflict studies in academia and was a technical lead at the Joint Warfare Analysis Center, where she earned the Command's top award for technical excellence. A global speaker, Andrea has presented extensively at a range of academic, government, and industry conferences, including Black Hat and RSA, and her research has been published in dozens of media outlets. Andrea holds a PhD in Political Science from the University of Colorado at Boulder and a BA from Bowdoin College.

Matt Stamper, CISA, CISM, CRISC, CDPSE, CIPP-US, QTE, is a multi-time CISO with extensive experience in cybersecurity, information security, cloud security, IT service management, audit, risk management, privacy, AI security, and governance. Matt is a former research director and security analyst at Gartner (NYSE:IT), with extensive experience in cloud services and IT service management, including international experience in Latin America and China. Throughout his career, Matt has spoken to hundreds of CISOs, CIOs, and other corporate leaders and boards of directors. Matt's experience spans early-stage startups and large, multinational public companies across multiple industries, including managed services, managed security services, global telecom, and advisory services. Matt excels at conveying complex cybersecurity and technology concepts to boards of directors, executive management, professional service providers, cybersecurity personnel, and vendors in the cybersecurity industry. His executive-level experience with managed services, cybersecurity, data centers, network services, and ITSM provides a unique perspective on the fast-changing world of enterprise IT, AI, IoT, and cloud services.

Matt is a co-author of the *CISO Desk Reference Guide: A Practical Guide for CISOs, Volumes 1 and 2,* as well as the *CISO Desk Reference Guide Executive Primer: An Executive's Guide to Security Programs,* which he co-authored with Bill Bonney and Gary Hayslip. Matt is also the co-author of the *Data Privacy Program Guide: How to Build a Privacy Program that Inspires Trust*, which he co-wrote with David Goodman and Justine Phillips.

Matt is an IT Sector Chief for the San Diego chapter of the FBI InfraGard program and a Board member of the San Diego ISACA chapter. Matt also chairs the FBI InfraGard's national CISO Cross-Sector Council.

Matt holds a Bachelor of Arts degree from the University of California at San Diego, graduating Cum Laude and with Honors and Distinction in Political Science. He holds a Master of Arts in Pacific International Affairs from the University of California, San Diego, and a Master of Science degree in Telecommunications, sponsored by AT&T. He is fluent in Spanish and has held executive roles in Latin America.

LinkedIn Profile: https://www.linkedin.com/in/stamper

www.ingramcontent.com/pod-product-compliance
Lightning Source LLC
Chambersburg PA
CBHW071406230926
51846CB00001B/20
* 9 7 8 1 9 5 5 9 7 6 2 8 2 *